HANDBOOK OF RESEARCH ON ENTREPRENEURSHIP AND REGIONAL DEVELOPMENT

T0319569

Handbook of Research on Entrepreneurship and Regional Development

National and Regional Perspectives

Edited by

Michael Fritsch

Chair of Business Dynamics, Innovation, and Economic Change, Friedrich Schiller University Jena, Germany

Edward Elgar

Cheltenham, UK • Northampton, MA, USA

Published by
Edward Elgar Publishing Limited
The Lypiatts
15 Lansdown Road
Cheltenham
Glos GL50 2JA
UK

Edward Elgar Publishing, Inc.
William Pratt House
9 Dewey Court
Northampton
Massachusetts 01060
USA

A catalogue record for this book
is available from the British Library

Library of Congress Control Number: 2011925779

ISBN 978 1 84844 264 1 (cased)

Typeset by Servis Filmsetting Ltd, Stockport, Cheshire
Printed and bound by MPG Books Group, UK

Contents

Contributors

Zoltan J. Acs, George Mason University, Washington, DC, USA.

Thomas Åstebro, HEC, Paris, France.

David B. Audretsch, Institute for Development Strategies, Indiana University, Bloomington, IN, USA.

Navid Bazzazian, HEC, Paris, France.

Niels Bosma, Utrecht University, The Netherlands.

Maryann P. Feldman, University of North Carolina, Chapel Hill, NC, USA.

Michael Fritsch, Friedrich Schiller University Jena, Germany.

Isabel Grilo, DG Economic and Financial Affairs, European Commission, Brussels, Belgium.

Magnus Henrekson, Research Institute of Industrial Economics (IFN), Stockholm, Sweden.

Dan Johansson, The Ratio Institute, Stockholm, Sweden.

Lauren Lanahan, University of North Carolina, Chapel Hill, NC, USA.

Jennifer M. Miller, University of North Carolina, Chapel Hill, NC, USA.

Rolf Sternberg, University of Hanover, Germany.

A. Roy Thurik, Erasmus School of Economics, University of Rotterdam and EIM/Panteia, Zoetermeer, The Netherlands.

1 The role of new businesses in regional development: introduction and overview
Michael Fritsch

FORMATION OF NEW BUSINESSES, POLICY, AND REGIONAL GROWTH

Politicians expend a great deal of effort on attempting to reduce unemployment and stimulate economic growth. Policy programs specifically intended to create additional employment can be found at the regional, national, and supranational levels. Historically, such measures focused on the performance of large incumbent firms and more or less ignored the role that new businesses play in economic development. It was not until the late 1970s that policymakers became conscious of the important contributions that new businesses make to employment and growth. The last few decades have witnessed a considerable amount of empirical research on entrepreneurship, particularly on the formation and effects of new businesses, leading to substantial progress in this important field.

One important result of recent research is that the factors that influence entrepreneurship vary considerably between nations and, particularly, between regions. Entrepreneurship is a regional event. Region-specific characteristics influence not only the level of new business formation, but also the type of new business that is created, for example innovative, knowledge-intensive, or high-growth start-ups. Moreover, the effects of entrepreneurship on development can also vary between nations and regions. In fact, in some countries or regions, new business formation is accompanied by significant employment growth, while the effect on employment may be negligible or even negative in other countries or regions. Currently, this variation in the effect of certain types of entrepreneurship on economic development and the role of the spatial environment are not well understood.

OVERVIEW OF THE CONTRIBUTIONS

The contributions found in this book provide an overview of the current state of research into the role new business formation plays in regional development. They survey the state of knowledge, present own results, provide interpretations, and suggest important avenues for further research. This chapter provides an overview of the contributions and their main results.

In Chapter 2, David B. Audretsch, Isabel Grilo, and A. Roy Thurik analyze the impact of ongoing globalization on the role of entrepreneurship and, in turn, entrepreneurship's role in regional development. Globalization has resulted in massive changes in the comparative advantages of countries and regions, one important result of which is the shift experienced by high-wage countries toward knowledge-intensive activity. In analyzing the reasons behind ongoing globalization, Audretsch et al. emphasize two developments. First, technological advancements in the field of information technology made many types of information ubiquitous and allowed high-quality telecommunication over long distances at decreasing costs. The second development the authors find important involves the political arena. In particular, the end of the Cold War and increased political stability of many countries made the spread of technological improvements feasible, resulting in a massive readjustment of the global division of labor.

Audretsch et al. particularly stress the increasing role of entrepreneurship in these developments, and see the process of global adjustment as a shift from a 'managed economy' to an 'entrepreneurial economy', a shift that is especially evident in many highly developed countries. The emergence of a more entrepreneurial society was supported, possibly in some cases even induced, by the development of small-scale technologies such as computer numerical controlled (CNC) machinery and the micro-computer, which led to a serious erosion of the cost advantages of large-scale production and allowed small firms to compete ever more successfully. The result was considerable corporate downsizing resulting in a shift in firm-size distribution toward small firms and the growing importance of new businesses. These developments had important consequences for the regional distribution of production and, especially, innovation activity. In particular, the importance of region-specific factors to the location and performance of economic activity has increased considerably, a trend often termed 'glocalization'. While spatial proximity became largely unimportant for certain activities, it became of increasing importance to others. Audretsch et al. point out that in a knowledge economy, entrepreneurship can play a key role in regional competitiveness, particularly at the local level.

Rolf Sternberg deals with new business formation and its determinants at the regional level (Chapter 3). In the first part of his contribution, Sternberg surveys a number of regional factors that may explain differences in start-up levels, with a particular focus on the role of new ventures in regional innovation systems. This pursuit leads him to look specifically at knowledge-based start-ups in technologically advanced and creative industries. In the second half of his contribution, Sternberg reports empirical evidence on how region-specific factors may influence the success of new businesses.

A key observation underscoring the importance of region-specific factors for new business formation is that start-up rates vary greatly across regions. That the level of new business formation and the respective interregional differences tend to be quite stable over time also demonstrates the importance of region-specific factors to entrepreneurship. Moreover, regional factors have a pronounced effect on an individual's propensity to become a 'nascent' entrepreneur, that is, someone who is planning to found a new business. One particularly interesting finding in this respect is that regional entrepreneurship seems to be self-energizing: the probability of becoming a nascent entrepreneur is heavily influenced by the availability of role models, that is, the presence of other (nascent) entrepreneurs in the same region. Other important factors that have a significantly positive impact on the regional level of new business formation are a high education level of the regional workforce, a high proportion of small business employment, and high population density. Thus, relatively high start-up rates in agglomerations can be explained by these regions' endowment with a high level of knowledge spillover which results from the amount and density of economic activity that takes place within them. The regional level of R&D also seems to have a positive impact on new business formation, especially in the case of innovative and knowledge-intensive start-ups.

Region-specific factors are important not only for the emergence of new businesses, but also to their success, as indicated, for example, by how long they survive. One finding common to the relevant empirical studies is that survival rates in high-density areas tend to be lower than in regions with lower population density, which may be due to higher intensity of intraregional competition. Sternberg's survey shows that the empirical results for regional determinants of start-ups' success are less clear than the empirical evidence for the regional determinants of their initiation. In summarizing the work in this field, Sternberg points to some important research gaps, especially the extant deficits in analyzing and understanding the effect of regional entrepreneurship policy.

Michael Fritsch reviews the results of empirical research on the effect of new business formation on regional employment, provides interpretations, draws some policy implications, and proposes a variety of avenues for further research (Chapter 4). Recent studies in this field have clearly shown that the employment effects of new businesses are rather a minor part of their overall effect on economic development: the indirect effects that arise via newcomers' competition with incumbent firms are far more important. Fritsch stresses that it is the interaction between the competitive challenge posed by the newcomers and the innovative response to it by incumbent firms that may lead to improved competitiveness and increasing regional employment. The range of such indirect effects varies considerably between regions, however. As a general trend, the effects of new business formation tend to be relatively pronounced in high-density areas and relatively weak in sparsely populated regions. Such interregional differences could be due to the intensity of competition on input and output markets and to the competitive pressure entries exert on incumbents. In this process, the quality of the new businesses plays a considerable role: the greater the competitive challenge, the stronger the reaction to it. There is some indication that large agglomerations have a relatively large share of high-quality start-ups, such as highly innovative or knowledge-intensive new businesses. This could to some degree explain the greater effects of new business formation in these regions.

The substantial role that the quality of entries plays in the competitive process with the incumbents implies that not all new businesses are of equal importance for job generation. Hence, simply maximizing the number of start-ups will not be an effective political strategy; rather, policy should be aimed at enhancing the quality of new businesses and ensuring that the market is working according to survival of the fittest. Fritsch concludes that if it turns out that more detailed studies confirm the supposition that only a small fraction of start-ups have a considerable effect on regional development, then analyses based on the overall start-up rate may be misleading because the share of new businesses that have a strong impact may vary considerably between regions. Therefore, it would be desirable to identify those characteristics of new businesses that induce a pronounced innovative response by incumbents, and then develop indicators for the formation of these types of start-ups. Such indicators would be valuable guidelines in designing regional entrepreneurship policy. Further avenues of research that Fritsch suggests concern investigating how market characteristics, regional conditions, and the institutional environment affect interaction between newcomers and incumbents. Research on these topics could result in substantial improvements to entrepreneurship policy aimed at stimulating regional growth.

In Chapter 5, Niels Bosma investigates the effect of different types of start-ups on labor productivity in regions of 17 European countries. He uses indicators for regional entrepreneurship that are based on information collected by the Global Entrepreneurship Monitor (GEM), an international project that inquires about entrepreneurial attitudes and activities in many countries of the world (for a description, see Reynolds et al., 2005). A main focus of his analysis is the role of urbanization economies in regional productivity, as previously investigated by Ciccone and Hall (1996) and Ciccone (2002). Based on a regional production function approach, Bosma asks what types of entrepreneurship, together with the spatial density of production activities, contribute to explaining regional productivity levels. Bosma shows high interregional variation in the levels of innovation-oriented entrepreneurial activity, as well as for high- and low-growth-oriented entrepreneurship. The levels of innovative and high-growth-oriented entrepreneurship are particularly high in regions with high labor productivity and a large share of the workforce with a tertiary degree. Interestingly, the rates for innovative and high-growth-oriented regional entrepreneurial activity are *not* significantly correlated with the measure for the overall level of regional new business formation. This underscores the necessity of developing indicators that are more focused on different types of entrepreneurship, particularly for those types of new businesses that have a significant impact on growth.

In his empirical analysis, Bosma first replicates Ciccone's (2002) analysis, showing the significantly positive effect of population density and of the share of population with a tertiary degree on regional labor productivity. In a next step, he includes indicators for the different types of entrepreneurship. According to the estimated coefficients, high-growth-oriented entrepreneurial activity has the strongest positive effect on regional levels of labor productivity, followed by innovative, medium-growth, and low-growth entrepreneurship. Including high-growth entrepreneurship in the model leads to the effect of employment density becoming insignificant. Bosma concludes that 'employment density alone may not give a sufficient picture of economic advantages to urbanization; regions also require entrepreneurs who can create employment *opportunities*' (original italics). He shows that the impact of innovative and high-growth-oriented entrepreneurship on labor productivity is quite homogeneous across countries. However, there are also country-specific effects that may have an influence on these relationships.

Zoltan J. Acs presents evidence on fast-growing high-impact firms, often called 'gazelles', in the USA (Chapter 6). He defines high-impact firms as those that at least doubled their revenues over a four-year period and experience comparatively high employment growth. These high-impact firms comprised between 5.2 and 6.5 percent of all private sector firms in the United States during the 1994–2006 period. His investigation into the characteristics of high-impact firms reveals that such firms are a rather heterogeneous group. Surprisingly, and in contradiction of a widespread prejudice, high-impact firms in the United States are not particularly young: only about 5.5 percent of the high-impact firms are four years old or younger. However, they are, on average, somewhat younger than the rest of the firm population. Moreover, there are both large and small high-impact firms: that is, size does not appear to be a limiting factor, in either direction. Acs shows that high-impact firms tend to have considerably higher labor productivity than the rest of the firm population. High-impact firms can be found in all industries, and are not especially concentrated in high-tech or knowledge-intensive industries. Although high-impact firms can be found in all types of regions, they tend to be located in or near city centers, but the difference between them and low-growth firms in this respect is small.

Most of the high-impact firms experienced a single period of extraordinary growth: the vast majority of the high-growth firms did not have exceptional growth rates in the years before the high-growth phase. However, a considerable number of the high-impact firms continued to enjoy substantial growth in the years subsequent to the high-growth phase. The analysis makes it clear that a high share of overall employment growth is generated by only a small number of firms. Since we cannot, and probably never will be able to, identify a high-impact firm as such before it enters its phase of extraordinary growth, it is not possible to predict the occurrence of such firms *ex ante*.

The contribution by Magnus Henrekson and Dan Johansson (Chapter 7) is an investigation of the effect of certain regulations on the emergence and performance of new businesses. The authors take a comprehensive perspective of 'structural transformation', taking into consideration the fact that growth entails considerable churning and restructuring. In particular, fast-growing firms need to attract factors of production from other firms, causing contraction and exit. Hence, fast-growing firms are only one part of the process that is initiated by entrepreneurship, which Joseph Schumpeter (1934, 1942) called 'creative destruction'. Henrekson and Johansson investigate how public provision, tax laws, social security regulation, and labor market regulation affect this process. In general, their findings lead them to argue for a lean government that leaves a great deal of room for private initiative and entrepreneurship. They argue that extensive labor market regulation will particularly hamper experimentation, reallocation of labor, and the emergence of high-growth firms that, by their very nature, need a large number of qualified workers. Labor market regulation, together with the social insurance system, may have a particularly negative impact on the decision to become an entrepreneur, thereby reducing the number of start-ups. After reviewing the effects of taxes on different types of firms, Henrekson and Johansson conclude that many tax regulations put a higher burden on small and young businesses than on large and long-established firms. Since many of these effects are currently only partly understood, the authors call for more research into these issues, with the hoped-for end result being better-designed tax systems that do not unduly hinder the emergence and development of high-growth firms.

The contribution by Maryann P. Feldman, Lauren Lanahan, and Jennifer M. Miller (Chapter 8) deals with the inadvertent consequences for entrepreneurship of certain public regulations. The effects on innovative firms are given special attention, although, unlike Henrekson and Johansson, Feldman et al. do not focus on only one type of start-up. The regulations they cover are covenants to compete, health insurance, size-based employment regulation, and antitrust regulation in the context of R&D joint ventures. Based on a number of empirical studies on the effects of covenants to compete, they conclude that this type of regulation has a negative effect on entrepreneurship that is particularly pronounced when it comes to the development of innovative clusters and industries. Investigation of the inadvertent consequences of health insurance regulation, sized-based exemptions from certain legislation, and antitrust regulations does not lead to comparably clear-cut results and recommendations; obviously, much depends on the specific details of these types of regulation. A great deal of research in this important field will be necessary before the effects of these regulations can be properly understood.

In the book's final chapter (Chapter 9), Thomas Åstebro and Navid Bazzazian provide an extensive review of the role universities play in local economic development. They begin with the history of university-based entrepreneurship, review university patenting, and investigate the number of new businesses that are directly spun off from universities. Generally, the number of new businesses founded by university employees or by recent post-graduates is relatively small. These few businesses, however, are only a small fraction of the businesses founded by persons with tertiary education, because many of these founders accumulate some experience in dependent employment before starting a business of their own. Due to there being more students than faculty, more academic new ventures are founded by former students. Åstebro and Bazzazian investigate the reasons behind the wide variation between universities in spin-off rates and students' propensity to start a firm later in the life course, with a specific focus on answering the question: what makes a university 'entrepreneurial'? They find that a university's (or that of one of its departments) 'commercialization culture' plays a prominent role. In their quest to discover the elements that make up such a culture and find out how entrepreneurship can be encouraged in both students and faculty, Åstebro and

Bazzazian focus on several universities (for example, the Massachusetts Institute of Technology in the United States; Halmstadt University and Chalmers University in Sweden) that have explicit strategies in this regard.

The empirical evidence reveals that many of the spin-offs founded by a university's students or faculty are located near to their alma mater, even if the local environment lacks important resources. Academic institutions can be an extremely important source of innovative entrepreneurship that may, particularly in the longer run, boost economic growth in their home regions. The strength of this effect, however, varies considerably between universities and regions. Much can be done to enhance the effect that universities have on regional development. We know some ingredients of a recipe for success in this respect, but a number of others and how to process them still need to be discovered. Among the known 'ingredients', a university's offer of entrepreneurship education is probably one of the most important. Technology transfer offices (TTOs) and incubators (science parks) may also make an important contribution, but much depends on how they are operated and what they offer.

CONCLUSIONS FOR POLICY

To summarize all the contributions this book makes to the field of entrepreneurship and economic growth, one can say that entrepreneurship in general and certain types of new businesses in particular may have a strong effect on regional development. The larger part of this effect is, however, rather indirect in nature and will take a relatively long time to manifest. Real-world examples, of which Silicon Valley is the most prominent, show that it may take several decades until the contribution of start-ups to regional development becomes fully evident. This process is characterized by a high degree of path-dependency: regional conditions have a considerable impact on the number and type of start-ups, as well as on their impact on growth. Although recent empirical research into the effects of new business formation on regional growth has made considerable progress, much remains to be discovered.

A number of recommendations for a growth-oriented entrepreneurship policy can be drawn from the current state of research. One general recommendation is to create favorable conditions for entrepreneurship, especially for innovative new businesses. Creating such an environment will involve at least three specific tasks. The first is to develop a knowledge base, which can be regarded as a necessary precondition for the emergence of innovative new firms. Since knowledge does not diffuse easily across space, knowledge bases are highly region specific. The second task is to build framework conditions that are conducive to start-ups or at least do not work to their disadvantage. This includes all types of regulations, such as, among others, labor market and health regulation, and competition policy. It also means securing the availability of adequate finance for innovative new businesses, for example, through a sufficiently well-working venture capital (VC) market. The third of these tasks, which may be the most difficult to accomplish, is to create an entrepreneurial culture. Since entrepreneurial culture is to a large degree place specific, just like the relevant knowledge base, policy measures need to take these specific characteristics into account and operate, to a considerable degree, at a regional level.

Another general policy recommendation is not to interfere with the market selection process, for example, by subsidizing particular firms, be they new or incumbent businesses. The main reason behind this recommendation is that many of the effects of new businesses on regional development, indeed, probably the most important of these effects, require that the market work according to survival of the fittest and any disturbance of this process has the potential to inhibit, if not destroy, the growth-enhancing effects of entry. This caveat particularly pertains to a 'pick the winner' strategy of providing special assistance to high-growth firms. Clearly, our current knowledge does not allow us to distinguish *ex ante* between those businesses that will make an important contribution to growth and those that will not. Although there is clear indication that such a contribution is more likely from innovative new businesses, even these innovative start-ups are a rather heterogeneous group and only a fraction of them will end up performing extraordinarily well (see particularly the contribution of Zoltan Acs to this book; Chapter 6). Hence, any attempt to 'pick winners' runs a high risk not only of wasting public resources but also of distorting market selection processes, thus reducing if not eliminating the positive effects of new business formation on growth.

The contributions to this book contain many suggestions for future research that have the potential to improve our knowledge about this very important field. This research may aid policymakers in designing appropriate and effective strategies.

REFERENCES

Ciccone, A. (2002), 'Agglomeration effects in Europe', *European Economic Review*, **46** (2), 213–27.

Ciccone, A. and R.E. Hall (1996), 'Productivity and the density of economic activity', *American Economic Review*, **86** (1), 54–70.

Reynolds, P.D., N.S. Bosma, E. Autio, S. Hunt, N. De Bono, I. Servais, P. Lopez-Garcia and

N. Chin (2005), 'Global Entrepreneurship Monitor: data collection design and implementation, 1998–2003', *Small Business Economics*, **24** (3), 205–31.
Schumpeter, J.A. (1934), *The Theory of Economic Development*, New Brunswick, NJ and London: Transaction Publishers.
Schumpeter, J.A. (1942), *Capitalism, Socialism and Democracy*, New York and London: Harper & Brothers.

2 Globalization, entrepreneurship, and the region[1]

David B. Audretsch, Isabel Grilo and
A. Roy Thurik

INTRODUCTION

Perhaps one of the less-understood phenomena accompanying the increased globalization during the first decade of the twenty-first century has been a shift in the comparative advantage of high-wage countries towards knowledge-based economic activity. An important implication of this shift in this comparative advantage is that much of the production and commercialization of economic knowledge is less associated with footloose multinational corporations and more associated with high-tech innovative regional clusters, such as Silicon Valley in California, the Cambridge area in the UK, and the Montpellier area in France. Only two decades ago the conventional wisdom predicted that globalization would render the demise of the region as a meaningful unit of economic analysis. Yet the obsession of policymakers around the globe to 'create the next Silicon Valley' reveals the increased importance of geographic proximity and regional agglomerations as well as of the role of small and medium-sized enterprises (SMEs) and entrepreneurial activity. The purpose of this chapter is to resolve the paradox of globalization by explaining the emergence of entrepreneurship and geographic localization as the two key organizational platforms because of and not in spite of a globalizing economy.

That globalization is one of the defining changes at the turn of the century is clear from a reading of the popular press. Like all grand concepts, a definition for globalization is elusive and elicits criticism. That domestic economies are globalizing is a cliché makes it no less true. In fact, the shift in economic activity from a local or national sphere to an international or global orientation ranks among the most vehement changes shaping the current economic landscape.

The driving force underlying the emerging globalization has been technology. While there are many different aspects to the technological revolution, the advent of the microprocessor combined with its application in telecommunications has altered the economic meanings of national borders and distance.

The present chapter analyzes the linkages between globalization, entrepreneurship and the role of regions. It is organized as follows. First, the meaning of globalization is dealt with. Second, the regional dimension of the response to globalization is described where downsizing, knowledge spillovers and agglomeration are the essential phenomena. Third, it is shown how these developments have led to the emergence of new entrepreneurial activities. Fourth, more details are given on the effects of the information and communication technology (ICT) revolution on the organization of industry in a globalized economy. Finally, we conclude that policies promoting both knowledge investments as well as entrepreneurship have become prominent for many regions in the most developed countries.

THE MEANING OF GLOBALIZATION

This section deals with what is meant by the death of distance predicted by the advent of the microprocessor revolution, and with the geopolitical consequences of this revolution. Finally, it provides some figures concerning globalization.

The Death of Distance

Observing the speed at virtually no cost with which information can be transmitted across geographic space via the Internet, cell phones, and electronic communication superhighways, *The Economist* proclaimed on its title page of an influential issue (30 September 1995) in the mid-1990s, 'The Death of Distance'. The new communications technologies have triggered a virtual spatial revolution in terms of the geography of production. According to *The Economist*, 'The death of distance as a determinant of the cost of communications will probably be the single most important economic force shaping society in the first half of the next century'. What the telecommunications revolution has done is to reduce the cost of transmitting information across geographic space to virtually zero. At the same time, the microprocessor revolution has made it feasible for nearly everyone to participate in global communications. There are many statistics about the increase of international trade and transactions. Inferences about the degree of and increase in globalization based on international trade statistics miss an important point – it is the quality and not just the quantity of international transactions that has changed. Interaction among individuals adds a very different quality to the more traditional measures of trade, foreign direct investment (FDI), and capital flows and also has very different implications for the development of economic activities. This additional quality contributed by the transnational interactions of individuals, and not just arm's-length transactions by corporations, exposes people to ideas and experiences that were previously inaccessible.

The Political Dimension of Globalization

Globalization would not have occurred to the degree that it has if the fundamental changes were restricted to the advent of the microprocessor and telecommunications. It took a political revolution in large parts of the world to reap the full benefits from these technological changes. The political counterpart of the technological revolution was the increase in democracy and concomitant stability in areas of the world that had previously been inaccessible. The Cold War combined with internal political instability rendered potential investments in Eastern Europe and much of the developing world risky and impractical. During the period since the Second World War, most trade and economic investment were generally confined to Europe and North America, and later a few of the Asian countries, principally Japan and the Asian Tigers. Trade with countries behind the iron curtain was restricted and in some cases prohibited. Even trade with Japan and other Asian countries was highly regulated and restricted. Similarly, investments in politically unstable countries in South America and the Middle East resulted in episodes of national takeovers and confiscation where foreign investors lost their investments. In other words, the energy and focus devoted to maintain geopolitical balance was freed up to boost geo-economic growth.

The fall of the Berlin Wall in 1989 and subsequent downfall of communism in Eastern Europe and the former Soviet Union was a catalyst for stability and accessibility to parts of the world that had previously been inaccessible. Within just a few years it has become possible not just to trade with, but also to invest in these countries, as well as in many others such as China, Vietnam, India, and Indonesia. For example, India became accessible as a trading and investment partner after opening its economy in the early 1990s. Trade and investment with the developed countries quickly blossomed, reflecting the rapid change in two dimensions. First, India was confronted with sudden changes in trade and investment, not to mention a paradigmatic shift in ways of doing business. Second, to some foreign partners, taking advantage of opportunities in India also meant downward pressure on wages, and even plant closings in the home country. Of a much higher order of magnitude was the effect of China's new market orientation which has, since the beginning of the current century, brought China into the international arena and made it a major player in the international division of labor.

With the opening of some of these areas to participation in the world economy for the first time in decades, the equilibrium which dominated the economic landscape since the Second World War came to a sudden end. This created the opportunities associated with gaping disequilibria. Consider the large differentials in labor costs: as long as the Berlin Wall stood, and countries such as China and Vietnam remained closed, large discrepancies in wage rates could be maintained without eliciting responses in trade and FDI. The low wage rates in China or parts of the former Soviet Union neither invited foreign companies to build plants nor resulted in large-scale trade with the West based on access to low production costs. Investment by foreign companies was either prohibited by local governments or considered to be too risky by the companies. Similarly, trade and other restrictions limited the capabilities of firms in those countries from being able to produce and trade with Western nations.

The gaping wage differentials existing while the Berlin Wall stood and much of the communist world was cut off from the West were suddenly exposed in the early 1990s. There were not only unprecedented labor cost differentials but also massive and willing populations craving to join the high levels of consumption that had become the norm in Western Europe and North America. For example, in the early part of the 1990s, the daily earnings of labor were estimated to be \$90 in the United States and \$80 in the European Union (EU). This was a sharp contrast to shortly after the Berlin Wall fell and wages were only some \$6 in Poland and the Czech Republic. In Asia, the wage gap was even greater, where the daily earnings were \$1.50 in China, \$2.50 in India, and \$1.25 in Sri Lanka. The potential labor force in countries like China, with some 450 million workers, and India with some 350 million workers, dwarfs the workforce in North America and Europe.[2]

Of course, the productivity of labor is vastly greater in the West, which compensates to a significant degree for such large wage differentials. Nevertheless, given the magnitude of these numbers, both trade and investment have responded to the opportunities made possible by the events of 1989.

Globalization: Some Figures

While the most salient feature of globalization involves interaction and interfaces among individuals across national boundaries, the more traditional measures of transnational activity reflect an upward trend of global activities. These traditional measures include trade (exports and imports), FDI (inward and outward), international capital flows, and intercountry labor mobility. The overall trend for all of these measures has been strongly positive. The world trade of goods and services increased fivefold between 1985 and 2007 and has more than doubled since 1996 (OECD, 2008 and 2009), while trade in goods experiences even higher growth rates. The trade of services increased by more than three times over this time period. The increases in investment income, direct investment, and portfolio investment (UNCTAD, 2007) are also sizable. But the increase in all of these measures within just over a decade reflects the increasing degree of globalization.

The degree of world trade, measured by exports and imports, has increased over time. World exports increased from $1.3 trillion in 1970 to nearly $5 trillion in 1999 and to $12 trillion in 2006, in real terms (WTO, 2007). While some of this increase in the world export rate is attributable to an increased participation in international trade by countries that had previously been excluded, export rates in the leading industrialized countries have also increased over the past three decades. For example, US exports and imports have increased from 13 percent of GDP in 1985 to more than 21 percent by 1996 and to almost 30 percent in 2007 (OECD, 2007) while the corresponding openness values for the EU are 49, 79, and 123 percent, respectively. The increase in world trade is also not attributable to the influence of just a few industries or sectors, but rather is systematic across most parts of the economy. A different manifestation of globalization involves (inward) FDI, which has increased for all world countries from an average of $0.5 trillion in the last decade of the last century to $1.5 trillion in 2006 in real terms. The increase in global FDI has also not been solely the result of a greater participation by countries previously excluded from the world economy. In the EU (inward) FDI as a percentage of gross fixed capital formation increased from an average of 12 percent for the last decade of the last century to 18 percent in 2006. For the US this percentage stayed constant (7 percent), whereas for the UK it nearly doubled from 18 percent to 34 percent. The stock of FDI for all world countries as a percentage of gross domestic product increased from an average of 8 percent in the last decade of the last century to 25 percent in 2006 (UNCTAD, 2007). Transnational private capital flows have also increased in the past two decades. For instance, total net capital flows to developing countries increased from an average of US$120 billion (2006) in the 1995–2000 period to nearly US$200 billion in 2007 (IMF, 2007).

THE REGIONAL RESPONSE

It is generally believed that the United States has been much quicker to absorb the consequences of globalized production than Europe, based upon the different growth rates of the United States when compared to European nations over the last 20 years. Indeed, the European countries have been relatively slow to move from the *managed* to the *entrepreneurial* economy (Audretsch and Thurik, 2001 and 2004). Clearly, the European response varied across countries. Nevertheless, by and large five distinct stages can be discerned of the evolution of the European stance towards the entrepreneurial economy (Audretsch et al., 2002, pp. 4–6). The first stage was denial. During the 1980s and early 1990s, European policymakers looked to Silicon Valley with disbelief. Europe was used to facing a competitive threat from the large well-known multinational American corporations; but not from nameless and unrecognizable start-up firms in exotic industries such as software and biotechnology. Twenty years ago the emerging firms such as Apple Computer and Intel were interesting but irrelevant competitors in the automobile, textile, machinery, and chemical industries – then the obvious engines of European competitiveness.

The second stage, during the mid-1990s, was recognition. Europe recognized that the entrepreneurial economy in Silicon Valley delivered a sustainable long-run performance. But it held to its traditional products while embracing the theory of comparative advantage and channeling resources into traditional moderate technology industries. During this phase Europe's most important economy, Germany, would provide the automobiles, textiles, and machine tools. The entrepreneurial economy of Silicon Valley, Route 128, and the Research Triangle would produce the software and microprocessors. Each continent would specialize according to its comparative advantage and then trade with each other.

The third stage, during the second half of the 1990s, was envy. As Europe's growth stagnated and unemployment soared, the capacity of the American entrepreneurial economy to generate both jobs and higher wages became the object of envy. The United States and Europe adhered to different doctrines: as the entrepreneurial economy diffused across the United States, European policymakers, particularly in large countries such as Germany and France, despaired that European traditions and values were simply inconsistent and incompatible with the entrepreneurial economy. They should have concluded that the concept of comparative advantage had yielded to the different, but better, concept of dynamic competitive advantage.

The fourth stage, during the last years of the twentieth century, was consensus. European policymakers reached a consensus that – in the terminology of Audretsch and Thurik (2001 and 2004) – the new entrepreneurial economy was superior to the old managed economy and that a commitment had to be forged to creating a new entrepreneurial economy. A broad set of policies were instituted to create a new entrepreneurial economy. European policymakers looked across the Atlantic and realized that if places such as North Carolina, Austin, and Salt Lake City could implement targeted policies to create the entrepreneurial economy, European cities and regions could as well. After all, Europe had a number of advantages and traditions, such as a highly educated and skilled labor force, world-class research institutions and its variety in cultures, and hence innovative approaches to new products and organizations. These phenomena would provide a perfect framework for absorbing the high levels of uncertainty inherent to the entrepreneurial economy (Audretsch and Thurik, 2001).

The fifth stage is attainment. The entrepreneurial economy is finally emerging in Europe. Consider the Green Paper on Entrepreneurship of the European Commission (European Commission, 2003) which aimed to stimulate debate among policymakers, businesses, representative organizations, journalists, and scientific experts on how to shape entrepreneurship policy.[3] More recently, the adoption in 2008 of the Small Business Act for Europe has provided a comprehensive SME policy framework for the EU and its member states in which initiatives to foster an entrepreneurial economy feature prominently (European Commission, 2008). See Audretsch et al. (2002) for further information on the five stages and some country studies on the determinants of entrepreneurship.

Downsizing: An Old Phenomenon

Confronted with lower-cost competition in foreign locations, producers in the high-cost countries have four options apart from doing nothing and losing global market share: (i) reduce wages and other production costs sufficiently to compete with the low-cost foreign producers, (ii) substitute equipment and technology for labor to increase productivity, (iii) shift production out of the high-cost location and into the low-cost location, and (iv) formulate a strategy away from using traditional inputs such as land, labor, and capital and toward knowledge.

Many of the European and American firms that have successfully restructured resorted to alternatives (ii) and (iii). Substituting capital and technology for labor, along with shifting production to lower-cost locations, has resulted in waves of corporate downsizing throughout Europe and North America well before the more recent restructuring triggered by the financial crisis of 2008/09. For example, already between 1979 and

1995 more than 43 million jobs were lost in the United States as a result of corporate downsizing.[4] This includes 25 million blue-collar jobs and 18 million white-collar jobs. Similarly, the 500 largest US manufacturing corporations cut nearly five million jobs between 1980 and 1993, or one-quarter of their workforce (Audretsch, 1995). Perhaps most disconcerting, the rate of corporate downsizing has apparently increased over time in the United States, even as the unemployment rate has fallen. During most of the 1980s, about one in 25 workers lost a job. In the 1990s this has risen to one in 20 workers.

Although at its most intense in the late 1980s and early 1990s, this wave of corporate downsizing has continued (Burke and Cooper, 2000).[5] The cries of betrayal and lack of social conscience on the part of the large corporations have died in the twenty-first century because the virtues of the new entrepreneurial economy become clear, but they were ubiquitous in the last century.[6] It is a mistake to blame the corporations for this wave of downsizing that has triggered massive job losses and rising unemployment in so many countries. These corporations are simply trying to survive in an economy of global competitors who have access to lower-cost inputs.

Much of the policy debate responding to the twin forces of the telecommunications revolution and increased globalization has revolved around a trade-off between maintaining higher wages but suffering greater unemployment versus higher levels of employment but at the cost of lower wage rates. There is, however, an alternative. It does not require sacrificing wages to create new jobs, nor does it require fewer jobs to maintain wage levels and the social safety net. This alternative involves shifting economic activity out of the traditional industries where the high-cost countries of Europe and North America have lost the comparative advantage, and into those industries where the comparative advantage is compatible with both high wages and high levels of employment – knowledge-based economic activity (Audretsch and Thurik, 1999). This shift is one of the reasons why entrepreneurship starts playing a vital role and the modern economy is often described as the 'entrepreneurial economy'.

The Knowledge Response

Globalization has rendered the comparative advantage in traditional moderate technology industries incompatible with high wage levels. At the same time, the emerging comparative advantage that is compatible with high wage levels is based on innovative activity. For example, employment increased by 15 percent in Silicon Valley between 1992 and 1996, even though the mean income is 50 percent greater than in the rest of the country.[7]

Thus, the regional response to globalization has been the emergence of strategic management policy – not for firms, but for regions. As long as corporations were inextricably linked to their regional location by sub-stantial sunk costs, such as capital investment, the competitiveness of a region was identical to the competitiveness of the corporations located in that region. A quarter-century ago, while the proclamation, 'What is good for General Motors is good for America' may have been controversial, few would have disagreed that 'What is good for General Motors is good for Detroit.' And so it was with US Steel in Pittsburgh and Volkswagen in Wolfsburg. As long as the corporation thrived, so would the region.

As globalization has not only changed the degree to which the tradi-tional economic factors of capital and labor are sunk, but also shifted the comparative advantage in the high-wage countries of North America and Europe toward knowledge-based economic activity, corporations have been forced to shift production to lower-cost locations. This has led to a delinking between the competitiveness of firms and regions. The advent of the strategic management of regions has been a response to the realization that the strategic management of corporations includes a policy option not available to regions – changing the production location.

Knowledge Spillovers

That knowledge spills over is barely disputed. While disputing the impor-tance of knowledge externalities in explaining the geographic concentra-tion of economic activity, Krugman (1991) and others do not question the existence or importance of such knowledge spillovers. In fact, they argue that such knowledge externalities are so important and forceful that there is no compelling reason for a geographic boundary to limit the spatial extent of the spillover. According to this line of thinking, the concern is not that knowledge does not spill over but that it should stop spilling over just because it hits a geographic border, such as a city limit, state line, or national boundary. The claim that geographic location is important to the process linking knowledge spillovers to innovative activity in a world of e-mail, cell phones, fax machines, and cyberspace may seem surprising and even paradoxical. The resolution to the paradox posed by the localization of knowledge spillovers in an era where the telecommunications revolu-tion has drastically reduced the cost of communication lies in a distinction between knowledge and information. Information, such as the price of gold on the New York Stock Exchange, or the value of the yen in London, can be easily codified and has a singular meaning and interpretation. By con-trast, knowledge is vague, difficult to codify, and often only serendipitously recognized (Audretsch et al., 2000). While the marginal cost of transmitting information across geographic space has been rendered invariant to distance by the telecommunications revolution, the marginal cost of transmitting knowledge, and especially tacit knowledge, rises with distance.

Von Hippel (1994) demonstrates that high-context, uncertain knowledge, or what he terms a 'sticky' knowledge, is best transmitted via face-to-face interaction and through frequent and repeated contact. Geographic proximity matters in transmitting knowledge, because as Kenneth Arrow (1962) pointed out nearly half a century ago, such tacit knowledge is inherently non-rival in nature, and knowledge developed for any particular application can easily spill over and have economic value in very different applications. As Glaeser et al. (1992, p. 1126) have observed, 'Intellectual breakthroughs must cross hallways and streets more easily than oceans and continents'.

The importance of local proximity for the transmission of knowledge spillovers has been observed in many different contexts. It has been pointed out that, 'business is a social activity, and you have to be where important work is taking place'.[8] See Jacobs (1969), Jaffe (1989), Saxenian (1990), Feldman (1994), Venables (1996), and Audretsch (1998) for some of these contexts.

Not only does Krugman (1991, p. 53) doubt that knowledge spillovers are not geographically constrained, but he also argues that they are impossible to measure because 'knowledge flows are invisible, they leave no paper trail by which they may be measured and tracked'. However, an emerging literature (Jaffe et al., 1993) has overcome data constraints to measure the extent of knowledge spillovers and link them to the geography of innovative activity. See also Audretsch and Feldman (1996), Audretsch (1998), Breschi and Lissoni (2001), Bottazi and Perri (2003), and Audretsch and Lehmann (2005).

Empirical evidence suggests that location and proximity clearly matter in exploiting knowledge spillovers. Not only have Jaffe et al. (1993) found that patent citations tend to occur more frequently within the state in which they were patented than outside of that state, but Audretsch and Feldman (1996) found that the propensity of innovative activity to cluster geographically tends to be greater in industries where economic knowledge plays a more important role.[9] Prevenzer (1997) and Zucker et al. (1998) show that in biotechnology, which is an industry based almost exclusively on knowledge, the firms tend to cluster together in just a handful of locations. This finding is supported by Audretsch and Stephan (1996), who examine the geographic relationships of scientists working with biotechnology firms. The importance of geographic proximity is clearly shaped by the role played by the scientist. The scientist is more likely to be located in the same region as the firm when the relationship involves the transfer of knowledge rather than of information. However, when the scientist is providing a service to the company that does not involve knowledge transfer, local proximity becomes much less important.

There is reason to believe that knowledge spillovers are not homogeneous across firms. In the face of a wave of studies identifying vigorous innovative activity emanating from small firms in certain industries, the question is: how are these small, and frequently new, firms able to generate innovative output while undertaking generally negligible amounts of investment into knowledge-generating inputs, such as research and development (R&D)? The answer appears to be through exploiting knowledge created by expenditures on research in universities and on R&D in large corporations. The findings of Acs et al. (1994) suggest that the innovative output of all firms rises along with an increase in the amount of R&D inputs, both in private corporations as well as in university laboratories. However, R&D expenditures made by private companies play a particularly important role in providing knowledge inputs to the innovative activity of large firms, while expenditures on research made by universities serve as an especially key input for generating innovative activity in small enterprises. Apparently, large firms are more adept at exploiting knowledge created in their own laboratories, while their smaller counterparts have a comparative advantage at exploiting spillovers from university laboratories.

Spillovers, Agglomeration, and the Role of Regions

Once a city, region, or state develops a viable cluster of production and innovative activity why should it ever lose the first-mover advantage? One answer, provided by Audretsch and Feldman (1996), is that the relative importance of local proximity and therefore agglomeration effects is shaped by the stage of the industry life cycle. A growing literature suggests that who innovates and how much innovative activity is undertaken is closely linked to the phase of the industry life cycle (Klepper, 1996). Audretsch and Feldman (1996) argue that an additional key aspect to the evolution of innovative activity over the industry life cycle is where that innovative activity takes place. The theory of knowledge spillovers, derived from the knowledge production function, suggests that the propensity for innovative activity to cluster spatially will be the greatest in industries where tacit knowledge plays an important role. As argued above, it is tacit knowledge, as opposed to information that can only be transmitted informally, and that typically demands direct, trustful and repeated contact. The role of tacit knowledge in generating innovative activity is presumably the greatest during the early stages of the industry life cycle, before product standards have been established and a dominant design has emerged. Audretsch and Feldman classify 210 industries into four different stages of the life cycle. The results provided considerable evidence suggesting that the propensity for innovative activity to spatially cluster is shaped by the stage of the industry life cycle. On the one hand, new economic knowledge embodied in skilled workers tends to raise the propensity for innovative activity to spatially cluster throughout all phases of the industry life cycle. On the other hand, certain other sources of new economic knowledge, such as university research, tend to elevate the propensity for innovative activity to cluster during the introduction stage of the life cycle, but not during the growth stage, and then again during the stage of decline.

Perhaps most striking is the finding that greater geographic concentration of production actually leads to more, and not less, dispersion of innovative activity. Apparently, innovative activity is promoted by knowledge spillovers that occur within a distinct geographic region, particularly in the early stages of the industry life cycle, but as the industry evolves toward maturity and decline, innovation may be dispersed by additional increases in concentration of production that have been built up within that same region. The evidence suggests that what may serve as an agglomerating influence in triggering innovative activity to spatially cluster during the introduction and growth stages of the industry life cycle, may later result in a congestion effect, leading to greater dispersion in innovative activity. While the literature on economic geography has traditionally focused on factors such as rents, commuting time, and pollution as constituting congestion and dissipating agglomeration economies (Henderson, 1986), this type of congestion refers to lock-in with respect to new ideas. While there may have been agglomeration economies in automobiles in Detroit in the 1970s and computers in the Northeast Corridor in the 1980s, a type of intellectual lock-in made it difficult for Detroit to shift out of large-car production and for IBM and DEC to shift out of mainframe computers and into mini-computers. Perhaps it was this type of intellectual congestion that led to the emergence of the personal computer in California, about as far away from the geographic agglomeration of the mainframe computer as is feasible on the mainland of the United States. Even when IBM developed its own personal computer, the company located its fledgling PC facility in Boca Raton, Florida, way outside of the mainframe agglomeration, in the Northeast Corridor. Thus, there is at least some evidence suggesting that spatial agglomerations, just as other organizational units of economic activity, are vulnerable to technological lock-in, with the result being in certain circumstances that new ideas need new space.

THE KNOWLEDGE PRODUCTION FUNCTION AND THE EMERGENCE OF ENTREPRENEURSHIP

That SMEs would emerge as becoming more important seems to be contrary to many of the conventional theories of innovation. The starting point for most theories of innovation is the firm. In such theories the firms are exogenous and their performance in generating technological change is endogenous (Arrow, 1962). For example, in the most prevalent model found in the literature of technological change, the model of the knowledge production function, formalized by Zvi Griliches (1979), firms exist exogenously and then engage in the pursuit of new economic knowledge as an input into the process of generating innovative activity. The most decisive input in the knowledge production function is new economic knowledge. Knowledge as an input in a production function is inherently different from the more traditional inputs of labor, capital, and land. While the economic value of the traditional inputs is relatively certain, knowledge is intrinsically uncertain and its potential value is asymmetric across economic agents.[10] The most important, although not the only source of new knowledge is considered to be R&D. Other key factors generating new economic knowledge include a high degree of human capital, a skilled labor force, and a high presence of scientists and engineers.

There is considerable empirical evidence supporting the model of the knowledge production function. This empirical link between knowledge inputs and innovative output apparently becomes stronger as the unit of observation becomes increasingly aggregated. For example, at the unit of observation of countries, the relationship between R&D and patents is very strong. The most innovative countries, such as the United States, Japan, and Germany, also tend to undertake high investments in R&D. By contrast, little patent activity is associated with developing countries, which have very low R&D expenditures. Similarly, the link between R&D and innovative output, measured in terms of either patents or new product innovations, is also very strong when the unit of observation is the industry. The most innovative industries, such as computers, instruments, and pharmaceuticals also tend to be the most R&D intensive. Audretsch (1995) finds a simple correlation coefficient of 0.74 between R&D inputs and innovative output at the level of four-digit standard industrial classification (SIC) industries. However, when the knowledge production function is tested for the unit of observation of the firm, the link between knowledge inputs and innovative output becomes weakly positive in some studies and even non-existent or negative in others. The model of the knowledge production function becomes particularly weak when small firms are included in the sample. This is not surprising, since formal R&D

is concentrated among the largest corporations, but a series of studies (Acs and Audretsch, 1988) have clearly documented that small firms account for a disproportional share of new product innovations given their low R&D expenditures.

The breakdown of the knowledge production function at the level of the firm raises the question, where do innovative firms with little or no R&D get the knowledge inputs? This question becomes particularly relevant for firms that, because small and new, undertake small absolute amounts of R&D themselves, yet contribute considerable innovative activity in newly emerging industries such as biotechnology and computer software (Audretsch, 1995). One answer that has emerged in the economics literature is from other, third-party firms or research institutions, such as universities: economic knowledge may spill over from the firm conducting the R&D or the research laboratory of a university.

The Emergence of Entrepreneurship

Why should knowledge spill over from the source of origin? At least two major channels or mechanisms for knowledge spillovers have been identified in the literature. Both of these spillover mechanisms revolve around the issue of appropriability of new knowledge. First, Cohen and Levinthal (1989) suggest that existing firms develop the capacity to adapt new technology and ideas developed in other firms and are therefore able to appropriate some of the returns accruing to investments in new knowledge made externally.

Second, Audretsch (1995) proposes shifting the unit of observation away from exogenously assumed firms to individuals, such as scientists, engineers, or other knowledge workers – agents with endowments of new economic knowledge. When the lens is shifted away from the firm to the individual as the relevant unit of observation, the appropriability issue remains, but the question becomes: how can economic agents with a given endowment of new knowledge best appropriate the returns from that knowledge? If the scientist or engineer can pursue the new idea within the organizational structure of the firm developing the knowledge and appropriate roughly the expected value of that knowledge, he (or she) has no reason to leave the firm. On the other hand, if he places a greater value on his ideas than do the decision-making bureaucracy of the incumbent firm, he may choose to start a new firm to appropriate the value of his knowledge. In the metaphor provided by Albert O. Hirschman (1970), if voice proves to be ineffective within incumbent organizations, and loyalty is sufficiently weak, a knowledge worker may resort to exit the firm or university where the knowledge was created in order to form a new company.

In this spillover channel the knowledge production function is actually reversed. The knowledge is exogenous and embodied in a worker. The firm is created endogenously in the worker's effort to appropriate the value of his/her knowledge through innovative activity.

What emerges from the new evolutionary theories and empirical evidence on innovation as a competitive strategy deployed by SMEs is that markets are in motion, with many new firms entering the industry and many existing firms exiting. But is this motion horizontal, in that the bulk of firms exiting comprise firms that had entered relatively recently, or vertical, in that a significant share of the exiting firms had been established incumbents that were displaced by younger firms? In trying to shed some light on this question, Audretsch (1995) proposes two different models of the evolutionary process of industries over time. Some industries can be best characterized by the model of the conical revolving door, where new businesses are started, but there is also a high propensity to subsequently exit from the market. Other industries may be better characterized by the metaphor of the forest, where incumbent establishments are displaced by new entrants. Which view is more applicable apparently depends on three major factors – the technological conditions, scale economies, and demand (ibid., p. 171).

When SMEs deploy a strategy of innovation, they typically start at a very small scale of output. They are motivated by the desire to appropriate the expected value of new economic knowledge. But, depending upon the extent of scale economies in the industry, the firm may not be able to remain viable indefinitely at its start-up size. Rather, if scale economies are anything other than negligible, the new firm is likely to have to grow to survive. The temporary survival of new firms is presumably supported through the deployment of a strategy of compensating factor differentials that enable the firm to discover whether or not it has a viable product (Audretsch et al., 2001).

The empirical evidence has found that the post-entry growth of firms that survive tends to be spurred by the extent to which there is a gap between the minimum efficient scale (MES) level of output and the size of the firm. However, the likelihood of any particular new firm surviving tends to decrease as this gap increases. Such new SMEs deploying a strategy of innovation to attain competitiveness are apparently engaged in the selection process. Only those SMEs offering a viable product that can be produced efficiently will grow and ultimately approach or attain the MES level of output. The remainder will stagnate, and depending upon the severity of the other selection mechanism – the extent of scale economies – may ultimately be forced to exit out of the industry. Thus, in highly innovative industries, there is a continuing process of entry of new

SMEs into industries and not necessarily the permanence of individual SMEs over the long run. Although the skewed size distribution of firms persists with remarkable stability over long periods of time, a constant set of SMEs does not appear to be responsible for this skewed distribution. Rather, by serving as agents of change, SMEs provide an essential source of new ideas and experimentation that otherwise would remain untapped in the economy.

ENTREPRENEURSHIP IN THE GLOBALIZED ECONOMY

Above we explained how globalization has ushered in an increased role for the entrepreneurial organization as well as an increased importance of geographic location. The emergence of entrepreneurship is due to the shift towards knowledge-intensive industries where SMEs play an increasing role in the modern knowledge production function as a conduit of knowledge spillovers and the evolution of industries as learning mechanisms serving as agents of change. This suggests that through the process of taking knowledge created in an incumbent organization that might otherwise have remained unused and dormant, and using that knowledge to launch a new enterprise, entrepreneurship serves as an important mechanism for the spillover of knowledge.[11]

In addition, changes in technology may have shifted the competitive advantage away from larger-scale organizations to smaller-scale organizations. In particular, the advent of the ICT revolution directly favored SMEs and entrepreneurship (Nooteboom, 1999 and 2000).

Any economic regime switch based upon a radical new technology is accompanied by the arrival of numerous small firms. There are two reasons. First, since a new technology creates new markets by definition, it destroys incumbent market positions and the entry barriers typical for the older technology and its market. Hence, entry is made easy. Second, in the early stages of new markets, price elasticity is low because of the novelty of the product. The small firm of the typical entrant has no disadvantage because there is no competitive pressure to fight the battle of scale economies.

ICT and the Competitive Advantage of Small Firms

The specific nature of ICT-driven regime switch leads to two more reasons why the competitive advantages of large firms decrease. First, ICT tools and the practically free access to the Internet created a worldwide platform for relations between firms irrespective of their size. Small firms in particular need these relationships to compensate for their narrow set of competencies. The second has to do with the scale effects in transaction costs (Nooteboom, 1993) when firms engage in deals, try to do so, or want to monitor them. Transaction costs are higher for small firms when compared to large firms. This has to do with the fixed costs involved with setting up information systems for search, evaluation, control and enforcement. These fixed costs consist of necessary hardware, software and mastering their use. The arrival of the ICT tools which are generally cheap, small and easy to use together with the practically free access to the Internet has significantly reduced the fixed cost part in the transaction costs of any deal.

In the newer knowledge-intensive economy there is more need for the exploration side of doing business as well as the skills and knowledge side. A well-known conflict in the strategic renewal of firms is whether to engage in product or process innovation. This difficult choice between the exploration and the exploitation emphasis is made easier because, as we explained above, Western firms hardly have a competitive advantage when it comes to exploiting scale economies by fine tuning the production process. This fine tuning is a process of extreme focus, eliminating every redundant part in the production process using division of labor and mechanized tasks and the smooth interplay of the labor and machines involved. Once an optimum given a certain product is reached, little prevents the forces of the globalized world from moving this optimum to wherever labor costs are lowest. Exploration is an entirely different activity requiring openness, flexibility and experimentation instead of focus and elimination. It thrives in environments where variety and cooperation can be made useful to break the knowledge filter. These are typically 'industrial district'-like and 'open source'-oriented environments with many small firms and much turbulence.

Another aspect is the removal of one of the major scale effects in the exploitation stage of the product life cycle: easy to use and cheap ICT tools in part destroy the fruits of large scale. Scale effects in distribution are threatened by the above-mentioned drop in the fixed part of the transaction costs. Lastly, there is the reputation effect which indeed protects many Western businesses, for instance in the fashion or lifestyle industries. Another cause of the decreased importance of the exploitation stage of the product life cycle is the increased wealth of the global consumer, who can afford to behave whimsically and individualistically so that the exploitation period of any given product decreases when compared to the exploration stage. Finally, the discrimination between the exploitation and exploration sides of doing business decreases. This is the world of prototypes, beta versions, simulations, and so on. This merger between the exploitation and exploration stages is necessary because of demand pressures but also made possible by the introduction of numerical controlled machines, that is, robots (Acs et al., 1991). Computer-aided design facilitates vertical cooperation and the speed with which products can be brought to the market.

The fine tuning of the production process involves skills and knowledge as well as physical capital. In the knowledge-intensive economy the emphasis is on skills and knowledge rather than on physical capital since globalization together with the whimsical and individualistic consumer makes investments in inflexible physical capital less desirable. Rejuvenation of labor by training or replacement and improvement of knowledge by joining loose networks of businesses or cooperation with research institutes is easier than rebuilding factories and plants. By and large, the shape of factories in the service industry differs from that in manufacturing where investments in physical capital are closely connected to a specific product. In the services, physical capital takes the shape of buildings and offices which can be used for different and changing portfolios of skills and knowledge. This is one of the reasons why Western countries have not lost their competitive advantage in the service industries. The higher orientation towards skills and knowledge creates more room for SMEs in many industries.

The Declining Role of 'Leakage'

Traditionally, 'leakage' is the most important impediment for businesses to cooperate. Leakage is the unwanted spillover of knowledge or competencies which is detrimental to the specific capabilities of a firm. A firm's competitive position can be negatively affected by leakage if the knowledge or competencies spill over beyond the boundaries of a specific cooperative effort and its partners towards potential competitors. Of course, a solution is the contracting and maintenance of exclusivity. This again has several disadvantages. First, many modern forms of cooperation have ill-defined goals and means by definition, since they aim for novelty. Second, the transaction costs involved in setting up, monitoring, and enforcing exclusivity contracts can be high because of their complexity and uncertainty. Lastly, exclusivity contracts limit the spontaneity of the process of learning which is essential in the process of joint learning. 'Leakage' is less of a problem in the globalized economy with its fast-changing consumer tastes and its fast-changing technological opportunities. First, these fast changes limit the time for competitors to absorb the potential fruits of a third-party cooperative effort. By the time they understand, imitate, implement, and commercialize the original cooperative effort, the first mover may already work on further developments and improvements. Second, as described above, more and more competitive advantage consists of the potential to combine processes of exploitation and exploration. This combination is a way of rejuvenation which is deeply engrained in a firm's organizational culture and cannot be easily imitated. In short, an essential part of the competitive advantage of modern firms is their ability to bring about change in products and technology and less to understand the virtues of existing products and technologies. Protection of what already exists as well as 'leakage' of its deeper characteristics has become less important. This protection was more difficult for SMEs.

So, there are many avenues by which the ICT revolution stimulated the competitive advantages of SMEs and generated new emphasis on the role of entrepreneurship. These avenues go beyond the effects of globalization which urged modern economies to shift towards knowledge-intensive activities. The increased emphasis on SMEs and entrepreneurship leads to a shift in policy focus towards their individual promotion as well as their collective support on the 'industrial district' level.

CONCLUSIONS

Globalization is shifting the comparative advantage in the OECD countries away from being based on traditional inputs of production, such as land, labor, and capital, toward knowledge. This chapter has focused on two important implications, both of which emanate from the shift in comparative advantage revolving around knowledge-based economic activity. The first implication involves the organizational context for the commercialization of that knowledge and the second implication involves the spatial or geographic context.

As what has been commonly characterized as the 'Swedish Paradox' and the 'European Paradox' suggests, investments in knowledge alone may not suffice to generate innovative activity and ultimately economic growth and employment. Rather, there are both theoretical and empirical reasons for challenging the assumption that investments in knowledge automatically lead to innovation and economic growth. The existence of the knowledge filter impedes the automatic spillover of knowledge. Entrepreneurial activity, in the organizational context of a new firm, can play a key role in generating economic growth by providing a conduit for the spillover of knowledge from the organization where it is created to a new organization where it is actually commercialized and transformed into innovative activity. Thus, entrepreneurship emerges as an important organizational form when the comparative advantage is based on knowledge, because it provides the link between the creation of that knowledge and its transformation into innovative activity.

A large literature has provided compelling evidence that knowledge spillovers tend to be localized within close geographic proximity to the source of that knowledge. In other words: entrepreneurial activity accordingly tends to spatially cluster within close geographic proximity to the knowledge source. This suggests that one of the apparent paradoxes of globalization is the (re-)emergence of regions as a source of knowledge and entrepreneurial activity that is localized and requires a presence in that region both to access the knowledge as well as to commercialize it. Thus, policies that promote both knowledge investments as well as entrepreneurship have become prominent for many regions in the most developed countries. While much of the recent attention has been devoted to the financial and economic crises, there is little reason to think that, as long as the trends towards globalized economic activity increase, the important role played by entrepreneurship within a regional context will diminish.

NOTES

1. The preparation of this document benefited from visits of Isabel Grilo to IDS in Bloomington and the Max Planck Institute in Jena. It has been written in cooperation with the research program SCALES, carried out by EIM and financed by the Dutch Ministry of Economic Affairs. Haibo Zhou provided research assistance.
2. The data are adopted from Jensen (1993).
3. It analyzes a range of policy options and asks, within the proposed context for entrepreneurship policy, a number of questions suggesting different options on how to reach progress.
4. 'The Downsizing of America', *New York Times*, 3 March 1996, p. 1.
5. The disadvantages of downsizing have also been documented. See Dougherty and Bowman (1995).
6. As the German newspaper, *Die Zeit* (2 February 1996, p.1) pointed out in a front page article, 'When Profits Lead to Ruin – More Profits and More Unemployment: Where is the Social Responsibility of the Firms?', the German public has responded to the recent waves of corporate downsizing with accusations that corporate Germany is no longer fulfilling its share of the social contract.
7. 'The Valley of Money's Delights', *The Economist*, 29 March 1997, special section, p. 1.
8. 'The Best Cities for Knowledge Workers', *Fortune*, 15 November 1993, p. 44.
9. Economic knowledge is here proxied by R&D activity.
10. Arrow (1962) pointed out that this is one of the reasons for inherent market failure. See also Audretsch et al. (2000).
11. The partly endogenous character of entrepreneurial activity is best shown in Acs et al. (2009) where the knowledge spillover theory of entrepreneurship is presented.

REFERENCES

Acs, Z.J. and D.B. Audretsch (1988), 'Innovation in large and small firms: an empirical analysis', *American Economic Review*, **78** (4), 678–90.

Acs, Z.J., D.B. Audretsch and B. Carlsson (1991), 'Flexible technology and firm size', *Small Business Economics*, **3** (4), 307–19.

Acs, Z.J., D.B. Audretsch and M.P. Feldman (1994), 'R&D spillovers and recipient firm size', *Review of Economics and Statistics*, **76** (2), 336–40.

Acs, Z.J., P. Braunerhjelm, D.B. Audretsch and B. Carlsson (2009), 'The knowledge spillover theory of entrepreneurship', *Small Business Economics*, **32** (1), 15–30.

Arrow, K. (1962), 'Economic welfare and the allocation of resources for invention', in R. Nelson (ed.), *The Rate and Direction of Inventive Activity*, Princeton, NJ: Princeton University Press, pp. 609–25.

Audretsch, D.B. (1995), *Innovation and Industry Evolution*, Cambridge, MA: MIT Press.

Audretsch, D.B. (1998), 'Agglomeration and the location of innovative activity', *Oxford Review of Economic Policy*, **14** (2), 18–29.

Audretsch, D.B. and M.P. Feldman (1996), 'R&D spillovers and the geography of innovation and production', *American Economic Review*, **86** (4), 253–73.

Audretsch, D.B., P. Houweling and A.R. Thurik (2000), 'Firm survival in the Netherlands', *Review of Industrial Organization*, **16** (1), 1–11.

Audretsch, D.B. and E.E. Lehmann (2005), 'Does the knowledge spillover theory hold for regions?', *Research Policy*, **34** (8), 1191–202.

Audretsch, D.B. and P. Stephan (1996), 'Company-scientist locational links: the case of biotechnology', *American Economic Review*, **86** (4), 641–52.

Audretsch, D.B. and A.R. Thurik (1999), *Innovation, Industry Evolution and Employment*, Cambridge: Cambridge University Press.

Audretsch, D.B. and A.R. Thurik (2001), 'What is new about the new economy: sources of growth in the managed and entrepreneurial economies', *Industrial and Corporate Change*, **10** (1), 267–315.

Audretsch, D.B. and A.R. Thurik (2004), 'A model of the entrepreneurial economy', *International Journal of Entrepreneurship Education*, **2** (2), 143–66.

Audretsch, D.B., A.R. Thurik, I. Verheul and A.R.M. Wennekers (2002), *Entrepreneurship: Determinants and Policies in the New Economy*, Boston, MA and Dordrecht: Kluwer Academic Publishers.

Audretsch, D.B., G. van Leeuwen, B.J. Menkveld and A.R. Thurik (2001), 'Market dynamics in the Netherlands: competition policy and the response of small firms', *International Journal of Industrial Organisation*, **19** (5), 795–821.

Bottazzi, L. and G. Peri (2003), 'Innovation and spillovers in regions: evidence from European patent data', *European Economic Review*, **47** (4), 687–710.

Breschi, S. and F. Lissoni (2001), 'Knowledge spillovers and local innovation systems: a critical survey', *Industrial and Corporate Change*, **10** (4), 975–1005.

Burke, R.J. and C.L. Cooper (2000), *The Organisation in Crisis: Downsizing, Restructuring and Privatisation*, Oxford: Blackwell.

Cohen, W. and D. Levinthal (1989), 'Innovation and learning: the two faces of R&D', *Economic Journal*, **99** (3), 569–96.

Dougherty, D.J. and E.H. Bowman (1995), 'The effects of organizational downsizing on product innovation', *California Management Review*, **37** (4), 28–44.

European Commission (2003), *Green Paper: Entrepreneurship in Europe*, available at: http://ec.europa.eu/enterprise/entrepreneurship/green_paper/index.htm (accessed December 2009).

European Commission (2008), '"Think small first", a "Small Business Act" for European Brussels', available at: http://ec.europa.eu/enterprise/policies/sme/small-business-act/index_en.htm (accessed December 2009).

Feldman, M. (1994), *The Geography of Innovation*, Boston, MA: Kluwer.

Glaeser, E., H. Kallal, J. Scheinkman and A. Shleifer (1992), 'Growth of cities', *Journal of Political Economy*, **100**, 1126–52.

Griliches, Z. (1979), 'Issues in assessing the contribution of R&D to productivity growth', *Bell Journal of Economics*, **10**, 92–116.

Henderson, V. (1986), 'Efficiency of resource usage and city size', *Journal of Urban Economics*, **19** (1), 47–70.

Hirschman, A.O. (1970), *Exit, Voice, and Loyalty*, Cambridge, MA: Harvard University Press.

IMF (2007), 'World economic outlook: globalization and inequality', WEO Reports, International Monetary Fund, available at: http://www.imf.org/external/pubs/ft/weo/2007/02/index.htm (accessed December 2009).

Jacobs, J. (1969), *The Economy of Cities*, New York: Random House.

Jaffe, A. (1989), 'Real effects of academic research', *American Economic Review*, **79**, 957–70.

Jaffe, A., M. Trajtenberg and R. Henderson (1993), 'Geographic localization of knowledge spillovers as evidenced by patent citations', *Quarterly Journal of Economics*, **63**, 577–98.

Jensen, M.C. (1993), 'The modern industrial revolution, exit, and the failure of internal control systems', *Journal of Finance*, **48**, 831–80.

Klepper, S. (1996), 'Entry, exit, growth, and innovation over the product life cycle', *American Economic Review*, **86** (4), 562–83.

Krugman, P. (1991), *Geography and Trade*, Cambridge, MA: MIT Press.

Nooteboom, B. (1993), 'Firm size effects on transaction costs', *Small Business Economics*, **5** (4), 283–95.

Nooteboom, B. (1999), *Interfirm Alliances: Analysis and Design*, London: Routledge.

Nooteboom, B. (2000), *Learning and Innovation in Organizations and Economies*, Oxford: Oxford University Press.

OECD (2007), *OECD Economic Outlook No. 81*, Paris: Organisation for Economic Co-operation and Development.

OECD (2008), *Main Economic Indicators*, Paris: Organisation for Economic Co-operation and Development.

OECD (2009), *OECD Economic Outlook No. 85,* Paris: Organisation for Economic Co-operation and Development.

Prevenzer, M. (1997), 'The dynamics of industrial clustering in biotechnology', *Small Business Economics*, **9** (3), 255–71.

Saxenian, A. (1990), 'Regional networks and the resurgence of Silicon Valley', *California Management Review*, **33**, 89–111.

UNCTAD (2007), *World Investment Report 2007, Transnational Corporations, Extractive Industries and Development*, New York and Geneva: United Nations Conference on Trade and Development, available at: http://www.unctad.org/wir (accessed December 2009).

Venables, A.J. (1996), 'Localization of industry and trade performance', *Oxford Review of Economic Policy*, **12** (3), 52–60.

Von Hippel, E. (1994), 'Sticky information and the locus of problem solving: implications for innovation', *Management Science*, **40**, 429–39.

WTO (2007), 'World Trade 2006, Prospects for 2007: Risks Lie Ahead Following Stronger Trade in 2006', WTO Press/472, World Trade Organization, available at: http://www.wto.org/english/news_e/pres07_e/pr472_e.htm#chart1 (accessed December 2009).

Zucker, L., M. Darby and J. Armstrong (1998), 'Geographically localized knowledge: spillovers or markets?' *Economic Inquiry*, **36** (1), 65–86.

3 Regional determinants of entrepreneurial activities – theories and empirical evidence
Rolf Sternberg

CONCEPTUALIZATION OF ENTREPRENEURSHIP FROM A REGIONAL PERSPECTIVE

This chapter offers theoretical arguments and empirical evidence to support the hypothesis that entrepreneurial activities are to a large extent a 'regional event' (Feldman, 2001). It is argued that regional, that is, subnational, determinants are relevant for both an individual's decision to start a new business and a start-up's success. As Figure 3.1 illustrates, entrepreneurial activities are influenced by regional (and non-regional) determinants and have regional (and non-regional) effects.

For example, entrepreneurs need the primarily regional, informal network of friends, former colleagues and bosses, relatives, and first

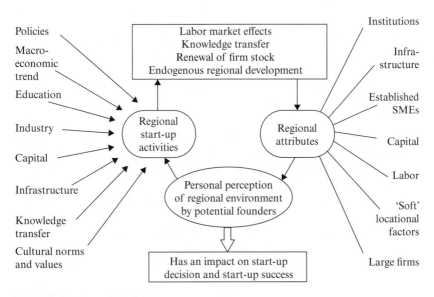

Source: Sternberg (2009, 245).

Figure 3.1 Causes and effects of regional entrepreneurship

customers to be able to realize their start-up idea at all, particularly at the first attempt. Not only the causes, but also the economic effects of entrepreneurial activities can primarily be felt locally and regionally, at least in a start-up's early days (see Figure 3.1). Only when several start-ups actually develop into forcefully growing new firms, can employment and other effects then be felt on a national scale. In each case, empirical research shows that the concentration of start-ups (particularly knowledge-intensive ones) in space and time has made a decisive contribution to the economic rise of regions that were previously anything but leading economic regions. This is demonstrated not only by the much quoted Silicon Valley (of the 1950s, Lee et al., 2000), but also by the cases of Munich (Germany) (see Sternberg and Tamásy, 1999) or Cambridgeshire (UK) (Segal Quince Wicksteed Ltd, 1985) over the past two decades.

Entrepreneurship is a particular regional or local phenomenon because people usually start businesses where they were born, have worked, or already reside (Stam, 2007). Therefore, a region rather than a nation seems to be a better unit for understanding the most proximate factors affecting entrepreneurship (see Sternberg and Rocha, 2007; Stam, 2009). Due to this 'geographic inertia' (Sorenson and Audia, 2000) as well as the spatial immobility of most entrepreneurs and their start-ups (Malecki, 1997), such start-ups are in theory elements of the regionally endogenous development potential (Johansson et al., 2001) and therefore contributing factors to endogenous regional development (Sternberg, 2009).

In many countries, the number of research projects, publications and academics dealing with (regional) entrepreneurship has increased considerably since about the mid-1990s. Large-scale public basic research programs have generated important stimuli for entrepreneurship research in several countries such as the 'Interdisciplinary Entrepreneurship Research' priority program of the German Research Foundation (DFG) between 1998 and 2004, resulting in numerous publications (see the related edited volumes by Fritsch and Grotz, 2002; Fritsch and Niese, 2004; Fritsch and Schmude, 2006; and Sternberg, 2006).

Every study on entrepreneurship needs a definition of what is understood by this term since there is no single, generally accepted definition of entrepreneurship or of regional entrepreneurship in the research community (for example, Sternberg and Wennekers, 2005). I understand entrepreneurship as a combination of behavioral entrepreneurship with some aspects of occupational entrepreneurship, making new venture creation the hallmark of entrepreneurship (Cooper, 2003). More specific definitions are needed for empirical work, however. For the purposes of this chapter the definition of entrepreneurship is adapted from the Global Entrepreneurship Monitor (GEM). Reynolds et al. (2005) define entrepreneurially active people as adults in the process of setting up a business if they (partly) own and/or currently own and manage an operating young business. The specific indicators of entrepreneurial activity (in the sense of new venture creation) are oriented toward the process character of entrepreneurship (Lumpkin and Dess, 1996). Four phases and three transition points between them can be differentiated: the conception phase ('latent entrepreneurs', see Grilo and Irigoyen, 2006), the gestation or start-up phase ('nascent entrepreneurs', see Davidsson, 2006), the creation of an operational business (owner-managers of young firms), and the aging of the start-up firm (established firms). See Bosma et al. (2009) for GEM operational definitions for individuals in each of the four phases. I intend to concentrate in this chapter primarily on start-ups as autonomous and independent businesses (not including subsidiaries and intrapreneurship). The regional determinants of the number of independent start-ups per region and the number of new subsidiaries per region clearly differ considerably (Bosma et al., 2008).

Comparative empirical research on regional entrepreneurship is restricted by the fact that there is no universally accepted set of statistics in most countries and subnational regions on the scope and dynamism of entrepreneurial activities in the sense defined. Empirical research, which relies on data that are as realistic as possible, must therefore generate the necessary data for itself (survey data). This is labor intensive, expensive and, due to the differing understanding of entrepreneurial activities, far from trivial. Various data sources therefore compete for the favor of academia and politics in many countries (see, for example, the presentation of alternative data sources in Germany by Fritsch and Niese, 2002). When regional analyses (covering all regions in a country) are to be carried out, large sample sizes need to be gathered. This led to the important differentiation between macro-level data, individual (micro-level) data, and a combination of both types of data within the same analysis (multi-level analysis). The last is still rare in entrepreneurship research (Davidsson and Wiklund, 2001) and mostly ignores the problem of ecological fallacies (see Schmude and Leiner, 1999).

Whereas macro-data analyses long dominated regional entrepreneurship (see Davidsson and Wiklund, 2001), analyses based on individual data (mainly survey data) have increased in recent years. Individual survey data make it possible to record context variables (for example, networks) and individual perceptions. Numerous empirical research attempts based on case studies succeeded in this respect – focused on either the individual entrepreneur within a certain region or the individual region (for example, Sternberg, 2006). In most cases, however, it is not possible to compare these results with those in other regions, that is, to carry out interregional comparisons. Davidsson et al. (2001, 13) are right when they criticize the laziness of many empirical entrepreneurship researchers who prefer to 'work with data that are readily available rather than data that are most important', in other words, with secondary data as opposed to survey data. This is particularly true of many regional issues such as contextual or cultural variables, which are relatively rarely recorded (see Malecki, 1997).

THEORY-BASED ARGUMENTS FOR THE REGIONAL CONTEXT IMPACT

Determinants of the Start-up Decision and Start-up Growth

'Today the phenomenon of entrepreneurship has lacked . . . a conceptual framework' (Shane and Venkataraman, 2000, 217). In its essence, this is also true of theories on regional entrepreneurship. Entrepreneurship research still largely ignores the spatial implications despite the increasing significance of contextual aspects of entrepreneurship, whereas the disciplines that are by definition interested in spatial issues, such as regional science or economic geography, barely touch on the subject of entrepreneurship, at least from a theoretical point of view (see Malecki, 1997, and Sternberg, 2004). Consequently, it can be no surprise that most theoretical entrepreneurship research uses theories that have been developed for the purpose of other disciplines.

Analysis of start-up activities and the propensity to launch new firms was for a long time dominated by approaches concentrating on the supply side and factors relating to the person of the entrepreneur, with the emphasis in particular on the motivation and motives for launching a company. However, personal factors alone cannot explain the entrepreneurship event; a wide range of contextual factors are becoming more relevant. In effect, the consideration of environmental factors in a broad sense, including spatial proximity and features of the regional environment, is becoming ever-more prevalent and popular. The intention is not to give the impression that absolutely all entrepreneurship activity is influenced by regional contexts or context variables. Some framework conditions that are suited to explaining entrepreneurship activities are national, meaning they differ more between countries, rather than between regions within a country (for example, areas of tax legislation); others are defined by characteristics of the individuals themselves. However, in addition to nationally more or less similar framework conditions, there are also a large number of other framework conditions that vary between regions of the same country and which influence the individual decision for or against self-employment. The frequently used term 'entrepreneurial climate' unifies many of these regionally specific characteristics which are at least potentially capable of influencing the individual decision of the local population for or against launching a start-up and may even influence the future success or failure of said start-up.

Entrepreneurship is a process of emergence. All phases of this process are influenced by various determinants. It makes sense to break down these determinants according to national (or macro) environment, micro environment and regional (or meso) environment (see Sternberg and Rocha, 2007). National factors are supraregional and they include cultural, social, political, and financial conditions as well as the system of education and research, the infrastructure, and the economic structure. The regional environment includes the same elements as the national one, except that in this case the question is of the characteristics of the individual region and not the entire country. As for the micro level, social environmental factors include, in particular, the social and professional backgrounds and the egocentric networks of the potential entrepreneurs. These elements can also be shaped by primarily regional (for example, private networks) or primarily supraregional (for example, a large number of professional networks) influences. Personal factors relating to the actual or potential founder such as entrepreneurial motivation (push versus pull factors), demographic factors (age and gender), as well as personality traits (for example, efficiency and the willingness to take risks) do not belong to the three types of environment. Rather, they can exert a direct influence on the perception of the three environments and therefore on the start-up decision and the success of the start-up.

Every individual filters the environmental signals he or she receives. The totality of individual entrepreneurial activities in a particular region determines the entrepreneurial activity of the region. Macro and micro factors are operative in all nations and in all regions of a nation. They have a clear regional dimension, however, because they come into play to varying degrees and thus operate differently in different regions. Even pure industrial economists now accept that 'the presence of substantially different geographical environments further increases the variability in the determinants and post-entry impact of new firm formation' (Santarelli and Vivarelli, 2007, 465). The high degree of spatial immobility of academic entrepreneurs is correctly interpreted as one piece of evidence of the importance of the regional environment for start-ups (see Wagner and Sternberg, 2004; Stam, 2009). The geographical proximity of actors potentially relevant for entrepreneurial processes, however, often does not guarantee true entrepreneurial activities if other kinds of proximity, such as cognitive proximity, are lacking (see Boschma, 2005, and Sternberg, 2007).

Entrepreneurship and Regional Growth Theories

Most of the older regional growth theories (see Capello and Nijkamp, 2009 for an overview) do not explicitly consider entrepreneurship (see Malecki, 1983, for a valuable review of these older theories), although there are some remarkable exceptions (for example, Sweeney, 1987; Malecki, 1997). Of course, Joseph Schumpeter (1942) had developed an influential framework explaining why and how entrepreneurship is favorable for innovation and economic growth. However, his framework was dedicated to the national level and to large firms. Some of the more recent theories of innovation-based regional growth, for example the industrial district approach, the theory of flexible production and specialization, and the concept of the innovative milieu, consider small-firm entrepreneurship more explicitly as a determinant of regional, technology-based growth (see Sternberg, 1996, for a review). Most of these approaches emphasize the role of regional innovation processes for regional economic growth. Actor-oriented explanations of regional innovation processes have gained in importance. The launch of new firms (rather than innovation within incumbent firms) nowadays plays a more important role for regional innovation processes than in the 'old economy'. Consequently, in many theories and concepts explaining regional innovation processes, we see the emphasis shift from firms and institutions to individuals. Thus, individual entrepreneurs in start-ups grow in relevance.

Regional growth theories are expected to answer the question 'why do some regions grow faster than others?'. Following Acs and Varga (2002), we consider three strands of literature that address exactly this question: the new economic geography (NEG) developed by Krugman (1991), the new growth theory designed by Romer (1990) and the new economics of innovation, created as a systematic approach first at the national level (national innovation systems, see Lundvall, 1992, and Nelson, 1993) and later at the regional level (regional innovation systems (RISs), see Cooke et al., 2004). All three approaches have been the subject of intense and controversial discussion in the literature (for NEG, see Martin and Sunley, 1996; for the new growth theory, see Martin and Sunley, 1998; for innovation system approaches, see Oinas and Malecki, 2002).

However, Krugman's theory of spatial concentration does not seem to be suitable for explaining technology-led regional development because it does not model spatially relevant knowledge spillovers (Acs, 2002). The main merit of the new growth theory is that it explicitly considers innovation as an engine of economic growth. It also acknowledges that the immigration of new creative people (that is, employees incorporating new knowledge) may have a positive impact on economic growth. However, it is not really a *regional* growth theory, although some 'regional' (that is, nation states) interpretations exist (see Grossman and Helpman, 1991). More importantly, new growth theory underestimates the role of tacit knowledge which plays an important role in the creation of innovation and for innovation-led regional development (Maskell and Malmberg, 1999).

Entrepreneurship and Regional Innovation Systems

Due to their actor-centricity and the strong emphasis on networks between these actors (including those of entrepreneurs), the systemic approaches to regional innovation processes are potentially good candidates to explain the role of entrepreneurship in regional economic development. The regional innovation system (see Cooke et al., 2004; Asheim and Gertler, 2005) approach takes into consideration the systemic character of the innovation process, which corresponds with the finding that innovation processes increasingly involve sharing work. According to Edquist (2005, 182), a system of innovation comprises all determinants of the innovation process, that is, all important economic, social, political, organizational, institutional, and other factors that influence the development, diffusion, and use of innovations. The constituents of systems of innovation are components and relations among these components. The main components in an innovation system are organizations (players or actors, including entrepreneurs) and institutions (sets of common habits, norms, routines, and so on that regulate the relations and interactions between individuals, groups, and organizations). An RIS considers all components and relations among these organizations and institutions relevant in and for a selected region.

Surprisingly enough, the growing number of studies concerning the impact of entrepreneurship on regional innovation-based growth has not yet been included in the RIS debate (see Sternberg, 2007). In line with literature on innovation systems, firms neither operate in an atomistic fashion nor do they interact with others based only on business considerations. Any business activity is embedded in a broader socio-institutional context, and therefore the economic dimensions or relationships cannot be separated from the socio-institutional ones. Saxenian's (1994) comparison of Silicon Valley and Greater Boston shows that several very different RISs with similarly differing roles played by local entrepreneurs and significant cultural differences can exist within the same national innovation system.

There is clear theoretical and empirical evidence that an interdependent relationship between the regional environment (or regional growth) and entrepreneurial activities exists, which makes entrepreneurship a highly relevant topic of RISs. Entrepreneurship, particularly in the form of innovative new businesses, has a positive influence on the RIS in various ways (see Koschatzky, 2001, and Sternberg, 2007). First, these firms are among the main actors of innovation creation within a region. They may also contribute to the development of region-specific knowledge. Second, they enjoy stronger growth on average than other new firms and established firms; overall, therefore, they may be drivers of the dynamics of an RIS – although this does not apply to every single start-up. Third, there is a close correlation between the learning capability of (other) regional innovative actors and the number of new innovative firms within an RIS. This promotes regional learning processes which are an important impulse for the emergence and liveliness of RISs (see Lawson and Lorenz, 1999). Thus, entrepreneurial activities support the sectoral and technological changes within an RIS. Fourth, new venture creation is obviously a superior method of penetrating the regional 'knowledge filter' over incumbent innovative firms. The idea of a 'knowledge filter' between new knowledge and new economic knowledge empirically tested by Acs and Plummer (2005) sheds light on the problem that not all new knowledge in the form of products, processes, and organizations leads to commercial exploitation and, consequently, economic growth. Due to the fact that the ability to produce, identify, and exploit knowledge depends on the existing knowledge stock and the absorptive capacity of actors such as employees in firms and researchers at universities and research institutions, the existing knowledge stock will never be commercialized to its full extent. Regions or selected firms within a region need transmission channels which help to separate knowledge that is economically useful from knowledge that is not. New innovative firms are especially suitable as such a knowledge filter (see Mueller, 2006, for German regions). Finally, small innovative firms tend to have the strongest intraregional connections if one compares them with other innovative actors such as research institutes, established and large manufacturing firms, or large firms of the service sector (Sternberg, 1999). Due to their great spatial immobility, their mainly intraregional innovation linkages and personal networks, they contribute significantly to the endogenous development potential of a region. While start-ups are mostly a regional phenomenon, in the case of start-ups by return migrants or transnational entrepreneurs, the international background of the founder can help to reduce the risk of lock-in effects for the RIS in which they settle (see Müller and Sternberg, 2008, and Saxenian, 2006).

Urban Agglomeration, Cities and Entrepreneurship

In fact, it is not easy to distinguish theories of regional economic growth in general from theories of urban economic growth, that is, of economic agglomeration. Most of the theoretical arguments in favor of agglomeration (in an economic sense) also hold true for economic growth in *all* region types (see McCann and van Oort, 2009). Urban areas and their cores, the cities, are actually only one of several region types. But there are many theoretical indications and empirical findings demonstrating the particularly comprehensive entrepreneurship activities in such urban areas. Two theoretical concepts in particular point to the special role of urban areas (see Acs et al., 2011): agglomeration theory and Richard Florida's (2002a,b) argument in favor of creativity and the 'geography of talent'.

As for agglomeration theory, the new growth theory directly models the knowledge-based element of the growth process as a result of profit-motivated choices of economic agents. Recently published findings in entrepreneurship, the geography of innovation, and the new economic geography suggest that the extent to which a country or a region is 'entrepreneurial' and its economic system is 'agglomerated' could be a factor that explains technological change. If knowledge necessary for technological change is not codified but tacit, the flow of knowledge can only be facilitated by personal interactions. Spatial proximity of knowledge owners and potential users therefore appears to be critical for the transmission of tacit knowledge (Polanyi,1966). This favors new firms in agglomerated urban areas. Geographical proximity is therefore of key importance for the flow of tacit knowledge in particular. Various empirical studies clearly demonstrate the distance-sensitivity of knowledge spillovers (for example, for the US by Jaffe et al., 1993, and Varga, 1998).

In addition, the spillover impact in knowledge production is positively related to the size of the region due to richer network linkages and a wider selection of producer services in larger areas. All this results in more entrepreneurship activities (also in relative terms), the larger the population of the urban area. The very recent 'knowledge spillover theory of entrepreneurship' (Audretsch et al., 2006; Audretsch and Keilbach, 2007) builds on these findings. A high level of regional research and development (R&D) activity increases regional opportunities to start new knowledge-based businesses, and such a high level of R&D intensity is supposed to increase the creation of new technological knowledge and, through localized knowledge spillovers, the level of opportunities for start-ups in knowledge-based industries. Consequently, ideas and knowledge flow faster and the provision of ancillary services and inputs is also greater in large cities – and one effect of this phenomenon is that entrepreneurial activity should be higher in more densely populated regions.

According to the 'economic geography of talent' hypothesis put forward by Florida (2002a,b), highly qualified people tend to live in close spatial concentration. Such regions are characterized by low barriers to entry for well-educated, young workers who are attracted in particular by cultural diversity and openness toward the new and the 'different'. The hitherto small number of empirical studies on the spatial mobility and entrepreneurial activities of the members of Florida's 'creative class' (Florida, 2002b; Boschma and Fritsch, 2009) show that they are highly mobile in a spatial sense, very discriminating when choosing locations and that they represent a high level of entrepreneurial potential. In Germany the number of creative people in a region seems to be positively correlated with a high share of immigrants, of innovations per employment and of start-ups (Fritsch and Stuetzer, 2009). Florida (2002a) stresses the attractiveness of urban areas for highly creative individuals. They either stay in such creative regions if they were born there or they leave other less creative regions. Given the fact that creative people are more inclined to economic independence, it seems to be plausible that they have a higher propensity to start a company than non-creative people. Consequently, regions with a higher proportion of creative people (that is, urban areas) should also be characterized by higher start-up rates than rural areas. Creative people therefore are potentially able to create a self-enforcing intraregional process of economic growth that is knowledge based and perpetuated by new firms, the founders of which are normally creative persons from within the region. In her seminal contribution to the role of cultural differences, Saxenian (1994) combined the role of entrepreneurship, culture, and competition to explain why the *regional* advantage matters – in favor of Silicon Valley and against the Greater Boston area.

EMPIRICAL EVIDENCE FROM STUDIES IN INDUSTRIALIZED COUNTRIES

Preconditions for Empirical Analyses of Regional Entrepreneurship

Empirical studies on regional entrepreneurship require the appropriate empirical data. Cross-sectional analyses of all regions in a given country need data that can be compared for all regions. If these data originate from official sources (register-based, secondary data), more complete documentation of entrepreneurial activities is probable, meaning that smaller regional areas can also be delineated without this necessarily leading to secrecy problems. Intertemporal comparisons are often also possible with such data. Examples of this kind of empirical study based upon secondary data include Audretsch and Fritsch (1994, 2002), Acs and Armington (2004), Braunerhjelm and Borgmann (2004), and Fritsch and Mueller (2004).

If such official secondary data are not available, very labor-intensive and therefore expensive surveys (primary data) are indispensable. Advantages of such surveys include: explicit documentation of entrepreneurship activities and related issues; and faster availability and regional delineation is oriented toward the research aims. These advantages are bought at the cost of disadvantages such as high price, small sample sizes per region (often leading to larger-scale regionalization) or the sacrifice of nationwide coverage, and a low level of comparability with other official data within the same country. The data used by GEM are survey data and originally intended for comparisons of entire countries. In Germany, Spain, and the UK, the large sample sizes with the pooling of data over several years certainly do, however, allow nationwide regional analysis, too (see Bergmann and Sternberg, 2007, for Germany and Vaillant and Lafuente, 2007, for Spain).

Case studies of individual regions, or only a few regions, within a country place considerably smaller demands on the quantity of data than cross-sectional comparisons of regions and usually make no claim to be representative of the country in question. They do allow more detailed analyses of the individual region than is possible with most cross-sectional studies. The best studied region is the Silicon Valley (for example, Kenney, 2000; Lee et al., 2000; Zhang, 2003). There are also edited volumes, however, that investigate entrepreneurial activities not in a single region, but in many entrepreneurial regions of the same country (for example, Sternberg, 2006, for Germany) or several countries (Bresnahan and Gambardella, 2004).

Distribution of Entrepreneurial Activities Across Subnational Regions

This subsection is intended to demonstrate whether and to what extent interregional disparities in entrepreneurship activities actually exist. It is clear that, in view of the great variety of regional delineations as well as the different economic geographies within different countries and varying methods for measuring entrepreneurship activities, the results may be comparable only to a limited extent. A particularly high number of empirical studies of regional entrepreneurship activities in regions in Germany, in the US, and in the Netherlands have been published in recent years, which is why the focus should be on these countries.

A great many empirical studies of German regions have been published recently, using various data sources and definitions of entrepreneurship (see the compilations of Fritsch and Grotz, 2002, Fritsch and Niese, 2004, and Fritsch and Schmude, 2006). Brixy and Grotz (2007) use data from the IAB Establishment Register of the Institute for Employment Research and calculate new-firm formation rates related to the number of employees between 15 and 65 years of age and for the 74 western German planning regions. Data stem from a long time period of 14 years (1984–97). The median birth rate (defined as the number of newly founded firms per 1,000 employees) for western Germany is 6.0. Most of the urbanized planning regions show a birth rate above the median, with some exceptions in the Ruhr area, in Lower Saxony, and in Northern Bavaria. The work of the Regional Entrepreneurship Monitor (REM, see Bergmann et al., 2002; Lückgen et al., 2006) demonstrates considerable differences in entrepreneurial activities between the 11 (out of 96) German planning regions in terms of nascent and young entrepreneurship. In some regions, the proportion of the population for both indicators is more than double that in other regions. Fornahl (2007) uses data from the Centre for European Economic Research (ZEW) for 49 (out of 440) German districts, specifically only those that include at least one firm that was listed in the NEMAX 50 (New Market Stock Index of the Frankfurt stock exchange). Average firm founding intensity (foundings per 10,000 inhabitants per year and for the 1990–2001 period) among these 49 regions varies between 25.7 and 105.2. Despite the lower level of spatial aggregation, these differences are lower than in the other studies of regional entrepreneurship activities in German regions cited here.

There is a rich collection of empirical literature on regional entrepreneurship for the US (see, for example, Reynolds et al., 1995; Reynolds, 2007). This country has a very different economic geography from Germany. Using data for two different two-year periods in the mid-1970s and the mid-1990s, Reynolds (2007) shows that highest firm birth rates were 10 times as high as in the labor market areas (LMAs) with the lowest firm birth rates. LMAs with the highest birth rates are concentrated on the coasts (Florida), the rural regions of the west and in some growing urban centers. Also on the basis of the 394 LMAs, Armington and Acs (2002) use the Longitudinal Establishment and Enterprise Microdata (LEEM) file of the Bureau of the Census with data from 1989 to 1996. They found significant differences in firm formation rates (new firms per 1,000 labor force) between industrial regions and technologically progressive regions. The US average is 3.85 for the labor market approach and 13.0 for the ecological approach. Values for the individual US states vary between 5.50 (Colorado) and 2.91 (Pennsylvania) for the labor market approach, and 18.7 (Nevada) and 8.5 (District of Columbia) for the ecological approach. As expected, the ranges between the extreme values of the LMAs are larger and the South and the West have the highest start-up rates, while the Northeast and the Midwest continue to lag behind the rest of the country. The authors (ibid., 37) state that 'regional firm birth rate varies greatly across regions'.

Relatively good data on regional entrepreneurship are available in the Netherlands, although, similar to Germany, various data sources compete with each other and use varying definitions of entrepreneurship. Bosma et al. (2008) use a regional panel dataset on annual numbers of independent start-ups (and new subsidiaries, not considered here), identifying 40 regions at the NUTS 3 level in a 14-year period (1988–2002). New entries are concentrated within the central and highly urbanized area of the Netherlands known as the Randstad. The country's two largest cities, however, Amsterdam and Rotterdam, do not belong to the highest-level category of entrepreneurial activity, which seems not to be implausible in this relatively homogeneous country. Some years before, van Oort et al. (1999) found a similar result with some suburban localities in particular and some fringes of central cities recording high scores. Nonetheless, the highest new firm density is to be found in the largest cities of the Randstad (The Hague, Rotterdam, Utrecht; see Huisman and van Wissen, 2004). Stam (2005) produced similar results for the regional distribution of particularly high-growth start-ups. International and at the same time interregional comparative findings are relatively rare. Exceptions have been produced by Reynolds et al. (1994), Bosma and Schutjens (2007) on regions in European countries, and Acs et al. (2011). The empirical results seem to support the importance of urbanization for entrepreneurship. The few empirical studies of the dynamic of interregional disparities in terms of entrepreneurial activities show that at least for more short-term comparisons (less than a decade), the stability is quite high (Armington and Acs, 2002, and Reynolds, 2007, for US regions, Fritsch and Mueller, 2006, for German regions and Mueller et al., 2008, for British regions).

Regional Attributes and Regional Disparities of Entrepreneurial Activities

This subsection deals with the influence of regional determinants on the number of start-ups in a region and on the individual decisions in favor of or against a start-up. Empirical literature mainly differentiates between the four groups of determinants that exert an influence on the individual decision to launch a start-up and the frequency of start-ups within regions. We are only interested in those factors that are regionally specific.

For German regions, several empirical studies have been published that use data from REM. Wagner and Sternberg (2004) demonstrate that regional factors such as the economic growth, the price of building land, housing density, or the level of other entrepreneurs in the region influence an individual's likelihood of launching a start-up. Based on REM and in a combination of micro data (for example, for entrepreneurial activity, demographics, entrepreneurial attitudes) and macro data, Sternberg and

Wagner (2005) in their multilevel analysis use a version of the logit model that takes into account the rare events nature of becoming a nascent entrepreneur as well as the regional stratification of the data. The authors find no stable relationship with the individual propensity to take the step to self-employment for the regional variables. One of the explanations is that the planning region does not describe the spatial unit relevant to that decision from the individual's point of view. When talking about impacts of the regional environment, the subject should be the region that is relevant from the point of view of a nascent entrepreneur – relevant both in terms of his/her earnings and in terms of his/her costs resulting from the two alternatives of self-employment or dependent employment. It is clear that the relevant region can vary widely from one case to another. If the relevant region diverges between potential start-up ideas, then the prevailing regional conditions, and those that influence the individual decision, cannot be adequately described using variables that are measured at a uniform spatial level of aggregation.

An interesting question is what influences entrepreneurial attitudes and to what extent regional characteristics play a part. Bergmann (2004) shows that entrepreneurial attitudes are primarily influenced by person-related determinants such as gender, age, educational attainment, and role models in the individual's social environment, but only to a limited extent by regional characteristics. But the probability of being positively influenced by such role models as a nascent entrepreneur is higher in regions with high start-up rates than in other regions. Role models are also relevant in Mueller's (2006) study designed as a combination of micro data on entrepreneurial activity and macro data (regional level). She shows that individuals are deeply embedded in their regional entrepreneurial environment. The probability of becoming a nascent entrepreneur is heavily influenced by the availability of role models, that is, other nascent or young entrepreneurs, in the same region: each additional new firm per 1,000 inhabitants in this region increases the probability of being a nascent entrepreneur by a factor of 1.24.

The network-founding hypothesis (Brüderl and Preissendörfer, 1998) also deals, at least implicitly, with the impacts of the regional environment on entrepreneurial activities by emphasizing the positive effect of involvement in a network. The results of empirical studies of this question are not consistent (see Davidsson and Honig, 2003). Rabe (2007, 206), in her work on regional support infrastructure and the related individual egocentric support network of 40 founders of knowledge-intensive start-ups in the Karlsruhe region, concludes correctly that 'entrepreneurship is a social role, embedded in a social *and a regional* context' (added italics).

In studies using aggregated data for entire regions, highly entrepreneurial regions stand out in particular in the areas of high educational attainment, a high proportion of employment in small businesses (Reynolds et al., 1994), and high population density. The impact of the regional unemployment rate is inconsistent (see the discussion in Bosma et al., 2008, and Stam, 2009). A positive impact is shown by Reynolds et al. (1994) and Johnson and Parker (1996), a negative one by Carree (2002) and Sutaria and Hicks (2004). The results, to a degree, depend on the definition of the new firm formation rate (ecological versus labor market method). To conclude, unemployed persons tend to have a lower propensity to start a firm than employed people. For 394 LMAs and three different time periods, Reynolds et al. (1995), Acs and Armington (2004), and Reynolds (2007) show that regional characteristics such as population growth, a more highly educated population of young adults and great sector diversity, and flexible policies regarding the hiring and firing of employees have a positive impact on firm birth rate.

Agglomeration effects obviously contribute to new firm formation via increased local market opportunities in terms of customers and required inputs (Fritsch et al., 2006; Bosma et al., 2008). This subject has been very thoroughly investigated for Dutch regions in particular (Bosma et al., 2008; Bosma, 2009).

Within the debate on agglomeration effects on regional entrepreneurial activities, it makes sense to differentiate between localization economies (associated with benefits derived from *intra*industry externalities) and urbanization economies (resulting from interindustry, but intraregional externalities). Bosma et al. (2008) show for Dutch regions that localization economies are important for the creation of independent new ventures – at least more important than urbanization economies. For independent start-ups, in contrast to subsidiaries, there are obviously large benefits (in particular, knowledge spillovers) of clustering together with firms from the same sector. Urbanization economies are positively correlated with the population size of the city because a greater number of new firms increases the probability of interindustry connections and spillover effects – and the last two aspects again have a positive regional impact on the firm birth rate in the region (Nyström, 2005). Several interregional empirical studies in different countries have shown that a positive relationship between population density and new firm formation exists (see, for example, Audretsch and Fritsch, 1994; Reynolds et al., 1994; Fotopoulos and Spence, 1999; Armington and Acs, 2002). However, it is not always clear whether city size or population density alone are adequate indicators of urbanization effects (or whether they are always combined with localization effects). Regional determinants that are directly or indirectly related to agglomeration are regional demand by consumers, regional income growth, regional wages, population growth, and regional economic growth such as growth in GDP (see Bosma et al., 2008). Most of the empirical studies mentioned above show positive impacts of these variables on regional entry rates. For regional wages, however, the empirical results are not uniform (Ashcroft et al., 1991). The access to and the availability of (highly) skilled labor has a positive effect on new firm formation (Fotopoulos and Spence, 1999; Armington and Acs, 2002).

Falck (2007) and Fritsch and Falck (2007) in the scope of a multidimensional analysis focus on new firms in 74 West German regions, and show that the regional dimension plays a key role in the new firm formation process. The technological regime of the region (innovation intensity, innovation behavior, number of inventions) and the entrepreneurial character of an industry are positively linked to the start-up rate. The authors interpret this as evidence of entrepreneurs being a part of the regional innovation system.

In survey-based studies, entrepreneurial attitudes and perceptions within the region play an important part in explaining entrepreneurial activities. Opportunity recognition, an example of entrepreneurial perceptions, differs from one region to another. Taken across all the people of a region, entrepreneurial attitudes can also influence individual start-up decisions in principle as regional determinants. Tamásy (2005) reports significant regional differences in entrepreneurial attitudes, and their impact is more relevant for entrepreneurial activities than regional entrepreneurial framework conditions (such as government programs, education, labor market or taxes and regulations). As sobering as some of the results of macro analyses may be at first glance – they do not contradict the Feldman thesis (2001) that entrepreneurship is primarily a 'regional event'. The results of many studies intended to explain regionally varying start-up rates that use only regional variables in their econometric analyses should be interpreted with care as they ignore the ultimately more important individual influence of the person.

Regional Attributes and Entrepreneurial Success

Regional attributes are also significant in principle for the success of a start-up. But there are very few empirical studies that attempt explicitly to analyze this regional impact. Empirical studies on the impact of regional attributes on entrepreneurial success can be divided into those using data on just one spatial level (for example, the level of the individual firm or the level of the county) and those using two or more different levels (for example, micro data of the firm for the dependent variable and macro data of the region for the independent ones). Let us start with the first group of empirical studies. Tamásy (2005) investigates the influences of the regional environment on the success of 462 start-ups in three German regions (Cologne, Munich, Stuttgart). She shows that the entrepreneurial framework conditions of the three regions primarily have an indirect effect on the success of start-ups. The regional entrepreneurial climate has a direct positive influence on the *subjective* start-up success (that is, on the individual perception of firm success), but not on the survival rates. The influence of agglomeration effects on start-up success is not unambiguously demonstrated in the literature. Works that confirm a positive influence (for example, Fotopolous and Louri, 2000) are countered by others (for example, Brixy and Grotz, 2007) that report a negative influence, or no influence at all. For urban agglomerations the majority of the empirical studies show lower survival rates, but higher growth of the surviving start-ups, compared with start-ups outside urban agglomerations (see, for example, Fritsch et al., 2006; however, this is an example of a multi-level analysis; more on this in the next paragraph). As for the network-success hypothesis, again, empirical research does not give a consistent answer to the question of whether involvement in regional networks really has a positive influence on start-up success (see Bloodgood et al., 1995; Scott and Stuart, 2002). The unmistakably interdependent relationship between regional environment and start-up success is demonstrated particularly clearly by the fact that spin-offs are a frequent characteristic of growing regional economies (Assimakopoulos et al., 2003).

Multidimensional analyses use a different methodology to achieve new insights on the role of regional effects on start-ups' success. The few empirical studies of regional survival rates show that these rates really do differ to a considerable extent. Fritsch et al. (2006) show that the average five-year survival rates differ significantly between West German regions and between larger cities (low survival rates) and other regions. Here there appears to be a considerable difference between the regional influence on the start-up decision on the one hand (large urban areas enjoy a clear advantage over rural areas in this respect) and start-up survival on the other (large urban areas offer poorer framework conditions for the majority of start-ups than rural regions due to the strong intraregional competition). Falck (2007) shows for the 74 West German planning regions that characteristics of the regional environment are of considerable importance for the survival of start-ups. Among these regional determinants, the number of other start-ups, the population density, and the employment growth rate increase the chance of business survival over time, while the number of new businesses in the same industry located in the respective federal state had a negative impact on new-firm survival. This is confirmation of the market density hypothesis, which has been demonstrated for many highly entrepreneurial regions. If a meso-level approach (a group of start-ups of the same cohort) is used, similar regional determinants show a positive relationship with survival rates of start-ups in a region (see Fritsch et al., 2006). Also Weyh (2006) finds pronounced differences in the development of alternative start-up cohorts across regions, and several regional characteristics have a significant impact on the success of start-ups. For US labor market regions, Acs et al. (2008) show a positive relationship between regional human capital stocks and new-firm survival; however, results differ between time periods.

CONCLUSIONS

This chapter assessed some theoretical arguments supporting the idea that entrepreneurial activities are influenced in many cases by the attributes of the region (defined as a subnational spatial unit) where the potential founder of a firm was or is located. There are still significant research gaps in terms of adequate regional theories of entrepreneurship. Most of the traditional theories of regional economic growth do not explicitly consider the role of entrepreneurship, in particular the crucial missing element in their institutional arrangement is the role of entrepreneurship in the innovation process (Acs, 2000). More recent approaches of regional economic growth theories are slightly better, considering entrepreneurial activities. The strength of the regional innovation systems concept is that it explicitly considers regional innovation actors (including entrepreneurs) and their linkages and networks. Such networks – either intra- or interregional – help to internalize the knowledge externalities of the innovation process. However, the RIS concept cannot explain where new innovations are created and how they and the founders of start-ups contribute to innovation-led regional growth. Agglomeration theories focus on agglomeration effects which are the main argument why cities should have higher start-up rates than non-urban regions. Furthermore, cities offer a great range of infrastructure, which is of interest especially for younger and/or more highly educated people. So, besides the enhancement of demand, cities also have larger proportions of highly educated people, which increases the pool of potential entrepreneurs. Thus, agglomeration theory offers some convincing argument why entrepreneurial activities should differ between regions, namely between urbanized and more rural or less densely populated areas in a country.

As for the empirical perspective, there are a great number of studies in the past decade that explore the interdependent relationship between regional environment and entrepreneurial activities. The results are quite heterogeneous, as are the environments between regions within and especially between countries. However, it is rather clear now that the regional environment as an important context variable must not be ignored any further when exploring the determinants of firm creation and of new firm growth. As for the regional variation of entrepreneurial activities, three findings seem to be unambiguous. First, there are obviously interregional differences in the scope of entrepreneurial activities, which are also mostly statistically significant in cases where survey data were used. Second, in most countries, urban areas clearly have higher start-up rates than the other region types. This may be attributable to regional causes, but also to determinants that have nothing to do with regional attributes. Third, the interregional differences in the start-up rates are rather stable over time. As for the regional influence on entrepreneurial activities within the same region, macro-analyses do not produce consistent results, but the positive effect is predominant here, too. Regional factors may also have an impact on the individual decision to become involved in new firm creation and on the gestation of an operating new firm. The regional impact on start-up survival and growth appears, however, to be weaker than on entrepreneurial activity. In other words, the influence decreases as the entrepreneurship process progresses. Thus, it makes sense in empirical studies to differentiate between start-up activity and start-up growth (Stuart and Sorenson, 2003).

Some final remarks on research gaps in regional entrepreneurship research are needed. The research gaps are currently greatest in research on regional entrepreneurship policies, an issue not discussed in this contribution but important for regional entrepreneurship as well (see Sternberg 2009). The numerous entrepreneurship support programs by supranational, national, regional, and local governments open up a rich field of activity for entrepreneurship researchers in coming years.

Countless studies have been carried out in recent years for many countries and regions in the field of empirical research on regional entrepreneurship. The research gap in empirical research on regional entrepreneurship rightly bemoaned a decade ago is now significantly smaller. Considerable progress has been made in methodical terms. It remains a challenge, in addition to innumerable and meaningful case studies of selected regions and/or industries in specific regions, to create interregionally comparable studies of the impact of regional entrepreneurship and the effect of regional entrepreneurship activities to at least look for results that can be generalized. As long as such studies do not exist, one finding of regional case studies remains obvious: despite various commonalities among the regions analyzed, there are so many differences in terms of the determinants of entrepreneurship activities, the role of politics and, for example, the role of regional-sectoral clusters that researchers should refrain from drawing generally applicable conclusions. Supposedly positive framework conditions for high levels of entrepreneurship activities, such as economic prosperity, low levels of unemployment, active entrepreneurship support policies, the lack of large, dominant companies or the existence of sectoral-regional industry clusters are evident both in regions with high current start-up rates and in those with low start-up rates. They are therefore neither necessary nor adequate as conditions for an entrepreneurial region.

As far as theoretical research is concerned, the quotation from Shane and Venkatamaran (2000, 217), 'Today the phenomenon of entrepreneurship has lacked . . . a conceptual framework' remains correct for large parts of regional entrepreneurship research. There is still no single grand theory that could satisfactorily explain regional entrepreneurship. Instead, there are a range of approaches that originated outside entrepreneurship research and were developed for other purposes before being used for regional entrepreneurship research. Whether this lack of a grand theory of regional entrepreneurship is perceived as an opportunity for new research or has just to be accepted may differ from researcher to researcher.

REFERENCES

Acs, Z.J. (ed.) (2000), *Regional Innovation, Knowledge and Global Change*, London: Pinter.

Acs, Z.J. (2002), *Innovation and the Growth of Cities*, Cheltenham, UK and Northampton, MA, USA: Edward Elgar.

Acs, Z.J. and C. Armington (2004), 'Employment growth and entrepreneurial activity in cities', *Regional Studies*, **39** (8), 911–27.

Acs, Z.J., C. Armington and T. Zhang (2008), 'The determinants of new-firm survival across regional economies: the role of human capital stock and knowledge spillover', *Papers in Regional Science*, **86** (3), 367–91.

Acs, Z.J., N. Bosma and R. Sternberg (2011), 'Entrepreneurship in world cities', in Maria Minniti (ed.), *The Dynamics of Entrepreneurial Activity*, Oxford: Oxford University Press, pp. 125–51.

Acs, Z.J. and L.A. Plummer (2005), 'Penetrating the "knowledge filter" in regional economics', *Annals of Regional Science*, **39**, 439–56.

Acs, Z.J. and A. Varga (2002), 'Geography, endogenous growth and innovation', *International Regional Science Review*, **25**, 132–48.

Armington, C. and Z.J. Acs (2002), 'The determinants of Regional Variation in new firm formation', *Regional Studies*, **36**, 33–45.

Ashcroft, B., J.H. Love and E. Malloy (1991), 'New firm formation in the British counties with special reference to Scotland', *Regional Studies*, **25**, 395–409.

Asheim, B.T. and M.S. Gertler (2005), 'The geography of innovation: regional innovation systems', in Jan Fagerberg, David C. Mowery and Richard R. Nelson (eds), *The Oxford Handbook of Innovation*, Oxford: Oxford University Press, pp. 291–317.

Assimakopoulos, D., S. Everton and K. Tsutsui (2003), 'The semiconductor community in the Silicon Valley: a network analysis of the SEMI Genealogy Chart (1947–1986)', *International Journal of Technology Management*, **25**, 181–99.

Audretsch, D.B. and M. Fritsch (1994), 'The geography of firm births in Germany', *Regional Studies*, **28** (4), 359–65.

Audretsch, D.B. and M. Fritsch (2002), 'Growth regimes over time and space', *Regional Studies*, **36** (2), 113–24.

Audretsch, D.B. and M. Keilbach (2007), 'The localization of entrepreneurship capital: evidence from Germany', *Papers in Regional Science*, **86** (3), 351–65.

Audretsch, D.B., M.C. Keilbach and E.E. Lehmann (2006), *Entrepreneurship and Economic Growth*, New York: Oxford University Press.

Bergmann, H. (2004), *Gründungsaktivitäten im regionalen Kontext, Gründer, Gründungseinstellungen und Rahmenbedingungen in zehn deutschen Regionen* [Start-up activities in a regional context, founders, entrepreneurial attitudes and framework conditions in ten German regions], Cologne: Institute of Economic and Social Geography (Kölner Forschungen zur Wirtschafts- und Sozialgeographie, 57).

Bergmann, H., A. Japsen and C. Tamásy (2002), *Regionaler Entrepreneurship Monitor (REM). Gründungsaktivitäten und Rahmenbedingungen in zehn deutschen Regione*, Köln, Lüneburg: Universität zu Köln, Universität Lüneburg.

Bergmann, H. and R. Sternberg (2007), 'The changing face of entrepreneurship in Germany', *Small Business Economics*, **28**, 205–21.

Bloodgood, J.M., H.J. Sapienza and A.L. Carsrud (1995), 'The dynamics of new business start-ups: person, context and process', in Jerome A. Katz and Robert H. Brockhaus (eds), *Advances in Entrepreneurship, Firm Emergence and Growth*, Amsterdam: JAI Press, pp. 123–44.

Boschma, R.A. (2005), 'Proximity and innovation: a critical assessment', *Regional Studies*, **39**, 61–74.

Boschma, R.A. and M. Fritsch (2009), 'Creative class and regional growth in Europe', *Economic Geography*, **85**, 391–423.

Bosma, N. (2009), 'The geography of entrepreneurial activity and regional economic development', Utrecht (PhD dissertation).

Bosma, N., Z. Acs, E. Autio, A. Coduras and J. Levie (2009), *Global Entrepreneurship Monitor 2008 Executive Report*, Wellesley, MA and Santiago de Chile: Babson College, Universidad del Desarrollo, Global Entrepreneurship Research Consortium (GERA).

Bosma, N. and V. Schutjens (2007), 'Patterns of promising entrepreneurial activity in European regions', *Tijdschrift voor ecconomische en sociale Geografie*, **98** (5), 675–86.

Bosma, N., A. van Stel and K. Suddle (2008), 'The geography of new firm formation: evidence from independent start-ups and new subsidiaries in the Netherlands', *International Entrepreneurship and Management Journal*, **4** (2), 129–46.

Braunerhjelm, P. and B. Borgmann (2004), 'Geographical concentration, entrepreneurship and regional growth: evidence from regional data in Sweden, 1975–1999', *Regional Studies*, **38** (8), 929–48.

Bresnahan, T. and A. Gambardella (eds) (2004), *Building High-tech Clusters*, Cambridge and New York: Cambridge University Press.

Brixy, U. and R. Grotz (2007), 'Regional patterns and determinants of the success of new firms in Western Germany', *Entrepreneurship and Regional Development*, **19** (4), 293–312.

Brüderl, J. and P. Preisendörfer (1998), 'Network support and the success of newly founded businesses', *Small Business Economics*, **10**, 213–25.

Capello, R. and P. Nijkamp (eds) (2009), *Handbook of Regional Growth and Development Theories*, Cheltenham, UK and Northampton, MA, USA: Edward Elgar.

Carree, M.A. (2002), 'Does unemployment affect the number of establishments? A regional analysis for US states', *Regional Studies*, **36** (2), 389–98.

Cooke, P., M. Heidenreich and H.J. Braczyk (eds) (2004), *Regional Innovation Systems*, London and New York: Routledge.

Cooper, A.C. (2003), 'Entrepreneurship: the past, the present, the future', in Zoltan J. Acs and David B. Audretsch (eds), *Handbook of Entrepreneurship Research*, Boston, MA and Dordrecht: Kluwer Academic Publishers, pp. 21–36.

Davidsson, P. (2006), 'Nascent entrepreneurship: empirical studies and developments', *Foundations and Trends in Entrepreneurship*, **2**, 1–76.

Davidsson, P. and B. Honig (2003), 'The role of social and human capital among nascent entrepreneurs', *Journal of Business Venturing*, **18** (3), 301–31.

Davidsson, P., M.B. Low and M. Wright (2001), 'Editor's introduction. Low and MacMillan ten years on: achievements and future directions for entrepreneurship research', *Entrepreneurship: Theory and Practice*, **25** (4), 5–15.

Davidsson, P. and J. Wiklund (2001), 'Levels of analysis in entrepreneurship research: current research practice and suggestions for the future', *Entrepreneurship: Theory and Practice*, **25** (4), 81–99.

Edquist, C. (2005), 'Systems of innovation: perspectives and challenges', in Jan Fagerberg, David C. Mowery and Richard R. Nelson (eds), *The Oxford Handbook of Innovation*, Oxford: Oxford University Press, pp. 181–208.

Falck, O. (2007), *Emergence and Survival of New Businesses*, Heidelberg: Physica.

Feldman, M.P. (2001), 'The entrepreneurial event revisited: firm formation in a regional context', *Industrial and Corporate Change*, **10**, 861–91.

Florida, R. (2002a), 'The economic geography of talent', *Annals of the Association of American Geographers*, **92**, 743–55.

Florida, R. (2002b), *The Rise of the Creative Class*, New York: Basic Books.

Fornahl, D. (2007), *Changes in Regional Firm Founding Activities*, London and New York: Routledge.

Fotopoulos, G. and H. Louri (2000), 'Location and survival of new entry', *Small Business Economics*, **14**, 311–21.

Fotopoulos, G. and N. Spence (1999), 'Spatial variations in new manufacturing plant openings: some empirical evidence from Greece', *Regional Studies*, **33**, 219–29.

Fritsch, M., U. Brixy and O. Falck (2006), 'The effect of industry, region and time on new business survival – a multi-dimensional analysis', *Review of Industrial Organization*, **28**, 285–306.

Fritsch, M. and O. Falck (2007), 'New business formation by industry over space and time: a multi-dimensional analysis', *Regional Studies*, **41**, 157–72.

Fritsch, M. and R. Grotz (eds) (2002), *Das Gründungsgeschehen in Deutschland – Darstellung und Vergleich der Datenquellen*, Heidelberg: Physica.

Fritsch, M. and P. Mueller (2004), 'Effects of new business formation on regional development over time', *Regional Studies*, **38**, 961–75.

Fritsch, M. and P. Mueller (2006), 'The evolution of regional entrepreneurship and growth regimes', in Fritsch and Schmude (eds), pp. 225–44.

Fritsch, M. and M. Niese (2002), 'Vergleichende Gegenüberstellung der Informationen zum Gründungsgeschehen: Vergleich auf gesamtwirtschaftlicher und sektoraler Ebene', in Michael Fritsch and Reinhold Grotz (eds), *Das Gründungsgeschehen in Deutschland. Darstellung und Vergleich der Datenquellen*, Heidelberg: Physica, pp. 141–64.

Fritsch, M. and M. Niese (eds) (2004), *Gründungsprozess und Gründungserfolg*, Heidelberg: Physica.

Fritsch, M. and J. Schmude (eds) (2006), *Entrepreneurship in the Region*, International Studies in Entrepreneurship, New York: Springer.

Fritsch, M. and M. Stuetzer (2009), 'The geography of creative people in Germany', *International Journal of Foresight and Innovation Policy*, **5**, 7–23.

Grilo, I. and J.-M. Irigoyen (2006), 'Entrepreneurship in the EU: to wish and not to be', *Small Business Economics*, **26**, 305–18.

Grossman, G.M. and E. Helpman (1991), *Innovation and Growth in the Global Economy*, Cambridge, MA: MIT Press.

Huisman, C. and L. van Wissen (2004), 'Localization effects of firm start-ups and closures in the Netherlands', *The Annals of Regional Science*, **38** (2), 291–310.

Jaffe, A., M. Traijtenberg and R. Henderson (1993), 'Geographic localization of knowledge spillovers as evidenced by patent citations', *Quarterly Journal of Economics*, **63**, 577–98.

Johansson, B., C. Karlsson and R.R. Stough (eds) (2001), *Theories of Endogenous Regional Growth, Lessons for Regional Policies*, Berlin: Springer.

Johnson, P. and S.C. Parker (1996), 'Spatial variations in the determinants and effects of firm births and deaths', *Regional Studies*, **30** (7), 679–88.

Kenney, M.G. (ed.) (2000), *Understanding Silicon Valley. The Anatomy of an Entrepreneurial Region*, Stanford, CA: Stanford University Press.

Koschatzky, K. (2001), *Räumliche Aspekte im Innovationsprozess*, Münster, Hamburg and London: Lit.

Krugman, P. (1991), *Geography and Trade*, Cambridge, MA: MIT Press.

Lawson, C. and E. Lorenz (1999), 'Collective learning, tacit knowledge and regional innovation capacity', *Regional Studies*, **33**, 305–17.

Lee, C.-M., W.F. Miller, M.G. Hancock and H.S. Rowen (eds) (2000), *The Silicon Valley Edge. A Habitat for Innovation and Entrepreneurship*, Stanford, CA: Stanford University Press.

Lückgen, I., D. Oberschachtsiek, R. Sternberg and J. Wagner (2006), 'Nascent entrepreneurs in German regions', in Fritsch and Schmude (eds), pp. 7–35.

Lumpkin, G.T. and G.G. Dess (1996), 'Clarifying the entrepreneurial orientation construct and linking it to performance', *Academy of Management Review*, **14** (1), 135–72.

Lundvall, B.-A. (ed.) (1992), *National Systems of Innovation*, London: Pinter.

Malecki, E.J. (1983), 'Technology and regional development. A survey', *International Regional Science Review*, **8**, 89–125.

Malecki, E.J. (1997), 'Entrepreneurs, networks, and economic development: a review of recent research', in Jerome A. Katz (ed.), *Advances in Entrepreneurship, Firm Emergence and Growth*, Greenwich: JAI Press, pp. 57–118.

Martin, R.A. and P. Sunley (1996), 'Paul Krugman's geographical economics and its implications for regional development theory: a critical assessment', *Economic Geography*, **72**, 259–92.

Martin, R.A. and P. Sunley (1998), 'Slow convergence? The new endogenous growth theory and regional development', *Economic Geography*, **74**, 201–27.

Maskell, P. and A. Malmberg (1999), 'Localized learning and industrial competitiveness', *Cambridge Journal of Economics*, **23**, 167–85.

McCann, P. and F. van Oort (2009), 'Theories of agglomeration and regional economic growth: a historical review', in Capello and Nijkamp (eds), *Handbook of Regional Growth and Development Theories*, Cheltenham, UK and Northampton, MA, USA: Edward Elgar, pp. 19–32.

Mueller, P. (2006), 'Exploring the knowledge filter: how entrepreneurship and university–industry relationships drive economic growth', *Research Policy*, **35**, 1499–508.

Mueller, P., A.J. van Stel and D.J. Storey (2008), 'The effects of new firm formation on regional development over time: the case of Great Britain', *Small Business Economics*, **30** (1), 59–71.

Müller, C. and R. Sternberg (2008), 'The role of Chinese return migrants for enhancing China's innovative capacity', in Henry S. Rowen, Marguerite Gong Hancock and William F. Miller (eds), *Greater China's Quest for Innovation,* Stanford, CA: Walter H. Shorenstein Asia-Pacific Research Center Books, pp. 231–52.

Nelson, R.R. (ed.) (1993), *National Innovation Systems. A Comparative Analysis*, New York and Oxford: Oxford University Press.

Nyström, K. (2005), 'Determinants of regional entry and exit in industrial sectors', CESIS Electronic Working Paper series, 33.

Oinas, P. and E.J. Malecki (2002), 'The evolution of technologies in time and space: from national and regional to spatial innovation systems', *International Regional Science Review*, **25**, 102–31.

Polanyi, M. (1966), *The Tacit Dimension*, New York: Doubleday.

Rabe, C. (2007), *Unterstützungsnetzwerke von Gründern wissensintensiver Unternehmen*, Heidelberg: Geographisches Institut der Universität Heidelberg.

Reynolds, P.D. (2007), *Entrepreneurship in the United States*, New York: Springer.
Reynolds, P.D., N. Bosma, E. Autio, S. Hunt, N. De Bono, I. Servais, P. Lopez-Garcia and N. Chin (2005), 'Global Entrepreneurship Monitor: data collection and implementation 1998–2003', *Small Business Economics*, **24**, 205–31.
Reynolds, P.D., B. Miller and W.R. Maki (1995), 'Explaining regional variation in business births and deaths: US 1976–88', *Small Business Economics*, **7**, 389–407.
Reynolds, P.D., D. Storey and P. Westhead (1994), 'Cross-national comparisons of the variation in new firm formation rates – an editorial overview', *Regional Studies*, **28**, 343–6.
Romer, P. (1990), 'Endogenous technological change', *Journal of Political Economy*, **98**, 71–102.
Santarelli, E. and M. Vivarelli (2007), 'Entrepreneurship and the process of firms' entry, survival and growth', *Industrial and Corporate Change*, **16** (3), 455–88.
Saxenian, A. (1994), *Regional Advantage: Culture and Competition in Silicon Valley and Route 128*, Cambridge, MA: Harvard University Press.
Saxenian, A. (2006), *The New Argonauts: Regional Advantage in a Global Economy*, Cambridge, MA: Harvard University Press.
Schmude, J. and R. Leiner (1999), 'Zur messung des unternehmensgründungsgeschehens: theoretische Überlegungen und empirische Befunde', in Lutz von Rosenstiel and Thomas Langvon Wins (eds), *Existenzgründungen und Unternehmertum*, Stuttgart: Schaeffer-Poeschel, pp. 109–28.
Schumpeter, J.A. (1942), *Capitalism, Socialism and Democracy*, New York: Harper Collins.
Scott, S. and T. Stuart (2002), 'Organizational endowments and the performance of university-start-ups', *Management Science*, **48** (1), 154–70.
Segal Quince Wicksteed Ltd (1985), *The Cambridge Phenomenon: The Growth of High Technology Industry in a University Town*, Cambridge (UK).
Shane, S. and S. Venkataraman (2000), 'The promise of entrepreneurship as a field of research', *Academy of Management Review*, **25** (1), 217–26.
Sorenson, O. and P.G. Audia (2000), 'The social structure of entrepreneurial activity: geographic concentration of footwear production in the United States 1940–1989', *American Journal of Sociology*, **106** (2), 424–62.
Stam, E. (2005), 'The geography of gazelles in the Netherlands', *Tijdschrift voor Economische en Sociale Geografie TESG*, **96**, 121–7.
Stam, E. (2007), 'Why butterflies don't leave. Locational behavior of entrepreneurial firms', *Economic Geography*, **83** (1), 27–50.
Stam, E. (2009), 'Entrepreneurship', in Rob Kitchin and Nigel J. Thrift (eds), *The International Encyclopedia of Human Geography*, Oxford: Elsevier Science, pp. 492–8.
Sternberg, R. (1996), 'Regional growth theories and high-tech regions', *International Journal of Urban and Regional Research*, **20** (3), 518–38.
Sternberg, R. (1999), 'Innovative linkages and proximity – empirical results from recent surveys of small and medium-sized firms in German regions', *Regional Studies*, **33** (6), 529–40.
Sternberg, R. (2004), 'Entrepreneurship research – the relevance of the region and tasks facing economic geography', *Geographische Zeitschrift*, **92** (special issue), 18–38.
Sternberg, R. (ed.) (2006), *Deutsche Gründungsregionen*, Hamburg and Münster: Lit (Wirtschaftsgeographie, 38).
Sternberg, R. (2007), 'Entrepreneurship, proximity and regional innovation systems', *Tijdschrift voor Economische en Sociale Geografie TESG*, **98** (5), 652–66.
Sternberg, R. (2009), 'Regional dimensions of entrepreneurship', *Foundations and Trends in Entrepreneurship,* **5** (4), 211–340.
Sternberg, R. and H.O. Rocha (2007), 'Why entrepreneurship is a regional event: theoretical arguments, empirical evidence, and policy consequences', in Mark P. Rice and Timothy G. Habbershon (eds), *Entrepreneurship: The Engine of Growth*, London and Westport, CT: Praeger, pp. 215–38.
Sternberg, R. and C. Tamásy (1999), 'Munich as Germany's No.1 high technology region – empirical evidence, theoretical explanations and the role of small firm/large firm relationships', *Regional Studies*, **33**, 367–77.

Sternberg, R. and J. Wagner (2005), 'Zur Evidenz regionaler Determinanten im Kontext individueller Gründungsaktivitäten. Empirische Befunde aus dem Regionalen Entrepreneurship Monitor (REM)', *Zeitschrift für Wirtschaftsgeographie*, **49** (3/4), 167–84.

Sternberg, R. and S. Wennekers (2005), 'Determinants and effects of new business creation using Global Entrepreneurship Monitor data', *Small Business Economics*, **24**, 193–203.

Stuart, T. and O. Sorenson (2003), 'The geography of opportunity: spatial heterogeneity in founding rates and the performance of biotechnology firms', *Research Policy*, **32** (2), 229–53.

Sutaria, V. and D. Hicks (2004), 'New firm formation: dynamics and determinants', *Annals of Regional Science*, **38**, 241–62.

Sweeney, G.P. (1987), *Innovation, Entrepreneurs and Regional Development*, London and New York: Macmillan/St. Martin's Press.

Tamásy, C. (2005), *Determinanten des regionalen Gründungsgeschehens*. Hamburg, Münster: Lit (*Wirtschaftsgeographie*, 27).

Vaillant, Y. and E. Lafuente (2007), 'Do different institutional frameworks condition the influence of local fear of failure and entrepreneurial examples over entrepreneurial activity?', *Entrepreneurship and Regional Development*, **19** (4), 313–37.

van Oort, F.G., B. van der Knaap and W. Sleegers (1999), 'New firm formation, employment growth and the local environment', in Jouke van Dijk and Piet H. Pellenbarg (eds), *Demography of Firms*, Groningen: Faculteit der Ruimtelijke Wetenschappen Rijksuniversiteit Groningen, pp. 173–204.

Varga, A. (1998), *University Research and Regional Innovation: A Spatial Econometric Analysis of Academic Technology Transfers*, Boston, MA: Kluwer Academic Publishers.

Wagner, J. and R. Sternberg (2004), 'Start-up activities, individual characteristics, and the regional milieu: lessons for entrepreneurship support policies from German micro data', *Annals of Regional Science*, **38**, 219–40.

Weyh, Antje (2006), 'What characterizes successful start-up cohorts?', in Fritsch and Schmude (eds), pp. 61–74.

Zhang, J. (2003), *High-tech Start-ups and Industry Dynamics in Silicon Valley*, Berkeley, CA: Public Policy Institute of California.

4 The effect of new business formation on regional development: empirical evidence, interpretation, and avenues for further research[1]
Michael Fritsch

THE LINK BETWEEN NEW BUSINESS FORMATION AND GROWTH

There seems to be a widespread belief that new business formation leads to economic growth (Wennekers and Thurik, 1999). This belief has motivated politicians in many countries to promote entrepreneurship in order to stimulate growth (see, for example, the contributions in Audretsch et al., 2007; and Leitao and Baptista, 2009). Remarkably, however, the theoretical as well as the empirical foundation for this belief is rather weak. Empirical research on the issue started late and only quite recently have researchers tried to assess the effects of new businesses on economic development in more detail.

This chapter provides an overview of the current state of knowledge about the effect of new business formation on regional development. It begins with a brief sketch of the extant research on this topic. I then report main results of studies that have analyzed the development of small and young firms, and discuss their merits and shortcomings. One objection to this type of analysis is that it does not account for possible indirect effects of new business formation, which may be important and require a macro-level analysis of the relationships. Based on an exposition of such indirect effects of new business formation on development, I turn to the findings of analyses that investigate the relationship between new business formation and regional development. After describing the overall pattern that has been found, I deal with the relative magnitude of the direct and indirect effects, the results by type of entry and by industry, and with differences in the effects that have been found for different types of regions. Finally, I provide an interpretation of the results, draw some conclusions for policy, and define important questions for further research.

EMERGENCE OF THE RESEARCH FIELD

In the eighteenth and nineteenth centuries, early writers on entrepreneur-ship, such as Richard Cantillon and Jean-Baptiste Say, described the role of the entrepreneur as an organizer of often risky business endeavors, but it was Joseph A. Schumpeter who began to fully recognize the impor-tance of entrepreneurship and new business formation for economic development. In his book *Theory of Economic Development*, published first in German in 1911, and again in his 1939 book *Business Cycles*, he analyzed the effect that some dynamic entrepreneurs had on growth and structural change, providing a number of empirical examples. Schumpeter was particularly interested in those entrepreneurs who made a strong impact on the economy by introducing radical innovation. According to Schumpeter, it was the dynamic entrepreneur who initiated radical structural change and growth, a process he described as 'creative destruc-tion'. Examples of this type of innovative entrepreneurship include the emergence of the cotton industry in England and the introduction of the mechanical loom and steam engine during the Industrial Revolution of the eighteenth century, as well as construction of the railway system that extended the geographic scope of markets, leading to the phenomenon of mass production and labor division in the nineteenth century. Schumpeter specifically described and highlighted the indirect growth-enhancing effects these cases of innovative entrepreneurship had in different parts of the economy.

Schumpeter recognized that dynamic entrepreneurs were rare, and that the absence of entrepreneurship could be regarded as an important barrier to economic development. However, in his focus on these rare cases of dynamic entrepreneurship, he did not say much about the ordinary, more commonplace business founder or about business owners in general.

One result of Schumpeter's writings was the emergence of business history as an academic discipline dealing with the development of firms and, thereby, with entrepreneurship. However, in the first decades fol-lowing Schumpeter's contribution, entrepreneurship did not attract a great deal of attention. Although the occurrence of larger groups of innovative new businesses, for example, in Silicon Valley, California, attracted some interest in the issue, the main starting point of systematic empirical analyses of the effects of new business formation on economic development was a study conducted by David Birch (1979) entitled 'The job generation process', which circulated as a mimeographed research report and was never formally published (see also, however, Birch, 1981, 1987). Birch declared that according to his analysis, small and, particu-larly, new businesses were the main job generator in the US economy.

This statement received responses ranging from enthusiastic praise for a new solution to employment problems to pronounced skepticism (for a review of initial reaction to the Birch study, see, for example, Storey, 1994). Most importantly, however, the study stimulated numerous follow-up analyses for the United States as well as for many other countries.

One main innovation of the Birch study was that it analyzed longitudinal micro-level data that covered nearly the entire US economy. In investigating the development of the US economy, the study followed the development of business cohorts of a certain age or size over the years. Unfortunately, reliable information on new business formation and longitudinal micro-level data, which would have allowed employment in firms and establishments[2] to be tracked over the years, was rarely available at the time,[3] and considerable effort had to be expended on making existing data sources accessible for research and on the creation of new ones. In this respect, also, the Birch study had an enormous impact.

The bulk of the empirical research motivated by the work of David Birch comprised micro-level studies that focused on the development of young and small firms. It soon became clear that small firms do not generally grow faster than larger firms; some small firms do, but most continue with only a few employees and face a relatively high risk of exit. A number of studies found that the age of a firm is much more important in explaining its development than its size, and that younger firms seem to have higher growth prospects than older ones.[4] This recognition finally directed attention to newly founded businesses and, consequently, to entrepreneurship. Compared to the micro-level studies of business development that have been initiated by Birch's work, analyses on a more macro level that related new business formation to the development of industries and regions as a whole are relatively few, many of them having been conducted only recently. The next section reviews the studies that assess the development of start-up cohorts and discusses their merits and limitations. The following sections then provide an overview of the results of analyses that investigated the effect of new business formation on economic development based on a more macro-level approach.

THE DEVELOPMENT OF NEW BUSINESSES

Birch's (1979) empirical approach was to follow the development of groups (cohorts) of businesses over time. His statements about the main drivers of development in the US economy were based on comparisons of the performance of business cohorts. A crucial issue in this type of analysis is selection of the sample, which should be representative of the entire population of firms. This requires datasets containing information about the businesses at several points in time. Simple surveys that gather data on current and previous performance at only one point of time are not sufficient because even if the information is representative of all businesses during the period in which the survey is conducted, information for those businesses that existed in an earlier period but are no longer in existence will nearly always be unavailable. Calculating average growth rates only for the firms that were active in both periods ignores those firms that exited the market and the rates thus suffer from a 'survivor bias' that implies a too optimistic picture of development. Hence, cohort analyses of the development of new businesses require information about those businesses that exited the market after some time.

The German Employment Statistics, a comprehensive database that covers all businesses in the private sector (for details, see Spengler, 2008), provides information about representative cohorts of the vast majority of new businesses in Germany over periods of up to 29 years.[5] I illustrate the findings of analyses of start-up cohorts with results based on this database because of the exceptional long time period that is covered. Many results derived from these data are in line with work using other kinds of data and for other countries.[6] Analyzing the German Employment Statistics for West Germany, Fritsch and Weyh (2006) and Schindele and Weyh (2011) showed that overall employment in entry cohorts first rises but then declines from the second or third year on (Figure 4.1). After about eight years, it falls below the initial level and after 20 years the overall number of employees in a cohort is slightly less than 80 percent of that in the year the new businesses were set up. After 29 years, the maximum length of the currently available time series, the overall number of employees is about 50 percent of the initial number of employees. Since most of the start-up activity takes place in the service sector, employment development in services is quite similar to the pattern observed in the private sector as a whole. The results for manufacturing are somewhat different. The number of employees in the manufacturing start-up cohorts remains above the initial level for a longer period of time than it does in the service sector. From year 18 onward, employment declines until it reaches 55 percent of the initial level in year 29. During their first years, the manufacturing start-ups are also more successful than those in services, in that peak employment is about 160 percent of the initial level as compared to 130 percent for services.

In the service sector, the remaining 55 percent of initial employment after 29 years is in just 15 percent of the initial cohort plants, that is, only 15 percent of all newly founded businesses survive the entire observation

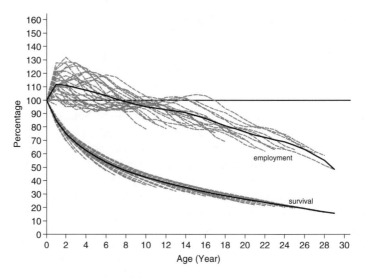

Source: Schindele and Weyh (2011).

Note: Thin dotted lines: individual cohorts; dark thick line: average value over all cohorts for which information in the respective year is available.

Figure 4.1   Evolution of employment and survival rates in entry cohorts

period. In manufacturing, nearly 20 percent of the start-ups endure for the entire 29 years. At the end of the period of analysis, in the year 2004, about 37 percent of all private sector jobs are in the start-ups of the previous 29 years. This share is higher in services (47 percent) than in manufacturing (26 percent) (ibid.).

It is a common observation of such cohort studies that only a small proportion of the new businesses create a considerable number of jobs; the vast majority remains rather small.[7] Accordingly, Schindele and Weyh find that after 10 years, about 23 percent of the jobs are concentrated in the largest 1 percent of the initial start-ups, 45 percent of employment is in the largest 5 percent, and more than 82 percent of the employees work for the largest 25 percent of the initial start-ups. Over time there is a continuously increasing employment concentration for the largest 25 percent of surviving businesses. The relatively few high-growth businesses, often termed 'gazelles', have attracted considerable interest (for a review of respective studies, see Henrekson and Johansson, 2010 and Acs, ch. 6 in this volume). One important result of these studies is that there is a slight tendency for gazelles to be relatively young, but that also quite a number of older firms can be found in this category. Moreover, gazelles are *not* concentrated in innovative manufacturing industries but can be found in all industries, particularly in the service sector (see also the contribution of Acs, ch. 6 in this volume).

The analyses of start-up cohorts clearly show that new businesses do create a considerable number of jobs, but that the share of employment in new businesses in overall employment is not overwhelming. Moreover, many new firms exit the market soon after entry; only a small fraction of start-ups exhibit considerable growth. Why these few gazelles succeed is still unclear and deserves further investigation. Having in mind Schumpeter's examples of innovative entrepreneurs that initiate radical changes with important indirect effects on other firms and other sectors of the economy (Schumpeter, 1939), the development of start-ups tells only part of the story. Hence, even if the number of jobs provided by gazelles or the amount of value they add does make up a considerable part of a region or sector, attempts to assess the impact of new business formation on development should try to account for indirect effects also. It is a severe disadvantage of cohort analyses that they do not account for possible indirect effects of new business formation such as the displacement of incumbent businesses or the effect of the innovative products they introduce. Such possible indirect effects are reviewed in the next section.

POSSIBLE INDIRECT EFFECTS OF NEW BUSINESS FORMATION ON ECONOMIC DEVELOPMENT

New firms introduce new capacities into the market and therefore are an essential element of the market process. The evolution of the newcomers, for example, as measured by how many employees they have or their market share, may be termed the 'direct effect of new capacities'. Due to competition and market selection, only a fraction of start-ups survive for a longer period of time, and those that do succeed in establishing themselves in the market may displace incumbents. Two types of market exit may result from the entry of new businesses. First, a considerable number of new businesses fail to be sufficiently competitive and thus are forced to exit the market. Second, displacement of incumbents by new competitors leads to declining market shares or market exit. Such crowding-out effects may occur in the output market because the entrants gain market share, as well as in the input market due to the additional demand for resources made by new businesses that can lead to scarcity of inputs and increasing factor prices.

These crowding-out effects are somewhat indirect. Given that market selection works according to a survival-of-the-fittest scenario, firms with

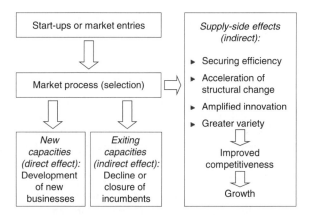

Figure 4.2   New business formation and the market process

relatively high productivity will remain in the market, whereas those with low productivity will have to either reduce their output or exit. At a constant output level, this market selection process should lead to a *decline* in employment, instead of the creation of jobs, because fewer resources are needed to produce the given amount of goods and services at a higher productivity level. Hence, although starting a new business means creating additional capacities that require personnel to operate them, the effect of new business formation on the number of jobs in the economy will not necessarily be positive but could just as well be negative.

However, a well-functioning market process is not a zero-sum game in which the gains of one actor are necessarily at the expense of the other actors. There are several ways in which competition by entry of new businesses can stimulate competitiveness on the supply side of the market and lead to employment growth. The main supply-side effects of entry could include (see Figure 4.2):

- *Securing efficiency and stimulating productivity by contesting established market positions*   Not only actual entry but also the very possibility of entry can force incumbents to perform more efficiently (Baumol et al., 1988).
- *Acceleration of structural change*   Quite frequently, structural change is mainly accomplished by a turnover of the respective economic units, that is, by the entry of new firms and the simultaneous exit of established incumbents. In this case, the incumbents do not undergo necessary internal changes, but are replaced by newcomers.[8] This type of process has been emphasized by Schumpeter's

(1911 [1934], 1942) concept of creative destruction and by Alfred Marshall's (1920) analogy of a forest in which the old trees must fall to make way for new ones.

- *Amplified innovation*, particularly the creation of new markets. There are many examples of radical innovations introduced by new firms (Audretsch, 1995; Baumol, 2004). One major reason for this pronounced role of new firms in introducing radical innovation could be that incumbent suppliers are more interested in exploiting the profit possibilities of their given product program versus searching for new opportunities, particularly if the new products may compete with their established ones (Klepper and Sleeper, 2005; Klepper, 2009). Due to the reluctance that these types of incumbent firms show toward the adoption of new ideas, setting up one's own business may appear to be the only or the most promising possibility for inventors seeking to commercialize their knowledge (Audretsch, 1995; Klepper, 2009).

- *Greater variety of products and problem solutions* If the product program of a newcomer differs from those of the incumbents, or if an entrant introduces significant process innovation, it will result in a greater variety of available goods and problem-solving methods. Such increased variety implies a higher probability of customers finding a better match for their preferences. Increased variety due to new supplies may intensify the division of labor as well as follow-up innovation and, therefore, can generate significant economic development (Boschma, 2004; Saviotti and Pyka, 2004).

Like the crowding-out effects, the supply-side effects are somewhat indirect. They are not necessarily limited to the industry to which the start-up belongs, but may also occur in completely different industries that use the improved supply as an input. Nor are they restricted to the region in which entry occurs, but can emerge in other regions, for example, those regions in which competitors are located. The indirect supply-side effects are the drivers of competitiveness in the respective industries, which may induce employment growth and increasing welfare. They are why one should expect positive employment effects of new business formation.

It is important to note that supply-side effects of new business formation do not necessarily require the newcomers to be successful and survive in order to occur. As long as entry induces improvements on the side of the incumbents, it will lead to enhanced competitiveness even if most of the new businesses fail and exit the market soon after entry. Indeed, even failed start-ups can make a significant contribution to growth.[9] A high degree of failure of new businesses, however, can also have a discouraging effect on market entry, and this possibility should not be ignored.

This review of the different impacts of new business formation on market processes makes very clear that the evolution of new businesses is only a portion of their total effect on development. Many important influences that start-ups have on growth and employment are of an indirect nature and occur on the supply side of the market. If the market is indeed a survival-of-the-fittest arena, the direct employment effects, that is, the growth of new businesses, as well as the displacement of incumbents, should actually result in a decline in employment. Under a properly functioning market regime, growth from new business formation can only be expected from improvements on the supply side. If, however, the process of market selection is not working as it should and allows the survival of relatively unproductive competitors, the economy's competitiveness will decline and, thus, cause the supply-side effects to become negative.

It is plausible to assume that the challenge to competitors made by a new business critically depends on its quality. Quality of a new business can be defined in many ways, of course, and may include aspects such as the entrepreneurial skills of the founder, the knowledge base and other resources of the new business, and its innovativeness. Therefore, the entry of innovative businesses led by well-prepared entrepreneurs who have the requisite knowledge and necessary resources can be expected to have a stronger effect and, particularly, lead to larger supply-side improvements than entry by non-innovative businesses run by persons lacking appropriate skills and unsuccessful at sufficiently accessing the relevant factors of production. High-quality start-ups that successfully challenge incumbents may then exhibit considerable growth and may become gazelles. It could also be expected that the supply-side effects will be relatively large in markets characterized by a high intensity of competition because of greater pressure for improvements. Moreover, supply-side effects may be larger in global product markets, compared to local markets, due to the greater number of direct competitors affected by the challenge of an entrant.

THE EFFECT OF NEW BUSINESS FORMATION ON REGIONAL DEVELOPMENT: AGGREGATE ANALYSES

This section provides an overview of the results of analyses that investigated the effect of new business formation on an aggregate level, particularly regions and countries. I first highlight some methodological issues involved in such an approach and then review the main results of recent studies. A special emphasis is on the relative importance of direct and indirect effects of entries, on the characteristics of the new businesses, on differences in the effects between regions as well as on differences between industries.

Methodological Issues

As I mentioned above, micro-level analyses are not well suited for examining the indirect effects of new business formation. To account for such indirect effects, the relationship between level of new business formation activity and some aggregate performance measure, such as change in employment, change in gross domestic product (GDP), or change in productivity in the respective country, region, or industry, must be analyzed. To date, work on the effects of new business formation on economic development has mainly focused on employment creation, possibly due to the importance placed by policymakers on job generation and the prevention of unemployment. Another reason may be the better availability of information on employment as compared to other performance indicators.

For a meaningful comparison of regions or industries of different size or economic potential, the number of start-ups needs to be related to a measure of economic potential, that is, a start-up rate should be used. Most commonly, the number of employees or the regional workforce (including the unemployed persons) is chosen as the denominator of start-up rates, what Audretsch and Fritsch (1994) term the 'labor market' approach. This kind of start-up rate is based on the notion that each member of the workforce is faced with the decision to either work as a dependent employee in someone else's business or start his or her own firm. According to the labor market approach, the entry rate may be viewed as the propensity of a member of the regional workforce to start an own business.[10] Many of the analyses of the effect of new business formation on regional development have used sector-adjusted start-up rates that account for the fact that start-up rates differ systematically across industries.[11]

The results derived from an analysis of the relationship between start-up rates and the development of employment or turnover at the level of industries can be very difficult to interpret. The problem is that if industries follow a life cycle, then the number of entries and the start-up rate will be relatively high in the early stages of the life cycle when the industry is growing, and relatively low in later stages when the industry is in decline (Klepper, 1997). Can the resulting positive correlation between the start-up rate and development of the industry in subsequent periods be regarded as an *effect* of entry on growth? Probably not – and, indeed, entirely different results are found if, for example, the relationship between the level of start-ups and subsequent employment change is analyzed at the level of regions or at the level of industries (see Fritsch, 1996). This clearly demonstrates that geographical units of observation are much better suited for such an analysis than are industries.

Empirical studies that have analyzed the impact of new business formation on the development of regions or countries employ a start-up measure that is based on gross entry as an indicator of the level of new business formation activity. Sometimes, net entry, calculated as the change in the number of business owners, is used, mainly for reasons of data availability (for example, Carree and Thurik, 2008; Dejardin, 2011). Another variant is to analyze the effect of turbulence, defined as the number of entries plus number of exits, on economic development (for example, Bosma et al., 2011), which can be regarded as an indicator of the level of creative destruction that takes place in the respective industry or region. Studies based on data from the Global Entrepreneurship Monitor (GEM) (for example, Bosma, ch. 5 in this volume) use 'total entrepreneurial activity' (TEA), which is the percentage of the adult population between 18 and 64 years old that is either actively involved in starting a new venture or is the owner/manager of a young business (for details, see Reynolds et al., 2005).

Most studies simply regress the effect of the indicator of new business formation activity on a performance measure with some control variables; however, some studies have applied an explicit production function framework that also contains indicators for the contribution of other inputs to growth (Audretsch and Keilbach, 2004; Wong et al., 2005; Audretsch et al., 2006). In this type of approach, entrepreneurship is regarded as a production factor that introduces resources, such as initiative and opportunity recognition, as well as willingness and ability to take risk, into the model. The advantage of analyzing the contribution of entrepreneurship within the framework of a production function, as compared to a simple regression of indicators for entrepreneurship on measures of development, is that doing so more systematically accounts for other determinants of growth, and it has a foundation in production theory. However, entrepreneurs do not accomplish success and growth by spirit and initiative alone; they must hire labor and make capital investments. Hence, in a production function framework that includes the inputs of labor and capital, parts of the impact of entrepreneurship on development may be attributed to labor and capital and not to the entrepreneur who made the decisions regarding their use. Therefore, the effect of entrepreneurship may well be underestimated in this sort of analysis. However, those empirical studies that more or less solely relate the start-up rate to growth are in danger of overestimating the effect of entrepreneurship due to the neglect of other factors.

A severe problem of applying the production function approach involves the data to be used. For example, data on the capital stock must generally be regarded as of questionable reliability and are, in many countries, rarely available at the regional level. Moreover, causal interpretation of these results can be problematic if the empirical analyses are related to the *level* of GDP or productivity, not to their development. To date, none of the available approaches using a production function framework has used longer time lags of the entrepreneurship indicators, which turns out to be of crucial importance, as will be shown in the next section.

Neglect of longer time lags is also a critical issue in nearly all of the available job-turnover analyses that try to assess the relative contribution that new, incumbent and exiting businesses make to the development of employment (for example, Davis et al., 1996; Spletzer, 2000; Neumark et al., 2006). Without accounting for such time lags, these approaches have more the character of a descriptive job-growth accounting exercise than of a causal analysis of the effects of start-ups. The inclusion of longer time lags for new business formation particularly allows for the identification of indirect effects of entry on incumbent employment (for such an approach, see Fritsch and Noseleit, 2009a and b).

Overview of the Empirical Evidence

The effect of new business formation on the performance of regions and industries
The first systematic analyses of the relationship between the level of new business formation and regional employment change were conducted by Reynolds (1994, 1999) for the United States. Reynolds found a pronounced positive effect. However, performing the analysis for different time periods revealed considerable variation in the outcome. A positive relationship between the regional level of start-ups and subsequent growth was confirmed by Ashcroft and Love (1996) for the United Kingdom, by Acs and Armington (2002) for the United States, by Brixy (1999) for East Germany, and by Fölster (2000) and Braunerjhelm and Borgman (2004) for Sweden. But a number of other studies could not identify such a positive relationship between the level of start-ups and regional employment growth (EIM, 1994; Audretsch and Fritsch, 1996; Fritsch, 1996, 1997). In an international cross-section analysis of 36 countries participating in the GEM project, van Stel et al. (2005) found some confirmation for a positive effect of TEA on GDP growth in highly developed countries, but not in the low-income countries of the sample. Audretsch et al. (2006) included the

start-up rate into a Cobb–Douglas production function and identified a positive effect on the level of GDP and labor productivity, as well as on the growth of labor productivity, in West German regions. In a study based on GEM data for 37 countries, Wong et al. (2005) divided the indicator of total entrepreneurial activity into several groups. A significantly positive impact on GDP growth was found for 'high growth potential' TEA[12] but not for overall TEA, necessity TEA, or opportunity TEA.[13] This result may be regarded as an indication of the important role quality plays in generating start-up effects.

Bosma et al. (2011) investigated the effect of entry and turbulence on total factor productivity for the 40 Nuts III regions of the Netherlands. Turbulence is defined as the number of entries plus the number of exits and is intended to measure the level of business dynamics understood as 'creative destruction'. The number of entries was lagged by two years; the number of exits was taken from the current year. Bosma et al. found an effect of business dynamics in the service sector but not for start-ups and turbulence in manufacturing. According to their estimates, the effect of entry and turbulence in the service sector on the growth of total factor productivity decreases with a rising level of business dynamics. They identify an optimum rate of turbulence at which the effect on productivity growth reaches a maximum.

One reason for the somewhat mixed results of studies analyzing the impact of new business formation on employment change could be that the entry and turnover of establishments (firms) may lead to a productivity increase (see Baldwin, 1995; Foster et al., 2001; Disney et al., 2003; OECD, 2003) that compensates for the employment effect. Another reason may be that not all the effects of new business formation on employment emerge immediately at the time the newcomers enter the market. Due to data restrictions, the analyses mentioned above did not include any or only rather short time lags between the founding of the start-ups and the respective effect on output and therefore may have assessed the effects on regional development only incompletely. In an analysis for West German regions, Audretsch and Fritsch (2002) did, indeed, find evidence for positive long-term effects of new business formation. In this study, new business formation activity in the early 1980s could not explain regional employment change in the rest of the decade, but did provide an explanation of employment change in the 1990s. Van Stel and Storey (2004) analyzed the relevance of such time lags more systematically and estimated a time-lag structure of the effects of new business formation on regional employment growth with data for Great Britain. They confirmed that there are considerable time lags between new business formation and its effect on regional development, which they found to be positive.

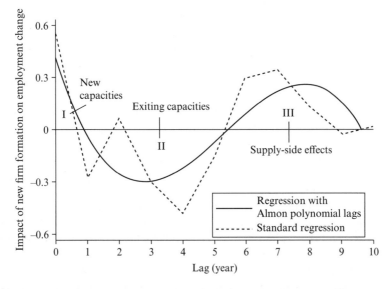

Figure 4.3   Effects of new business formation on employment change over time in West Germany – regression coefficients for start-up rates and the results of the Almon lag procedure assuming a third-order polynomial

The 'wave' pattern

A severe problem in analyzing the lag structure of the effect of new business formation on growth emerges from a high correlation between yearly start-up rates. Because of this high correlation, the original estimates may not reflect the 'true' lag structure. In dealing with this problem, van Stel and Storey (ibid.) applied the Almon polynomial lag procedure. This procedure attempts to approximate the lag structure by a polynomial function (for a detailed description of this method, see Greene, 2008). In this type of analysis, an assumption must be made about the order of the polynomial to be used for estimating the lag structure. Fritsch and Mueller (2004) applied the Almon polynomial lag procedure in an analysis of the effect of new business formation on regional development in West Germany. They found that a statistically significant effect of new business formation on employment is restricted to a period of about 10 years. Van Stel and Storey (2004) assumed a second-order polynomial for estimating the lag structure of new business formation rates; however, Fritsch and Mueller (2004) also applied higher-order polynomials. With a third- and higher-order polynomial, they found a 'wave' pattern of the effects (see Figure 4.3).

Figure 4.3 depicts the original regression coefficients that have been found without application of the Almon lag procedure as well as the coefficients that result from this procedure by assuming a third-order polynomial. The resulting smoothened lag structure suggests that new business formation during the current year has a positive impact on employment change. For years $t-1$ to $t-5$, the effect is negative, with a minimum in $t-3$. For entries in years $t-6$ to $t-9$, a positive relationship is found, with a maximum between years $t-7$ and $t-8$. The magnitude of the effect then decreases and becomes slightly negative in the last year of the sample $(t-10)$.[14] This type of wave pattern of the lag structure has been confirmed for a number of countries, including Belgium (Dejardin, 2011), the Netherlands (van Stel and Suddle, 2008; Koster, 2011), Portugal (Baptista et al., 2008; Baptista and Preto, 2011), Spain (Arauzo-Carod et al., 2008), Sweden (Andersson and Noseleit, 2011), the United Kingdom (Mueller et al., 2008), and the United States (Acs and Mueller, 2008), as well as for a sample of 23 OECD countries (Carree and Thurik, 2008).

Fritsch and Mueller (2004) suggest an interpretation of this wave pattern that builds on the systematization of direct and indirect effects, as discussed in a previous section. According to this interpretation, the positive employment impact for start-ups in the current year can be understood as the additional jobs created by the newly founded businesses at the time of inception. This direct employment effect is indicated in Area I in Figure 4.3. It is well known from a number of analyses that employment in entry cohorts tends to be stagnant or even decline from the second or the third year onward (Boeri and Cramer, 1992; Schindele and Weyh, 2011). Therefore, new firm formation activity in year $t-3$ and more distant time periods should not lead to any significant direct employment effect of the cohort as a whole. As soon as a new business is set up, it is subject to market selection and may gain market shares from incumbent suppliers. Thus, the negative impact of the start-ups in years $t-1$ to $t-5$ (Area II in Figure 4.3) is probably a result of market exit, that is, new businesses that fail to be competitive and displacement of incumbents. The positive impact of new business formation on employment for years $t-6$ to $t-10$ (Area III in Figure 4.3) is probably due to a dominance of indirect supply-side effects, that is, increased competitiveness of the regional suppliers resulting from market selection. After about nine or ten years, the impact of new business formation on regional employment fades away.

When they assumed a second-order polynomial for the Almon lag procedure, Fritsch and Mueller (2004) found the resulting lag structure to be 'u'-shaped. The interpretation of the u-shaped lag structure is similar to that for the wave pattern that resulted from assuming a higher-order polynomial. According to Fritsch and Mueller, the initial increase in

employment can be regarded as the direct employment effect of new business formation, which is followed by a period during which the crowding-
out effects prevail, before the employment-increasing supply-side effects
finally start to dominate. What is different between the two patterns is
that these supply-side effects then become stronger and stronger without
decreasing again in the more distant years. However, such an increase
is highly implausible given the statistical insignificance of start-up rates
during these periods. The increase in the curve for the later periods is
probably caused by the very nature of a second-order polynomial, which
by definition possesses only one inflection point. If the interpretation of
the lag structure proposed by Fritsch and Mueller (ibid.) is correct, both
patterns imply that the indirect employment effects as indicated in Areas I
and II of Figure 4.3 are more important than the direct effect, that is, the
initial employment created in the newly founded businesses (Area I).

Identifying and comparing direct and indirect effects of new business formation

Fritsch and Noseleit (2009a) tried to identify the indirect effects of new
business formation on employment and compare the magnitude of the
two types of effects – direct and indirect. Using the information on total
employment change (ΔEMP_{total}) and on employment in new businesses
(ΔEMP_{new}), they calculate the employment change of incumbents as:

$$\Delta EMP_{inc} = \Delta EMP_{total} - \Delta EMP_{new}.$$

This employment change in incumbent businesses encompasses the indirect effects of the new businesses – displacement and supply-side effects
– as well as other influences that are not caused by the start-ups. They
then estimated the indirect effect of new business formation by regressing
the start-up rate of the preceding 10 years on the change in incumbent
employment.

Fritsch and Noseleit (ibid.) calculated the direct contribution of new
businesses to overall employment as:

$$\Delta Emp_{direct_{t=n}} = \frac{Emp_{cohort_{t=n}} Emp_{cohort_{t=n-1}}}{Emp_{total_{t=n-1}}} * 100$$

with ΔEmp_{cohort_t} giving the number of employees in a certain cohort in year
t and where ΔEmp_{total_t} is the overall regional employment in year t.[15] The
pattern of the direct employment effect identified this way is surprisingly
similar for the different start-up cohorts in the sample. In the year the start-
ups enter the market, they account for an employment increase of about

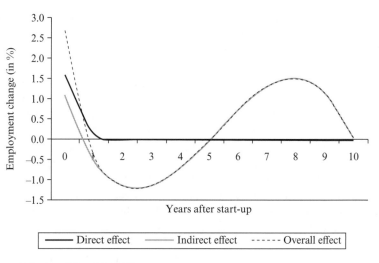

Source: Fritsch and Noseleit (2009a)

Figure 4.4   Impact of start-ups on regional employment change – direct and indirect effects

1.5 to 1.8 percent. In the first year after entry, this effect is also positive but much smaller. Because the start-up cohorts tend to experience an employment decline in later years, their direct contribution to employment change becomes slightly negative. Hence, the largest direct contribution of start-ups to employment change occurs in the year they are set up (see Figure 4.4).

Estimating the indirect effect of new business formation by regressing the start-up rates of the preceding 10 years on the change in incumbent employment, Fritsch and Noseleit (ibid.) found a wave pattern (see Figure 4.4). After applying a weighing procedure that allowed them to express employment change in incumbents as a share of overall employment change, they compared the magnitude of the direct effect and the indirect effects. The resulting curve for the overall effect (Figure 4.4) corresponds well to the findings of earlier studies for Germany (Fritsch and Mueller, 2004, 2008). As Figure 4.4 clearly shows, the largest part of the overall employment induced by new businesses is due to indirect effects on incumbents. The main deviation between the two curves is that the aggregate indirect effect is considerably lower than the overall effect in the first two years, which is due to the direct effect of new business formation on regional employment in this early period.

Based on their analysis for West Germany, Fritsch and Noseleit (2009a) estimate that the overall effect of start-ups on regional employment over the period of analysis is an increase of about 3.8 percent. This means that in the average West German region, start-ups of a certain vintage have led to a nearly 4 percent increase in employment over a period of 11 years.[16] About 40 percent of this increase is attributable to employment in new businesses; the other 60 percent is due to the indirect effects. Hence, nearly two-thirds of the employment change generated by new business formation arises from the interaction between newcomers and incumbents in the region. Employment in the start-ups is clearly the smaller part of the overall effect. This result was confirmed by using another way of identifying direct and indirect effects of new business formation (Fritsch and Noseleit, 2009b). A simple explanation for the larger indirect employment effects may be seen in the greater number of incumbents compared to entries. If many more incumbents react to the challenge posed by a much fewer number of newcomers, it could produce more employment.

In order to identify indirect effects of new business formation on regional growth, Koster et al. (2010) used a market mobility measure that reflects the change in the ranking of establishments with five or more employees in terms of employment size. They found a pronounced correlation between this market mobility measure and the start-up rate, indicating significant effects of entry on the regional market structure. Including the start-up rate and the market mobility measure in a model for explaining regional employment growth shows a statistically significant effect of both indicators. This result seems to be driven by the development of the service sector. When running the analysis for manufacturing only, the start-up rate as well as the market mobility measure have no statistically significant effect on regional employment growth.

Characteristics of new businesses: the quality of entry

The currently available datasets that allow us to assess the regional level of new business formation provide only modest information about the characteristics of start-ups that may be indicative of quality. One piece of information about new businesses that is available in some data is their size at the time of entry or their organizational status, for example, whether a start-up is part of a larger firm or whether it can be viewed as independent. Other characteristics that can be found in the GEM data are based on a self-estimation by founders concerning their growth prospects and the innovativeness of their venture. Another method of identifying start-ups of a certain quality uses information on their industry affiliation. For example, start-ups in industries classified as 'high tech' or 'low tech' may be regarded, respectively, as highly innovative or non-innovative. Results of such analyses are reported below in the section about differences between industries.

Koster (2011) investigated whether independent new firms, as compared to establishments started by existing firms (organizational foundings), in the Netherlands have different effects on regional employment change. Such different effects might very well be expected since new establishments set up by existing firms can rely on the resource base of their parent firm, which makes them less vulnerable and can result in relatively high survival and growth rates (Brüderl et al., 1992; Tübke, 2004).[17] Koster finds that the lag structure for the effects of organizational foundings on regional employment indicates a positive direct effect on regional employment, but that this positive impact rapidly tapers off until it is close to zero and non-significant; specifically, he does not find the positive third part of the typical wave pattern that Fritsch and Mueller (2004, 2008) viewed as an indication of supply-side effects. However, a statistically significant third part of the wave was found for independent start-ups. This supports the idea that the organizational status of entries makes a difference to their potential effect on regional development.

In an analysis employing data on Portugal, Baptista and Preto (2010) studied the time-lag structure of different types of new businesses. They found that start-ups with foreign capital involved, which are a very small share of the total number of new businesses, have a strong displacement effect on employment as well as pronounced supply-side effects, whereas the impact of start-ups without foreign capital is very weak, resulting in only a low amplitude of the wave. According to Baptista and Preto, the overall employment effect of start-ups with foreign capital is clearly positive. Distinguishing between new businesses that enter with an above-average size and the smaller start-ups leads to similar results: the larger entries have a pronounced effect and show the usual wave pattern of the time-lag structure with a rather high amplitude, while the impact of smaller start-ups is minor. However, it remains rather unclear whether the larger start-ups lead to an increase or a decrease of regional employment over the observation period.

In comparable research, Acs and Mueller (2008) investigated the effect of different kinds of start-ups on employment in US Metropolitan Statistical Areas. According to their estimates, the start-up of firms having fewer than 20 employees, of which the vast majority can be assumed to be independent new businesses, has a positive initial, but quickly disappearing, effect on regional employment; no positive third part of the wave pattern indicating dominant supply-side effects could be found for these small start-ups. However, Acs and Mueller did find a pronounced third part of the wave for entry firms having between 20 and 499 employees. New businesses set up with 500 and more employees, the majority of which are plausibly assumed to be subsidiary establishments, have a rather pronounced negative employment effect that probably indicates considerable displacement of incumbents. This negative effect is largest about three years after start-up and then becomes weaker. Unfortunately, the time series available to Acs and Mueller allowed them to estimate a lag structure of the effects of new business formation on regional employment for a period of only six years, so they cannot say whether the effect of the start-up of large firms becomes positive in later years. The authors speculate that the entry of larger firms induces massive restructuring of the regional economy, leading to a pronounced reduction of labor inputs during the first years after start-up.[18]

Using GEM data for 127 Nuts III regions of 17 European countries, Bosma (ch. 5 in this volume) draws distinctions between start-ups based on the ambitions and expectations of entrepreneurs, that is, between those with low growth ambitions (expect to have none or at most one employee in the next five years), those with modest growth ambitions (expect to have between two and nine employees in the next five years), those with high growth ambitions (expect to have 10 or more employees in the next five years), and those with innovative ambitions (assume that at least some customers will consider their product or service new and that not many other businesses offer the same product or service). He finds that the regional rate (TEA) of young entrepreneurs with high growth ambitions has a much closer relationship with the regional level of labor productivity than does the regional rate of less ambitious start-ups or the TEA for innovative entrepreneurship.

Another indication that not all entries are equally important to economic development but that the quality of the newcomers may play a decisive role is provided by empirical work that distinguishes between new businesses according to how long they remain in the market. In an empirical analysis at the level of German industries, Falck (2007) found that new businesses that survived for at least five years ('long-distance runners') had a significantly positive impact on GDP growth, whereas the effect of entries that stayed in the market for only one year ('mayflies') was statistically insignificant or significantly negative. Fritsch and Noseleit (2009b) arrived at a similar result in an analysis at the level of West German regions. They found that the positive effect of new business formation on incumbent employment is nearly entirely caused by start-ups that are able to survive for at least four years. The employment effect of new businesses that exit the market within the first four years is much weaker or statistically insignificant.

The available evidence on the effect of entries with different characteristics clearly suggests that not all start-ups are of equal importance for economic development but that the quality of the newcomers plays a decisive role. However, the results are by no means completely uniform. For example, while Acs and Mueller (2008) as well as Baptista and Preto (2010) found relatively pronounced effects on regional employment from larger start-ups, many of which are probably subsidiaries of larger companies, Koster (2011) identified a slightly lower impact from organizational foundings, that is, new subsidiaries of already existing firms. According to Acs and Mueller (2008) as well as Baptista and Preto (2010) large start-ups induce strong displacement effects but it is unclear whether they lead to an increase or a decrease of overall employment in the long run. Moreover, it is not entirely clear what the set-up of subsidiary establishments of large firms means in terms of challenge to incumbent establishments in the region. On the one hand, it could lead to increased competition for scarce resources on the local input market; on the other, it could be an important source of regional growth (ibid.). Presumably, much depends on the type of activity conducted by the new establishment and on the regional economic environment (for example, the intensity of competition for local inputs). However, despite some ambiguity in interpreting results, it is fairly clear from the available evidence that small and short-lived new businesses have very little effect on regional development, probably because they do not constitute a strong enough challenge to incumbents. The intensity of the challenge may also explain why entry by ambitious entrepreneurs who expect to grow has a stronger impact than that of start-ups with low growth expectations.

Clearly, it would be helpful to have data that allow for a much more differentiated characterization of entry in attempting to discover more about how the quality of a new business affects the direct and indirect contribution it will make to economic development.

Regional Differences

Empirical findings
Regions may differ considerably with regard to the characteristics of their new and incumbent businesses, as well as with regard to their ability to absorb the positive effects of new business formation. Fritsch and Mueller (2004, 2008) analyzed three types of German planning regions: the highly agglomerated areas, the moderately congested regions, and the rural regions. The analysis showed that new business formation in agglomerations not only creates relatively pronounced positive short-term (direct) effects, but also leads to comparatively high, positive long-term (supply-side) effects (Figure 4.5). Also, the negative medium-term (displacement) effects are slightly stronger in agglomerations. Generally, the effects of new business formation on employment change are much more pronounced in

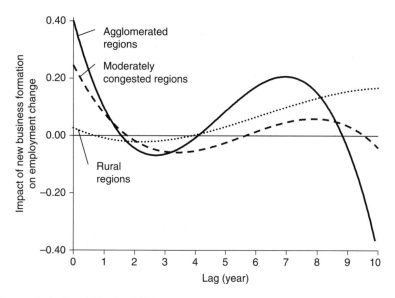

Source: Fritsch and Mueller (2008).

Figure 4.5   *Impact of new business formation on regional employment change in agglomerations, moderately congested regions, and rural regions*

agglomerations than in the other two types of regions.[19] A similar result was found by van Stel and Suddle (2008) for urban and rural regions of the Netherlands, and by Baptista and Preto (2011) for highly and modestly agglomerated regions of Portugal. Mueller et al. (2008) showed that the effects of new business formation on regional employment are much more pronounced in England compared to either Wales or, particularly, Scotland.

Fritsch and Noseleit (2009a) investigated the direct and indirect effects of new business formation in agglomerations, moderately congested areas, and rural regions in West Germany, applying the decomposition procedure described above. They found only minor differences in direct effects between the three types of regions, but differences in the indirect effects were found to be considerable and well suited for explaining the patterns detected by Fritsch and Mueller (2008). Figure 4.6 displays the results of their analysis. The basic shape of the curve for the aggregate indirect effect in agglomerations is quite similar to the shape of the curve for moderately congested regions, the main difference being that the amplitude of the wave is more pronounced in agglomerations, indicating a higher intensity of indirect effects. This higher intensity of indirect effects

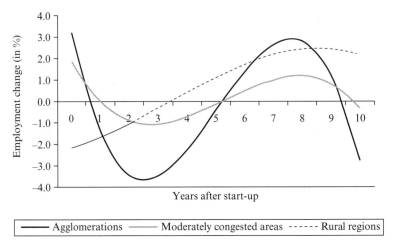

Source: Fritsch and Noseleit (2009a).

Figure 4.6   *Average effects of new business formation on incumbent employment in different types of regions*

of new business formation on incumbents in agglomerations suggests a higher level of economic interaction in these regions, which may directly result from higher density, particularly the spatial proximity of relatively many actors. The pronounced negative indirect effect in agglomerations between year 1 and year 6 after start-up suggests higher displacement effects, which may be due to more intense competition in these regions. In turn, this relatively intense competition and selection in agglomerations may explain the more pronounced supply-side effects that dominate the third phase of the wave.

Another main difference between agglomerations and moderately congested areas, on the one hand, and rural regions on the other, is the direction of the aggregate indirect effects in the first years. In agglomerations and moderately congested areas, the early indirect effect is positive, suggesting that demand-side effects of the resources purchased by the newly founded businesses are much stronger than the displacement effects. In rural regions, the early indirect effects are significantly negative, a possible explanation for which could be that because of poor local supply, an increased demand for resources the rural start-ups need is chiefly met by suppliers in other areas. That the values for the coefficients of the aggregate indirect effect in rural areas do not decrease in the last periods as is the case for agglomerations and moderately congested areas should be interpreted with great caution because the unrestricted regression coefficients for the start-up rate in later periods almost never prove to be statistically significant if included in the model (indicated by the dotted character of the respective curve).

Fritsch and Schindele (2011) investigated in more detail the regional differences in direct employment effects of new business formation in West Germany. They used two indicators to measure the contribution new businesses made to employment growth. The first is the *short-term employment contribution* of the start-up cohorts after a period of two years to total employment in the year prior to start-up. The second indicator is the *long-term employment contribution* of a start-up cohort after 10 years that is also related to overall employment in the year before the new businesses were set up. Fritsch and Schindele found that, on average, an entry cohort of a particular year adds 1.8 percent to overall employment after two years (short-term employment contribution) and 1.56 percent after 10 years. The difference between the long- and the short-term employment contribution reflects the development of start-up cohorts over these years. There is noteworthy variation in the employment contribution of new businesses across regions. The minimum value for the long-term employment contribution for all private industries is 0.84 percent; the maximum value is about eight times as high (6.56 percent). For short-term employment contribution of new businesses, the maximum value (4.71 percent) is more than four times larger than the minimum value of 0.95 percent.

Regression analyses by Fritsch and Schindele explaining the impact of regional characteristics on the direct employment contribution of new businesses showed that the start-up rate, the survival rate, the employment growth of new businesses, a large share of small businesses engaged in regional innovation activity, a highly educated regional workforce, and good availability of moderately priced labor have a significantly positive impact. Population density also has a positive effect, which can be partly explained by the fact that agglomerations are home to a relatively well-educated workforce. Remarkably, Fritsch and Schindele did not find any indication that growth of new businesses is at the expense of incumbents; in fact, the development of both new businesses and incumbent firms appears to be positively interlinked. All in all, their analysis suggests that the *quality* of young firms, in terms of survival and success, has more influence on regional employment than does the *quantity* of start-ups. This indicates that simply trying to increase the number of regional start-ups will not suffice to create employment growth.

Fritsch and Schroeter (2011b) analyzed the influence of region-specific factors on the overall effect of start-up activity on employment change using the regression:

Average employment change$_{r,\,t0\,to\,t+2}$ $= a + b_1{}^*$ *average start up rate*$_{r,\,t-1\,to\,t-10}$

$+ b_2{}^*$ *average start up rate*$^2_{r,\,t-1\,to\,t-10}$ $+ b_3{}^*$ *variable* $l_{r,\,t-1} + b_4{}^*$ *variable* $l_{r,\,t-1}$

**average start up rate*$_{r,\,t-1\,to\,t-10}$ $+ b_5{}^*$ *variable* $ll_{r,\,t-1} + b_6{}^*$ *variable* $ll_{r,\,t-1}$

**average start up rate*$_{r,\,t-1\,to\,t-10}$ $+$ *industry shares*$_{r,\,t-1}$ $+$ *time dummies* $+ u_{r,\,t}$

where r indicates the regions and t time. The *average start-up rate* is calculated as the mean over a 10-year period, that is, from $t - 10$ to $t - 1$. A
period of 10 years was used to account for the relevant long-term effects
found in a number of other analyses. The squared value of the start-up
rate was included to account for a nonlinear relationship with employment
change. Fritsch and Schroeter found a positive coefficient for the average
start-up rate, but a significantly negative coefficient for its squared value,
indicating that the marginal effect of new business formation on regional
employment declines with the number of start-ups. This suggests that
regions with a relatively low level of start-ups may benefit more from an
increase in the start-up rate than will regions in which the start-up rate is
already high.

The estimated coefficients of the start-up rates and the potential growth
determinants indicate their direct influence on employment change. The
coefficients of the interaction terms can be regarded as a measure of the
impact the respective variable has on the employment effect of the new
businesses. This makes it possible to distinguish between the direct effects
of several regional characteristics and the impact that these potential
determinants of regional growth may have through new business formation activity. For example, because employment in West German
agglomerations grew less than it did in other types of regions during
the period of analysis, Fritsch and Schroeter (ibid.) found a negative
coefficient for the effect of population density on employment change.
However, interaction of the start-up rate with population density showed
a strongly positive relationship, indicating that new business formation has a much larger effect in high-density areas than in rural regions.
According to Fritsch and Schroeter, this population density effect is
rather dominant. Other region-specific factors that lead to a relatively
pronounced effect of new business formation on employment growth are
a large share of medium-skilled workers and a high level of innovative
activity. Although the total unemployment rate appears to be unimportant, a high share of short-time unemployed had a negative influence on
the employment effect of start-ups. Moreover, the growth impact of new
businesses turns out to be negatively related to the employment share
in small establishments. The regional share of highly skilled employees,

labor productivity, and the entrepreneurial character of the technological regime were insignificant factors in the employment growth effects of new business formation.

In their analysis of the effect of entry and turbulence on the total factor productivity in a region, Bosma et al. (2011) identified a significantly higher effect in regions with high population density, particularly those regions in which the industry structure is characterized by a high level of *related variety* (for this concept, see Frenken et al., 2007). 'Related variety' of regional industry structure means that the region's industries are diverse but technologically related so that they share at least some portion of the same knowledge base. For example, technological relatedness of industries can be assumed if one firm produces goods normally produced by several different industries (Neffke and Svensson, 2008). Such technological relatedness may be conducive to the emergence of new combinations of ideas among different industries, which could be viewed as a special case of Jacobs externalities (Jacobs, 1969).

What explains the dominance of density?
Many empirical analyses have found that the effect of new business formation on growth is considerably more pronounced in high-density areas as compared to rural regions. When investigating the reasons for regional differences of the effects for West German regions, Fritsch and Schroeter (2011b) found that population density played an important role. There are at least two strands of argument that may explain why density is so important with regard to the effect of new business formation:

- First, high-density areas tend to be a breeding ground for relatively high-quality start-ups, such as innovative new businesses. A main reason for this is the pronounced knowledge base of larger cities, manifested by the presence of universities and other research institutes. This explanation is supported by empirical evidence showing that innovative new businesses are particularly likely to be set up close to such research institutions (Bade and Nerlinger, 2000; Baptista and Mendonça, 2010). Moreover, many agglomerations have an abundant high-skilled workforce that can be viewed as a reservoir of high-quality entrepreneurs, not to mention an important input for innovative new firms. Other factors that may stimulate the emergence and success of high-quality start-ups in high-density areas include spatial proximity to other actors and the resulting knowledge spillovers, as well as diversity of activity (Jacobs externalities).

- Second, the high intensity of local competition, particularly on the input markets, may lead to relatively strong selection effects that spur regional productivity. The argument for a higher intensity of selection in agglomerations is in line with the observation that survival rates of new businesses are significantly lower in these regions compared to other areas (Renski, 2009; Fritsch et al., 2011). The argument is also consistent with the results of Fritsch and Mueller (2004, 2008) as well as those of Fritsch and Noseleit (2009a), who showed that displacement effects tend to be more severe in agglomerations, but that positive supply-side effects are also considerably more pronounced (see Figures 4.5 and 4.6).

Thus, there are some plausible explanations for the relatively pronounced effect of new business formation on regional development in high-density areas, but the reasons behind this phenomenon are not yet well understood. In particular, we do not know whether these differences are due to a different quality of the regional entries or what role local competition plays. If the intensity of local competition contributes to explaining the regional effects, this could be a clue as to which is more important – competition on the output market or competition for local inputs. Moreover, the dominant effect of density is a phenomenon that holds for a sample of regions *on average*; there are also empirical examples of high-density areas where new business formation has no such strong effect.[20]

Regional growth regimes

Audretsch and Fritsch (2002) suggested that there may be considerable differences between regions with regard to the role that new firms and entrepreneurship play in development. In introducing the concept of regional growth regimes, they extended the idea of the technological regime (Winter, 1984; Audretsch, 1995, 39–64; Marsili, 2002) from the unit of observation being the industry to a geographic unit of observation (see also Fritsch, 2004). By analogy to the common concept of a technological regime, the growth regime in a region is called 'entrepreneurial' if growth results from a high level of new firm start-ups and a turbulent enterprise structure. In contrast, regions where above-average growth is accompanied by relatively stable large incumbent enterprises are regarded as having a 'routinized' growth regime (Figure 4.7). In the routinized regime, new businesses do not play an important role, and their chances for survival and growth are much lower than in an entrepreneurial regime.

Audretsch and Fritsch (2002) characterized regions with relatively low growth rates but above-average start-up rates as 'revolving-door' growth regimes (see also Fritsch and Mueller, 2006). They conjectured that under

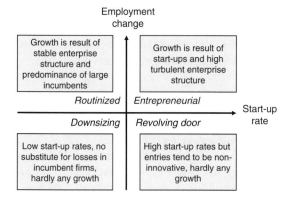

Figure 4.7   Regional growth regime types and their characteristics

such a regime, entries will tend to be non-innovative, supplying basically the same products and using nearly the same technology as the incumbent firms. Finally, relatively low-growth regions, which are characterized by a below-average level of start-up activity, are classified as 'downsizing growth' regimes. In such regions, the number and quality of start-ups is not sufficient to provide enough new jobs or income to substitute for the losses in incumbent firms.

In analyzing transitions between the different growth regimes, Fritsch and Mueller (2006) identified some patterns. They found that while downsizing as well as entrepreneurial growth regimes tend to be rather stable over time, the other two types of regime appear to be more temporary. Moreover, if a region with a downsizing regime experiences an increase in new business formation, it will most probably become a revolving-door regime before it eventually reaches the stage of being an entrepreneurial growth regime. Correspondingly, if regions with an entrepreneurial growth regime experience a decline in start-ups, they will first assume the character of a routinized growth regime before they eventually turn into a downsizing regime. These findings suggest that the effect of new business formation on growth occurs with a time lag that may be considerably longer than the lag suggested by the wave pattern. It may take a long time before the growth effects of an increased level of entrepreneurship become evident and even if the start-up rate begins to decrease, the growth benefits of higher start-up rates in a region will continue to prevail for some time.

In comparing entrepreneurship and growth in former socialist East Germany to the long-established market economy of West Germany, Fritsch (2004) concluded that the two parts of the country experienced different growth regimes during the period under inspection, the 1990s and the early 2000s. Despite quite similar formal institutions in both parts of the country, differences with regard to entrepreneurship culture, level of economic development, and policy, to name just a few, seem to have had a relatively strong effect on how the two regions developed.

Differences between Industries

Why should there be differences in the effect of new business formation on regional growth between industries?
Differences in the effects of start-ups in different industries on regional growth are interesting for two reasons. First, industry affiliation may be regarded as an indicator for certain characteristics of new businesses so that the results of the respective analyses may help us assess the importance of the quality of start-ups on their effects on growth. Second, market conditions, particularly the intensity of competition and the importance of particular parameters in the competitive process such as price and quality, may vary considerably between industries, resulting in differences in the direct and indirect effects of entry.

Acemoglu et al. (2006) and Aghion et al. (2009) argued that the distance of an industry or firm from the technological frontier may be decisive with regard to how incumbents will react to the challenge of new competition. According to this view, firms or industries that are relatively advanced and can be regarded as close to the technological frontier tend to react to entry with innovation (escape-entry effect), whereas the entry of new competition discourages more-backward firms or industries from innovation activity. Aghion et al. presented empirical evidence as to the effects of entry by foreign competitors on a sample of UK firms that is in line with this hypothesis.

Another set of predictions about the divergent effects of entry in different industries is based on the notion of an equilibrium rate of business ownership (Carree and Thurik, 1999; Audretsch et al., 2002; Hartog et al., 2010), a concept sometimes referred to as a market's 'carrying capacity' in the organization ecology literature (Hannan and Freeman, 1977). If there is such a thing as an equilibrium rate of business ownership, then 'excessive entry' may lead to 'market overcrowding'.[21] Hence, business ownership rates that exceed the equilibrium rate will be unstable and tend to develop toward the equilibrium rate. This implies that the effect of new business formation on growth depends on the actual number of competitors, not the equilibrium number. If the actual number of firms in a market is equal to or greater than the equilibrium number, positive net entry will not increase long-term overall employment in the firms operating in this market. However, entry may lead to growth if the actual business ownership rate is below the equilibrium rate (Hartog et al., 2010).

Despite some empirical evidence (most of which is on the whole-nation level rather than covering a particular industry[22]) in support of this market 'overcrowding' idea (Audretsch et al., 2002; Carree et al., 2007; Hartog et al., 2010), the concept suffers a number of drawbacks. First, many markets are geographically much larger than a region or a country and it thus may be rather questionable as to whether one can determine an optimal number of firms for a certain region or country. Second, the assumption that a market has a given carrying capacity is a static one in that it implies given levels of product, costs of production, and demand. These assumptions ignore possible supply-side effects of new businesses and may be appropriate chiefly in the case of non-innovative entry. If entry is innovative, that is the new firm introduces new products or better methods of production or distribution that stimulate innovation by incumbent firms, it may induce considerable change in the equilibrium number of firms. Clearly, for the case of innovative entry, the notion of excessive entry and overcrowding is of limited value, and even in the case of non-innovative entry, the argument is weak, especially in the event that incumbents respond to the newcomers' challenge by engaging in innovation.

A number of *ad hoc* hypotheses about divergent effects of entry into different industries may apply. For example, it is plausible to assume that the effect of entry is relatively strong in industries that are knowledge intensive and require relatively high qualification (for example, high-tech manufacturing, knowledge-intensive business services) because the entries into such industries are generally of high quality. One may particularly assume a relatively positive employment development for new ventures, that is, a pronounced direct effect, in innovative industries as they benefit from a new and growing demand for their products or services. Nevertheless, innovations are always subject to uncertainty as to market success and, if they involve research and development (R&D), also with respect to the success, cost, and duration of the R&D. If innovative new firms do survive, however, it is plausible to expect them to grow rapidly and to generate a relatively strong direct employment effect in the respective region. However, the regional incidence of the indirect effect does depend on the spatial distribution of competitors. It can be relatively pronounced within regional clusters of the respective industry but it may be rather weak if the number of local competitors is small.

How certain barriers, such as minimum efficient size and capital requirements, affect entry is a priori unclear. On the one hand, one may assume that a certain minimum efficient size leads to larger-size entries, which will tend to have a more pronounced effect than smaller entries (Acs and

Mueller, 2008). Hence, start-ups in the manufacturing sector, which is characterized by a relatively large minimum efficient size, have a stronger effect on growth than new businesses in small-scale industries such as many types of consumer-oriented services. On the other hand, entry rates tend to be higher in industries with a low minimum efficient size (Fritsch and Falck, 2007), which should lead to higher intensity of competition and, hence, more pronounced supply-side effects.

Empirical evidence of industry differences
There are only a few empirical studies investigating the employment effect of start-ups differentiated by their sector affiliation. Concerning the direct employment effect of new businesses, empirical analyses for Germany provide evidence that there is a great deal of variation between manufacturing and the service sector. For example, while the number of employees in start-up cohorts of service firms falls below the initial level after a period of eight years, in the case of new manufacturing businesses, the number of employees stays above the initial number for 18 years (Fritsch and Weyh, 2006; Schindele and Weyh, 2011).

Empirical results on the survival of innovative firms are mixed. Studies by Audretsch (1995) for the United States and by Audretsch et al. (2000) for the Netherlands indicated a relatively greater risk of failure for start-ups in industries with high R&D levels. In contrast, Cefis and Marsili (2005) for the Netherlands, Metzger and Rammer (2009) as well as Fritsch et al. (2011) for Germany presented evidence for higher survival rates for new ventures in innovative industries as compared to other industries in Germany. Metzger and Rammer also showed that new businesses in innovative manufacturing industries and knowledge-intensive services created, on average, more jobs per start-up than entries in non-innovative and non-knowledge-intensive industries, at least in the case of Germany.

Applying a regional production function approach, Audretsch et al. (2006) included the start-up rate as an input together with capital, labor, and R&D investment. In their analysis for West Germany, they found that new business formation in high-tech manufacturing industries and in information and communication industries had a considerably stronger impact on the regional growth of labor productivity than did the overall start-up rate or the level of start-ups in low-tech industries.

Analyses of the overall effect of new business formation on regional employment growth have found much stronger effects for start-ups in manufacturing than for start-ups in the service sector (Fritsch and Mueller, 2004; van Stel and Suddle, 2008; Andersson and Noseleit, 2011; Fritsch and Schroeter, 2011a). Distinguishing between several parts of the service sector, van Stel and Suddle (2008) identified the lowest effect for new business formation in trades. According to Fritsch and Schroeter (2011a), start-ups in knowledge-intensive business services had the strongest impact on overall employment growth in West Germany, while the effect of new businesses in innovative manufacturing remained statistically insignificant. However, studies using performance indicators based on GDP figures have found contradictory results. Dejardin (2011), in a study of Belgium, identified a positive effect of net entry on GDP growth only for services, while the effect of net entry into manufacturing industries was non-significant. Bosma et al. (2011), in their analysis for regions of the Netherlands, found a positive effect of entry and turbulence on the growth of total factor productivity only for services, not for manufacturing.

Analyzing the effect of new business formation on regional employment in Portugal, Baptista and Preto (2011) found that the overall effect on regional employment was substantially larger for new businesses in knowledge-based industries than for start-ups in other sectors. In their study, 'knowledge-based' industries include innovative manufacturing and knowledge-intensive services (for example, communications, finance, insurance, real estate, and business services) (OECD, 2002). Specifically, the displacement effects as well as the supply-side effects of new businesses in knowledge-based industries were much more pronounced than in non-knowledge-intensive industries.

The wave pattern observed for the effects of new businesses on employment implies that start-ups may induce a considerable reallocation of resources in the respective regional economy. Andersson and Noseleit (2011), in an analysis of Sweden, focused on such intersectoral effects. In a first step, they confirmed the well-known wave pattern for the Swedish economy as a whole. In a second step, the model was run for three sectors: manufacturing, low-end services, and high-end services. Andersson and Noseleit found that in all three sectors new business formation resulted in an employment increase. Analyzing the effect on overall employment change, start-ups in manufacturing had the strongest impact, followed by new business formation in low-end services. The effect of start-ups in high-end services, defined to include knowledge-intensive services, on overall employment change, however, was hardly statistically significant. Andersson and Noseleit clearly showed the presence of indirect effects by regressing new business formation in a certain sector on employment change in other sectors of the economy. These indirect effects were strongest for start-ups in manufacturing, again followed by start-ups in low-end services, with high-end service industries again bringing up the rear.

In short, the results of empirical studies on how new business formation in different industries affects growth are far from being monolithic. The only point of agreement among these studies is that start-ups in manufacturing tend to have a stronger impact on employment than do new businesses in the service sector, which may be explained by the larger average size of manufacturing start-ups. However, in analyses with GDP or productivity as the dependent variable, only entry into the service sector had a statistically significant effect. With regard to entries in innovative industries, some analyses found lower probabilities of survival, whereas studies for other countries showed relatively high survival rates in these industries. The results on the overall impact on regional employment of start-ups in innovative or knowledge-intensive industries are also inconclusive. In some studies, start-ups in these industries had a pronounced impact, while in others this effect was statistically insignificant.

There are a number of explanations for these diverse empirical results. One reason may be that industry classifications are not well suited for distinguishing between entries that have a different impact on regional development. A second reason could be that there are considerable differences between certain industries in specific countries or types of regions that have implications for the effects of entry on development. Differences in the results between countries or regions may have to do with how close the firms under study are to their technological frontiers (Aghion et al., 2009). Also unclear is how the method of analysis and the choice of the dependent variable shape the results. For example, that Audretsch et al. (2006), applying a production function approach, identified a strong positive effect of new business formation in the German high-tech manufacturing industries on the development of labor productivity, while, for the same country and sector, Fritsch and Schroeter (2011a) found no significant effect on employment needs explanation. More research is also needed into the effect on employment and total factor productivity of start-ups in the manufacturing and the service sector in the Netherlands (van Stel and Suddle, 2008; Bosma et al., 2011). Obviously, considerable further research is needed before we completely understand how economic development is affected by start-ups in different industries.

IS NEW BUSINESS FORMATION A CAUSE OR A SYMPTOM OF REGIONAL DEVELOPMENT?

The review of research on the effect of entry on regional development has shown that there is compelling empirical evidence in favor of a positive relationship. However, given that economic growth creates entrepreneurial opportunities, which, in turn, is accompanied by an increasing number of firms, entry may also be viewed as a symptom of development. If growth stimulates the emergence of new businesses, ignoring this relationship may lead to overestimating the effect that start-ups have on economic development.[23] In an extreme case, new business formation would simply be a byproduct of growth processes that take place independently of new business formation.

However, viewing new business formation as only a byproduct of economic development is rather implausible. Such a stance would have to ignore numerous examples of the pioneering role some exceptional entrepreneurial personalities have played in economic development. Even if one made the rather strong assumption that historical developments obviously largely initiated by new ventures – for example, the Industrial Revolution of the eighteenth century or development of the micro-computer and emergence of the Internet economy – would have occurred anyway, such a stance cannot explain the geography of these developments. On the other hand, however, without an adequate empirical analysis of the relationships, the possibility of such an effect of economic development on new business formation cannot be ignored. The question, therefore, is: does economic growth truly have such a significant impact on new business formation and, if so, does this situation lead to overestimating the effect of entry on development in subsequent periods?

A first indication of the extent to which the emergence of new business is a result of growth processes can be drawn from studies that have analyzed the determinants of entry. Many of these studies have found such a positive effect of growth, particularly population growth, on entry, but in most cases the relationship was not very strong.[24] Audretsch et al. (2006) simultaneously estimated the effect of regional performance on the level of new business formation, as well as the effect of new business formation on the growth of regional labor productivity, using a production function framework. While they found that the growth of GDP per head had a statistically significant positive impact on new business formation in subsequent periods, the effect of start-ups on the increase in labor productivity remained statistically significant. This clearly suggests that new business formation has a distinct positive effect on development that is independent of an overall growth trend.

In a recent paper, Anyadike-Danes et al. (2011) analyzed this relationship for Irish regions between 1988 and 2004, a time span that includes the period of rapid economic growth Ireland enjoyed between 1994 and 2000. The authors found that during the period of analysis, the number of businesses in Ireland almost tripled. However, the number of start-ups in relation to the number of incumbent businesses remained fairly constant in the longer run. The same holds for the number of new businesses in relation to the number of employees. Relating the time series of new business formation and employment showed no statistically significant effect of employment growth on the level of start-ups, but did show a weak effect of gross entry on employment.

These statistical tests were, however, restricted by the limited length of the two time series. Anyadike-Danes et al. found that the stock of businesses per regional population is fairly constant across regions, supporting the idea of an equilibrium number of businesses per population at a certain point in time. The authors suggested that relatively high start-up rates in a region might be regarded as a process of catching up to this equilibrium rate.

Hartog et al. (2010) investigated the possible two-way relationship between changes in the business ownership rate (net entry) and growth for 21 OECD countries for the 1981–2006 period, employing a simultaneous empirical approach. They identified a link between the national welfare level and the business ownership rate, but found that development during the previous periods had no statistically significant effect. Analyzing the effect of changes in the business ownership rate on GDP growth, Hartog et al. concluded that there are decreasing marginal returns in terms of growth effects to entrepreneurship, which confirms the results of Fritsch and Schroeter (2011b) for German regions. Hartog et al. (2010) explained this result with the notion of an equilibrium business ownership rate: an increasing level of entrepreneurship will have relatively pronounced effects on growth if the initial business ownership rate is below the equilibrium rate; the effects will be considerably smaller if the initial rate is above the equilibrium rate. A main limitation of Hartog et al.'s study is that it contains no information on gross entry and thus nothing can be learned about the effects of the number of entries on turbulence in the stock of businesses and its effects on economic development.

In summary, work to date has not identified any, or only a relatively weak, effect of growth in previous periods on the level of new business formation; the effect of new business formation on economic development, however, is found to be considerably pronounced. Based on this evidence, we can conclude that start-ups do have a distinct impact on growth independent of any long-term growth trajectory that might exist. New business formation is more a cause than a symptom of growth. However, assessing the effect of new business formation on economic development without simultaneously accounting for a possible effect of growth on the level of start-ups may lead to some overestimation of the effects of start-ups.

ENTRY, MARKET SELECTION, AND REGIONAL PERFORMANCE: INTERPRETATION AND SPECULATION

Empirical evidence as to the effects of new business formation on economic development clearly indicates that start-ups need to be understood as an integral part of the market process. According to this view, new businesses are a challenge to incumbents and may induce improvement of overall economic performance, given that market selection is working on a survival of the fittest basis. This implies that the consequences of new business start-ups for growth depend on a number of factors, including:

- quality of the newcomers in terms of the competitive pressure that they exert on incumbents,
- the way incumbent firms react (for example, by product innovation, process innovation, outsourcing to low-wage regions), as well as
- the functioning of the market selection process, which, in turn, depends on several other factors, such as the number of competitors, demand conditions, technological developments, barriers to entry and exit, and so on.

Market selection processes are at work in both output and input markets. Given the interregional or even global scope of many output markets, improvements on the part of incumbents that were originally motivated by pressure from local start-ups may not occur in the same region where the local start-up is but elsewhere. Since many input markets, such as markets for low-end services, floor space, and labor, are much more local in character than output markets, one may expect that the competition effects induced by start-ups on input markets will more often occur in the same region as the start-up compared to the consequences of competition on output markets. For example, intense competition for inputs could explain why survival rates of start-ups in regions with high population density are lower and that displacement effects are more pronounced. This would point to a relatively high importance of regional input market conditions to the effect of new business formation on regional development as compared to the regional market for the respective products and services.

The above-discussed factors make it uncertain that new business formation will necessarily lead to additional employment in the same region where the start-up takes place. Indeed, there are several examples of regions in which the effect of new business formation on employment is insignificant or even negative. However, on average and in most regions, start-ups *do* create more employment in their region, particularly in the longer run. Why there is such variation between regions in this regard, however, is still rather unclear.

IMPLICATIONS FOR ENTREPRENEURSHIP POLICY

Although our understanding of the effects of new business formation on regional development is still incomplete, the current state of knowledge suggests a number of important implications for an entrepreneurship policy aimed at stimulating regional growth.

It has been shown that new business formation may produce a number of important indirect effects that have a strong impact on regional competitiveness and growth. These competitiveness-enhancing supply-side effects of new business formation rely on markets operating according to survival of the fittest principles. If the market does not operate according to these principles, which when functioning properly force less productive firms to exit, entry may not stimulate growth. Therefore, any growth-oriented entrepreneurship policy should ensure that the market truly is determined by survival of the fittest. Policymakers should take particular care to avoid any action that will interfere with this selection process, such as direct support of new businesses by means of special subsidies that are not available to incumbents.

A number of analyses clearly suggest that it is not the mere number of start-ups, but their ability to compete successfully with incumbents and to survive, that is important for their effect on regional development. Hence, increasing the number of start-ups may not be an appropriate strategy for an entrepreneurship policy aimed at stimulating growth; rather, such a policy should focus on improving the quality of start-ups and on increasing the number of high-quality new businesses. Hence, to be truly effective, the policy must concern itself with the quality of the start-ups it encourages. This implies that start-up rates or business ownership rates that include all types of businesses are of only limited relevance for assessing the level of growth-relevant entrepreneurship in a region.

Policy intended to stimulate high-quality start-ups should be firmly based on the preconditions necessary to successful entrepreneurship, such as general as well as entrepreneurship education, and provide qualified advice to potential founders. Entrepreneurship education, in particular, could be very useful in helping people make a more realistic assessment of their ability to run a business and, in the best case, dissuade those ill suited to such a venture from embarking on it (von Graevenitz et al., 2010). The empirical results particularly indicate that a highly educated regional workforce and good availability of moderately priced labor are generally conducive to the employment contribution of new businesses. Moreover, policy should be especially designed to include measures aimed at the regional knowledge base, which is an important source of spatially bounded knowledge externalities that may enhance the recognition of promising entrepreneurial opportunities and the emergence of high-quality start-ups. Trying to increase the number of high-quality start-ups means actively creating an entrepreneurial culture. For innovative start-ups, this includes building a high-quality university system that provides cutting-edge scientific knowledge and technology, facilitates access to higher education by talented people, and effective technology transfer.

The results of recent research clearly show that region-specific factors play an important role in the development of new businesses and their contribution to employment. Growth conditions for new businesses and their role in regional development will vary according to the characteristics of the regional environment, and thus different regions may well have quite different types of growth regimes (Audretsch and Fritsch, 2002; Fritsch, 2004; Fritsch and Mueller, 2006). This suggests that policy measures aimed at creating an environment for successful entrepreneurship should be region specific and take into consideration both the advantages and disadvantages of a region's economic structure.

AVENUES FOR FURTHER RESEARCH

Recent empirical analyses of the effects of new businesses on economic development have produced a number of interesting results. This work has substantially improved our understanding of the underlying forces, but there is considerable room for further investigation. In what follows, I sketch some important avenues for further research in the field.

Alternative Performance Measures

Most analyses of the effect of new business formation on regional development have used employment change as a measure for performance for reasons of data availability. Only very few studies used GDP-based indicators such as GDP growth or productivity, quite often with considerably different results from analyses using employment growth figures. Such divergent results deserve further investigation. Since productivity can be regarded as a catch-all variable that should particularly reflect improvements in performance that do not result in more employment (for example, labor-saving process innovations), the effect of new business formation on productivity should be more pronounced than the effect on employment. Moreover, since the wave pattern that has been found for the effect of new business formation on employment change suggests that market selection begins to work rather soon after entry, the positive effect of entry on GDP and productivity should occur considerably earlier than the effect on employment.

Quality of Entry

The quality of a new business may be indicated by factors such as the innovativeness of the supplied goods and services, the qualification of the entrepreneur, her or his motivations (for example, opportunity versus necessity start-ups) and growth ambitions, the marketing strategy pursued, the amount and quality of resources mobilized for the new business, its productivity, survival over a certain period of time, and so on. Since high-quality start-ups put greater competitive pressure on incumbents, the market-process-oriented view expressed above implies that they should have a stronger effect on overall development than start-ups of a lower quality. However, nearly nothing is known about those characteristics of new businesses that make them particularly challenging to incumbents. Only a few studies have analyzed the factors that are conducive to the emergence of high-quality entry such as innovative start-ups or new businesses with high growth expectations. To derive policy recommendations for increasing the number of high-quality start-ups, much more needs to be known about the determinants of this type of entry.

Gazelles

Fast-growing new businesses (gazelles) are a special case of high-quality start-ups. Although these firms have attracted a fair amount of attention and research in recent years (Henrekson and Johansson, 2010; Acs, ch. 6 in this volume), not much is known about them. This holds particularly in regard to their effect on the respective industry and region. What regional conditions are conducive to the emergence of gazelles? What impact do these fast-growing new businesses have on overall regional development? Does the emergence of gazelles lead to a particularly pronounced response by incumbents?

Indicators for Growth-relevant New Businesses

All the studies on how new business formation affects regional development are based on start-up rates for the entire regional economy or for different sectors. If it is correct that only a small portion of new businesses has a significant effect on regional development, then start-up rates that include all new businesses produce a rather diffuse picture and are not well suited to assess the level of growth-relevant entrepreneurship in a region.

More informative indicators for this type of entrepreneurship should be developed.

Effects of Entry on Competition in Input and Output Markets

The available evidence as to the competitive processes induced by the new-comers is still incomplete and somewhat speculative. For example, it is still a largely open question as to why we can observe such pronounced supply-side effects of new business formation in many regions when output markets are interregional or even global. Is the effect of start-ups on such interregional markets concentrated in the respective region? Moreover, what is the relative importance of competition on output markets compared to competition for local inputs such as floor space and labor? To what degree do the indirect effects of new business formation that occur in the region rely on input market competition? If input markets play a considerable role in this respect, what can policy do to stimulate positive effects of new business formation on regional development?

Characteristics of Output Markets

Entry conditions and the competitive process vary considerably with the characteristics of the industry such as the stage of the industry life cycle (Audretsch, 1995; Klepper, 1997). Such characteristics of output markets should have consequences for the performance of newcomers as well as for the effect of new business formation on overall development. They may also have some influence on the quality of entry. Empirical evidence as to the impact of start-ups in different industries on overall economic performance, however, is not very clear and partly contradictory. And nothing is known about the influence that the intensity of competition and the importance of particular parameters in the competitive process of a certain market, such as price and quality, have on the direct and the indirect effects of entry.

Institutional Environment

Generally, the role the institutional environment plays in entrepreneurship is a research 'blind spot'. This is particularly true for the effects of new business formation on development. Formal as well as informal institutions may be important at all stages of the entrepreneurial process and can affect the number and quality of start-ups as well as their impact on input and output markets (for a more detailed treatment of this topic, see Henrekson and Johansson, ch. 7 and Feldman et al., ch. 8 in this volume).

Regional Characteristics

A number of studies have clearly shown that regional characteristics can play a considerable role in the employment effects of new business formation. Particularly, population density seems to have a dominant effect in this respect. These regional differences are not yet well understood and should be further investigated. Among the factors that might explain such regional differences are:

- the regional economic and political history, wealth level, and development in previous years;
- the characteristics of the regional knowledge base;
- the scale and type of entrepreneurship culture prevalent in the region;
- the quality of the regional start-ups;
- the qualification of the workforce, the availability of labor, and the regional wage level;
- the local availability and price of other inputs, such as finance and business-oriented services;
- the regional industry composition;
- the size structure of the regional economy;
- regional policy measures such as subsidies for start-ups and incumbent businesses;
- the presence of supportive networks; and
- the intensity of regional competition on input and output markets.

Combinations of such region-specific factors may lead to particular regional growth regimes.

Entry as a Cause or as a Symptom of Growth?

Research in this important field is particularly hampered by the lack of appropriate data. Time series are often too short for adequately investigating this important issue. Although the few available studies clearly indicate that start-ups can have an effect on subsequent growth that is independent from long-term development trajectories, more such studies for countries of different wealth levels would be desirable. It would be particularly interesting to know whether it is possible to identify types of new businesses that are mainly induced by increasing domestic demand and have no significant effect on future development (start-ups as a symptom of growth). Accordingly, it would be desirable to know what types of new ventures are growth initiators and to what extent their emergence is a result of development processes.

Universities and Other Research Institutions as Incubators

Although our knowledge about the characteristics of those new businesses that are of particular importance for regional growth processes is incomplete, there are sufficient indications that the regional knowledge base, particularly universities and other research institutions, plays an important role in this respect. Hence the role of these knowledge sources as incubators of new businesses should be further investigated (for a review of this field, see the contribution of Astebro and Bazzazian, ch. 9 in this volume). A more comprehensive understanding of the role played by these institutions could be particularly helpful in deriving appropriate policy recommendations.

Entrepreneurship Policy

Finally, all the research directions proposed above should lead to the design of an appropriate growth-oriented entrepreneurship policy. A large part of the entrepreneurship policy currently observed in many countries and regions is motivated by stimulating regional growth. However, these policy instruments have been designed more or less *ad hoc*, without a sufficient understanding of the underlying processes. The effects of the current strategies should be analyzed and considerable effort should be devoted to carefully transform the research results into appropriate and effective policy strategies.

FINAL REMARKS

How new business formation affects regional development is still a largely underresearched field. This is remarkable given the importance of the issue, particularly since regional development is often given as a justification for policy measures intended to promote the emergence of new ventures. Recent research has shown that new business formation can indeed further regional development, but it would be naive to expect that all or even most of these new businesses create a substantial number of jobs. Many and probably the most important effects of new business formation on growth are indirect in nature and much depends on factors such as the quality of the start-ups and the regional environment. Our knowledge about these influences has increased considerably in recent years, but a great deal of research is necessary before we arrive at an understanding of the effects that is sufficiently comprehensive to be useful.

This survey of research in the field has highlighted a number of open questions that are ripe for further research. I very much hope that further research will lead to answers (and, of course, more questions) that will be particularly helpful in designing appropriate and effective policies in this field.

NOTES

1. I am indebted to Florian Noseleit and Michael Wyrwich for helpful comments on an earlier version of this survey.
2. A start-up can be either a new firm or a new establishment of a multi-plant enterprise. The term 'new business' is used here as an overall category that encompasses the set-up of a new headquarters as well as the creation of a new subsidiary establishment.
3. Birch (1979) used microdata from the Dun & Bradstreet credit rating agency for the United States in the 1969–76 period.
4. Evans (1987), Davis et al. (1996), Sutton (1997), Audretsch et al. (2004), Haltiwanger et al. (2010), Stangler and Kedrosky (2010).
5. The statistic is limited to those businesses that have at least one employee, that is, start-ups consisting only of owners are not included.
6. See, for example, Horrell and Litan (2010) and Stangler and Kedrosky (2010) for the USA.
7. See, for example, Storey (1994, pp. 113–19) for a review of the cohort studies that were available until the early 1990s.
8. Such a process could, for example, be observed in the transformation of former socialist economies of Central and Eastern Europe, where new firms – the bottom-up component – had a considerably stronger impact on structural change (see Brezinski and Fritsch, 1996; Pfirrmann and Walter, 2002).
9. Thus, even in a 'revolving-door' market regime in which the vast majority of entries soon exit the market (Audretsch, 1995), start-ups may have an important effect to the extent that they pose a challenge to incumbents.
10. Because start-ups are usually located close to the residence of the founder (Stam, 2007), the regional workforce can be regarded as an appropriate measure of the number of potential entrepreneurs.
11. For example, start-up rates are higher in the service sector than in manufacturing industries. This means that the relative importance of start-ups and incumbents in a region is confounded by the composition of industries in that region. If this fact is not appropriately taken into consideration, the result will be an overestimation of the level of entrepreneurship in regions that are home to a large number of industries for which start-ups play an important role, and an underestimation of the role of new business formation in regions that are home to a high share of industries characterized by relatively low start-up rates. To correct for the confounding effect of the regional composition of industries on the number of start-ups, a shift-share procedure is employed to obtain a sector-adjusted measure of start-up activity (for details, see Audretsch and Fritsch, 2002, Appendix). This sector-adjusted number of start-ups is defined as the number of new businesses in a region that could be expected if the composition of industries were identical across all regions. Thus, the measure adjusts the raw data by imposing the same composition of industries upon each region. This procedure leads to somewhat clearer results and higher levels of determination than the estimates using the non-adjusted start-up rate. However, the basic relationships are left unchanged.
12. A venture was classified as having a 'high growth potential' if it fulfilled four criteria: (i) the venture plans to employ at least 20 employees in five years; (ii) the venture indicates

at least some market creation impact; (iii) at least 15 percent of the venture's customers normally live abroad; and (iv) the technologies employed by the venture were not widely available more than a year ago (Wong et al., 2005, 345).

13. Necessity entrepreneurship is understood as a start-up that is founded due to a lack of alternatives (for example, the founder cannot find any other kind of job). A new business that is set up to pursue an opportunity is classified as 'opportunity' entrepreneurship. See Reynolds et al. (2005) for details.

14. The overall effect of new business formation on employment change can be measured by the sum of the regression coefficients for the start-up rates of the different years (Gujarati, 2009), which are depicted by the three areas in Figure 4.3.

15. Thus, start-ups of the 1984 cohort, for example, which entered the market with 230,138 employees, accounted for an employment change of 1.47 percent in the initial year because:

$$\Delta EMP_{direct_{1984}} = \frac{230,138 - 0}{15,677,496} * 100 = 1.47.$$

Since these businesses did not exist in the prior period, the share of employees in the cohort over all employees in $t - 1$ gives the percentage change of employment that the 1984 start-up cohort contributed in that year. In 1985, employment in this cohort grew from 230,138 to 236,236. Thus, the contribution of the 1984 start-up cohort to overall employment change in the year 1985 is calculated as:

$$\Delta EMP_{direct_{1985}} = \frac{236,236 - 230,138}{15,522,385} * 100 = 0.039 \text{ percent.}$$

16. This result corresponds quite well to the estimates of Fritsch and Mueller (2008), according to whom one additional start-up per 1,000 employees leads to an overall employment increase of about 0.46 percent in the average region. Given an average start-up rate of about nine new businesses per 1,000 employees, an employment increase of 4.14 percent can be attributed to new business formation.

17. The number of organizational foundings in Koster's data is about half the number of independent start-ups (Koster, 2011).

18. More than 10 percent of the entries were firms with fewer than 20 employees, about 8 percent were firms with between 20 and 499 employees, and the larger firms made up a little more than 10 percent of all new establishments.

19. The results for the rural regions, however, should be viewed with caution because only two of the 11 coefficients for start-up rates in the unrestricted model proved to be statistically significant and the coefficients for the Almon lags remained insignificant.

20. This holds, for example, for large sections of the old-industrialized Ruhr area in Germany.

21. The common explanation for why entrepreneurs enter markets that are already crowded is that they are overconfident with regard to their chances and risks (Arabsheibani et al., 2000; Koellinger et al., 2007). Such overconfidence does indeed seem to be common among firm founders, and one may even argue that it is a necessary ingredient of new ventures, given the high risk of failure that would otherwise deter entry (ibid.). Excessive entry can occur in markets with low barriers to entry (for example, certain service industries) or if public subsidies are available that lead to reduced costs of venture creation. Individuals particularly prone to founding such types of business may be those individuals who face relatively low opportunity costs, for example, due to being unemployed.

22. An exception is the analysis by Carree and Thurik (1999) of the Dutch retailing sector.

23. Economic growth can stimulate new business formation in at least three ways. First, previous growth may generate a relatively large number of new entrepreneurial opportunities. Second, positive expectations about future growth can encourage individuals

to start an own business. Third, overall growth makes it easier for start-ups to survive their first critical years and to become established on the market.
24. See, for example, Reynolds et al. (1994), Sutaria and Hicks (2004), Audretsch and Keilbach (2007), and Fritsch and Falck (2007).

REFERENCES

Acemoglu, Daron, Philippe Aghion and Fabrizio Zilibotti (2006), 'Distance to frontier, selection, and economic growth', *Journal of the European Economic Association*, **4**, 37–74.
Acs, Zoltan J. and Catherine Armington (2002), 'The determinants of regional variation in new firm formation', *Regional Studies*, **36**, 33–45.
Acs, Zoltan J. and Pamela Mueller (2008), 'Employment effects of business dynamics: mice, gazelles and elephants', *Small Business Economics*, **30**, 85–100.
Aghion, Phillippe, Richard W. Blundell, Rachel Griffith, Peter Howitt and Susanne Prantl (2009), 'The effects of entry on incumbent innovation and productivity', *Review of Economics and Statistics*, **91**, 20–32.
Andersson, Martin and Florian Noseleit (2011), 'Start-ups and employment dynamics within and across sectors', *Small Business Economics*, **36**, 461–83.
Anyadike-Danes, Michael, Mark Hart and Helena Lenihan (2011), 'New business formation in a rapidly growing economy: the Irish experience', *Small Business Economics*, **36**, 503–16.
Arabsheibani, Gholamreza, David de Meza, John Maloney and Bernard Pearson (2000), 'And a vision appeared unto them of a great profit: evidence of self-deception among the self-employed', *Economic Letters*, **67**, 35–41.
Arauzo-Carod, Josep-Maria, Daniel Liviano-Solis and Mònica Martin-Bofarull (2008), 'New business formation and employment growth: some evidence for the Spanish manufacturing industry', *Small Business Economics*, **30**, 73–84.
Ashcroft, B. and J.H. Love (1996), 'Firm births and employment change in the British counties: 1981–1989', *Papers in Regional Science*, **25**, 483–500.
Audretsch, David B. (1995), *Innovation and Industry Evolution*, Cambridge, MA: MIT Press.
Audretsch, David B., Martin Carree, André van Stel and Roy Thurik (2002), 'Impeded industrial restructuring: the growth penalty', *Kyklos*, **55**, 81–98.
Audretsch, David B. and Michael Fritsch (1994), 'On the measurement of entry rates', *Empirica*, **21**, 105–13.
Audretsch, David B. and Michael Fritsch (1996), 'Creative destruction: tubulence and economic growth', in Ernst Helmstädter and Mark Perlman (eds), *Behavioral Norms, Technological Progress, and Economic Dynamics: Studies in Schumpeterian Economics*, Ann Arbor, MI: University of Michigan Press, pp. 137–50.
Audretsch, David B. and Michael Fritsch (2002), 'Growth regimes over time and space', *Regional Studies*, **36**, 113–24.
Audretsch, David B., Isabel Grilo and Roy Thurik (eds) (2007), *Handbook of Research on Entrepreneurship Policy*, Cheltenham, UK and Northampton, MA, USA: Edward Elgar.
Audretsch, David B., Patrick Houweling and Roy Thurik (2000), 'Firm survival in the Netherlands', *Review of Industrial Organization*, **16**, 1–11.
Audretsch, David B. and Max Keilbach (2004), 'Entrepreneurship capital and economic performance', *Regional Studies*, **38**, 949–59.
Audretsch, David B. and Max Keilbach (2007), 'The localisation of entrepreneurship capital: evidence from Germany', *Papers in Regional Science*, **86**, 351–65.
Audretsch, David B., Max Keilbach and Erik Lehmann (2006), *Entrepreneurship and Economic Growth*, Oxford: Oxford University Press.
Audretsch, David B., Luuk Klomp, Enrico Santarelli and Roy Thurik (2004), 'Gibrat's Law: are the services different', *Review of Industrial Organization*, **24**, 301–24.
Bade, Franz-Josef and Eric Nerlinger (2000), 'The spatial distribution of new technology based firms: empirical results for West-Germany', *Papers in Regional Science*, **79**, 155–76.

Baldwin, John (1995), *The Dynamics of Industrial Competition*, Cambridge: Cambridge University Press.

Baptista, Rui, Vitor Escária and Paulo Madruga (2008), 'Entrepreneurship, regional development and job creation: the case of Portugal', *Small Business Economics*, **30**, 49–58.

Baptista Rui and Joana Mendonça (2010), 'Proximity to knowledge sources and the location of knowledge-based start-ups', *Annals of Regional Science*, **45**, 5–29.

Baptista, Rui and Miguel Torres Preto (2010), 'Long-term effects of new firm formation by type of start-up', *International Journal of Entrepreneurship and Small Business*, **11**, 382–402.

Baptista, Rui and Miguel Torres Preto (2011), 'New firm formation and employment growth: regional and business dynamics', *Small Business Economics*, **36**, 419–42.

Baumol, William J. (2004), 'Entrepreneurial enterprises, large established firms and other components of the free-market growth-machine', *Small Business Economics*, **23**, 9–21.

Baumol, William J., John C. Panzar and Robert D. Willig (1988), *Contestable Markets and the Theory of Industry Structure*, rev. edn, San Diego, CA: Harcourt Brace Jovanovich.

Birch, David L. (1979), 'The job generation process', mimeo, MIT Program on Neighborhood and Regional Change, Cambridge, MA.

Birch, David L. (1981), 'Who creates jobs?', *The Public Interest*, 3–14.

Birch, David L. (1987), *Job Creation in America: How Our Smallest Companies Put the Most People to Work*, New York: Free Press.

Boeri, Tito and Ulrich Cramer (1992), 'Employment growth, incumbents and entrants – evidence from Germany', *International Journal of Industrial Organization*, **10**, 545–65.

Boschma, Ron (2004), 'Competitiveness of regions from an evolutionary perspective', *Regional Studies*, **38**, 1001–14.

Bosma, Niels, Erik Stam and Veronique Schutjens (2011), 'Creative destruction and regional productivity growth: evidence from the Dutch manufacturing and services industries', *Small Business Economics*, **36**, 401–18.

Braunerhjelm, Pontus and Benny Borgman (2004), 'Geographical concentration, entrepreneurship, and regional growth – evidence from regional data in Sweden 1975–1999', *Regional Studies*, **38**, 929–47.

Brezinski, Horst and Michael Fritsch (eds) (1996), *The Economic Impact of New Firms in Post-Socialist Countries: Bottom Up Transformation in Eastern Europe*, Cheltenham, UK and Northampton, MA, USA: Edward Elgar.

Brixy, Udo (1999), *Die Rolle von Betriebsgründungen für die Arbeitsplatzdynamik*, Nuremberg: Bundesanstalt für Arbeit.

Brüderl, Joseph, Peter Preisendörfer and Rolf Ziegler (1992), 'Survival chances of newly founded business organizations', *American Sociological Review*, **57** (2), 227–42.

Carree, Martin and Roy Thurik (1999), 'The carrying capacity and entry and exit flows in retailing', *International Journal of Industrial Organization*, **17**, 985–1007.

Carree, Martin and Roy Thurik (2008), 'The lag structure of the impact of business ownership on economic performance in OECD countries', *Small Business Economics*, **30**, 101–10.

Carree, Martin, André van Stel, Roy Thurik and Sander Wennekers (2007), 'The relationship between economic development and business ownership revisited', *Entrepreneurship and Regional Development*, **19**, 281–91.

Cefis, Elena and Orietta Marsili (2005), 'A matter of life and death', *Industrial and Corporate Change*, **14**, 1167–92.

Davis, Steven J., John C. Haltiwanger and Scott Schuh (1996), *Job Creation and Destruction*, Cambridge, MA: MIT Press.

Dejardin, Marcus (2011), 'Linking net entry to regional economic growth', *Small Business Economics*, **36**, 443–60.

Disney, Richard, Jonathan Haskell and Ylva Heden (2003), 'Restructuring and productivity growth in UK manufacturing', *Economic Journal*, **113**, 666–94.

EIM (1994), *Kleinschalig ondernemen 1994, deel II: regionaleconomische dynamiek en werkgelegenheidscreatie*, EIM Small Business Research and Consultancy, Zoetermeer.

Evans, David S. (1987), 'The relationship between firm growth, size, and age: estimates for 100 manufacturing industries', *Journal of Industrial Economics*, **35**, 567–81.
Falck, Oliver (2007), 'Mayflies and long-distance runners: the effects of new business formation on industry growth', *Applied Economic Letters*, **14**, 1919–22.
Fölster, Stefan (2000), 'Do entrepreneurs create jobs?', *Small Business Economics*, **14**, 137–48.
Foster, Lucia, John Haltiwanger and Chad Syverson (2001), 'Aggregate productivity growth: lessons from microeconomic evidence', in Charles R. Hulton, Edwin R. Dean and Michael J. Harper (eds), *New Developments in Productivity Analysis*, Chicago, IL: University of Chicago Press, pp. 303–63.
Frenken, Koen, Franz van Oort and Thijs Verburg (2007), 'Related variety, unrelated variety and regional economic growth', *Regional Studies*, **41**, 685–97.
Fritsch, Michael (1996), 'Turbulence and growth in West-Germany: a comparison of evidence by regions and industries', *Review of Industrial Organization*, **11**, 231–51.
Fritsch, Michael (1997), 'New firms and regional employment change', *Small Business Economics*, **9**, 437–48.
Fritsch, Michael (2004), 'Entrepreneurship, entry and performance of new businesses compared in two growth regimes: East and West Germany', *Journal of Evolutionary Economics*, **14**, 525–42.
Fritsch, Michael and Oliver Falck (2007), 'New business formation by industry over space and time: a multi-dimensional analysis', *Regional Studies*, **41**, 157–72.
Fritsch, Michael and Pamela Mueller (2004), 'The effects of new business formation on regional development over time', *Regional Studies*, **38**, 961–75.
Fritsch, Michael and Pamela Mueller (2006), 'The evolution of regional entrepreneurship and growth regimes', in Michael Fritsch and Jürgen Schmude (eds), *Entrepreneurship in the Region*, New York: Springer, pp. 225–44.
Fritsch, Michael and Pamela Mueller (2008), 'The effect of new business formation in regional development over time: the case of Germany', *Small Business Economics*, **30**, 15–29.
Fritsch, Michael and Florian Noseleit (2009a), 'Investigating the anatomy of the employment effects of new business formation', Jena Economic Research Paper 2009–001, Friedrich Schiller University and Max Planck Institute of Economics, Jena.
Fritsch, Michael and Florian Noseleit (2009b), 'Start-ups, long- and short-term survivors and their effect on regional employment growth', Jena Economic Research Paper 2009–081, Friedrich Schiller University and Max Planck Institute of Economics, Jena.
Fritsch, Michael, Florian Noseleit and Yvonne Schindele (2011), 'Success or failure? Business-, industry- and region-specific determinants of survival – a multidimensional analysis for German manufacturing', mimeo, Friedrich Schiller University, Jena.
Fritsch, Michael and Yvonne Schindele (2011), 'The contribution of new businesses to regional employment – an empirical analysis', *Economic Geography*, **87**, 153–80.
Fritsch, Michael and Alexandra Schroeter (2011a), 'Does quality make a difference? Employment effects of high- and low-quality start-ups', Jena Economic Research Paper 2011–001, Friedrich Schiller University and Max Planck Institute of Economics, Jena.
Fritsch, Michael and Alexandra Schroeter (2011b), 'Why does the effect of new business formation differ across regions?', *Small Business Economics*, **36**, 383–400.
Fritsch, Michael and Antje Weyh (2006), 'How large are the direct employment effects of new businesses? An empirical investigation', *Small Business Economics*, **27**, 245–60.
Greene, William (2008), *Econometric Analysis*, 6th edn, Upper Saddle River, NJ: Pearson Prentice-Hall.
Gujarati, Damodar N. (2009), *Basic Econometrics*, 5th edn, Boston, MA: McGraw-Hill.
Haltiwanger, John, Ron S. Jarmin and Javier Miranda (2010), *Who Creates Jobs? Small vs. Large vs. Young*, Washington, DC: US Census Bureau, Center for Economic Studies (CES 10–17).
Hannan, Michael T. and John Freeman (1977), 'The population ecology of organizations', *American Journal of Sociology*, **82**, 929–64.

Hartog, Chantal, Simon Parker, André van Stel and Roy Thurik (2010), 'The two-way relationship between entrepreneurship and economic performance', Scales report H200822, Zoetemer: EIM.

Henrekson, Magnus and Dan Johansson (2010), 'Gazelles as job creators: a survey and interpretation of the evidence', *Small Business Economics*, **35**, 227–44.

Horrell, Michael and Robert Litan (2010), *After Inception: How Enduring is Job Creation by Startups?*, Kansas City, MO: Kauffman Foundation.

Jacobs, Jane (1969), *The Economy of Cities*, New York: Random House.

Klepper, Steven (1997), 'Industry life cycles', *Industrial and Corporate Change*, **6**, 145–81.

Klepper, Steven (2009), 'Spinoffs: a review and synthesis', *European Management Review*, **6**, 159–71.

Klepper, Steven and Sally Sleeper (2005), 'Entry by spin-offs', *Management Science*, **51**, 1291–306.

Koellinger, Philipp, Maria Minniti and Christian Schade (2007), ' "I think I can, I think I can": overconfidence and entrepreneurial behavior', *Journal of Economic Psychology*, **28**, 502–27.

Koster, Sierdjan (2011), 'Individual foundings and organizational foundings: their effect on employment growth in the Netherlands', *Small Business Economics*, **36**, 485–501.

Koster, Sierdjan, André van Stel and Mickey Folkeringa (2010), 'Start-ups as drivers of market mobility: an analysis at the region-sector level for the Netherlands', Scales Research Report # H200905, Zoetemeer: EIM.

Leitao, Joao and Rui Baptista (eds) (2009), *Public Policies for Fostering Entrepreneurship: A European Perspective*, Dordrecht: Springer.

Marshall, Alfred (1920), *Principles of Economics*, 8th edn, London: Macmillan.

Marsili, Orietta (2002), 'Technological regimes and sources of entrepreneurship', *Small Business Economics*, **19**, 217–15.

Metzger, Georg and Christian Rammer (2009), *Unternehmensdynamik in forschungs- und wissensintensiven Wirtschaftszweigen in Deutschland* (Firm dynamics in research- and knowledge intensive industries in Germany), Mannheim: ZEW (Studien zum deutschen Innovationssystem Nr. 05–2009).

Mueller, Pamela, André van Stel and David J. Storey (2008), 'The effect of new firm formation on regional development over time: the case of Great Britain', *Small Business Economics*, **30**, 59–71.

Neffke, Frank and Henning M. Svensson (2008), 'Revealed relatedness: mapping industry space', Papers in Evolutionary Economic Geography #08.19, University of Utrecht.

Neumark, David, Junfu Zhang and Brandon Wall (2006), 'Where the jobs are: business dynamics and employment growth', *Academy of Management Perspectives*, **20**, 79–94.

Organisation for Economic Co-operation and Development (OECD) (2002), *OECD Science, Technology and Industrial Outlook*, Paris: OECD.

Organisation for Economic Co-operation and Development (OECD) (2003), *The Sources of Economic Growth in OECD Countries*, Paris: OECD.

Pfirrmann, Oliver and Günther H. Walter (2002), *Small Firms and Entrepreneurship in Central and Eastern Europe: A Socio-economic Perspective*, Heidelberg: Physica.

Renski, Henry (2009), 'New firm entry, survival, and growth in the United States – a comparison of urban, suburban, and rural areas', *Journal of the American Planning Association*, **75**, 60–77.

Reynolds, Paul D. (1994), 'Autonomous firm dynamics and economic growth in the United States, 1986–90', *Regional Studies*, **27**, 429–42.

Reynolds, Paul D. (1999), 'Creative destruction: source or symptom of economic growth?', in Zoltan J. Acs, Bo Carlsson and Charlie Karlsson (eds), *Entrepreneurship, Small and Medium-Sized Enterprises and the Macroeconomy*, Cambridge: Cambridge University Press, pp. 97–136.

Reynolds, Paul D., Niels Bosma, Erkko Autio, Steve Hunt, Natalie De Bono, Isabel Servais, Paloma Lopez-Garcia and Nancy Chin (2005), 'Global Entrepreneurship Monitor: data collection design and implementation 1998–2003', *Small Business Economics*, **24**, 205–31.

Reynolds, Paul D., David J. Storey and Paul Westhead (1994), 'Cross-national comparisons of the variation in new firm formation rates', *Regional Studies*, **28**, 443–56.
Saviotti, Pier Paolo and Andreas Pyka (2004), 'Economic development, variety and employment', *Revue Économique*, **55**, 1023–49.
Schindele, Yvonne and Antje Weyh (2011), 'The direct employment effects of new businesses in Germany revisited – an empirical investigation for 1976–2004', *Small Business Economics*, **36**.
Schumpeter, Joseph A. (1911 [1934]), *Theorie der Wirtschaftlichen Entwicklung*, Leipzig 1911: Duncker & Humblot; rev. English edn: *The Theory of Economic Development*, Cambridge, MA: Cambridge University Press.
Schumpeter, Joseph A. (1939), *Business Cycles: A Theoretical, Historical, and Statistical Analysis of the Capitalist Process*, New York: McGraw-Hill.
Schumpeter, Joseph A. (1942), *Capitalism, Socialism and Democracy*, New York: Harper & Row.
Spengler, Anja (2008), 'The Establishment History Panel', *Schmollers Jahrbuch / Journal of Applied Social Science Studies*, **128**, 501–9.
Spletzer, James R. (2000), 'The contribution of establishment births and deaths to employment growth', *Journal of Business and Economic Statistics*, **18**, 113–26.
Stam, Erik (2007), 'Why butterflies don't leave: locational behaviour of entrepreneurial firms', *Economic Geography*, **83**, 27–50.
Stangler, Dane and Paul Kedrosky (2010), *Neutralism and Entrepreneurship: The Structural Dynamics of Startups, Young Firms, and Job Creation*, Kansas City, MO: Kauffman Foundation.
Storey, David J. (1994), *Understanding the Small Business Sector*, London: Routledge.
Sutaria, Vinod and Donald A. Hicks (2004), 'New firm formation: dynamics and determinants', *Annals of Regional Science*, **38**, 241–62.
Sutton, John (1997), 'Gibrat's legacy', *Journal of Economic Literature*, **35**, 40–59.
Tübke, A. (2004). *Success Factors of Corporate Spin-offs*, Boston, MA: Kluwer Academic Publishers.
van Stel, André, Martin Carree and Roy Thurik (2005), 'The effect of entrepreneurial activity on national economic growth', *Small Business Economics*, **24**, 311–21.
van Stel, André and David J. Storey (2004), 'The link between firm births and job creation: is there a Upas tree effect?', *Regional Studies*, **38**, 893–909.
van Stel, André and Kashifa Suddle (2008), 'The impact of new firm formation on regional development in the Netherlands', *Small Business Economics*, **30**, 31–47.
von Graevenitz, Georg, Dietmar Harhoff and Richard Weber (2010), 'The effects of entrepreneurship education', *Journal of Economic Behavior and Organization*, **76**, 90–112.
Wennekers, Sander and Roy Thurik (1999), 'Linking entrepreneurship and economic growth', *Small Business Economics*, **13**, 27–55.
Winter, Sidney G. (1984), 'Schumpeterian competition in alternative technological regimes', *Journal of Economic Behavior and Organization*, **5**, 287–320.
Wong, Poh Kam, Yuen Ping Ho and Erkko Autio (2005), 'Entrepreneurship, innovation and economic growth: evidence from GEM data', *Small Business Economics*, **24**, 335–50.

5 Entrepreneurship, urbanization economies, and productivity of European regions
Niels Bosma

INTRODUCTION

The literature of regional economic growth has established that differences in regional productivity can to a large extent be explained by the density of economic activity. This effect of 'urbanization economies' has been documented for regions in the United States (Ciccone and Hall, 1996) and Europe (Ciccone, 2002). Micro-level foundations of urbanization economies have been investigated since the 1980s and an overview of today's knowledge is provided in reviews by Rosenthal and Strange (2003, 2004) and Duranton and Puga (2004). Other authors have related urbanization economies to specific characteristics of the labor force in cities such as human capital (Glaeser et al., 1992) and creative class (Florida, 2002).[1] In addition, in the tradition of Romer (1986, 1990) and Lucas (1988), urbanization economies have been connected to knowledge, innovation, and technology (Audretsch and Feldman, 1996). An important regional-level mechanism that feeds urbanization effects is knowledge spillovers taking place via Jacobs externalities (Jacobs, 1969). Duranton and Puga (2004) conclude that the different microeconomic mechanisms that may be used to justify the existence of cities generally lead to very similar outcomes. They argue that, while this equivalence means that the concept of 'urban agglomeration economies' is robust for many different specifications and microeconomic mechanisms, the problem remains that identifying and separating these mechanisms empirically becomes very difficult.

An emerging contribution to regional growth theory comes from the entrepreneurship literature. The reasoning of the importance of entrepreneurship and the surprisingly low attention paid to entrepreneurship in economic literature had already been signaled in the 1960s by William Baumol using the often-cited words (Baumol, 1968, p. 68): 'The theoretical firm is entrepreneurless – the Prince of Denmark has been expunged from the discussion of Hamlet'. In the very same issue of the *American Economic Review*, Leibenstein (1968, p. 72) argued that 'the standard competitive model hides the vital function of the entrepreneur'. It was, however, only after the rediscovery of Joseph Schumpeter's works in the 1980s and the publication of David Birch's findings about the importance of the small-business sector for job growth (Birch, 1979) that data collection on entrepreneurship really took off. This data collection has enabled empirical testing so that now entrepreneurship is included more explicitly in economic modeling. Audretsch and Keilbach (2004, 2005) see entrepreneurial processes as an additional factor that enables the productive use and combinations of labor, capital, and knowledge. Acs et al. (2003) see entrepreneurs as agents who filter the available stock of knowledge in the region and turn this into promising new ventures. They argue that it is the combination of research and development (R&D) and entrepreneurship in particular that leads to economic growth.

This expanding body of literature takes as its point of departure that most new firms are embodied by the entrepreneurs. However, it is clear that there are many types of entrepreneurs and it can be argued that different types of entrepreneurship may impact on the regional economy differently. Indeed, Leibenstein (1968, pp. 72–3) made a plea 40 years ago for the identification of different types of entrepreneurship, separating *routine entrepreneurship* as a type of management from Schumpeterian or *new* type of entrepreneurship. Sternberg and Wennekers (2005) argue that different types of entrepreneurship will impact on economic growth differently. Since the empirical literature clearly documents spatial unevenness in entrepreneurship rates (Reynolds et al., 1994; Audretsch and Fritsch, 2002; Bergmann and Sternberg, 2007; Glaeser, 2007; Bosma and Schutjens, 2009) it becomes clear that, conceptually, the individual level and the regional level should be explicitly modeled when linking entrepreneurship to economic growth.

In addition to an emphasis on the individual, identifying the *stage* of entrepreneurship is important. Entrepreneurship is not an event, but a process. In line with Schumpeter (1942), the early stage of entrepreneurship, including the phase from before to after the birth event of the firm, is widely recognized as the most relevant entrepreneurial stage for economic growth. Davidsson (2006) makes a plea for investigating the pre-birth processes of entrepreneurship, also known as 'nascent entrepreneurship' (see Davidsson and Gordon, 2009 for a recent overview of empirical findings). Whether a potential high-impact firm succeeds in reaching the market depends on numerous factors. However, even if nascent entrepreneurs do not succeed in getting their business started, their efforts will probably not be lost. Good ideas will be picked up by others, or returned to by the same entrepreneur who experienced what went wrong in the first attempt. The chances that the knowledge spillovers will remain lingering in the region are high (Michelacci and Silva, 2007). We therefore hypothesize that early-stage entrepreneurial activity, and in particular the ambitious types of early-stage entrepreneurial activity, contribute to regional economic performance.

In this chapter, we contribute to the literature by describing a model in which entrepreneurship impacts on regional levels of growth in addition to the traditional inputs of labor, capital, and knowledge. The model presumes that different types of entrepreneurship are identified at the individual level. The model also recognizes that the odds of being engaged in (types, stages of) entrepreneurship are not exogenous. Individual characteristics are believed to exert a significant influence on the odds of being entrepreneurially active. Regional characteristics are believed to provide an additional effect. Our combined individual- and regional-level focus allows us to investigate which types of entrepreneurship complement urbanization economies in explaining regional variation in labor productivity and which types of entrepreneurship unravel effects equivalent to other microlevel explanations of agglomeration effects (Duranton and Puga, 2004).

In our empirical analysis, we draw on an extensive database extracted from the Global Entrepreneurship Monitor (GEM). It allows us to explore the entrepreneurial perceptions and behavior of more than 370,000 individuals over 136 regions in 17 European countries. In our methodology, as our point of departure we have taken Ciccone's (2002) model – designed for establishing the effect of urbanization economies in European regions. We introduce different types of early-stage entrepreneurship as additional explanations of regional variation in labor productivity. Our results indicate that in particular regional levels of high-growth-oriented early-stage entrepreneurship are indicators of higher levels of regional labor productivity. This finding is in line with, for example, those of Audretsch and Keilbach (2004), Acs et al. (2005) and Wong et al. (2005). However, we also find a weakly significant positive link for low-growth-oriented entrepreneurship. Importantly, when including high-growth-oriented entrepreneurship in our equation, the estimated effect of urbanization economies decreases, suggesting that high-growth-oriented entrepreneurship is a type that can be linked to urbanization economies. The impact of innovation-oriented entrepreneurship, however, complements urbanization economies rather than affords an explanation.

ENTREPRENEURSHIP, URBANIZATION ECONOMIES, AND THE PRODUCTIVITY OF REGIONS: EVIDENCE FROM REGIONAL MODELS

In specifying the link between entrepreneurship, urbanization economies, and regional productivity levels, we can conveniently take the model proposed by Ciccone (2002), also applied to European regions, as a point of departure. Ciccone examines a production function relating the output of an acre of land to the amount of human capital (the number of workers employed on the acre multiplied by the average level of the human capital of the workers on the acre), the amount of physical capital used on the acre, and an index of total factor productivity in the region. A regional perspective is added by conditioning the production function on a basic regional feature: the total production of the region divided by the total acreage of the region. In this model, spatial externalities are driven by the density of production in the region; the elasticity of output per acre is assumed to be constant. The approach concentrates exclusively on explaining regional variation in production; dynamic effects are not considered.[2]

What is the role of entrepreneurship in such a model? Audretsch and Keilbach (2004) argue that entrepreneurship is an additional relevant factor in models of economic growth. Knowledge is not enough in itself for economic growth; new ideas have to be turned into economic outputs in order to affect the economic performance of regions and countries. Entrepreneurship involves the capacity for economic agents to generate new firms or new activities in existing firms, an essential condition for turning new ideas into economic outputs. Empirical studies have confirmed to some extent the importance of entrepreneurship in economic growth (Carree and Thurik, 2003; Audretsch et al., 2006). Analyses of German data show that entrepreneurship is an even more important factor for (regional) economic growth than the regional knowledge base (Audretsch and Keilbach, 2004).

From an evolutionary economics perspective, the long-term competitiveness of a region depends on its ability to upgrade its economic base (i) by creating new economic variety (that is, new combinations of resources introduced into a market) and (ii) by selection (that is, the destruction of the weaker economic entities in the existing supply) (Boschma, 2004).[3] New economic variety emanates from investments in R&D by incumbent firms, but also through the start-up of new firms; economic variety can accordingly be expressed in terms of differences in the regional levels of entrepreneurship (Audretsch and Keilbach, 2004).

The above lines of thought have resulted in formal economic models that take entrepreneurship into account. One of the most ambitious models was proposed by Acs et al. (2003). They formally model the interplay between knowledge workers (researchers) and entrepreneurs and arrive at a macro-level growth equation where entrepreneurship is an explanatory variable additional to labor, capital, and knowledge. In an empirical exercise, the same authors found evidence for the importance of entrepreneurship in explaining national economic growth (see Acs et al., 2005).[4] In this chapter, we adopt some of the views put forward by Acs et al. (2003), that is, that entrepreneurship may constitute a relevant additional explanation for the performance of regions. However, we focus on the role of distinct *types* of entrepreneurship for regional performance in a specific spatial and economic context: urbanization economies.

In this chapter, we concentrate on two major types of entrepreneurship: growth oriented and innovation oriented. Both types are well documented in the literature. Growth-oriented entrepreneurship is particularly important, because it has been found that fast-growing firms (also known as 'gazelles') form a minority of the business stock, but account for a large share of employment growth. Henrekson and Johansson (2010) provide a thorough review of studies investigating the significance of gazelles for national and regional economies. The importance of innovative entrepreneurship can be traced back to Schumpeter's work on creative destruction: he saw entrepreneurs as agents challenging the existing markets, creating disequilibria, and thus moving the production frontier forward (Schumpeter, 1942). Aghion and Howitt (1992) formally introduced the creative-destruction mechanism in economic modeling by explicitly focusing on the degree of innovation with which entrepreneurship is associated in the theory of creative destruction.

For both of the types distinguished, the *early stage* of the entrepreneurial process is of the utmost importance. Gazelles are most often found among start-ups and the increasing importance of new firms is reflected in the increasing share of young firms in listings such as Fortune 500. Autio (2007) charts the job-growth expectation for early-stage entrepreneurs and finds that 12 percent of the individuals involved in early-stage entrepreneurial activity account for 78 percent of the total expected job growth created by early-stage entrepreneurs. The early stage is also the most relevant phase for innovation-oriented entrepreneurial activity; as Schumpeter (1942) argues, most creative destruction can be expected from entrepreneurs entering existing markets or exploring new markets. Here the expected returns for the regional economy are not as direct as with growth orientation. Regions in particular will benefit from new, innovative ventures by virtue of the spillover processes. The nascent or pre-start-up phase is also very important; while a new idea may invoke innovation, that is no guarantee for success. The new business may even fail; however, economically viable ideas will be picked up by others who may be better equipped to exploit them, attract investors, and target the right markets.

Summarizing, we consider the role of entrepreneurship for regional performance in what we feel are crucial elements. We concentrate on the occurrences of specific types of entrepreneurship in the early-stage phase. The types of early-stage entrepreneurship are determined at the individual level, but their regional prevalence rates exhibit significant regional variation. Our first two basic hypotheses at the regional level are accordingly:

H1:   The regional level of high-growth-*oriented early-stage entrepreneurial activity explains the variation in regional productivity.*

H2:   The regional level of innovation-*oriented early-stage entrepreneurial activity explains the variation in regional productivity.*

A relatively new insight into modeling entrepreneurship as a driver of regional economic performance is the idea that some regional features may have an impact on the magnitude of the measured effect. The urban features of a region may be particularly important. Thus, not only may levels of entrepreneurship in cities exceed those at the country level (see Acs et al., 2011 for initial evidence on world cities), but also the consequences for economic growth may be higher in cities (see Becker and Henderson, 2000). In particular, Fritsch and Schroeter (2011) find that, for densely populated areas in Germany, the long-term impact of regional firm-formation rates on employment growth exceeds the impact found for rural areas. Bosma et al. (2011) report a similar conclusion for the Dutch services sector and declared that the effect was more pronounced if related variety is examined rather than population density.[5] They showed that related variety is positively correlated with population density. These findings suggest that part of urbanization economies, captured in Ciccone and Hall (1996) by estimating the impact of employment density on labor productivity, may be accounted for by entrepreneurial activity. In other words, inserting entrepreneurship in the regression would result in a lower estimated impact of employment density on regional productivity. In our framework, the remaining question is whether specific types of entrepreneurship would cause such an effect. High job-expectation entrepreneurship is most directly related to employment density and employment creation. Since Acs et al. (2011) also present evidence for the *entrepreneurial advantage of cities*, especially where high degrees of growth orientation are concerned, we expect the effect for this type of early-stage entrepreneurship in particular.

H3:   High-growth-oriented entrepreneurial activity captures part of the estimated degree of urbanization economies.

MODELING ENTREPRENEURSHIP, URBANIZATION ECONOMIES, AND REGIONAL PRODUCTIVITY

Following Ciccone (2002), we model a regional productivity function where Q denotes value added at the level of Nuts3 regions, N captures employment, and A the acreage of the region in square kilometers. The derived equation to be estimated at the regional level (see Ciccone, 2002, p. 218) is as follows:

$$\log Q_{ci} - \log N_{ci} = \text{Country/Regional Dummies} + \vartheta (\log N_{ci} - \log A_{ci})$$

$$+ \sum_k \delta_k F_{kci} + u_{ci}, \qquad (5.1)$$

where c denotes the country and i the region. F_k represents the share of educational attainment of type k. The dummy variables entering the regression – at the country, Nuts1 or Nuts2 levels – control for potential regional differences in total factor productivity at that particular country or regional level. In Ciccone's computations, the inclusion of regional dummies for different spatial scales did not affect the estimated effect of urbanization economies. Ciccone (p. 217) explains that the estimated coefficient ϑ does not measure the strength of spatial externalities; rather, it measures the effect of the regional density of employment and human capital on regional productivity. While Ciccone uses the term 'agglomeration effects' for this measure, we denote it the 'urbanization effect'.[6] In Ciccone's analysis, urbanization effects are consistently estimated at a rate ranging between 4.0 and 4.5 percent.[7] In this chapter we introduce regional levels of early-stage entrepreneurship as additional explanatory variables. Three of the measures reflect entrepreneurship along a growth-expectation classification (low growth, moderate growth, high growth). The fourth measure captures the innovative ambitions of early-stage entrepreneurship.

Adding entrepreneurship to equation (5.1) in a similar fashion to education, we have:

$$\log Q_{ci} - \log N_{ci} = \text{Country/Regional Dummies} + \vartheta (\log N_{ci} - \log A_{ci})$$

$$+ \sum_k \delta_k F_{kci} + \gamma_p E_{pci} + \mu_{ci}, \qquad (5.2)$$

where p denotes the type of entrepreneurship. In principle, multiple types of entrepreneurship may be modeled simultaneously in equation (5.2). In this chapter, we consider only one type of entrepreneurship in each regression.

EMPIRICAL APPLICATION

Data

For analyzing equation (5.2), we require data on value added, employment, education, the acreage of each region, and several types of entrepreneurship. Data on value added and employment are available at the Nuts3 level and are drawn from the Cambridge Econometrics database on European Regions.[8] Data on education are obtained from Eurostat's regional database, which distinguishes three major categories of education. We included the shares of the number of people who have tertiary education in 2003 (the denominator is the population aged between 25 and 64).[9] These indicators are only available for the Nuts2 regions; we have therefore assumed that the shares at the Nuts2 level are similar to those at the Nuts3 level. This assumption is less restrictive in our applications using the Nuts1/3 classification, since the regions defined by Nuts3 only form a minor share of the total number of regions (see Appendix 5A for the regions included in our analysis). The square kilometers for the acreage of the Nuts3 regions are also drawn from Eurostat.

Our entrepreneurship indicators are derived from the Global Entrepreneurship Monitor (see Reynolds et al., 2005; Bosma and Levie, 2010). The indicators are based on telephone surveys among the adult population. A key GEM indicator is the early-stage entrepreneurial activity (ESEA) rate.[10] This measure is defined as the prevalence rate (in the 18–64 population) of individuals who are involved in either nascent entrepreneurship or as an owner–manager in a new firm in existence for up to 42 months. 'Nascent entrepreneurs' are identified as individuals who are, at the moment of the GEM survey, setting up a business. Moreover they have indicated (i) that they have 'done something to help start a new business, such as looking for equipment or a location, organizing a start-up team, working on a business plan, beginning to save money, or any other activity that would help launch a business'; and (ii) that they will be the single owner or a co-owner of the firm in gestation. Also, they have not paid any salaries, wages or payments in kind (including to themselves) for more than three months; if they have, they are considered to be an owner-manager of a (new) firm.

While the ESEA rate is an overall measure of early-stage entrepreneurial activity, identifying different types of ESEA is also possible. We draw distinctions between growth orientation (three categories) and innovation orientation.[11] The four types of early-stage entrepreneurial activity are as follows:

1. Early-stage entrepreneurial activity with low-growth ambitions (ESEAGR_LO): individuals in early-stage entrepreneurial activity who expect to have no employees or just one in the next five years.
2. Early-stage entrepreneurial activity with modest-growth ambitions (ESEAGR_MD): individuals in early-stage entrepreneurial activity who expect to have between two and nine employees in the next five years.
3. Early-stage entrepreneurial activity with high-growth ambitions (ESEAGR_HI): individuals in early-stage entrepreneurial activity who expect to have 10 or more employees in the next five years.
4. Early-stage entrepreneurial activity with innovative ambitions ESEAINNOV: individuals in early-stage entrepreneurial activity who expect (i) at least some customers to consider the product or service new and unfamiliar *and* (ii) not many businesses offering the same products or services.

We first take a look at the spatial variation in entrepreneurship rates relating to the first, third, and fourth types of entrepreneurial activity listed above. This regional pattern of the different types of entrepreneurship, as depicted in Figures 5.1–3, shows large differences, pointing to the relevance of distinguishing regions instead of merely countries.

The average non-growth regional entrepreneurship rate (ESEAGR_LO) shown in Figure 5.1 is 2.8 percent and ranges from 1.2 percent in the western part of France to 6.0 percent in Western Transdanubia (Hungary). The rate of high-growth-oriented ESEA in Figure 5.2 ranges from 0.6 percent in the French Parisien Bassin to 2.6 percent in the Hamburg area. We should note that, since the indicators are *estimates* rather than count data, there are confidence intervals attached to these estimates. Therefore, when examining the maps one should especially focus on general patterns and not so much on the outcome for one particular region.

Although we can still figure out national borders in these European maps, regional variations within countries are also large. Focusing on the main differences between lower ambitious types of entrepreneurship (Figure 5.1) and higher-growth ambitious types of entrepreneurship (Figure 5.2), we see some notable differences. In general, the growth-oriented entrepreneurship rates appear to be somewhat higher in or around strongly populated regions. Compared to other European regions, in many Spanish areas there are quite a number of early-stage entrepreneurs with low-growth expectations, but the rate of ambitious ones with respect to hiring employees is relatively low. The same goes for northern Portugal, Greece, and parts of France. Sweden is an example of a country showing low overall entrepreneurship rates, but performing

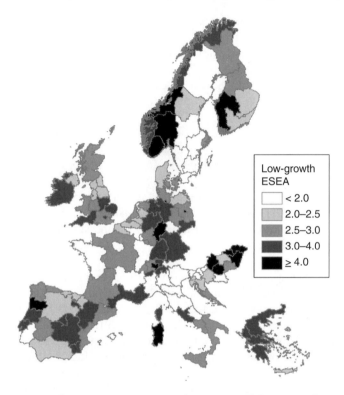

Figure 5.1   Early-stage entrepreneurial activity with low-growth orientation (0–1 employees in the next five years), percentage of population between 18 and 64 years, 2001–2006

better on growth-oriented entrepreneurship. This is even stronger for the northern part of Italy, where there is relatively little participation in ESEA with low-growth orientation, but the scores on growth ambitious entrepreneurship are clearly higher. In this respect the western part of Slovenia connects to northern Italy. Within France only the Paris and Mediterranean areas have relatively many growth-ambitious early-stage entrepreneurs, while this rate is low in all other regions. Regions performing relatively badly in all types of entrepreneurship are situated in the east of France, and to a lesser extent, some Swedish regions and the whole of Belgium.

The innovation-oriented early-stage entrepreneurship rates (Figure 5.3) show an even larger regional variation. In the UK, the London area and the eastern region (including Cambridge) outperform other regions with respect to innovation-oriented early-stage entrepreneurship rates. The

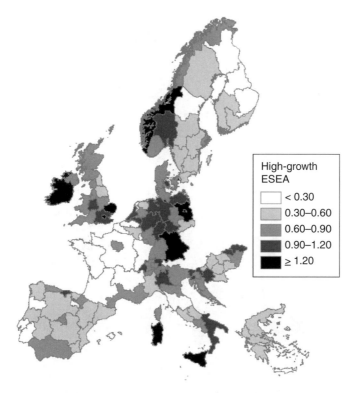

*Figure 5.2   Early-stage entrepreneurial activity with high-growth
orientation (10+ employees in the next five years), percentage
of population between 18 and 64 years, 2001–2006*

Mediterranean area (including Nice/Sophia-Antipolis) seems to be rather
innovative, as compared to the rest of France; Emilia-Romagna and
Sardinia show far higher innovative entrepreneurship rates than Sicily.
Sweden and Finland show high levels of innovation-oriented entrepreneurial activity; while especially in the latter country regional variation is
also large.

Each individual involved in innovation-oriented early-stage entrepreneurship is also classified in one of the three growth-orientation categories. As could be expected, innovation-oriented early-stage entrepreneurs
were relatively often in the category of high-growth orientation: of all the
high-growth-oriented individuals involved in ESEA, 25 percent were also
characterized as innovative, whereas the percentages for the medium and
low levels of growth orientation were 19 and 16, respectively.

Table 5.1 shows the means, standard deviations and correlations of all

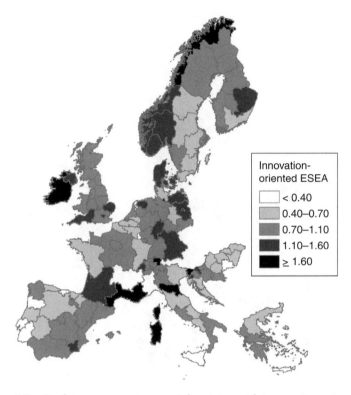

*Figure 5.3   Early-stage entrepreneurial activity with innovative orientation
(regardless of sector), percentage of population between 18
and 64 years, 2001–2006*

the variables concerned in the estimation of equation (5.2). The average
value of our dependent variable, regional labor productivity, equals 3.84.
Further inspection reveals that there are substantial differences between
countries (more so than within countries). The standard deviation *between*
countries equals 0.45, whereas the standard deviation *within* countries
equals 0.13. This result confirms that country borders need to be appreci-
ated in our empirical models explaining labor productivity. Nevertheless,
regional differences are important as the top-performing regions are situated in different countries: highest labor productivity rates are found in
Oslo and surroundings, the western parts of Switzerland, Île de France
(Paris), and the Stockholm and Copenhagen areas. Many urbanized areas
feature in the top 15 regions in terms of labor productivity. The bottom
15 consist of regions in Hungary, Portugal, Slovenia, and Extremadura
(Spain).

Table 5.1 Descriptive statistics

	Mean	Std dev.	Correlation table						
			1.	2.	3.	4.	5.	6.	7.
1. Labor productivity 2006 (ln)	3.84	0.41							
2. Employment density 2001– 2006 (ln)	−2.67	1.50	0.22*						
3. Acreage of the region (*1000)	27.18	31.52	0.08	−0.69*					
4. Entrepreneurship: low-growth expectation	2.81	0.87	−0.15	0.05	−0.07				
5. Entrepreneurship: mid-growth expectation	1.88	0.79	0.02	0.00	−0.07	0.28*			
6. Entrepreneurship: high-growth expectation	0.75	0.42	0.30*	0.43*	−0.34*	0.39*	0.26*		
7. Entrepreneurship: innovation	0.94	0.46	0.42*	0.16	0.02	0.30*	0.37*	0.61*	
8. Share tertiary education, 2003 (ln)	−1.64	0.36	0.59*	0.21*	−0.10	−0.03	0.29*	0.23*	0.39*

Notes: Regional level, $N = 127$; * $p < 0.05$.

Table 5.1 shows that high regional education levels, high-growth-oriented entrepreneurship and innovation-oriented entrepreneurship are positively correlated with regional levels of labor productivity. Also, high-growth-oriented entrepreneurship correlates with employment density, which gives some initial support for hypothesis 3. The correlation between high-growth-oriented entrepreneurship and innovation-oriented entrepreneurship equals 0.61, which could potentially lead to multicollinearity problems if they are both included in a model. We have therefore decided not to include two entrepreneurship measures in the same regression. Employment density is strongly correlated with its instrumental variable, the acreage of the region. The instrument is not correlated with labor productivity and therefore this assumption for proper instruments is not violated. We also calculated the correlations with overall regional ESEA rates. Interestingly, these rates do not correlate significantly with any of the four different types of ESEA. This finding confirms the relevance of identifying different types; the regional patterns turn out to differ from each other.

Results

In our empirical application we replicate Ciccone's analysis as a starting point (Ciccone, 2002, pp. 215–19) with two empirical adjustments. First, we estimated equation (5.2) for the year 2006, as this is the most recent year with reliable data on productivity rates, and our entrepreneurship measures span 2001–06. Ciccone's analysis was based on the year 1989. Second, where Ciccone's model controls for educational systems varying over countries, we used one single classification for educational attainment that is harmonized over EU countries and has only recently been made available by Eurostat. This procedure allows us to interpret the results concerning educational attainment better and seriously limits the loss of degrees of freedom when augmenting the number of countries from five to 16 in our analysis. We estimate equation (5.2) in several applications. First, we developed a model acknowledging the role of entrepreneurial activity and compatible with data availability. Second, we entered different types of regional levels of entrepreneurial activity.

Our results are shown in Table 5.2. The first model replicates Ciccone (2002) with country dummies and employment density instrumented with the acreage of the region. For 1989, Ciccone reported a coefficient for employment density equal to 0.046 with a robust standard error of 0.005. Whether he included Nuts0 (country), Nuts1 or Nuts2 regions as fixed effects did not make any difference in the estimated size of this coefficient. Our computation for effects on labor productivity in 2006 in model 1 produces very similar results: we arrived at a coefficient equal to 0.053. Augmenting the number of countries and adopting the regional level for which we have entrepreneurship leads to a decrease in the number of observations. We had 142 regions at our disposal, but we excluded 15 regions for which the sample size of adults from which entrepreneurship rates are derived is lower than 700. For the remaining 127 regions over 17 countries, the estimated effect in model 2 decreases somewhat to 4.3 percent (model 2a) and is significant at the 5 percent level. In this different spatial setting, the coefficient measuring the effect of education is now positive and significant. The standard errors are somewhat larger owing to the lower number of observations. This model has the features that allow us to include different types of early-stage entrepreneurial activity.

Table 5.2 *Estimation results: replication of Ciccone's (2002) analysis for 2006 and different spatial settings and estimation techniques (dependent variable: regional levels of labor productivity, 2006, in logarithm)*

	Model 1a	Model 1b	Model 2a	Model 2b
Employment density	0.053***	0.053***	0.043**	0.035*
(ln), Average 2001–2006	(0.008)	(0.008)	(0.020)	(0.019)
Share tertiary education	−0.02	−0.02	0.27***	0.32***
(ln), 2003	(0.03)	(0.03)	(0.09)	(0.09)
Constant	3.92***	3.92***	4.44***	4.53***
	(0.06)	(0.05)	(0.10)	(0.14)
No. of countries	5	5	17	17
No. of regions	766	766	127	127
Regional classification	Nuts3	Nuts3	Nuts1/3	Nuts1/3
Treatment country effects				
Country dummies	yes			
Fixed effects model		yes	yes	
Random effects model				yes
Hausman test χ^2 – null		71.44	3.50	
supporting use random effects model		($p < 0.01$)	($p = 0.17$)	
R-squared overall	0.356	0.189	0.313	0.339
Within countries		0.164	0.418	0.400
Between countries		0.473	0.422	0.463

Notes: * $p < 0.10$, ** $p < 0.05$, *** $p < 0.01$. Regions with a sample size lower than 700 have been excluded (15 regions). Acreage of the region enters the regressions as instrumental variable for employment density.

A Hausman test indicates that random effects estimation may also be used; here the estimated effect of urbanization economies becomes even lower. It can be seen that estimating with random effects improves the model fit between countries, but reduces the model fit within countries. As we are primarily interested in capturing regional effects we shall first proceed based on the fixed-effects estimation; however, we shall revisit random-effects modeling at the end of this section – but in a multilevel setting. Tests for spatial autocorrelation revealed that there were no problems to be expected due to spatial lags and spatial errors. Using a binary weight matrix with information on neighboring regions, the Getis–Ord statistic did not point at spatial lags for the dependent and independent variables, as well as the residuals from model 2b. In comparison to the

Table 5.3   Estimation results including measures of types of entrepreneurship (dependent variable: regional levels of labor productivity, 2006, in logarithm)

	Model 2a (repeated)	Model 3a	Model 3b	Model 3c	Model 3d
Employment density (ln),	0.043**	0.044**	0.044**	0.031	0.045**
Average 2001–2006	(0.020)	(0.019)	(0.019)	(0.018)	(0.019)
Share tertiary education	0.27***	0.26***	0.24***	0.25***	0.26***
(ln), 2003	(0.09)	(0.08)	(0.08)	(0.09)	(0.08)
Entrepreneurship, 2001–2006					
Low-growth ESEA		0.034*			
		(0.017)			
Medium-growth ESEA			0.049**		
			(0.023)		
High-growth ESEA				0.118**	
				(0.047)	
Innovation ESEA					0.084**
					(0.038)
Constant	4.44***	4.33***	4.30***	4.29***	4.15***
	(0.10)	(0.12)	(0.13)	(0.12)	(0.19)
No. of countries	17	17	17	17	17
No. of regions	127	127	127	127	127
Regional classification	Nuts1/3	Nuts1/3	Nuts1/3	Nuts1/3	Nuts1/3
R-squared overall	0.313	0.257	0.245	0.327	0.353
Within countries	0.418	0.439	0.443	0.437	0.450
Between countries	0.422	0.346	0.380	0.426	0.449

Notes: * $p < 0.10$, ** $p < 0.05$, *** $p < 0.01$. Fixed effects (country level) used in all models. Standard errors reported in parentheses. Regions with a sample size lower than 700 have been excluded (15 regions). Employment density instrumented with acreage of the region.

more often used Moran's I-statistic, the Getis–Ord statistic focuses on clustering of high and low values, but does not capture the presence of negative spatial correlation (see Getis and Ord, 1992). Considering the nature of our weight matrix and the low probability of negative spillovers, we opted for the Getis–Ord statistic.

We now turn towards the analysis, based on model 2b in Table 5.2 but including entrepreneurship measures. The first model in Table 5.3 repeats the results of model 2b for the sake of comparison. From the results in models 3a–d, entrepreneurial activity appears to be positive and significant at $p < 0.10$ for all four distinguished types of entrepreneurship, while we particularly expected the impact to be positive for high-growth and for innovation-oriented entrepreneurial activity. Our expectations are, however, confirmed in the sense that the regional variations in labor productivity are best explained by high-growth and innovation-oriented entrepreneurship. A possible explanation of the positive and weakly significant effect of low-growth-oriented entrepreneurial activity may be that we pick up some of the effects not captured by employment and education. Self-employment is not very often captured in employment statistics used to estimate growth models. In other words, the effect found for low-ambition self-employment may be very similar to the traditional effect of employment.

Interestingly, we find a distinctive result for high-growth-oriented entrepreneurship: this type exhibits the strongest interplay with employment density – controlling for national effects. Here we find support for the third hypothesis, since the estimated 'urbanization economies' effect drops from 4.4 percent (and statistically significant at $p < 0.05$) to 3.1 percent (and statistically insignificant at $p < 0.10$). Thus, employment density alone may not give a sufficient picture of economic advantages to urbanization; regions also require entrepreneurs who can create employment *opportunities*. Adding entrepreneurship to model 2d leads to a significant improvement for most of the models: the likelihood ratio test supports the relevance of the inclusion of early-stage entrepreneurial activity at $p < 0.05$ for models 3a–d.

Earlier on, from Table 5.2, we observed that treating countries as random effects (modeling a stochastic distribution for country-specific effects) was not inferior to treating countries as 'fixed' effects (modeling a constant for every single country). This result allows us to further explore model 3c in a genuine multilevel setting, with regions being hierarchically nested within countries and inclusion of a random intercept capturing the country-level random effects. The advantage of such an approach is (i) to acknowledge a hierarchical structure in our data, as regions' economic activities together 'shape' the countries' economic activities; and (ii) to examine whether there are also *random slope* effects with growth-oriented entrepreneurship and/or education.[12] Random slope effects capture differences in the estimated impact at the 'higher' level of the analysis, in our case differences in estimated impacts at the country level. In other words, we can test whether the estimated *impact* of employment density, education, and high job-expectation entrepreneurship on labor productivity is very similar across countries or whether the impact differs substantially across countries.

Table 5.4 shows a hierarchical structure of the results of these auxiliary regressions for high-growth-oriented entrepreneurship (models 4a–e), as

Table 5.4   *Estimation results: auxiliary random slope regressions (dependent variable: regional levels of labor productivity, 2006, in logarithm)*

	Model 4a	Model 4b	Model 4c	Model 4d	Model 4e	Model 4f
Employment density	0.029 (0.018)	0.018 (0.020)	0.044 (0.030)	0.017 (0.018)	0.025 (0.020)	0.029* (0.017)
Random slope: standard deviation			0.070** (0.029)			
Share tertiary education	0.37*** (0.08)	0.33*** (0.08)	0.21*** (0.08)	0.43*** (0.12)	0.29*** (0.07)	0.36*** (0.07)
Random slope: standard deviation				0.38*** (0.09)		
High-growth-expectation entrepreneurship		0.131*** (0.047)	0.128*** (0.046)	0.114*** (0.040)	0.132*** (0.051)	
Random slope: standard deviation					0.097 (0.053)	
Innovation-oriented entrepreneurship						0.135*** (0.047)
Random slope: standard deviation						0.116 (0.069)
Constant	4.58*** (0.14)	4.39*** (0.15)	4.33*** (0.13)	4.57*** (0.19)	4.35*** (0.15)	4.46*** (0.15)
No. of countries	17	17	17	17	17	17
No. of regions	127	127	127	127	127	127
Regional classification	Nuts1/3	Nuts1/3	Nuts1/3	Nuts1/3	Nuts1/3	Nuts1/3
Wald χ^2	49.99***	66.22***	40.82***	38.09***	60.44***	67.82***
Log likelihood	37.47	45.62	49.67	63.34	47.43	46.14
Likelihood ratio test for significance random slope			7.69**	35.43***	3.62	2.95

Notes: $* p < 0.10$, $** p < 0.05$, $*** p < 0.01$. Random intercepts for country level in all models. Standard errors reported in parentheses. Regions with a sample size lower than 700 have been excluded (15 regions). Employment density instrumented with acreage of the region.

well as for innovation-oriented entrepreneurship (model 4f). We should note that some care needs to be taken with these results, as we deal with a limited number of observations – especially *within* some of the countries included. From Table 5.4 it appears that acknowledging random slopes with employment density (model 4c) and education (model 4d) improves the model fit, whereas no improvement is reported for high job-expectation entrepreneurship and innovation-oriented entrepreneurship (models 4e and 4f). This suggests that the coefficients measuring the impact of high job-expectation entrepreneurship and innovation-oriented entrepreneurship on regional performance are quite homogeneous over countries, with an overall impact that is positive and significant. On the contrary, while the overall effect of education is positive and significant, we also find significant variation in this effect across countries.

Based on the estimates of the random slopes models in Table 5.4 we can explore which countries exhibit high and low impacts for each of the random slopes considered. The so-called 'best linear unbiased predictions' (BLUPs) of the country-level random slopes with education point at highest and positive impacts for Hungary, Norway (both above the estimated standard deviation), and Slovenia (slightly below the estimated standard deviation), perhaps suggesting that recent accession countries have, given regional variations, more return to education. They are estimated to be lowest for Germany and Greece (both above the estimated standard deviation).[13] From model 4c we see that acknowledging country-specific effects for employment density somewhat increases the estimated effects of urbanization economies. The BLUPs of the country-level random slopes with employment density showed that the country-specific random effect with unemployment density was particularly high for Hungary, Slovenia, and Portugal (all above the estimated standard deviation). None of the countries had a prediction that was very negative.

Without making too many inferences from these results, Table 5.4 in general suggests that – although there may be a general pattern across European regions – country differences should not be ruled out and can in fact conceal an underlying general pattern.

CONCLUDING REMARKS

In this chapter, we considered the role of entrepreneurship for regional performance in a specific spatial and economic context. We concentrated on the occurrences of specific types of entrepreneurship in the early-stage phase, when the venture is in the exploration phase (nascent entrepreneurship) or in the early years after start-up. The types of early-stage entrepreneurship are determined at the individual level, and their regional prevalence rates exhibit significant variation. We expected to find a positive link between high-growth- and innovation-oriented entrepreneurship and regional levels of labor productivity, controlling for regional differences in labor, capital, education, and national levels of total factor productivity.

In our empirical investigation we found confirmation for the importance of both high-growth- and innovation-oriented entrepreneurship in explaining regional variation in labor productivity. Moreover, we found in our analysis of European regions that the impact of growth-oriented entrepreneurship overrides an important part of the urbanization economies found by Ciccone (2002), who also examined European regions. Thus, urbanization economies can partly be explained by the effect of differentials in regional levels of growth-oriented entrepreneurship. In other words, individuals from the labor force who expect to *provide jobs* may be more important to regional welfare than the phenomenon of urbanization effects captured by employment density. We did not find this particular overriding effect for the other three identified types of entrepreneurship.

An interesting finding was also that regions with high levels of *low-growth-oriented* entrepreneurship (that is, early-stage entrepreneurs expecting to generate at most one job apart from their own over the next five years) were also associated with higher levels of labor productivity. Regions with a large number of such early-stage entrepreneurs, overall constituting over 50 percent of all early-stage entrepreneurs, may be more productive because there are more people who are responsible for their own income and therefore willing to work hard. In addition, these findings may reflect productivity gains stemming from the trend of increasing 'independent professionals' in service sectors. Many of these entrepreneurs are focused on increasing their earnings, basically under the condition that they will not grow in terms of employment. As a result, many of these independent professionals subcontract and, as a regional aggregate, their impact may be sizable in terms of regional productivity measures. Another explanation may be that the effect of low-growth entrepreneurship adds to the effect of labor, since in most statistics the number of employed excludes the self-employed. In this perspective, the positive effect found with low-growth-oriented entrepreneurship may be interpreted similarly to the contribution of the traditional factor of labor.

Some modifications and extensions may prove to be useful for future research. First, the literature suggests that a beneficial impact of entrepreneurship would particularly be found in interaction with R&D investments and output; R&D investments paired with the presence of innovative entrepreneurs who know how to commercialize new ideas (captured, for instance, by patent activity) should lead to higher regional economic performance. Second, dynamics in space and time can be made more explicit. It is conceivable that exceptional productivity in one region spills over to neighboring regions. In our analysis we did not find support for such spillover effects as our dependent variable and the residuals did not point at the presence of spatial lags from the Getis–Ord statistics. However, this may be due to the fact that we included rather large regions in our analysis.

As regards the time dimension, it may take a while for innovative entrepreneurship to impact on regional productivity. In this chapter, we were primarily interested in explaining differences in regional productivity. Regional variation in economic performance is often very persistent (Martin and Sunley, 2006), as are entry rates (Fritsch and Mueller, 2007; Brenner and Fornahl, 2008). Independent and dependent variables thus seem to reveal path-dependent processes, and our results indicate that entrepreneurship may be an important vehicle driving these processes at the regional level. Nevertheless, there are also signs that some economic convergence is taking place in the EU; using a sophisticated spatial panel data analysis, Bosker (2007) finds a negative coefficient for *change* in economic growth in highly urbanized areas, whereas for the regions surrounding highly urbanized areas he finds a positive coefficient. It is clear that further systematic collection of entrepreneurship data – preferably identifying types and phases – remains crucial for deriving the impact of (types of) entrepreneurship on growth and vice versa.

To conclude, our multilevel approach capturing information at the individual, firm and macro levels opens other avenues for further research. To some extent, we accounted for the interaction between human capital and growth-oriented entrepreneurship when we investigated the impact on urbanization economies, but this could be modeled more explicitly. For instance, the data also allow us to look at the impact of highly educated entrepreneurs on regional performance *vis-à-vis* the impact by lower-educated entrepreneurs. Similarly, one might contribute to the creativity debate by identifying entrepreneurial activity in sectors associated with the creative class, as proposed by Florida (2002). Preliminary results for world cities indeed suggest relatively high prevalence rates of this particular type of entrepreneur (Acs et al., 2011).

NOTES

1. Regional variations in human capital and creative class overlap, but are not the same. Boschma and Fritsch (2009) find that the measure of creative class dominates the human capital measure in explaining growth over European regions.

2. Estimating dynamic effects calls for spatial econometric applications; see, for example, Bosker (2007) who investigated space–time structures for growth in European regions using spatial panel data estimation techniques.
3. These two parts of the creative destruction process generally tend to go together. In a review, Caves (1998) concludes that entry and exit are highly correlated.
4. Interestingly, even though the empirical analysis takes place at the national level, the authors acknowledge the importance of spatial unevenness to some extent by instrumenting entrepreneurship on the degree of urbanization. However, this is applied in only one of their equations.
5. Frenken et al. (2007) define 'related variety' as a combination of sector diversity and the degree to which the sectors are related. Entropy statistics have been used to calculate this measure. Related variety is measured for each region as the weighted sum of industrial variety (over five-digit classes) within each of two-digit classes.
6. Agglomeration economies consist of urbanization and localization economies. Localization economies, that is, the strength of particular industries in agglomerations, are not considered here.
7. Here employment density has not been considered as an exogenous variable; it has been instrumented by the size of the region in square kilometers, in accordance with Ciccone (2002).
8. See www.camecon.com.
9. In terms of the ISCED classification (UNESCO, 1997), the third category includes levels 5 and 6. In other specifications we additionally included an indicator expressing the share with higher and post-secondary education. These did not improve the overall fit of the model.
10. This is the same measure as that known as 'TEA' in most GEM reports. We have chosen to use the abbreviation ESEA because it better reflects the early-stage nature of the measure.
11. All entrepreneurs have been asked to indicate if all, many or none of their (potential) customers would consider their product or service new and unfamiliar. Also, they have indicated if many, few or no other businesses are offering the same products or services to their (potential) customers.
12. See, for example, Hox (2002) for an extensive overview of the advantages of using multilevel analysis in these types of settings.
13. This analysis was based on an 'unstructured' variance–covariance between the random intercept (country levels) and the random slope (education).

REFERENCES

Acs, Z.J., D.B. Audretsch, P. Braunerhjelm and B. Carlsson (2003), 'The missing link: the knowledge filter and endogenous growth', Center for Business and Policy Studies, Stockholm.
Acs, Z.J., D.B. Audretsch, P. Braunerhjelm and B. Carlsson (2005), 'The knowledge spillover theory of entrepreneurship', CEPR Discussion Paper No. 5326, Centre for Economic Policy Research, London.
Acs, Z.J., N.S. Bosma and R. Sternberg (2011), 'Entrepreneurship in world cities', in M. Minniti (ed.), *The Dynamics of Entrepreneurial Activity*, Oxford: Oxford University Press, pp. 125–51.
Aghion, P. and P. Howitt (1992), 'A model of growth through creative destruction', *Econometrica*, **60** (2), 323–51.
Audretsch, D.B. and M.P. Feldman (1996), 'R&D spillovers and the geography of innovation and production', *American Economic Review*, **86** (3), 630–40.
Audretsch, D.B. and M. Fritsch (2002), 'Growth regimes over time and space', *Regional Studies*, **36** (2), 113–24.

Audretsch, D.B. and M.P. Keilbach (2004), 'Entrepreneurship capital and economic performance', *Regional Studies*, **38** (8), 949–59.

Audretsch, D.B. and M.P. Keilbach (2005), 'Entrepreneurship capital and regional growth', *Annals of Regional Science*, **39** (3), 457–69.

Audretsch, D.B., M.P. Keilbach and E.E. Lehmann (2006), *Entrepreneurship and Economic Growth*, Oxford: Oxford University Press.

Autio, E. (2007), *Global Entrepreneurship Monitor: 2007 Global Report on High-Growth Entrepreneurship*, Babson College, London Business School and Global Entrepreneurship Research Association (GERA).

Baumol, W.J. (1968), 'Entrepreneurship in economic theory', *American Economic Review*, **58** (2), 64–71.

Becker, R. and J.V. Henderson (2000), 'Intraindustry specialization and urban development', in Jean-Marie Huriot and Jacques-Francois Thisse (eds), *Economics of Cities: Theoretical Perspectives*, Cambridge: Cambridge University Press, pp. 138–66.

Bergmann, H. and R. Sternberg (2007), 'The changing face of entrepreneurship in Germany', *Small Business Economics*, **28** (2), 205–21.

Birch, D.L. (1979), 'The job generation process', mimeo, MIT Program on Neighborhood and Regional Change, Cambridge, MA.

Boschma, R. (2004), 'Competitiveness of regions from an evolutionary perspective', *Regional Studies*, **38** (9), 1001–14.

Boschma, R.A. and M. Fritsch (2009), 'Creative class and regional growth – empirical evidence from seven European countries', *Economic Geography*, **85** (4), 391–423.

Bosker, M. (2007), 'Growth, agglomeration and convergence: a space–time analysis for European regions', *Spatial Economic Analysis*, **2** (1), 91–108.

Bosma, N.S. and J. Levie (2010), *Global Entrepreneurship Monitor 2009 Executive Report*, Babson Park, MA: Babson College; Santiago, Chile: Universidad del Desarollo and Reykjavík, Iceland: Háskólinn Reykjavík University.

Bosma, N.S. and V.A.J.M. Schutjens (2009), 'Mapping entrepreneurial activity and entrepreneurial attitudes in European regions', *International Journal of Entrepreneurship and Small Business*, **7** (2), 191–213.

Bosma, N.S., E. Stam and V.A.J.M. Schutjens (2011), 'Creative destruction, regional productivity growth; evidence from the Dutch manufacturing and services industries', *Small Business Economics*, **36**.

Brenner, T. and D. Fornahl (2008), 'Regional path-dependence in start-up activity', Papers in Evolutionary Economic Geography, 08.12, Utrecht University, Utrecht.

Carree, M.A. and A.R. Thurik (2003), 'The impact of entrepreneurship on economic growth', in Zoltan J. Acs and David B. Audretsch (eds), *Handbook of Entrepreneurship Research*, New York: Springer, pp. 437–72.

Caves, R. (1998), 'Industrial organization and new findings on the turnover and mobility of firms', *Journal of Economic Literature*, **36** (4), 1947–82.

Ciccone, A. (2002), 'Agglomeration effects in Europe', *European Economic Review*, **46** (2), 213–27.

Ciccone, A. and R.E. Hall (1996), 'Productivity and the density of economic activity', *American Economic Review*, **86** (1), 54–70.

Davidsson, P. (2006), 'Nascent entrepreneurship: empirical studies and developments', *Foundations and Trends in Entrepreneurship*, **2** (1), 1–76.

Davidsson, P. and S.R. Gordon (2009), 'Nascent entrepreneur(ship) research: a review', http://eprints.qut.edu.au/19622/, Brisbane: Queensland University of Technology.

Duranton, G. and D. Puga (2004), 'Micro-foundations of urban agglomeration economies', in J. Vernon Henderson and Jacques-Francois Thisse (eds), *Handbook of Urban and Regional Economics*, Vol. 4, New York: North-Holland, pp. 2063–118.

Florida, Richard (2002), *The Rise of the Creative Class. And How It's Transforming Work, Leisure, Community, and Everyday Life*, New York: Basic Books.

Frenken, K., F. van Oort and T. Verburg (2007), 'Related variety, unrelated variety and regional economic growth', *Regional Studies*, **41** (5), 685–97.

Fritsch, M. and P. Mueller (2007), 'The persistence of regional new business formation-activity over time – assessing the potential of policy promotion programs', *Journal of Evolutionary Economics*, **17** (3), 299–315.

Fritsch, M. and A. Schroeter (2011), 'Why does the effect of new business formation differ across regions?', *Small Business Economics*, **36**.

Getis, A. and J.K. Ord (1992), 'The analysis of spatial association by use of distance statistics', *Geographical Analysis*, **24** (3), 189–206.

Glaeser, E.L. (2007), 'Entrepreneurship and the City', NBER Working Papers w13551, October.

Glaeser, E.L., H.D. Kallal, J.A. Scheinkman and A. Shleifer (1992), 'Growth in cities', *Journal of Political Economy*, **100** (6), 1126–52.

Henrekson, M. and D. Johansson (2010), 'Gazelles as job creators', *Small Business Economics*, **35**, 227–44.

Hox, Joop J. (2002), *Multilevel Analysis: Techniques and Applications*, Mahwah, NJ: Erlbaum.

Jacobs, J. (1969), *The Economy of Cities*, New York: Random House.

Leibenstein, H. (1968), 'Entrepreneurship and development', *American Economic Review*, **58** (2), 72–83.

Lucas, R.E. (1988), 'On the mechanics of economic development', *Journal of Monetary Economics*, **22** (1), 3–42.

Martin, R. and P. Sunley (2006), 'Path dependence and regional economic evolution', *Journal of Economic Geography*, **6** (4), 395–437.

Michelacci, C. and O. Silva (2007), 'Why so many local entrepreneurs?', *Review of Economics and Statistics*, **89** (4), 615–33.

Reynolds, P.D., N.S. Bosma, E. Autio, S. Hunt, N. De Bono, I. Servais, P. Lopez-Garcia and N. Chin (2005), 'Global Entrepreneurship Monitor: data collection design and implementation, 1998–2003', *Small Business Economics*, **24** (3), 205–31.

Reynolds, P., D.J. Storey and P. Westhead (1994), 'Cross-national comparisons of the variation in new firm formation rates', *Regional Studies*, **28** (4), 443–56.

Romer, P.M. (1986), 'Increasing returns and long-run growth', *Journal of Political Economy*, **94** (5), 1002–37.

Romer, P.M. (1990), 'Endogenous technological change', *Journal of Political Economy*, **98** (5), 71–102.

Rosenthal, S.S. and W.C. Strange (2003), 'Geography, industrial organization, and agglomeration', *Review of Economics and Statistics*, **85** (2), 377–93.

Rosenthal, Stuart S. and William C. Strange (2004), 'Evidence on the nature and sources of agglomeration economies', in J. Vernon Henderson and Jacques-Francois Thisse (eds), *Handbook of Urban and Regional Economics*, Vol. 4, New York: North-Holland, pp. 2119–72.

Schumpeter, J.A. (1942), *Capitalism, Socialism and Democracy*, New York: Harper & Row.

Sternberg, R. and S. Wennekers (2005), 'Determinants and effects of new business creation using Global Entrepreneurship Monitor data', *Small Business Economics*, **24**, 193–203.

UNESCO (1997), *International Standard Classification of Education* (ISCED 1997), Paris: UNESCO.

Wong, P.K., Y.P. Ho and E. Autio (2005), 'Entrepreneurship, innovation, and economic growth: evidence from GEM data', *Small Business Economics*, **24** (3), 335–50.

APPENDIX 5A   REGIONS INCLUDED IN THE EMPIRICAL ANALYSIS

Belgium (Nuts1)
Brussels
Vlaams Gewest
Region Wallone
   + Antwerp (Nuts2)
   + Ghent (Nuts2)

Denmark (Nuts2)
Copenhagen area
Sealand and Bornholm
Funen
Jutland
   + Aarhus area (Nuts3)

Finland (Nuts2)
Ita-Suomi
Etela-Suomi
   + Helsinki Area (Nuts3)
Lansi-Suomi
Pohjois-Suomi

France (Nuts1)
Ile de France
Parisien Bassin
East
West
South-West
Center-East
Meditéranée

Germany (Nuts1)
Baden-Württemberg
   + Stuttgart (ROR)
Bayern
   + München (ROR)
Berlin
Brandenburg
Hamburg
Hessen
   + Rhein-Main (ROR)
Mecklenburg-Vorpommern
Niedersachsen

Nordrhein-Westfalen
   + Duisburg-Essen
   (ROR) + Düsseldorf
   (ROR) + Köln
   (ROR)
Rheinland - Pfalz
Sachsen
Sachsen-Anhalt
Schleswig-Holstein
Thüringen

Greece (Nuts2–3)
Athens
Macedonia & Thrace
Thessaly & Epiros
Central + Ionian
Islands
Peloponnesus /Aegean/
Crete

Hungary (Nuts2)
Central Transdanubia
Western Transdanubia
Southern
Transdanubia
Northern Hungary
Northern Great Plain
Southern Great Plain
   + Budapest area
   (Nuts3)

Ireland (Nuts2)
Dublin
Border, Midl., Western
Southern and Eastern

Italy (Nuts1–2)
Nord-Ovest
Lombardia
Nord-Est
Centro
Campania

Sud
Sicilia

Netherlands (Nuts1)
Noord-Nederland
Oost-Nederland
West-Nederland
   + Utrecht (Nuts3)
   + Amsterdam (Nuts3)
   + The Hague (Nuts3)
   + Rotterdam (Nuts3)
Zuid-Nederland

Norway (~Nuts2)
North Norway
Middle Norway
West Norway
South Norway
Oslo and surroundings

Portugal (Nuts1)
Norte (incl Porto)
Centro
Lisboa e Vale de Tejo

Slovenia (Nuts2–3)
Kraska
Dolenjska,
Osrednjeslovenska,
Zasavska
Koroska, Savinjska,
Spodnjeposavska
Pomurska and Podravska

Spain (Nuts2)
Galicia
Asturias
Pais Vasco
Navarra
Aragon
Madrid
Castilla y León

APPENDIX 5A   (continued)

Castilla La Mancha	**Sweden (Nuts2)**	**United Kingdom (Nuts1)**
Extremadura	Stockholm area	Scotland
Catalunya	Östra Mellansverige	North East
+ Barcelona (Nuts3)	Sydsverige	North West
Comm Valenciana	Norra Mellansverige	Yorkshire Humberside
Baleares	Mellersta Norrland	East Midlands
Andalucia	Övre Norrland	West Midlands
+ Valencia (Nuts3)	Småland med öarna	East Anglia
+ Sevilla (Nuts3)	Västsverige	Greater London
+ Malaga (Nuts3)		South East
Murcia	**Switzerland (~Nuts1–2)**	South West
Canarias	North-East	Wales
	North-West	Northern Ireland
	South	
	West (French speaking)	

Note: Regions with sample sizes lower than 700 observations were excluded from the analysis.

+   Urban area has been abstracted from larger surrounding areas (these abstracted areas are not visualized in Figures 5.1–3).

ROR: 'Raumordnungsregionen'. This classification for German regions indicates labor market areas; its spatial scale lies between the European Nuts2 and Nuts3 classification.

6 High-impact firms: gazelles revisited
Zoltan J. Acs

INTRODUCTION

One aspect of Birch's work that is especially interesting focuses on the classification of different types (ages and sizes) of establishments. This focus yielded the findings on job creation for which he is best known. Birch finds that 'Of all the net new jobs created in our sample of 5.6 million businesses between 1969 and 1976, two-thirds were created by firms with 20 or fewer employees' (Birch, 1981, 7). Between 1976 and 1982, firms with fewer than 100 employees created 82 percent of the jobs. Birch goes on to say, 'Another distinguishing characteristic of job replacers is their youth. About 80 percent of the replacement jobs are created by establishments four years old or younger'. Finally, 'Whatever they are doing, however, large firms are no longer the major providers of new jobs for Americans' (p. 8).[1]

In 1994, Birch suggested that perhaps it is not large or small firms that are important for job growth but gazelles. One conclusion was that the distinction between small and large firms as job creators is of less importance – most jobs are created by gazelles, which are firms that are neither large nor small. 'These gazelles move between small and large quickly – at various times in either direction – and to classify them by their size is to miss their unique characteristics: great innovation and rapid job growth' (Birch and Medoff, 1994, 163). A conclusion of the Birch and Medoff study was that a small number (4 percent) of ongoing firms create a disproportionately large share of all new jobs in the United States (70 percent). In a second study, Birch et al. (1995) concluded that gazelles account for all new jobs in the whole economy. In fact, in a survey of almost 20 studies, Henrekson and Johansson (2010, 227) concluded:

> [N]et employment growth rather is generated by a few rapidly growing firms – so-called gazelles – that are not necessarily small and young. Gazelles are found to be outstanding job creators. They create all or a large share of net new jobs. On average, gazelles are younger and smaller than other firms, but it is young age more than small size that is associated with rapid growth.

What is less clear from all of these studies is what the role of firm age is. And second, what is the role of entry that is closely related to age?

133

Today we know that age of firm is a much more important issue in business dynamics than is size, and of course most new firms are small (Haltiwanger et al., 2010). However, what about rapidly growing firms that may have started not so small? While the theoretical literature suggests that noise selection plays an important role in industry dynamics, it does not provide much insight into what role different types of firms play. Noise selection implies that it is difficult to select winners from losers. We just do not know ahead of time. In other words, what is the impact on employment today of new firms, rapidly growing firms, and the establishments of large firms?

One of the purposes of this study is to revisit the Birch question of 'Who creates jobs: mice, gazelles, or elephants?'. Birch's most interesting insight was that rapidly growing firms, which he termed 'gazelles', were responsible for most of the employment growth in regional economies (Birch and Medoff, 1994). In contrast, mice are small firms that add little to employment (Shane, 2008), and elephants are large firms that shed jobs (Dertouzos et al., 1989). Very little is known about these rapidly growing firms, which we refer to in this study as 'high-impact firms'. We describe these firms as 'high impact' because they have a disproportionately large impact on employment growth, revenue growth, and, we contend, productivity.

As the theory suggests, and our statistical analysis bears out, high-impact firms play an especially important role in the process of job creation over time compared with either the plants of large existing firms or very small start-ups that tend not to grow. High-impact firms appear to be different from other firms. However, very little is known about where they come from. In other words, what are they before they become high-impact firms? Are they start-ups or are they non-growing enterprises that exist for years before they enter their growth phase?

This study recreates some of Birch's investigations of gazelles using new and better data. We use two datasets. First, we use the Business Information Tracking System (BITS) data to examine the roles of different types of entrants over time. We find that different entrants have different trajectories with respect to job creation. Second, we use the Corporate Research Board's American Corporate Statistical Library (ACSL) to better understand these high-potential firms' role in the economy. The ACSL is a longitudinal file linking microdata on virtually all US business establishments and enterprises over time. The ACSL enables us to identify and track high-impact firms from January 1, 1994, to January 1, 2006 (Parsons and Tracy, 2005). The data are updated every year.

Our study attempts to shed light on an important question: 'What are the characteristics of high-impact firms and how have they changed?'. One argument in the literature on evolution suggests that start-ups are important and that these entrants over time will become high-impact firms. But how long does that take? This question has never been addressed. The study should help inform regional policy to promote economic development. Most economic development money is spent attracting new plants, and most small-firm and entrepreneurship policy is focused on new firm start-ups or helping disadvantaged firms. Very little economic development money is spent on expanding or retaining existing firms, or what the literature today calls 'economic gardening' (US SBA, 2006, ch. 6).

Part of the reason for a lack of support for economic gardening is that very little is known about companies on their way to rapid growth. It is hoped that this study will lead to the development of policies tailored to helping regions retain and expand high-potential firms, since these are the firms that appear to create jobs in the long run. We shall examine four sets of questions. First, how do high-impact firms compare with all other firms? Second, where are they located, in terms of industry and geography? Third, what stage of development precedes the emergence of high-impact firms? And finally, what are the characteristics of high-impact firms in the years after their high-growth phase?

The next section presents the theoretical framework of the relationship between industry dynamics and employment growth, and respective empirical results. It also suggests why high-impact firms may be important to the understanding of job generation. We then discuss the methodology, period of analysis, the hypotheses to be tested, and present the results of the study. The final section concludes.

THE RELATIONSHIP BETWEEN NEW BUSINESS FORMATION AND EMPLOYMENT GROWTH

Theory

How do high-impact firms interact with the economy? This can happen in many ways but there are at least three ways in the economic literature: innovation, productivity growth, and employment change. High-impact firms either create innovations or they use them – Microsoft as opposed to Wal-Mart. Productivity impact is also important, but much harder to measure. Finally, employment changes are important and they are easier to measure. Therefore, the literature on firm dynamics (entry and exit) and employment growth is important because it relates the two activities.

While the literature on firm dynamics does not explicitly discuss the importance of high-impact firms, the implicit relationship implies that these firms are involved in activities that have a 'material' impact on the economy. As the literature reviews by Sutton (1997), Caves (1998), and Davis and Haltiwanger (1999) make clear, research on gross employment flows has a long tradition. However, it is only in the last two decades that economists and powerful computers have examined numerous census bureaus in different countries and organized the primary economic census data so that the births, deaths, survival, and growth of individual business units can be traced.

This research has borne fruit in the form of a great outpouring of stylized facts, where little more than impressions existed before. The interpretation of these facts is less clear. According to Caves (1998) while the importance of research on employment flows is manifest to the economy, its development has not been theory driven. In fact, figuring out which theoretical models the stylized facts shed light on 'is itself an exercise in hunting and gathering' (ibid., 1947). This literature can be interpreted through the lens of dynamic models and theories of industrial evolution and therefore should be of importance for evolutionary economics. Models of industry evolution can help us better understand the underlying patterns of gross job flows.[2] Much of the empirical analysis in recent studies of firm- and plant-level employment dynamics is explicitly couched in terms of this type of theory (Evans, 1987; Dunne et al., 1989). Davis and Haltiwanger (1992) looked at gross job flows for the 1978–83 period and found that learning and initial conditions provide a plausible explanation for the strong and pervasive relationship between job reallocation rates and plant age. These results lead to the conclusion that passive learning stories are quite useful for interpreting variations in job reallocation intensity across different types of plants and manufacturing industries.[3] Passive learning strategies assume that the firm learns, but it does not initiate any action to increase its learning capabilities, for example, engaging in research and development (R&D) or some similar activity.

These models all suggest that the enduring differences in the size distribution of firms and firm growth rates result less from the effects of the fixity of capital than from the effects of 'noisy' selection and incomplete information. If this is the case, then the persistence of jobs in the service sector should not be substantially different from that of the more capital-intensive manufacturing sector (Lucas and Prescott, 1971; Lucas, 1978). Jovanovic (1982) stresses the selection effects associated with passive learning about initial conditions. A firm's underlying efficiency level cannot be directly observed but is learned over time through the process of production. A firm that accumulates favorable information about its efficiency expands and survives, whereas a firm that accumulates sufficiently unfavorable information exits. Firms differ in size not because of the fixity of capital, but because some learn that they are more efficient than others. In this model, firms and potential entrants know the entire equilibrium price sequence, and based on it, they make entry, production, and exit decisions. A one-time entry cost is borne at the time of entry. Thereafter, only production costs are incurred, where efficient firms grow and survive and the inefficient decline and close.

Ericson and Pakes (1995) develop a theory of firm and industry dynamics in which investment outcome involves idiosyncratic uncertainty. The stochastic outcomes of an individual firm's investment coupled with competitor investment outcomes determine the probability distribution over future profitability streams. A plant's (establishment) investment outcome may improve its position relative to competitors, thus leading to expansion, or it may involve a relative deterioration, thus leading to contraction and possibly exit. Investment in the Ericson–Pakes model thus entails elements of active learning and selection. Active learning, as opposed to passive learning, implies that the firm has a strategy to increase its learning capabilities. This model builds in an explanation for perpetual entry and exit. Hence, the active learning theory embeds technical change into a rich model of firm-level heterogeneity and selection.

Lambson (1991) stresses differences in initial conditions, or uncertainties about future conditions, that lead firms to commit to different factor intensities and production techniques. These differences in turn lead to heterogeneity in firm-level responses to common cost and demand shocks. According to Hopenhayn (1992), even firms that produce identical products with identical technologies can face idiosyncratic cost disturbances. For example, energy costs and tax burdens are often heavily influenced by local conditions. Exogenous idiosyncratic cost disturbances lead to contraction at some firms and, simultaneously, expansion at other firms. The above theories account for several factors that would plausibly account for simultaneous job creation and destruction within narrowly defined sectors of the economy.

While interesting as a way to think about job flows, these models do not serve to predict how the patterns of job creation would differ across diverse sectors of the economy, such as services and manufacturing. However, it would follow from these dynamic models that if learning and noisy selection are more important than the fixity of capital, job growth and persistence should be similar for sectors with substantially different capital intensity, other things being constant. If fixity of capital is more

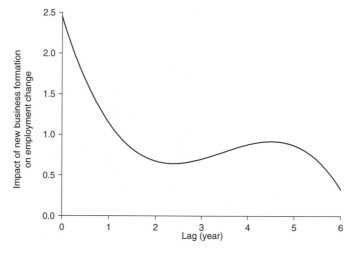

Figure 6.1   Distribution of employment effects – all start-ups

important than learning and selection, capital-intensive sectors should have higher persistence rates than less capital-intensive sectors because of sunk costs. Of course, one could easily imagine a noisy selection process with different entry fees and different means and variances of the efficiency parameters across sectors. This could generate very different employment flow patterns.

The Impact of Start-ups Over Time

What is the impact of new firms over time? While few studies have looked at the number of start-ups as a measure of industry dynamics in the past, recently there has been a host of studies examining the effect of business formation over time. For example, using data from the US Small Business Administration (SBA), Acs and Mueller (2008) found that the impact of new business formation on employment change in the United States shows a strong positive initial effect in year t (Figure 6.1).[4] Although the effect is decreasing in $t - 1$ and $t - 2$, the effect does not become negative. Therefore, we do not detect a negative employment effect of new business formation. In year $t - 3$ the employment effect increases again and it takes between four and five years until the effect is maximized again. Figure 6.1 shows clearly that the overall employment effect is positive, leading us to the conclusion that new business formation leads to employment growth in the short and medium terms.

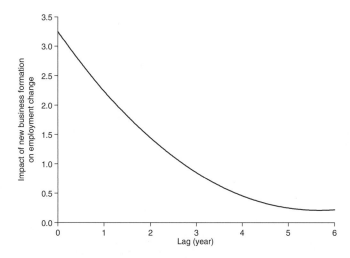

Figure 6.2 Distribution of employment effects – start-ups with fewer than 20 employees

It can be expected that the displacement effect of new businesses, which causes incumbents to reduce employment or exit the market, is more pronounced for new multi-unit establishments and larger new firms. First, new plants or branches of existing firms are most likely to be supported by their parent company, which gives them better starting conditions. Second, larger new firms have better survival chances and are more likely to stimulate better performance from incumbent firms, resulting in employment growth in their own firm and existing firms. To gain further insight into the relationship between new business formation and employment growth, a distinction is made between the results for the establishment of firms with fewer than 20 employees, between 20 and 499 employees, and more than 500 employees.

The results for each group of new establishments indicate that the three employment effects of new businesses depend on the size of the firm. By employment effects we mean with what impact and with what time lag the firm entry affects employment. Market entry of small new establishments (firms with fewer than 20 employees, almost exclusively single-unit establishments) results in a strong positive initial effect that decreases over time and is negligible after six years (Figure 6.2). We do not find a further induced effect in the long term.

New establishments of firms with 20 to 499 employees or new firms of this size are shown in Figure 6.3. The positive effect increases after one year and reaches a maximum after five years before it decreases again.

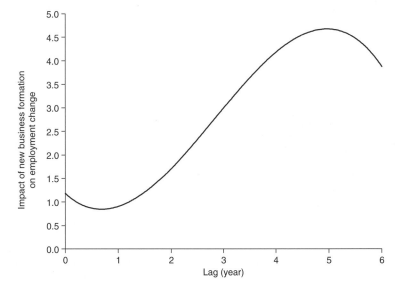

Figure 6.3   Distribution of employment effects – start-ups with 20–499 employees

These so-called 'gazelles' are able to increase their level of productivity sooner after entry due to their size and preconditions. Furthermore, they challenge existing firms and increase the competitiveness of surviving existing firms.

The distinction between the new establishments according to the size of the firm reveals that a negative employment effect may exist. The entry of firms or new establishments with at least 500 employees leads to a strong negative employment effect, which turns positive after six years (Figure 6.4). For this group of entrants, the long-term employment effect may be negative but it probably takes more than six years to become visible. One way of characterizing this phenomenon is to picture these entrants as new locations of large multi-unit corporations and that enter the market with a high productivity level. Their entry may not just challenge incumbent firms but even lead to market exits and employment losses in incumbent firms. Such entrants are termed 'elephants' since they demolish employment in the first years after entry. Nevertheless, it can be expected that their entry is important since they force inefficient establishments to leave the market and lead to an indirect positive effect in the long run.

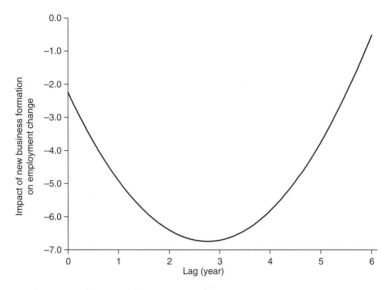

Figure 6.4   Distribution of employment effects – start-ups with at least 500 employees

METHODOLOGY

Data

A recent, comprehensive study of US government data collection conducted by the National Research Council (Haltiwanger et al., 2007) confirmed the shortage of data for the study of entrepreneurship and concluded that existing US business data are inadequate for the study of productivity, innovation, and firm creation. One of the report's central recommendations is 'to increase the statistical system's capacity to measure activities of nascent and young businesses – especially those positioned in fast-growing and innovative sectors of the economy – that are central to understanding business dynamics' (p. 4). While this report underscores the problem and offers specific recommendations to improve US data collection, attempts to measure entrepreneurial activity remain fraught with statistical difficulties. Nonetheless, we present here what we consider to be the best data available for the study of business dynamics.

We have developed a new richer dataset referred to as the American Corporate Statistical Library. The ACSL stitches together data from public and private sector sources over a 12-year period, allowing users to analyze discrete business patterns and broad economic trends in insightful ways. Its principal data sources are Dun & Bradstreet's (D&B) DUNS Market Identifier file, the Bureau of Labor Statistics' Industry Occupation Mix, and the Census Bureau's Public Use Microdata Sample file. See Acs et al. (2008, Appendix H) for a more complete description.

Traditional definitions of high-growth firms are based solely on sales growth. The concept was developed to appeal to marketing executives at large enterprises seeking to sell their products and services to companies with substantial revenue. A limitation of this concept is that it does not take into account employment growth – an important policy consideration for government. In fact, a nontrivial number of traditional high-growth firms (gazelles) do not contribute to employment growth. More recent studies have also looked at employment growth (Henrekson and Johansson, 2010). In this chapter we offer a variation of the gazelle concept that encompasses both revenue and employment considerations – what we call a 'high-impact firm'. A gazelle firm is defined as 'an enterprise whose sales have at least doubled for the most recent four year period'. We define a high-impact firm as an enterprise whose sales have at least doubled over the most recent four-year period and which has an employment growth quantifier (EGQ) of 2 or greater over the same period. The EGQ is the product of the absolute and percent change in employment over a four-year period of time, expressed as a decimal. The EGQ is used to mitigate the unfavorable impact of measuring employment change solely in either percent or absolute terms, since the former favors small companies and the latter large businesses.[5] We also divide the high-impact firms into three size classifications to compare with the ones used by the US Census Bureau/SBA: 1–19 employees, 20–499 employees, and 500-plus employees.

Period of Analysis

Our principal period of analysis is 1998–2002. A four-year period was required, given that by definition *a high-impact firm had to at least double its revenues over a four-year period.* We selected this four-year period because data on the preceding and following four-year periods were available, enabling us to analyze the nature of high-impact firms before their growth took off (1994–98) and the disposition of these firms after this four-year high-growth period (2002–06).

With the addition of the pre- and post-high-impact phases, the entire time period studied is 1994–2006, with a primary focus on 1998–2002. The entire period was a much more entrepreneurial period than the earlier period that Birch studied in the late 1970s. By 1994 the US economy had begun to rebound from the 1989–92 recession. Even California, which had been particularly hard hit by the recession due to military base realignments, had begun to recover by 1994. The macroeconomic period studied corresponds to a period that covers the longest peacetime expansion in US history, followed by the burst of the dot-com bubble, a short recession, then a period of slower growth after 2002. The economy grew by close to 4 percent a year between 1995 and 2000. The economy slowed to around 1 percent between 2000 and 2002. By 2003 the economy began to grow again (though not at the levels of the mid- to late 1990s) at a rate of about 3 percent a year.

The primary study period, 1998–2002, covers a four-year period of rapid growth and the dot-com collapse. While the firm birth rate was close to 11 percent in 1996, it had started to slow by the end of the 1990s, and by the end of 2002 it had slowed slightly to about 10 percent. This is evident in other indicators such as initial public offerings, which declined from 476 in 1999 to 66 in 2002. The time period includes the transition from the rapidly growing 1990s to a period of slower growth during the 2000s. This slowdown is also evident in macroeconomic trends such as the federal budget's shift from surplus to deficit, the increase in the unemployment rate, and the stock market decline.

Twelve research questions are analyzed in the following sections:

1. How have high-impact firms been defined? How do differences in definitions compare and contrast over time?
2. What share of new jobs do high-impact firms generate? Has this changed over time?
3. What share of revenue do high-impact firms generate? Has this changed over time?
4. What is the typical age range of a high-impact firm – young, mature, or older? Has this changed over time?
5. How big are high-impact firms (in employment terms) at the beginning of the period? Does size change over time?
6. In what industries are high-impact firms generally found? Does this change over time?
7. How efficient or inefficient are high-impact firms? How has this changed over time?
8. Where are high-impact firms located – in metropolitan, rural, or suburban areas? How far are they from central business districts? Has this changed over time?
9. What were high-impact firms before their growth surge – start-ups, slow growers, decliners, or volatile or stagnant firms? How has this changed over time?

10. What happens to high-impact firms after their intensive growth period? What percentages continue their growth surge; continue to grow but more slowly; or stagnate, decline, or go out of business? How has this changed over time?
11. Is there an opposite group of 'decliners' that net out the contribution of high-impact firms?
12. Which metropolitan statistical areas rank highest in share of high-impact firms?

We now turn to a detailed analysis of high-impact firms.

RESULTS

This section presents the results for the questions posed about high-impact firms. The answers are presented in each of the next four sections where we compare high-impact firms to all other firms in terms of age, size, and efficiency; determine where they are located (by industry and geographically); and identify what they were before and after being classified as high-growth firms.

Table 6.1 provides summary statistics on the two different definitions of high-impact firms. Gazelles, corresponding to Birch's definition, double their sales over a set time period, while high-impact firms double their sales and have an employment growth qualifier of two or greater (see above). The top panel of Table 6.1 shows employment and revenue growth for gazelles; the bottom half shows this for high-impact firms. The total numbers of firms that qualify as gazelles and as high-impact firms are not very different, and the two datasets do not exhibit any clear pattern. For example, in 1998–2002, there were 345,330 gazelles and 299,973 high-impact firms, while in 1994–98 there were 354,049 gazelles and 352,114 high-impact firms. These firms created 11.4 million and 11.7 million jobs, respectively, during the 1998–2002 period. While firms in the 1–19 employee firm-size category were most numerous, most of the jobs were created by the 500-plus firm-size class. In fact, the 500-plus firm-size class created almost as many jobs as both of the smaller firm-size classes combined during the first two time periods, although not in 2002–06.

The most striking differences between gazelles and high-impact firms are in the 500-plus firm-size class. There are fewer high-impact firms by almost two to one during the 2002–06 time period. However, the employment effect is greater for the smaller number of high-impact firms, 2,514,558 versus 2,966,826. The number of high-impact firms was smaller than the number of gazelles in the first two periods, but was greater in the third

Table 6.1   Gazelles and high-impact firms, by select variables

Number of employees	Period	Number of gazelles	Job change	Revenue change ($1,000s)
1–19	1994–1998	309,160	3,018,440	577,533,025
	1998–2002	301,275	3,573,918	716,504,242
	2002–2006	283,308	2,883,475	589,072,471
20–499	1994–1998	43,342	3,014,683	762,963,829
	1998–2002	42,390	3,291,048	957,923,241
	2002–2006	39,617	2,130,682	1,014,653,361
500 plus	1994–1998	1,547	5,063,517	1,195,977,664
	1998–2002	1,665	4,515,417	1,841,396,607
	2002–2006	1,485	2,514,558	1,663,635,336
Total	1994–1998	354,049	11,096,640	2,536,474,518
	1998–2002	345,330	11,380,383	3,515,824,090
	2002–2006	324,410	7,528,715	3,267,361,168

Number of employees	Period	Number of high-impact firms	Job change	Revenue change ($1,000s)
1–19	1994–1998	327,397	3,170,729	346,038,292
	1998–2002	278,190	3,577,111	423,042,570
	2002–2006	359,289	4,041,099	425,041,975
20–499	1994–1998	23,464	2,788,969	503,059,203
	1998–2002	20,601	2,966,647	570,102,604
	2002–2006	16,523	2,001,835	549,674,434
500 plus	1994–1998	1,253	5,501,049	1,110,073,562
	1998–2002	1,182	5,192,558	1,657,759,197
	2002–2006	793	2,966,826	1,060,128,527
Total	1994–1998	352,114	11,460,747	1,959,171,057
	1998–2002	299,973	11,736,316	2,650,904,371
	2002–2006	376,605	9,009,760	2,034,844,936

Source: Corporate Research Board, American Corporate Statistical Library (2007).

(Table 6.1). It is interesting that the number of high-impact firms exceeded the number of gazelles, given the more restrictive definition.

Table 6.2 presents summary statistics on the ratio of high-impact firms to all other firms for the 1994–2006 period. Between 1994 and 1998 there were 352,114 high-impact firms, for a US high-impact firm share of 6.3 percent. The high-impact share was 5.2 percent between 1998 and 2002 and 6.5 percent between 1994 and 1998. The high-impact firm share varies as much as it does because the absolute number of high-impact firms changes over time, reflecting changes in the total number of firms in the

Table 6.2   Ratio of high-impact firms to low-impact firms, 1994–2006

	1994–1998	1998–2002	2002–2006
High-impact firms	352,114	299,973	376,605
All other firms	5,579,177	5,697,759	5,787,631
High-impact firm ratio (%)	6.3	5.2	6.5

Source: Corporate Research Board, American Corporate Statistical Library (2007).

economy. The denominator used in Table 6.2 represents all employer firms in the BITS file. Of course, using a different denominator would yield a different rate. The BITS dataset has the advantage that both the numerator and the denominator contain employer firms.

How Do High-impact Firms Compare with All Other Firms?

Age
How old are high-impact firms? Firm age is an important issue in industrial organization and has received considerable attention in the literature. Many studies have found that new firms grow faster than older firms (Evans, 1987). Table 6.3a shows the age distribution of all high-impact firms in the three firm-size classes and allows us to compare them to low-impact firms (Table 6.3b). The average age of high-impact firms is surprisingly high.

For the 1–19 firm-size class the average age is about 17 years. This increases to about 25 years for the 20–499 size class and to 34 years for the 500-plus size class. This is surprising given previous findings in the literature. What about start-ups? Table 6.3a shows that the 0–4-year-old age class (where start-ups would be classified) accounted for only 2.8 percent of high-impact firms between 1998 and 2002. In fact almost 95 percent of high-impact firms are over five years old. No more than 5.5 percent of high-impact firms are start-ups (0–4 years old). In 1994–98, 16.8 percent of the high-impact firms in the 20–499 firm-size class are 11–14 years old and 13.9 percent of the 500-plus firm-size class is in the 15–19-year age range. As shown in Table 6.3b, low-impact firms are on average older than high-impact firms, but not by much. For the 1–19 firm-size class the difference is about five years (17 vs. 21), for the 20–499 firm-size class it is about seven years, and for the 500-plus size class it is about 12 years. In other words, as firms become larger the age spread between the high- and low-impact firms increases. Therefore, high-impact firms are on average younger than

Table 6.3a   *Distribution of high-impact firms by age range and firm size, selected periods (percent, except where noted)*

	1994–1998 Firm size (no. of employees)			1998–2002 Firm size (no. of employees)			2002–2006 Firm size (no. of employees)		
	1–19	20–499	500 plus	1–19	20–499	500 plus	1–19	20–499	500 plus
Age of firm									
0–4	0.83	0.67	0.56	0.13	0.9	1.35	0.55	0.89	0.38
5–7	6.72	7.94	4.89	2.42	9.89	9.73	3.26	10.19	6.2
8–10	6.81	11.49	7.94	5.46	11.56	7.7	7.3	13.04	10.63
11–14	7.85	16.82	14.6	5.08	13.92	9.98	4.34	13.82	10.76
15–19	5.22	16.19	13.95	3.75	16.09	15.57	1.95	14.41	13.04
20–24	0.51	11.49	9.22	0.61	11.68	11.68	0.59	12.44	9.75
25–29	0.75	9.13	9.3	0.24	8.43	6.77	0.09	8.62	7.72
30–39	0.62	9.96	11.39	0.54	10.72	10.58	0.74	10.97	10.89
40–49	0.32	6.12	6.82	0.98	5.75	5.33	0.67	5.47	6.96
50–69	0.42	6.31	10.67	0.4	6.3	8.63	0.27	5.46	9.49
70–99	0.95	3.9	10.67	0.94	3.4	7.02	0.86	3.2	7.85
100 plus	0	0	0	0.45	1.36	5.67	0.39	1.48	6.33
Average firm age (years)	17.4	24.3	32	17	25.2	33.5	17.4	24.7	35.7

Source: Corporate Research Board, American Corporate Statistical Library (2007).

low-impact firms. Of course it should be kept in mind that D&B has difficulty adding new firms; this should not alter the current analysis, however, as high-impact firms are basically by definition at least three years old and most likely around 20 years old.

Employment size of firm
How much did high-impact firms grow during the study period? Tables 6.4a–f compare high- and low-impact firms' distribution in terms of employment-size class and average firm size. As shown in Table 6.4b, for the 1–19 firm-size class the average employment size in 1998 was 3.4 growing to 16.3 in 2002. As shown in Table 6.4e, the average employment size of low-impact firms was 3.9 and 4.1 for the same time period. The average firm size of low-impact firms was virtually unchanged over the four-year period. The results were similar for the four-year periods before and after the primary study period.

*Table 6.3b   Distribution of low-impact firms by age range and firm size,
selected periods (percent, except where noted)*

	1994–1998 Firm size (no. of employees)			1998–2002 Firm size (no. of employees)			2002–2006 Firm size (no. of employees)		
	1–19	20–499	500 plus	1–19	20–499	500 plus	1–19	20–499	500 plus
Age of firm									
0–4	0.62	0.49	0.54	0.52	0.52	0.56	0.32	0.41	0.33
5–7	0.90	4.29	3.67	4.27	5.18	4.16	1.30	4.97	3.56
8–10	2.08	6.61	5.81	1.71	6.83	4.47	4.31	7.85	5.74
11–14	6.14	11.21	10.2	3.86	9.86	6.18	4.48	10.42	6.58
15–19	6.14	12.96	9.57	4.96	13.57	9.57	4.29	12.32	7.74
20–24	2.79	11.91	6.08	1.76	11.55	7.10	1.63	12.07	9.39
25–29	0.93	10.46	6.95	0.54	9.93	5.47	0.09	9.99	6.24
30–39	0.77	13.85	11.19	0.74	14.39	12.01	0.76	15.00	11.28
40–49	0.64	9.45	8.75	0.10	8.78	8.69	0.74	8.44	8.94
50–69	4.62	10.37	11.56	0.39	9.91	12.36	0.24	9.63	12.34
70–99	0.35	8.39	25.69	0.77	6.12	13.93	0.56	5.63	12.66
100 plus	0	0	0	0.38	3.37	15.49	0.26	3.26	15.20
Average firm age (years)	22.1	32.00	44.30	22.40	33.40	52.80	22.40	32.90	52.10

Source: Corporate Research Board, American Corporate Statistical Library (2007).

The distribution of employment size between high- and low-impact firms is also interesting. While almost 70 percent of the low-impact firms stayed in the 1–4 employee firm-size class between 1994 and 1998, only 30 percent of the high-impact firms remained in that category. This result is robust throughout the whole time period. The results are even more startling for the 20–499 firm-size class. For the 1994–98 period (Table 6.4a) the average employment size increased from 67 to 186; similar results were seen in the other two time periods, with average employment size increasing from 66 to 210 (Table 6.4b) and from 62 to 183 (Table 6.4c), respectively. For the low-impact firms, employment size increased slightly over the 1994–98 period (61 to 63) and the 1998–2002 period (59 to 63), and it decreased slightly over the 2002–06 period (58 to 57). However, what is important to note is that employment in the low-impact firms never declined over the period. This is consistent with our results above on the behavior of start-ups and employment growth. For

Table 6.4a   Percent of high-impact firms by employment size of firm, 1994–1998

Average number of employees	1–19		20–499		500 plus	
	Start of period	End of period	Start of period	End of period	Start of period	End of period
0–4	82.66	30.97	–	–	–	–
5–9	11.12	27.13	–	–	–	–
10–24	6.22	30.34	19.82	–	–	–
25–49	–	8.78	40.42	20.78	–	–
50–99	–	2.13	21.57	35.74	–	–
100–249	–	0.50	13.67	27.60	–	–
250–499	–	0.09	4.51	9.72	–	–
500–999	–	0.03	–	4.31	44.05	12.85
1,000–2,499	–	0.02	–	1.50	31.36	36.55
2,500–4,999	–	–	–	0.25	13.17	22.59
5,000–9,999	–	–	–	0.05	5.99	12.93
10,000–24,999	–	–	–	0.04	3.67	9.26
25,000–49,999	–	–	–	–	1.20	3.27
50,000 plus	–	–	–	–	0.56	2.55
Average size	3.30	13.00	66.80	185.70	2,915.50	7,305.80

Source: Corporate Research Board, American Corporate Statistical Library (2007).

both firm-size classes, 0–19 and 20–499, employment remained positive over time.

As shown in Table 6.4b, the average employment size of the largest firms (500-plus employees) increased from 3,648 in 1998 to 8,041 in 2002, a 120 percent increase. The results are even more dramatic for the non-recessionary periods before and after our focus period, during which average firm size went from 2,916 to 7,306 and 3,234 to 6,975, respectively. These results appear to be inconsistent with our results above that the 500-plus firm-size class loses employment from entry. The answer is found by looking at the low-impact firms' behavior. Tables 6.4d–f show that employment in large low-impact firms decreases by almost 40 to 62 percent in the periods studied. For example, in 1994–98, average firm size decreased from 7,340 to 2,794 (Table 6.4d). Large firm shrinkage is evident in Tables 6.4d–f as firms with more than 500 employees start to repopulate the smaller firm-size classes. While the two smaller size classes of low-impact firms exhibited almost no statistical trend, the 500-plus firm-size class exhibits a steady and persistent decline in employment. In fact, these tables show how the economy sheds jobs – the larger firms

Table 6.4b   *Percent of high-impact firms by employment size of firm,*
1998–2002

Average number of employees	1–19		20–499		500 plus	
	Start of period	End of period	Start of period	End of period	Start of period	End of period
0–4	81.01	20.78	–	–	–	–
5–9	12.18	32.35	–	–	–	–
10–24	6.81	32.46	21.48	–	–	–
25–49	–	10.07	39.70	19.56	–	–
50–99	–	3.09	21.07	35.51	–	–
100–249	–	0.99	13.31	28.00	–	–
250–499	–	0.15	4.44	10.20	–	–
500–999	–	0.06	–	4.48	41.71	12.10
1,000–2,499	–	0.03	–	1.72	31.30	35.87
2,500–4,999	–	0.01	–	0.37	13.54	21.74
5,000–9,999	–	–	–	0.10	6.68	14.13
10,000–24,999	–	–	–	0.04	4.31	10.58
25,000–49,999	–	–	–	–	1.52	2.88
50,000 plus	–	–	–	0.01	0.93	2.71
Average size	3.40	16.30	65.80	209.80	3,648.00	8,041.00

Source: Corporate Research Board, American Corporate Statistical Library (2007).

that do not grow shed large numbers of jobs in a relatively short period of time. The striking trend of rapidly growing employment in high-impact firms is almost canceled out by large, low-impact firms' decline in employment.

The results from Tables 6.4a–c are consistent with the results from the SBA data. Most, if not all, of the growth in employment comes from the 300,000 high-impact firms in the economy over any four-year period. Depending on the time period studied, this is about evenly split between firms with fewer than 500 employees and firms with more than 500 employees. Therefore, it would appear that both small and large firms contribute about equally to employment growth.

However, when one looks at the performance of low-impact firms another picture emerges. As shown in Tables 6.4d–f, while the low-impact firms in the 0–19 and the 20–499 firm-size class exhibit either no change or a slight increase in average employment size, the 500-plus firm-size class exhibits a persistent and steady decrease in average firm size, down by 62 percent between 1994 and 1998. The declines in average firm size were similar for the other two time periods. These results are consistent with the

Table 6.4c   Percent of high-impact firms by employment size of firm, 2002–2006

Average number of employees	1–19		20–499		500 plus	
	Start of period	End of period	Start of period	End of period	Start of period	End of period
0–4	87.21	25.55	–	–	–	–
5–9	8.22	34.38	–	–	–	–
10–24	4.56	27.66	22.24	–	–	–
25–49	–	8.62	41.60	20.76	–	–
50–99	–	2.99	20.52	36.76	–	–
100–249	–	0.62	11.80	27.54	–	–
250–499	–	0.11	3.85	9.01	–	–
500–999	–	0.04	–	3.82	38.59	12.74
1,000–2,499	–	0.02	–	1.62	32.41	32.03
2,500–4,999	–	0.01	–	0.24	14.88	23.96
5,000–9,999	–	–	–	0.15	7.57	15.64
10,000–24,999	–	–	–	0.09	5.42	10.21
25,000–49,999	–	–	–	0.01	0.76	3.40
50,000 plus	–	–	–	–	0.38	2.02
Average size	2.70	14.00	61.70	182.90	3,233.80	6,975.10

Source: Corporate Research Board, American Corporate Statistical Library (2007).

SBA data showing that the entry into the 500-plus firm-size class results on average in no employment gain over a five- or six-year period.

Productivity
Are high-impact firms more productive than low-impact firms? We use revenue per employee to provide an indication of labor productivity. Tables 6.5a and 6.5b present results on revenue per employee by one-digit industry for 1994–2006 for all high- and low-impact enterprises. For example, for the 2002–06 period, revenue per employee was $286,082 per year for high-impact firms with 500 or more employees and $203,892 per year for low-impact firms of this size. Revenue per employee was greater for high-impact firms in total for all time periods studied and firm-size categories. For 2002–06, the only two industries where low-impact firms outperformed high-impact firms were high-technology and wholesale trade. The gap between high- and low-impact firm productivity also seems to be increasing over time. These results are consistent with the theory that newer firms drive out older inefficient firms, resulting in higher productivity in new firms. (High-impact firms are on average younger than low-impact firms.)

*Table 6.4d   Percent of low-impact firms by employment size of firm,
1994–1998*

Average number of employees	1–19		20–499		500 plus	
	Start of period	End of period	Start of period	End of period	Start of period	End of period
0–4	70.56	70.93	–	3.20	–	3.34
5–9	19.56	18.53	–	2.09	–	1.71
10–24	9.88	9.78	21.46	20.88	–	2.68
25–49	–	0.61	42.33	36.91	–	2.90
50–99	–	0.11	20.94	20.92	–	3.34
100–249	–	0.03	11.56	11.93	–	5.90
250–499	–	0.01	3.70	3.50	–	6.91
500–999	–	–	–	0.50	41.65	30.24
1,000–2,499	–	–	–	0.05	30.28	25.92
2,500–4,999	–	–	–	0.01	11.49	8.54
5,000–9,999	–	–	–	–	6.59	4.35
10,000–24,999	–	–	–	–	5.43	2.63
25,000–49,999	–	–	–	–	2.02	0.87
50,000 plus	–	–	–	–	2.53	0.68
Average size	4.40	4.60	61.40	63.40	7,340.10	2,793.60

Source: Corporate Research Board, American Corporate Statistical Library (2007).

High-impact firms by industry
In what industries are high-impact firms most prevalent? Economists
have long debated the merits of having an economy that is specialized
versus one that exhibits high levels of diversity (Glaeser et al., 1992). The
empirical evidence suggests that economies that are more diversified will
grow more rapidly than ones that are more specialized. Table 6.6 shows
the percentage of high-impact firms aggregated by 2-digit SIC industry
for 1998–2006. The most striking observation is that high-impact firms
exist in virtually all of the 2-digit SIC codes for all of the years. Second,
the percentage of high-impact firms appears to be declining over time;
however, this is in part the result of the growth in overall number of firms
(the denominator).

The industries with the highest shares of high-impact firms in 1998 are
SIC 36, electronic equipment; SIC 30, rubber and plastics; and SIC 37,
transportation equipment. Disregarding the industries at the extremes,
the range is between 2 and 6 percent. When we compare years, we notice
that the percent of high-impact firms varies significantly over time. For
example in electronic equipment, the rate declined from 7 percent in 1998

Table 6.4e   *Percent of low-impact firms by employment size of firm,*
1998–2002

Average number of employees	1–19		20–499		500 plus	
	Start of period	End of period	Start of period	End of period	Start of period	End of period
0–4	74.13	73.52	–	1.85	–	1.91
5–9	16.79	16.79	–	1.54	–	1.13
10–24	9.08	9.09	22.53	22.10	–	2.04
25–49	–	0.45	42.46	38.66	–	1.98
50–99	–	0.10	20.45	20.52	–	2.15
100–249	–	0.03	11.11	11.47	–	4.10
250–499	–	0.01	3.45	3.39	–	6.38
500–999	–	–	–	0.41	44.89	35.57
1,000–2,499	–	–	–	0.05	29.89	26.04
2,500–4,999	–	–	–	0.01	10.96	9.37
5,000–9,999	–	–	–	–	6.29	4.74
10,000–24,999	–	–	–	–	4.30	2.80
25,000–49,999	–	–	–	–	1.72	1.02
50,000 plus	–	–	–	–	1.94	0.77
Average size	3.90	4.10	59.50	62.70	5,501.80	3,051.00

Source: Corporate Research Board, American Corporate Statistical Library (2007).

to 4.4 percent in 2002 and settled at 3.5 percent in 2006. The trend is similar for many industries. However, the range is roughly between 2 and 6 percent across industries and over time, with some exceptions.

At the more aggregate level, manufacturing as a whole does very well, with numbers that compare favorably with other sectors including finance, insurance, and real estate; transportation; and services in general. We can see why a diversified economy grows more rapidly than one that is less diversified. The industries that are rapidly growing, which are led by high-impact firms, seem to shift over time. Therefore, encouraging diversity as a policy seems to make much more sense than targeting select industries.

High-impact firms by geography
The location of economic activity is of great interest to economic development officials and communities alike. Several authors, including Jane Jacobs (1969), Michael Porter (1990), and Richard Florida (2002) have presented theses on how regional economies grow and prosper. At the heart of these models is the idea that economic and social inputs lead to rapidly growing companies. A large literature over the past decade has

Table 6.4f   Percent of low-impact firms by employment size of firm, 2002–2006

Average number of employees	1–19		20–499		500 plus	
	Start of period	End of period	Start of period	End of period	Start of period	End of period
0–4	79.06	79.18	–	3.63	–	2.97
5–9	13.55	13.42	–	1.64	–	1.12
10–24	7.39	7.13	22.91	23.44	–	1.76
25–49	–	0.21	42.57	38.89	–	1.90
50–99	–	0.04	20.47	19.03	–	2.16
100–249	–	0.01	10.83	10.12	–	3.33
250–499	–	–	3.22	2.97	–	4.70
500–999	–	–	–	0.23	46.98	37.68
1,000–2,499	–	–	–	0.03	28.17	26.00
2,500–4,999	–	–	–	0.01	10.41	8.96
5,000–9,999	–	–	–	–	6.18	4.68
10,000–24,999	–	–	–	–	4.52	2.70
25,000–49,999	–	–	–	–	2.03	1.22
50,000 plus	–	–	–	–	1.71	0.81
Average size	3.30	3.50	58.02	56.80	5,199.90	3,153.10

Source: Corporate Research Board, American Corporate Statistical Library (2007).

argued that these firms are located in high-tech regions and that most of them are also high-tech firms by nature (Lee et al., 2004).

We start by examining the distribution of high-impact firms by Census region. Table 6.7 provides data for all nine Census regions for the number of high-impact firms, the number of companies, the ratio of high-impact firms, and an index scaled from zero to 100. What we find as a first cut is that the distribution of high-impact firms shows some variation across regions, but not a lot. The rates are calculated as the number of high-impact firms divided by the total numbers of firms in the regions as defined by the ACSL. The Mountain region leads, with 29,893 high-impact firms or 2.33 percent of all firms. Table 6.7 shows the rankings of the other eight regions. However, the range is only 2.12 to 2.33 percent, showing only a slight variation among regions.[6]

Table 6A.1 in Appendix 6A ranks the 50 states and the District of Columbia. Again we see that the variation is not very large, ranging from 2.76 to 1.92 percent. However, at this lower level of aggregation the range is wider than in the regional distribution. The states with the highest ratios are Alaska, Arizona, Wyoming, South Carolina, North Dakota, and

Table 6.5a   *High-impact firm efficiency, by industry and employment size, selected periods (revenue per employee, in dollars)*

Industry	1994–1998			1998–2002			2002–2006		
	1–19	20–499	500 plus	1–19	20–499	500 plus	1–19	20–499	500 plus
Agriculture/forest/mining	63,261	190,960	159,502	68,201	246,583	407,686	90,296	637,717	832,423
Construction	119,666	199,275	230,306	144,676	159,947	295,062	125,695	210,304	862,301
Manufacturing	110,088	152,111	189,864	117,459	164,352	239,157	124,650	185,090	332,381
High-tech manufacturing	141,864	182,385	277,861	137,892	181,061	321,520	120,804	247,600	233,813
Communication/utilities	170,285	173,002	278,806	150,986	304,959	616,504	138,257	420,215	447,272
Distribution/wholesale	246,372	363,533	467,522	247,555	388,998	535,783	210,523	409,630	335,306
Retail	118,617	234,587	142,693	142,752	261,964	167,608	113,105	242,743	270,135
Eating/drinking retail	28,384	28,851	32,729	29,694	42,453	40,055	27,833	29,396	52,820
Financial/insurance/real estate	110,054	247,777	288,713	142,788	242,752	323,609	125,605	396,144	388,101
Services	42,013	58,352	65,247	43,978	51,531	66,536	43,369	84,323	64,560
Professional services	76,313	74,147	71,295	82,616	114,214	110,006	76,327	113,110	104,370
Total	101,690	156,440	177,123	110,745	168,396	254,923	99,439	224,786	286,082

Source: Corporate Research Board, American Corporate Statistical Library (2007).

Table 6.5b Low-impact firm efficiency, by industry and employment size, selected periods (revenue per employee, in dollars)

Industry	1994–1998			1998–2002			2002–2006		
	1–19	20–499	500 plus	1–19	20–499	500 plus	1–19	20–499	500 plus
Agriculture/forest/mining	70,556	111,179	455,757	67,556	79,248	419,929	65,961	96,816	712,840
Construction	109,846	153,937	196,926	117,275	158,409	228,623	107,255	149,299	226,547
Manufacturing	92,728	119,540	230,444	93,776	123,052	223,765	90,278	131,763	299,925
High-tech manufacturing	120,996	121,763	196,965	125,700	133,755	199,144	118,552	146,213	263,381
Communication/utilities	158,279	162,402	239,795	166,682	167,381	259,133	131,806	175,954	343,362
Distribution/wholesale	226,412	269,776	285,932	225,429	262,393	251,320	190,581	259,461	378,686
Retail	99,983	206,568	129,583	100,803	210,192	172,644	96,164	213,054	186,133
Eating/drinking retail	28,239	26,593	35,477	28,645	26,448	33,468	28,909	27,776	36,953
Financial/insurance/real estate	115,789	189,815	338,076	121,797	204,664	351,986	113,928	181,577	376,204
Services	39,880	49,345	63,745	42,329	54,457	66,536	42,189	52,709	61,738
Professional services	70,621	63,826	71,308	75,377	70,988	92,090	72,244	73,186	95,923
Total	92,867	113,744	163,316	93,656	117,306	170,733	85,691	116,145	203,892

Source: Corporate Research Board, American Corporate Statistical Library (2007).

156

Table 6.6   Share of high-impact firms by industry (percent)

SIC	Description	1998	2002	2006
1	Agriculture-crops	1.53	1.18	1.72
2	Agriculture-animals	1.21	1.34	1.86
7	Agriculture services	4.90	2.50	3.42
8	Forestry	4.34	2.60	2.79
9	Fishing, hunting	3.40	1.98	2.69
10	Metal mining	4.51	1.43	3.66
12	Coal, lignite mining	3.07	2.16	2.47
13	Oil, gas extraction	4.11	3.17	3.83
14	Non-metallic mining	4.98	3.93	2.94
15	General contractors	4.01	2.27	2.12
16	Heavy construction	6.13	4.52	4.60
17	Special trade contractors	4.94	3.08	2.93
20	Food, kindred products	4.96	3.40	3.36
21	Tobacco products	1.45	2.35	2.80
22	Textile mill products	4.02	2.89	2.45
23	Apparel, textiles	4.24	2.49	2.18
24	Lumber, wood products	4.99	2.69	2.63
25	Furniture, fixtures	5.98	3.70	2.97
26	Paper products	5.52	3.13	3.15
27	Printing, publishing	3.79	2.13	2.21
28	Chemical products	5.23	4.02	3.91
29	Petroleum, coal products	4.74	3.20	3.71
30	Rubber, plastics	7.18	4.04	3.36
31	Leather products	3.94	1.99	2.57
32	Stone, clay, glass	5.21	3.19	2.59
33	Primary metal industries	6.39	3.44	3.65
34	Fabricated metals	6.39	3.84	3.25
35	Machinery not electric	6.91	3.29	3.00
36	Electric, electronic	7.03	4.39	3.51
37	Transportation equipment	6.90	3.86	3.58
38	Instruments, related	6.06	4.29	3.98
39	Misc. manufacturing	3.93	1.75	2.12
40	Railroad transport	1.83	1.31	1.66
41	Transit	2.95	2.35	2.15
42	Trucking, warehouse	4.11	2.52	2.56
44	Water transportation	4.82	2.79	3.19
45	Air transportation	3.91	3.60	3.46
46	Pipelines, not gas	0.63	0.95	2.91
47	Transportation services	4.04	1.91	1.79
48	Communications	1.97	1.70	1.67
49	Utility services	4.79	3.45	3.68
50	Durable wholesale	4.37	2.89	2.77

Table 6.6   (continued)

SIC	Description	1998	2002	2006
51	Non-durable wholesale	4.10	2.62	2.48
52	Building, garden	3.73	2.49	2.67
53	General merchandise retail	2.06	1.38	1.40
54	Food stores	3.63	2.41	2.46
55	Automotive dealers	4.01	2.32	2.42
56	Apparel stores	2.06	1.50	1.53
57	Home furnishing retail	2.99	2.03	2.19
58	Eating, drinking	1.94	1.38	1.26
59	Miscellaneous retail	2.97	1.81	2.06
60	Banking	3.16	2.76	3.12
61	Non-bank credit	2.30	2.57	3.07
62	Securities brokers	3.41	2.52	2.22
63	Insurance carriers	3.33	2.26	3.17
64	Insurance agents	4.31	2.65	3.43
65	Real estate	4.04	2.53	2.27
67	Holding investments	4.17	0.98	0.88
70	Hotels and lodging	3.14	2.29	2.16
72	Personal services	4.33	1.78	2.18
73	Business services	3.54	1.69	2.01
75	Auto repair services	3.97	2.03	2.27
76	Misc. repair services	2.78	1.84	1.70
78	Motion pictures	3.33	1.52	1.46
79	Recreation services	3.82	2.09	2.59
80	Health services	5.39	2.64	3.67
81	Legal services	5.11	3.22	2.98
82	Educational services	1.23	0.96	1.84
83	Social services	6.30	3.69	4.35
84	Museums, gardens	0.00	0.00	0.00
86	Member organizations	0.33	0.15	0.20
87	Engineering, management	4.46	2.45	2.98
89	Miscellaneous services	1.38	0.34	0.92

Source: Corporate Research Board, American Corporate Statistical Library (2007).

Virginia. Preparing the data for the 52 top-tier metropolitan statistical areas (MSAs) shows the highest high-impact firm rate is Norfolk–Virginia Beach–Newport News, Virginia, with 2.58 percent high-impact firms (see Acs et al., 2008, Appendix B). The lowest is Orlando, Florida, with 1.93 percent. Once again, the range is not very large. For the mid-tier MSAs, the range is slightly greater: 1.81–2.81 percent (see ibid., Appendix B). The

Table 6.7   High-impact firm distribution by region, 2002–2006

Region	Rank	Number of high-impact firms	Total firms	Percent high-impact firms	Index value
Mountain	1	29,893	1,281,786	2.33	100.00
West North Central	2	26,895	1,195,553	2.25	60.37
East North Central	3	50,936	2,269,977	2.24	57.64
Pacific	4	64,108	2,888,440	2.22	45.91
South Atlantic	5	81,126	3,705,610	2.19	31.41
New England	6	18,786	865,929	2.17	21.90
East South Central	7	18,769	869,048	2.16	17.22
West South Central	8	39,952	1,860,120	2.15	11.51
Middle Atlantic	9	46,156	2,173,218	2.12	0.00

Source: Corporate Research Board, American Corporate Statistical Library (2007).

greatest variation is found in the lower-tier MSAs (ibid., Appendix D). Of this group, College Station, Pennsylvania, has 196 high-impact firms or 3.28 percent. The lowest is Danville, Virginia, with 266 high-impact firms or 1.8 percent.

High-impact firms' proximity to the central business district
The role that central business districts play in economic development and the growth of cities is an ongoing area of research. Of interest are the role of specialization versus diversity and of tolerance versus intolerance, as well as the role of density (Florida, 2002). Density is viewed as creating a fertile setting for the incubation of ideas, especially those that relate to innovation and productivity growth. So the location of high-impact firms with respect to the central business district is an interesting issue. Table 6.8a provides data on the share of high-impact firms located in metropolitan areas; these can be compared to low-impact firm locations (Table 6.8b).

There are four important observations. First, about 23 percent of high-impact firms are located in rural areas, and they exhibit a slight decline over time. This is a very high number; close to one-quarter of the firms that are important for growth are not located in metropolitan areas. Second, the percentage of high-impact firms located in the central business district has declined over the past 12 years, from 10.5 to 8.8 percent. The share of low-impact firms has likewise declined. Third, most high-impact firms are concentrated about 6 to 15 miles from the central business district. About 100,000 firms (close to one-third of the total) are in these concentric rings.

Table 6.8a   High-impact firm distribution by proximity to the central business district

Distance from central business district (miles)	1994–1998		1998–2002		2002–2006	
	Number	Percent	Number	Percent	Number	Percent
In CBD	36,758	10.48	28,085	9.38	33,249	8.84
1–5	31,771	9.06	27,547	9.20	33,966	9.03
6–10	59,279	16.90	50,357	16.82	63,458	16.88
11–15	35,154	10.02	31,476	10.52	39,269	10.45
16–20	26,307	7.50	23,018	7.69	30,169	8.02
21–25	27,998	7.98	24,197	8.08	30,383	8.08
26–30	15,579	4.44	13,507	4.51	18,014	4.79
31–35	10,377	2.96	9,661	3.23	12,866	3.42
36–40	10,180	2.90	8,941	2.99	11,046	2.94
41 or more	14,432	4.12	15,004	5.01	19,515	5.19
Rural	82,840	23.62	67,549	22.57	84,008	22.35

Source: Corporate Research Board, American Corporate Statistical Library (2007).

Table 6.8b   Low-impact firm distribution by proximity to the central business district

Distance from central business district (miles)	1994–1998		1998–2002		2002–2006	
	Number	Percent	Number	Percent	Number	Percent
In CBD	983,126	9.83	1,197,286	8.24	1,345,903	7.92
1–5	879,598	8.79	1,318,135	9.07	1,538,320	9.05
6–10	1,660,875	16.60	2,461,005	16.93	2,921,467	17.19
11–15	984,786	9.85	1,513,943	10.41	1,794,170	10.55
16–20	722,589	7.22	1,122,682	7.72	1,359,973	8.00
21–25	762,361	7.62	1,180,531	8.12	1,373,575	8.08
26–30	438,348	4.38	662,607	4.56	801,096	4.71
31–35	290,937	2.91	443,464	3.05	562,935	3.31
36–40	279,359	2.79	411,190	2.83	483,402	2.84
41 or more	434,649	4.35	714,863	4.92	877,225	5.16
Rural	2,566,109	25.65	3,513,281	24.16	3,941,502	23.19

Source: Corporate Research Board, American Corporate Statistical Library (2007).

Finally, the patterns of location of high- and low-impact firms are very similar; a discernible trend over the 12-year period is that both rural and central business districts appear to be losing firms to semi-rural areas.

What are high-impact firms like in their pre-growth phase?
Since it is clear that high-impact firms tend to be older rather than start-ups, the very interesting question arises, what do these firms look like before their growth surge? In the two and a half decades since the publication of Birch's work (1981), there has been an active line of research trying to answer questions about firm age, size, and growth (Dunne et al., 1989; Davis et al., 1996a and 1996b; and Acs and Armington, 2006). Data limitations and inconsistent theoretical models have hampered research in this area. In fact, Richard Caves (1998), in a review article described the efforts to sort out the empirical issues as an exercise in 'hunting and gathering' (p. 1947). One of the important issues in this chapter has been to try to get a better handle on where high-impact firms come from and what happens to them afterward. Perhaps the most important question has been the role of firm age.

Many theoretical models and empirical findings have suggested that firm age is important and that new firms grow faster than older firms. Moreover, it has been suggested that the timeline between a firm's birth and the point at which it starts to grow is almost instantaneous. This was articulated in Audretsch (1995) when he suggested that the 'trees-in-the-forest' metaphor of Marshall should be contrasted with the 'revolving door'. The trees-in-the-forest model suggests that firms will stay around for a long time and grow into high-impact firms. The revolving-door model suggests that firms enter and exit simultaneously, and some of these firms survive and grow.

To examine the question of what firms were before they became high-impact firms we classify them in six degrees of volatility:

- *Constant grower* The firm grew (had at least one job gain) in each two-year period of a four-year period of analysis.
- *Mixed grower* The firm grew in one two-year period of a four-year period of analysis, and declined or experienced no change during the other two-year period. The net result over four years was an increase.
- *Non-changer* The firm had zero change in each two-year period of a four-year period of analysis.
- *Volatile non-changer* The firm grew in one two-year period of a four-year period of analysis and declined in the other two-year period, with the overall four-year change netting out to zero.

Table 6.9a   *High-impact firm status and volatility in the preceding four years, 1994–1998*

	Firm size (number of employees)					
	1–19		20–499		500 plus	
	Number	%	Number	%	Number	%
Status						
Births	34,197	9.6	1,292	7.9	51	6.4
New listings	191,743	53.8	2,247	13.7	69	8.7
Growth	19,043	5.3	7,033	42.9	499	63.1
No change	70,166	19.7	4,479	27.3	70	8.8
Decline	41,582	11.7	1,334	8.1	102	12.9
High impact	4,894	1.4	2,131	13.0	192	24.3
Data missing	32	0.0	7	0.0	1	0.1
Volatility						
Constant growth	1,641	1.3	1,920	15.0	254	37.9
Mixed growth	17,047	13.2	5,024	39.3	242	36.1
Non-changer	66,857	51.7	4,370	34.2	70	10.4
Volatile non-changer	1,682	1.3	48	0.4	0	0.0
Mixed decline	40,188	31.1	1,303	10.2	83	12.4
Constant decline	1,870	1.4	129	1.0	21	3.1
Data missing	4,032	3.1	183	1.4	2	0.3

Source: Corporate Research Board, American Corporate Statistical Library (2007).

- *Mixed decliner*   The firm declined in one two-year period of a four-year period of analysis, grew or experienced no change during the other two-year period, and the net result over four years was a decrease.
- *Constant decliner*   The firm declined in each two-year period of a four-year period of analysis.

Next we identify all high-impact firms between the years 1998 and 2002 and divide them into three firm-size classes (1–19, 20–49, and 500-plus employees). Then we determine the status of these firms during the four-year period 1994–98. Tables 6.9a and 6.9b consider high- and low-impact firms in terms of growth status and volatility in the four years prior to the primary study period. Table 6.9a shows that 53 percent of the firms in the 1–19 firm-size class were born before 1994 but were not in the D&B file. (The term 'new listing' indicates that they existed before 1994 but entered

Table 6.9b   Low-impact firm status and volatility in the preceding four years, 1994–1998

| | Firm size (number of employees) | | | | | |
| | 1–19 | | 20–499 | | 500 plus | |
	Number	%	Number	%	Number	%
Status						
Births	786,148	6.6	26,457	3.7	692	3.1
New listing	5,808,553	48.4	116,583	16.3	1,389	6.1
Growth	884,417	7.4	243,481	34.1	11,331	50.0
No change	3,246,093	27.1	267,278	37.4	5,702	25.2
Decline	1,265,742	10.6	60,576	8.5	3,533	15.6
High impact	215,897	1.8	74,183	10.4	2,676	11.8
Data missing	27,383	0.2	22,254	3.1	1,881	8.3
Volatility						
Constant growth	57,151	1.1	38,553	7.0	2,938	15.7
Mixed growth	808,887	15.3	194,600	35.2	7,498	40.1
Non-changer	3,081,905	58.2	251,057	45.3	4,948	26.5
Volatile non-changer	64,541	1.2	2,237	0.4	84	0.4
Mixed decline	1,244,481	23.5	61,927	11.2	2,719	14.5
Constant decline	38,699	0.7	5,244	0.9	518	2.8
Data missing	151,087	2.9	11,008	2.0	148	0.8

Source: Corporate Research Board, American Corporate Statistical Library (2007).

the D&B file between 1994 and 1998.) Only 9 percent of the firms labeled 'high impact' in 1998–2002 were born between 1994 and 1998. A small portion, 1.4 percent or 4,894 firms, were high-growth firms in the 1994–98 period. The overwhelming majority of the small high-impact firms were born prior to 1994. As noted above, the average age of a high-impact firm for this firm-size class was 17.4 years (Table 6.3a).

Another interesting question is whether high-impact firms can be identified in the previous time period. The answer appears to be no. Table 6.9a identifies the volatility of the enterprises in the previous four-year period. In fact, 52 percent of firms exhibited no change in employment or revenue in the prior period, and 31 percent of enterprises were mixed decliners. In short, high-impact firms showed no signal or mixed signals as to their subsequent potential in the years preceding their growth surge. Table 6.9b provides comparable information for low-impact firms. The patterns of behavior of high- and low-impact firms are broadly similar.

The results are significantly different for the 20–499 firm-size class. First, 7.9 percent of high-impact firms in the study period were born in the previous four years and only 13 percent are new listings. Only 5.3 percent of the 1–19 firm-size class were growers, compared with 43 percent of the larger firm-size class. Only 1.4 percent of the 1–19 firm-size class were already high impact, but 13 percent of the 20–499 firm-size class were. Firms in the 1–19 firm-size class exhibited considerable volatility, but most of the larger firms (73 percent) were either mixed growers or non-changers. As noted earlier, the average age of high-impact firms in the 20–499 firm-size class is 24 years old (Table 6.3a). Among the largest firms (500-plus employees) fully 25 percent were already high-impact firms in the previous time period, and 63 percent were growth firms. Only 6.4 percent were born in the previous period. Volatility declines further for the 500-plus group: 38 percent experienced constant growth and 36 percent had mixed growth.

What happens to high-impact firms after their growth period?
What happens to high-impact firms in the years after their high-performance years? Do they remain in the high-impact firm category for a longer period of time, or do they move on to something else? Table 6.10a provides a glimpse into these questions by examining the four-year period (1998–2002) after our study period. We present comparable data to that found in Tables 6.9a and 6.9b for easy cross-referencing. The data in the bottom half of Tables 6.10a and 6.10b are smaller because the deaths and the high-impact firms have been eliminated.

Table 6.10a presents the status of 1–19 firm-size class of high-impact firms from 1998 to 2004, focusing on firm exit. If the earlier results are any indication of the symmetry of firm behavior, we would expect that firm exit would be higher for the smaller firm-size class than the larger ones. In fact after being classified as 'high impact' in 1998–2004, 6 percent exit the file two years later and another 4 percent exit by the end of four years. Another 60 percent exhibit no change. However, 2.4 percent remain high-impact firms. In fact, with the exception of a small number of firms that stay high impact or show mixed growth, most of the smallest firms exhibit some sort of decline. The results for the low-impact firms are even more striking, with more than one-quarter exiting (Table 6.10b). The results for the 20–499 firm-size class are similar to those for the 1–19 firm-size class, except that the exit rates are lower and almost 30 percent of the high-impact firms exhibit constant or mixed growth. Fifty percent showed no change.

There are important differences in the 500-plus firm-size class. First, the rate of high-impact firms that remain in a high-growth pattern is 8

Table 6.10a   *High-impact firm status and volatility after the study period, 2002–2006*

	Firm size (number of employees)					
	1–19		20–499		500 plus	
	Number	%	Number	%	Number	%
Status						
Deaths within 2 years	15,564	5.9	691	3.4	36	3.1
Deaths within 2–4 years	10,445	4.0	500	2.5	21	1.8
Growth	34,553	13.1	5,445	27.1	530	45.3
No change	160,499	60.9	9,667	48.1	282	24.1
Decline	42,651	16.2	3,784	18.8	301	25.7
High impact	6,419	2.4	703	3.5	95	8.1
Missing data	407	0.2	35	0.2	6	0.5
Volatility						
Constant growth	3,672	1.6	1,235	6.6	267	24.2
Mixed growth	30,478	12.9	4,175	22.2	260	23.6
Non-changer	158,814	67.2	9,536	50.8	275	24.9
Volatile non-changer	1,058	0.4	75	0.4	7	0.6
Mixed decline	40,395	17.1	3,343	17.8	201	18.2
Constant decline	1,969	0.8	401	2.1	93	8.4
Missing data	994	0.4	105	0.6	4	0.4

Source: Corporate Research Board, American Corporate Statistical Library (2007).

percent, more than double the rate for the smaller firm-size classes. In fact the number of firms that remain high-impact firms is larger than the number that exit after four years. Moreover, almost 50 percent exhibit either constant or mixed growth, and almost 75 percent of surviving firms exhibit no decline. A comparison of the survival of large high- and low-impact firms (Tables 6.10a and 6.10b) shows two discernible differences. First, the rate of constant growers is 25 percent for high-impact firms and only 8 percent for low-impact firms. Second, the rate of non-changers is twice as large for low-impact firms. Clearly, being a high-impact firm in the previous four years has a significant impact on firm performance in the subsequent four years, and the effect is more evident as firm-size class increases.

*Table 6.10b   Low-impact firm status and volatility after the study period,
2002–2006*

	Firm size (number of employees)					
	1–19		20–499		500 plus	
	Number	%	Number	%	Number	%
Status						
Deaths within 2 years	1,190,267	10.4	46,448	6.7	883	4.0
Deaths within 2–4 years	1,793,290	15.7	25,022	3.6	519	2.4
Growth	1,171,409	10.2	112,274	16.2	5,872	26.7
No change	6,385,655	55.9	391,769	56.6	10,107	45.9
Decline	890,504	7.8	116,948	16.9	4,646	21.1
High impact	354,395	3.1	15,912	2.3	698	3.2
Missing data	68,684	0.6	25,530	3.7	1,863	8.5
Volatility						
Constant growth	63,756	0.8	12,671	2.1	1,488	8.0
Mixed growth	1,071,988	13.0	88,803	15.0	3,964	21.2
Non-changer	6,169,259	75.0	380,294	64.1	8,840	47.3
Volatile non-changer	48,990	0.6	2,257	0.4	101	0.5
Mixed decline	845,524	10.3	101,212	17.1	3,447	18.4
Constant decline	25,175	0.3	8,128	1.4	861	4.6
Missing data	174,374	2.1	3,354	0.6	99	0.5

Source: Corporate Research Board, American Corporate Statistical Library (2007).

Do 'decliners' cancel out the contribution of high-impact firms?

How many dramatically declining firms exist that might cancel out the positive effect of high-growth companies in a given time period? Table 6.11 provides details on the decliners by both firm-size class and year. When we compare Table 6.11 with Table 6.1, we can see that, for example, there were 327,397 high-impact firms in the 1–19 employee firm-size class between 1994 and 1998. The decliners for that period were 90,016. So the net effect was 237,381. For each four-year period and each firm-size class, job creation was greater than the job destruction.

We next calculate the net employment effect of high-impact firms. In Table 6.12, (a) shows the gross employment change from high-impact firms aggregated from the 12 years calculated from Table 6.1; (b) shows the gross decline from fast decliners; and (c) shows the net change. The

Table 6.11   Dramatically declining firms

Employment size range	Period	Number of firms	Job change	Revenue change ($1,000s)
1–19	1994–1998	90,016	−498,161	−45,199,711
	1998–2002	64,422	−364,207	−35,969,588
	2002–2006	61,613	−366,674	−41,777,878
20–499	1994–1998	22,228	−902,145	−110,247,248
	1998–2002	18,641	−725,416	−119,861,091
	2002–2006	26,224	−1,097,147	−389,814,740
500 plus	1994–1998	737	−1,275,384	−177,153,624
	1998–2002	775	−1,602,940	−281,123,106
	2002–2006	867	−1,927,681	−623,710,585

Source: Corporate Research Board, American Corporate Statistical Library (2007).

Table 6.12   Net employment change from gazelles

<500	500+	Total	Percent <500
(a) Gazelle employment growth during the 3 periods			
18,546,390	13,660,433	32,206,823	57.6%
(b) Fast decliner employment lost during the 3 periods			
3,953,750	4,806,005	8,759,755	45.1%
(c) Net employment change = fast growth – fast decliners			
4,592,640	8,854,428	23,447,068	62.2%

Source: Corporate Research Board, American Corporate Statistical Library (2007).

most interesting finding is that small firms with fewer than 500 employees account for 57 percent of gross job creation and 62 percent of net job creation because large firms lose more employment. However, most of the firms that have more than 500 employees all have fewer than 5,000 employees.

CONTINUOUS PERFORMERS

What happens to high-impact companies after their high-performance years? To answer this question, we identified high-impact companies in the 1998–2002 period and tracked their performance over the subsequent four-year period of analysis (2002–06). We found that 7,217 firms continued to perform as high-impact companies. Given their exceptional performance from 1998 to 2006, this section takes a look at the disposition of these back-to-back high-impact companies as of the 2002–06 study period.

Of the 7,217 back-to-back high-impact companies, 6,419 had 1–19 employees at the start of the 1998–2002 period, 703 had 20–499 employees, and 95 had 500 or more employees. Tables 6.10a and b look at the disposition of these companies by employee-size segment and firm age at the end of the 2002–06 period. Of the 6,419 back-to-back high-impact companies, 3,132 (or about 50 percent) were 13–19 years old at the end of the 2002–06 period. Nearly 50 companies were acquired during the 2002–06 period and 162 died during the same period.

Of the 703 back-to-back high-impact companies that had 20–499 employees at the start of the 1998–2002 period, 254 (or about 35 percent) were 20–29 years old at the end of the 2002–06 period. And of the 500-plus companies, about 30 percent were 30–59 years old at the end of the most recent study period. Across all employee-size segments, about 80–90 percent of back-to-back high-impact companies were 13–59 years old at the end of the 2002–06 period.

We next show the disposition of back-to-back high-impact companies by employee-size segment and firm size at the end of the 2002–06 period. Of the 6,419 companies with 1–19 employees at the start of the 1998–2002 period, 82 had 1–4 employees at the end of the 2002–06 period. Another 2,315 had 5–19 employees. Most of the remaining firms had more than 19 employees, with the largest share employing 20–99 employees at the end of the most recent study period. Across all employee-size segments, 37 percent of back-to-back high-impact companies with 1–19 employees at the start of the 1998–2002 period still had 1–19 employees at the end of the 2002–06 period. By contrast, about 70 percent of back-to-back companies with 20–499 employees and 90 percent of companies with 500 or more employees still had 20–499 and 500 or more employees, respectively, at the end of the same period.

What is the disposition of back-to-back high-impact companies by employee-size segment and industry? Across all employee-size segments, the professional services industry contains the largest share of companies. Of the companies that had 1–19 employees at the start of the 1998–2002 period, about 24 percent were in the professional services industry. About 25 percent of companies with 20–499 employees and 17 percent of companies with 500 or more employees were in the same industry. The construction industry contained the second largest share of back-to-back companies with 1–19 and 20–499 employees, though not with 500 or more employees. It was the finance, insurance, and real estate industry that contained the second largest share of companies with 500 or more employees.

To sum up their performance, high-impact companies have had a remarkable 14 years. On average, they created about 10.7 million jobs in each of the four periods of analysis. Across all periods, the US economy would have lost about 16.3 million jobs had it not been for their contribution. High-impact companies are not only remarkable job generators. They are also efficient operators. On average, in every industry, employee-size segment, and period of analysis, they generated more revenue with the same share of human capital inputs.

CONCLUSION

The purpose of this study was to revisit earlier conclusions about the role of high-impact firms in the economy. First, we use the Business Information Tracking System (BITS) data to examine the role different types of entrants play over time. We find that different entrants have different trajectories with respect to job creation, with the 20–499 firm-size class exhibiting sustained job growth. However, the BITS database is not accessible enough to examine these high-impact firms in greater detail. To better understand the role of these high-potential firms in the economy, we used the American Corporate Statistical Library (ACSL), a database that contains over 130 variables on more than 18 million firms in the United States. By using the ACSL we are able to identify and track high-impact firms over a 12-year period from January 1, 1994, to January 1, 2006.

The results of this study shed light on the characteristics of high-impact firms and changes over time. Our results find consistencies with Birch's work and similar studies, namely that high-impact firms appear to account for the lion's share of the employment and revenue growth in the economy. Job creation is almost evenly split among small high-impact firms (fewer than 500 employees) and large ones (500-plus employees), with small firms creating about half the jobs and large ones creating the other half. Low-impact firms do not grow on average. Almost all of the job loss in the economy over any four-year period comes from the large low-impact firms. We found that the average high-impact firm while younger than all firms is not a new start-up; instead, the average age is around 17 years old and the median age is around 13 years old. These firms have been around for a long time before they make a significant impact on the economy.

Less than 3 percent of high-impact firms were born in the previous four-year period. Almost one-quarter of all high-impact firms in the study period had been high-impact firms during the previous four-year period as well. In other words, some enterprises have been doubling their revenues and adding jobs over an eight-year period. This trend accelerates among the largest firm-size class. Thus super high-impact firms account for a small percentage of firms but they still number in the thousands. In the four years after our study period, only about 3 percent of the high-impact firms died. Most continued and exhibited at least some growth. Most high-impact firms are not small or young. Therefore, we find little support for the original Birch findings with respect to firm age.

How can economic development policy affect these high-potential firms? The study should help us better understand economic policy that focuses on economic development. Local economic development officials should recognize the value of cultivating high-growth firms versus trying to increase entrepreneurship overall or trying to attract relocating companies when utilizing their resources.

ACKNOWLEDGMENT

The author gratefully acknowledges data and insights from Spencer Tracy and William Parsons of the Corporate Research Board and comments from Brian Headd. The author fully acknowledges financial support from the US Small Business Administration, Office of Advocacy (contract number SBAHQ-06-Q-0014).

NOTES

1. The Birch study did not distinguish between new jobs in a new plant (new jobs in an existing firm's new location) and new jobs in a plant set up by a newly started firm. By introducing this distinction, the US Small Business Administration (1983) found that 53 percent instead of 82 percent of new jobs were created by firms with fewer than 100 employees in the 1976–82 period.
2. See, for example, Jovanovic (1982), Lambson (1991), Hopenhayn (1992), Katsoulacos (1994), Dopfer (1995), and Ericson and Pakes (1995).
3. Davis and Haltiwanger (1992) examined job reallocation behavior and the passive learning story within the manufacturing sector. While learning about initial conditions provided a plausible explanation for the sharp and pervasive relationship between job reallocation rates and plant age, on the more fundamental matter of explaining the overall magnitude of job reallocation, the passive learning story is far less successful. Learning about initial conditions accounts for a small portion (11 to 13 percent) of total job reallocation.
4. Also see Fritsch and Mueller (2004); Acs and Mueller (2008); Mueller et al. (2008).
5. The number of new jobs necessary for firms of different sizes to achieve an EGQ of two or more are as follows:

Initial firm size	Minimum job increase necessary to achieve EGQ of 2 or more
1–4 jobs	2
5–7 jobs	3
8–12 jobs	4
13–17 jobs	5
18–24 jobs	6
25–31 jobs	7
32–40 jobs	8
41–49 jobs	9
20,000 jobs	200

6. The index value varies from 100 to zero for the percent of high-impact firms.

REFERENCES

Acs, Z.J. and C. Armington (2006), *Entrepreneurship, Geography and American Economic Growth*, Cambridge, MA: Cambridge University Press.
Acs, Z.J. and P. Mueller (2008), 'Employment effects of business dynamics: mice, gazelles and elephants', *Small Business Economics*, **30**, 85–100.
Acs, Z.J., W. Parsons and S. Tracy (2008), *High Impact Firms: Gazelles Revisited*, Office of Advocacy, US Small Business Administration, Washington, DC.
Audretsch, D. (1995), *Innovation and Industry Evolution*, Cambridge, MA: MIT Press.
Birch, D.L. (1981), 'Who creates jobs?', *The Public Interest*, **65**, 3–14.
Birch, D.L., A. Haggerty and W. Parsons (1995), *Who's Creating Jobs?*, Boston, MA: Cognetics Inc.
Birch, D.L. and J. Medoff (1994), 'Gazelles', in Lewis C. Solmon and Alec R. Levenson (eds), *Labor Markets, Employment Policy and Job Creation*, Boulder, CO: Westview Press, pp. 159–68.
Caves, R. (1998), 'Industrial organization and new findings on the turnover and mobility of firms', *Journal of Economic Literature*, **36**, 1947–82.
Davis, S. and J. Haltiwanger (1992), 'Gross job creation, gross job destruction, and employment reallocation', *Quarterly Journal of Economics*, **107**, 819–63.
Davis, S. and J. Haltiwanger (1999), 'Gross job flows', in Orley Ashenfelter and David E. Card (eds), *Handbook of Labor Economics*, Volume 3B, Amsterdam: Elsevier Science, pp. 2101–939.
Davis, S., J. Haltiwanger and S. Schuh (1996a), *Job Creation and Destruction*, Cambridge, MA: MIT Press.
Davis, S., J. Haltiwanger and S. Schuh (1996b), 'Small business and job creation: dissecting the myth and reassessing the facts', *Small Business Economics*, **8**, 297–315.
Dertouzos, L.M., R.K. Lester and R.M. Solow (1989), *Made in America*, Cambridge, MA: MIT Press.
Dopfer, K. (1995), Special issue: 'Global economic evolution: knowledge variety and diffusion in economic growth and development', *Journal of Evolutionary Economics*, **5**, 181–339.
Dunne, T., M. Roberts and L. Samuelson (1989), 'The growth and failure of US manufacturing plants', *Quarterly Journal of Economics*, **104**, 671–98.
Ericson, R. and A. Pakes (1995), 'Markov-perfect industry dynamics: a framework for empirical work', *Review of Economic Studies*, **62**, 53–82.
Evans, D. (1987), 'Tests of alternative theories of firm growth', *Journal of Political Economy*, **95**, 657–74.

Florida, R. (2002), *The Rise of the Creative Class*, New York: Basic Books.
Fritsch, M. and P. Mueller (2004), 'The effects of new business formation on regional development over time', *Regional Studies*, **38**, 961–75.
Glaeser, E., H. Kallal, J. Scheinkman and A. Shleifer (1992), 'Growth in cities', *Journal of Political Economy*, **100**, 1126–52.
Haltiwanger, J., R. Jarmin and J. Miranda (2010), 'Who creates jobs? Small vs. large vs. young', NBER Working Paper 16300, National Bureau of Economic Research, Cambridge, MA, August.
Haltiwanger, J., L.M. Lynch and C. Mackie (eds) (2007), *Understanding Business Dynamics*, Committee on National Statistics, National Research Council, Washington, DC: National Academies Press.
Henrekson, M. and D. Johansson (2010), 'Gazelles as job creators: a survey and interpretation of the evidence', *Small Business Economics*, **35**, 227–44.
Hopenhayn, H. (1992), 'Entry, exit and firm dynamics in long run equilibrium', *Econometrica*, **60**, 1127–50.
Jacobs, J. (1969), *The Economy of Cities*, New York: Vintage Books.
Jovanovic, B. (1982), 'Selection and the evolution of industry', *Econometrica*, **50**, 649–70.
Katsoulacos, Y. (1994), Special issue: 'Evolutionary and Neoclassical Perspectives on Market Structure and Economic Growth', *Evolutionary Economics*, **4**, 151–271.
Lambson, V. (1991), 'Industry evolution with sunk costs and uncertain market conditions', *International Journal of Industrial Organization*, **9**, 171–98.
Lee, S.Y., R. Florida and Z.J. Acs (2004), 'Creativity and entrepreneurship: a regional analysis of new firm formation', *Regional Studies*, **38**, 879–91.
Lucas, R.E. Jr. (1978), 'On the size distribution of business firms', *Bell Journal of Economics*, **9**, 508–23.
Lucas, R.E. Jr. and E.C. Prescott (1971), 'Investment under uncertainty', *Econometrica*, **39**, 659–81.
Mueller, P., A. van Stel and D.J. Storey (2008), 'The effects of new firm formation on regional development over time: the case of Great Britain', *Small Business Economics*, **30**, 59–71.
Parsons, W. and S. Tracy (2005), *American Corporate Statistical Library*, Washington, DC: Corporate Research Board, LLC.
Porter, M. (1990), *The Competitive Advantage of Nations*, New York: Free Press.
Shane, S. (2008), *The Illusion of Entrepreneurship*, New Haven, CT: Yale University Press.
Sutton, J. (1997), 'Gibrat's legacy', *Journal of Economic Literature*, **35**, 40–59.
US Small Business Administration (SBA) (1983), *The State of Small Business: A Report to the President*, Washington, DC.
US Small Business Administration (SBA) (2006), *The Small Business Economy: A Report to the President*, Washington, DC: US Government Printing Office. Chapter 6, 'Economic gardening: next generation applications for a balanced portfolio approach to economic growth', pp. 132–57.

APPENDIX 6A

Table 6A.1   Distribution of high-impact firms by state

State	Rank	Number of high-impact firms	Total firms	Percent high-impact firms	Index value
Alaska	1	1,117	40,468	2.76	100.00
Arizona	2	7,463	290,687	2.57	77.11
Wyoming	3	988	38,801	2.55	74.61
South Carolina	4	5,252	206,531	2.54	74.21
North Dakota	5	1,108	44,636	2.48	67.01
Virginia	6	9,284	376,337	2.47	65.18
Pennsylvania	7	14,147	577,328	2.45	63.22
Washington, DC	8	1,092	44,728	2.44	62.15
Rhode Island	9	1,297	53,625	2.42	59.45
Wisconsin	10	6,832	282,737	2.42	59.18
Montana	11	1,773	73,942	2.40	56.98
Ohio	12	12,878	541,169	2.38	54.82
Washington	13	8,919	376,102	2.37	53.84
New Mexico	14	2,313	97,713	2.37	53.33
Maine	15	1,836	77,867	2.36	52.23
North Carolina	16	11,253	479,124	2.35	51.14
Maryland	17	7,330	313,585	2.34	49.81
Idaho	18	2,458	105,246	2.34	49.58
West Virginia	19	1,591	68,188	2.33	49.31
South Dakota	20	1,300	56,067	2.32	47.58
Oregon	21	5,832	252,048	2.31	47.01
Hawaii	22	1,410	61,062	2.31	46.45
Minnesota	23	7,323	317,897	2.30	45.79
Vermont	24	1,005	43,842	2.29	44.45
Tennessee	25	7,016	306,755	2.29	43.84
Kansas	26	3,683	161,411	2.28	43.20
Delaware	27	979	43,086	2.27	42.06
Alabama	28	4,823	212,298	2.27	42.02
Colorado	29	7,928	350,608	2.26	40.76
Missouri	30	6,891	304,981	2.26	40.55
New Hampshire	31	1,891	84,329	2.24	38.53
Louisiana	32	5,677	253,725	2.24	37.94
Nebraska	33	2,409	108,349	2.22	36.27
New Jersey	34	10,300	463,976	2.22	35.86
Illinois	35	13,443	607,417	2.21	35.05
Utah	36	3,778	171,195	2.21	34.30
Indiana	37	6,777	307,631	2.20	33.84

Table 6A.1   (continued)

State	Rank	Number of high-impact firms	Total firms	Percent high-impact firms	Index value
Arkansas	38	3,077	140,945	2.18	31.49
California	39	46,830	2,158,760	2.17	29.85
Oklahoma	40	3,993	184,085	2.17	29.82
Massachusetts	41	8,098	378,452	2.14	26.34
Texas	42	27,205	1,281,365	2.12	24.36
Nevada	43	3,192	153,594	2.08	19.03
Michigan	44	11,006	531,023	2.07	18.37
Iowa	45	4,181	202,212	2.07	17.78
Florida	46	32,078	1,556,496	2.06	16.98
Mississippi	47	2,822	137,086	2.06	16.70
Connecticut	48	4,659	227,814	2.05	15.10
Georgia	49	12,267	617,535	1.99	8.14
Kentucky	50	4,108	212,909	1.93	1.37
New York	51	21,709	1,131,914	1.92	0.00

Source: Corporate Research Board, American Corporate Statistical Library (2007).

7 Firm growth, institutions, and structural transformation

Magnus Henrekson and Dan Johansson

INTRODUCTION

For a long time, large firms were considered to create new employment and economic growth, mainly due to economies of scale in production as well as in research and development (for example, Schumpeter, 1942; Galbraith, 1956, 1967). This conventional wisdom was challenged by Birch (1979) who in an empirical investigation claimed small firms to be the main job generators. Birch's results and his conclusions have been questioned and sparked up a debate; see Kirchhoff and Greene (1998) for a review of the discussion. Van Praag and Versloot (2008) summarize the empirical evidence on job creation by small firms, and conclude (p. 135) that it is an unambiguous result that small firms create more jobs on net than large firms, even when the methodology suggested by the critics is applied. Subsequent research shows that a fairly small number of high-growth firms (HGFs) – on average smaller and younger than other firms – contribute the bulk of net employment; see Henrekson and Johansson (2010) for a survey.

This chapter has its starting point in a generally overlooked part of the critique that certain firms – be they small, young or rapidly growing – are of particular importance for job creation and economic growth. This critique asserts that growth has to be understood in a broader perspective entailing considerable churning and restructuring (for example, Haltiwanger and Krizan, 1999).[1] In fact, rapid growth of some firms implies that they attract factors of production from other firms. Growth therefore requires contraction and exit of some firms to free up resources that can be reallocated to expanding firms. Entry and expansion are flipsides to exit and contraction. The process through which the factors of production are put into different use defines structural transformation.

It may therefore be misleading to simply focus on a particular piece of this process and claim that it alone contributes a disproportionately large share towards net job growth. This is not to refute that some type of firms may be more productive than others in creating new jobs and contributing to economic growth, in the same way that some entrepreneurs are more successful than others. In fact, the critique is in concordance with Schumpeter's (1942) description of capitalism as a process of creative destruction where novel ideas continuously challenge old structures, thereby giving rise to structural transformation when new successful innovations, products, firms, and industries arise while obsolete ones decline and vanish. It is also in line with evidence from recent research showing that the employment effect of new firm entry tends to follow a 'wave pattern'. Initially, employment increases due to hiring by entering firms, composing the direct effect. Thereafter employment declines as a result of exits by both failed newcomers and crowding out of incumbent firms that have lower productivity levels than the successful newcomers. Finally, positive supply-side effects increase employment in the long run (Fritsch and Mueller, 2004; Fritsch and Noseleit, 2009). Accordingly, the conditions for structural transformation are decisive for economic growth. Empirical studies point out HGFs[2] – or high-impact firms as Acs (ch. 6 in this volume) puts it – to be the main drivers of this process, which motivates in-depth analyses of HGFs.

Despite the heterogeneity across the studies in several dimensions, Henrekson and Johansson (2010) conclude that some general findings emerge:

- All studies report HGFs to be crucial for net job growth compared to non-HGFs. They generate a large share of all, or more than all (in the case where employment shrinks in non-HGFs), new net jobs. This is particularly pronounced in recessions when HGFs continue to grow, while non-HGFs decline or exit.
- Several studies, particularly the ones concerning the US, find that HGFs provide a large share of new net jobs relative to total job growth in the economy and total unemployment.
- Small firms are overrepresented among HGFs, but HGFs are of all sizes. In particular, larger firms are important job contributors in absolute terms. A small subgroup of large HGFs – sometimes called 'superstars' or 'super gazelles' – are major job creators.
- Age is of great importance. All studies reporting firm age conclude that HGFs are younger, on average. Super gazelles are also relatively young. HGFs are overrepresented in young and growing industries with a large inflow of new firms.
- Young and small HGFs grow organically to a larger extent than large and old HGFs, and therefore make a larger contribution to net employment growth.
- HGFs are present in all industries. There is no evidence that they are overrepresented in high-tech industries. If anything, HGFs appear to be overrepresented in service industries.

On the basis of this meta-analysis, we conclude that HGFs are instrumental to economic growth and net job creation, in particular those HGFs that start growing rapidly when young and small.

The purpose of this chapter is to discuss institutions and policies conducive to the expansion of HGFs and therefore to structural transformation. We use North's (1990, p. 3) definition of institutions: 'the rules of the game in society, or more formally, the humanly devised constraints that shape human interaction'.

Institutions can be both formal – 'hard' – (laws and regulations) and informal – 'soft' – (habits, norms, conventions, and so on). Here we almost exclusively deal with formal institutions. This is not to deny that informal institutions such as networks, culture, codes of conduct, and trust are also very important. Although limiting the analysis to formal institutions is admittedly a simplification, it is of less concern than one would expect for a number of reasons, for instance because informal institutions are harder both to enact and to analyze, and since informal rules are not imposed through explicit political/collective decisions they cannot be directly influenced by policy.[3]

Obviously, the institutions we analyze in this chapter also affect the non-HGFs. However, we still believe that it is warranted to focus on the HGFs. The reason is straightforward: if certain institutions affect HGFs relatively strongly and if HGFs are of crucial importance, then the effect of institutions on HGFs is of particular relevance for growth. At first sight, this seems to contradict the story concerning the direct and the indirect effects of new business formation on growth since the development of HGFs represents only the direct effect. However, strong start-ups represent a rather serious challenge for the incumbents and thereby induce indirect effects (Fritsch and Noseleit, 2009).

We use Schumpeter's (1934) theory of economic development as a starting point for the analysis. Long-run growth results from the introduction and diffusion of profitable new combinations – novel ideas – into the economic system. Schumpeter emphasized this to be a human-driven process and recognized inventors, entrepreneurs, creditors, and imitators to be key actors – each one performing a crucial economic function. We identify the constellation of actors with different but complementary competencies necessary to generate large-scale economic development and structural transformation.

Thereafter, we integrate institutional theory into the analysis. Institutions, and in particular private property rights, shape the incentives of economic actors and the functioning of markets. Modern societies are rich webs of formal and informal institutions that differ greatly. A complete analysis of the effects of institutions on HGFs and structural transformation is therefore an immense task, which is beyond the scope of this chapter. In three subsequent sections, we address three institutional systems identified as hampering HGFs and structural transformation. In what follows we shall in turn deal with the effect on potential HGFs and structural transformation of institutions affecting freedom of enterprising – as in the right and opportunity for the different types of actors to establish enterprises producing goods and services with the objective to make a profit, institutions governing the labor market, and the tax system. The chapter ends with some concluding remarks.

THE CRUCIAL AGENTS AND THEIR COMPETENCIES

Wealth, measured as gross domestic product (GDP) per capita, has developed slowly – if at all – for all but the most recent part of the history of humankind. The Industrial Revolution broke this trend in development and since then wealth has surged (Figure 7.1).

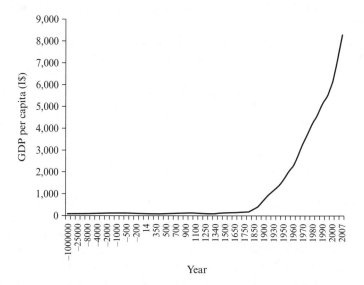

Sources: De Long/Kremer data from −1000000 to 1985 (extension of Maddison's estimates; Kremer, 1993), Maddison data from 1985 to 2005 (GDP per capita, 1990 International Dollars; Maddison, 2009), World Bank data for 2007 (GDP per capita, US$) from http://web.worldbank.org/WBSITE/EXTERNAL/DATASTATISTICS/0,,menuPK:2 32599~pagePK:64133170~piPK:64133498~theSitePK:239419,00.html.

Figure 7.1   Gross domestic product per capita for all history of humankind

In this chapter, we deal with two main explanations that have been put forward to explain this historical shift:

- First, the accumulation and use of new productive knowledge including a far-driven division and specialization of labor (Smith, 1776).
- Second, the establishment and protection of private property rights (North and Thomas, 1973; Rosenberg and Birdzell, 1986; Mokyr, 1990; Jones, 2001; Acemoglu et al., 2005).

Relating to the first point, Schumpeter (1934) asserts that producing the same goods in the same way results in a stagnant economy. *Change* is therefore a central concept for Schumpeter's theory and the purpose of his seminal book is to present a theory of economic development explaining change – and economic growth – as an endogenous process.[4] Change emanates from the generation, introduction, and dissemination of novel ideas on how to combine resources more efficiently.[5] Schumpeter distinguishes between novel ideas – inventions – and the introduction of these ideas into the economy – innovations. Economic development is defined as putting new combinations into use.[6] It is an endogenous process since it is driven by actors within the economic system. Schumpeter identifies four actors as critical according to the economic *function* they carry out: inventors who come up with novel ideas, entrepreneurs who introduce new combinations into the economic system, creditors who finance the enterprises of the entrepreneurs, and imitators who disseminate innovations through copying and commercializing them in competing firms. Hence, in order to achieve large-scale industrial growth, a set of actors with different but complementary competencies is required to generate, identify, select, and exploit new combinations.[7]

We extend Schumpeter's list and identify six key categories of actors:

1. *Inventors* fulfill the same function as in Schumpeter's theory. They have detailed knowledge about products and solve specific problems of a technical as well as an organizational and economic nature.
2. *Entrepreneurs* identify novel ideas about new combinations and introduce those with expected profitability into the market. They may be characterized as agents of change and fulfill a fundamental coordinating and judgmental function.[8] Compared to Schumpeter, the entrepreneur plays a more restricted role. Part of his/her function is carried out by the industrialists.
3. *Industrialists* are active after the entrepreneurial phase and organize the further commercialization of the innovation into large-scale businesses. They carry out the function of the Schumpeterian entrepreneur in later phases and the function of the Schumpeterian imitator.

The reason for unraveling the entrepreneurial function is that there is empirical evidence that the introduction of new ideas into the economy and the subsequent development of the original innovations into large-scale businesses generally require two separate competencies (Flamholtz, 1986; Baumol, 2004). Like in Schumpeter's theory, one individual can carry out more than one function, and the original entrepreneur may evolve into an industrialist.

4. *Financiers* supply capital in the form of equity or loans. We recognize the empirical evidence establishing the importance of distinct categories of investors specializing in investing in different phases of the life cycle of HGFs. We therefore prefer the term 'financiers' before the term 'creditors' to encompass these actors. In addition to capital, financiers provide management skills, industry-specific knowledge, and access to business networks necessary for rapid firm growth. *Venture capitalists* supply enterprises in early phases of business ventures with capital and *actors in the secondary markets* carry out similar functions, but at a later stage when entrepreneurs and venture capitalists want to exit from their investments. There are several types of actors in secondary markets, notably portfolio investors in publicly listed companies, private equity (PE) firms, and management buy-ins. Research also identifies *business angels* as providing a similar role as venture capitalists, but in an earlier phase.[9]

5. *Skilled labor* Economic development and economic growth require labor with relevant professional skills. The lack of individuals with specific skills may become a bottleneck for further expansion of HGFs and dampen structural transformation.

6. *Competent customers* provide the entrepreneur with information about their preferences. The ability to discern the preferences of the customers, so that highly valued goods and services are produced, is a key ingredient in successful entrepreneurship; see von Hippel (2007) and Bhidé (2008) for recent examples. Competent customers should be representative of large groups of customers and can be both firms and individuals. Large enterprises can also function as competent financiers and finance the development of particular products, as exemplified by the biotechnology industry (for example, Lerner and Merges, 1998; Audretsch and Feldman, 2003).

The actors start firms to exploit business ideas, and innovations are commercialized in both new and established firms. If the actors are successful their firms expand, but if they fail to generate sustainable profits their firms exit. Figure 7.2 schematically summarizes the role of the various actors in the process of fostering HGFs. The figure provides a

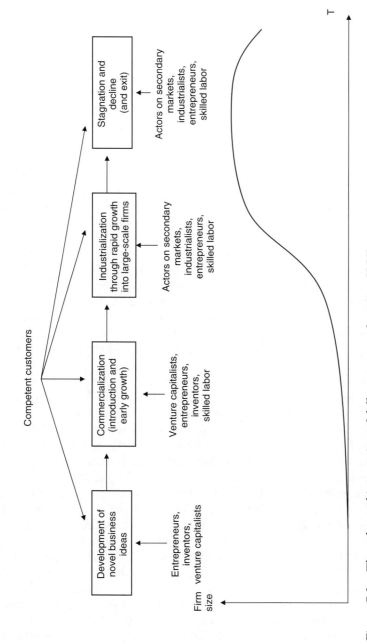

Figure 7.2   The roles and interaction of different actors fostering HGFs

181

stylized representation of the categories of actors needed in the various growth phases of HGFs (the development of a business idea, introduction, early growth, and rapid growth into a large-scale firm). Some categories may be important in several phases and a certain individual can fulfill several functions either simultaneously or at different points in the individual's or firm's life cycle. In a stylized form, the development of rapidly growing firms may be depicted as an S-shaped curve. Most HGFs do not display sustained growth, but follow a more complex pattern (Parker et al., 2010). The figure shows at which stage of a firm's growth different categories play a key role. The order in which the categories appear beneath the boxes indicates which actor has the main coordinating responsibility.

This is not a definite ranking, and in practice it differs across enterprises, but a stylized depiction of what we believe is the typical situation. In the first phase, entrepreneurs together with competent customers identify potential business opportunities. Inventors are engaged to solve specific problems. The first phase of commercialization (introduction and early growth of firms) involves entrepreneurs, while skilled workers are involved to a small extent only. Industrialists are active in the phase of industrialization and rapid growth, which also requires a great deal of skilled labor. Venture capitalists are important financiers in the earlier phases. In later phases when the firm is larger, this role is taken over by actors in secondary markets. Competent customers are typically involved in all phases and ultimately (together with other customers) determine the demand for the good.

The economic activities of the actors give rise to a dynamic process of creative destruction – channeled via firm entry, expansion, contraction, and exit – which brings about structural transformation in the perennial struggle between new and old structures. In what follows we focus on the effects of institutions on the establishment, growth and exit of HGFs. We aim to answer the question: how should institutions be designed to promote HGFs?

Our approach relates to the literature on 'technological regimes' pioneered by Winter (1984). In particular, a distinction has been made between 'entrepreneurial' and 'routinized' regimes (Audretsch, 1995). An entrepreneurial regime is found to apply in early stages of a product or industry life cycle, where knowledge is new and dispersed, development is driven by product innovation, firm entry, and entrepreneurship, while scale economies are of minor importance. By contrast, a routinized regime applies to later stages of an industry or a product life cycle, when products and knowledge have become more standardized. In this regime, scale economies and process innovation hold center stage, and large incumbent firms tend to predominate. The entrepreneurial regime relates to the early phases of the process of creative destruction when novel ideas are introduced and new technologies are discovered. The routinized regime relates to the later phases when the technologies are exploited. In the later phase, the industry has probably undergone a period of shake-out and is dominated by a small number of firms (see Klepper and Simons, 2005).

Audretsch and Fritsch (2002), Fritsch (2004) and Fritsch and Mueller (2006) have extended the use of the regimes concept to geographical units, notably regions, the idea being that the mode of production in a certain region may be distinct from the dominant modes of production in other regions. This suggests that regional growth may be spurred by different kinds of economic policies depending on the knowledge conditions underlying the industries represented in different regions.

Linking to our analysis, regional regime is not a choice variable; it can rather be seen as the outcome of a historical process of structural transformation and is therefore strongly path dependent. This is all the more clear since the formal institutional set-up is for the most part national rather than regional, and yet there could exist large regional differences in technological regimes.[10] Hence, the concept of regional growth regimes provides a good *ex post* characterization of how the production system has evolved in a particular region. We believe that our approach complements the concept of growth regimes and provides a useful tool for policy guidance, since it focuses on the interaction and complementarity of different categories of key actors necessary to build an HGF and their incentives.

FREEDOM OF ENTERPRISING AND/OR THE REGULATION OF PRODUCT MARKETS

Since HGFs are prime movers of structural transformation, we begin by discussing the effect of free enterprising restrictions on the prevalence of HGFs. By free enterprising we mean the right to establish profit-seeking firms producing goods and services. This gives consumers the option to buy preferred quantities and qualities at offered prices from different suppliers. In recent decades, developed countries have experienced a wave of deregulations aimed at increasing the contestability of markets and providing more opportunities for private entrepreneurship, for example, in telecommunications, transportation, and financial services. This can be expected to lead to greater scope for the emergence of HGFs.

However, one central segment of many advanced economies remains heavily regulated and in some cases even monopolized by the public sector: the provision of private-good social services such as health care,

care of children and the elderly, and education. The social benefits from further deregulations fostering HGFs in these areas are likely to be substantial (although the difficulties arising from asymmetric information and moral hazard are no doubt often greater here than in other areas). These industries already constitute a considerable share of GDP: about 20 percent of GDP in the OECD, and even more (about 30 percent) in the Scandinavian welfare states (Adema, 2001; Adema and Ladaique, 2005; Andersen, 2008). These industries will meet an increasing demand from aging and wealthier populations. The income elasticity of services provided by these industries has been estimated to be as high as 1.6 (Fogel, 1999). While several of these markets have been partially opened for private competition in recent years, many impediments are still in place, with private firms still producing only a fraction of total output. We discuss three combinations of restrictions separately: (i) the case where both production and financing are monopolized by government, that is, government controls production and prices and pays for the services; (ii) the case where production is monopolized by government, but private financing is allowed; and (iii) the case where private production is allowed but financing comes from the government.

Public Production and Public Financing

Private entrepreneurs cannot play any role if the provision of goods and services is monopolized by government. Business angels, venture capitalists, and actors in the secondary market will not be present, since there are no investment opportunities. The build-up of industrial competence is negligible when the acquisition and use of such competence is restricted. While research and development may be subsidized, the incentives for inventors themselves are weakened since there will be no competitive markets for potentially successful inventions. The labor market is monopsonized, that is, there is only one employer, which tends to lower wages for skilled workers, inducing a scarcity of skilled workers.[11] Competent customers will be scant and unable to affect production.

This will hamper structural transformation, since the essence of functions provided by entrepreneurs, industrialists, business angels, venture capitalists, and secondary market actors is to generate profit through the use of new productive knowledge commercialized in competitive markets. These competencies are acquired through individual learning by doing in profit-driven firms and can rarely be substituted by competence obtained in political organizations (Pelikan, 1993).[12] As a result, HGFs will not form, dampening structural transformation. Today, there are very few markets in democratic societies where government monopolizes both production and financing, with one notable exception: large parts of the educational sector.

Public Production and Private Financing

There are a few markets, mainly infrastructure, where government monopolizes production, but where private financing is allowed, even as the main source of funding. Electricity supply, garbage collection, telecommunications, postal services, public transportation, and water supply are still prime examples in many countries. Here too, we observe an ongoing deregulation. To exemplify: personal transports on railways were until recently monopolized in most European countries. Now a partial deregulation has taken place, opening up the market for private and international providers in many EU countries.

Revoking the restriction on private financing while keeping production under government control does not change the effect on HGFs and structural transformation compared to the case of government monopolization of both product and financing markets. In this setting, critical entrepreneurial competence can hardly exist. Public enterprises sometimes have intrapreneurs, for example, hospital managers, school principals, or college deans that improve performance through innovation and the build-up of structural capital. But in this system, establishments that are better managed or otherwise above average in performance have weak incentives and far fewer opportunities to expand and improve quality across the board. Business angel and venture capitalist competencies still cannot exist, and industrialist competencies are hard to acquire, attract, and utilize. State ownership makes management less interested in innovation activities, since it is more difficult for them to reap any benefits from these activities compared to private owners (for example, Shleifer, 1998).[13] This implies that it is difficult for inventors to earn returns on their efforts in excess of their salary, which in general is much less than the market value of potentially successful inventions.[14] The monopsonized labor market will also make the salaries lower than in a market with many competing producers, leading to poor incentives to acquire high skills.

Private Production and Public Financing

Welfare states increasingly recognize that ensuring access to health care and other social goods and services does not require government production of such goods, only public financing. Hence, market-type mechanisms[15] that combine private provision and public financing of these services are increasingly utilized. Outsourcing, vouchers, and public–private partnerships are the three most common arrangements. Deregulating markets previously closed to private entrepreneurship through these strategies increases the economy's potential to generate HGFs. But the remaining regulation may still cause problems for future HGFs. First, the government is a monopsonist. Consumers are entitled to specific goods or services at reduced costs or free of charge, but only from providers commissioned by government.[16] The providers typically have limited options to offer and charge for additional quality on top of what is granted through the tax-financed system. These restrictions bar customers from buying their preferred qualities or services in preferred quantities from preferred providers. The growth of potential HGFs may then slow down – or even stop altogether – due to restrictions on attracting customers. As a result, reallocation and structural transformation will be dampened.

Second, it is common that government crowds out private producers in markets such as health care and non-mandatory schooling. A common strategy is to offer services free of charge, financed through taxes in combination with the banning of customers from being eligible for any subsidies when buying from private suppliers. Such policies may imply a de facto ban on private entrepreneurship in these markets, even though not explicitly prohibited by law. This does not suggest that health care and other welfare services should not be publicly financed, rather it implies that the fostering of HGFs and structural transformation are encouraged by a policy where private producers are entitled to the subsidies if the patients or customers prefer a private producer to a public producer, that is, the subsidy should follow the patient/customer, like in a voucher system. In many instances opening previously monopolized markets to private providers has led to impressive performance of HGFs, suggesting that there is a large untapped potential for this in sectors such as health care, education, and care of children and the elderly. One such example is the voucher system for school choice that was introduced in Sweden in the early 1990s, which paved the way for several HGFs in the area. At about the same time, local and regional governments began to outsource health care, and from this a number of HGFs have emerged. Some of them have since become multinationals.[17]

Sometimes it is suggested that private firms providing publicly financed services should be prohibited from making a profit and required to reinvest all surplus in the firm.[18] Such provision constitutes no impediment for private non-profit foundations (such as universities and many US hospitals). However, a de facto ban on profit will have the same effect on HGFs and structural transformation as the government monopolizing production. Even though there will exist a strong demand for, for example,

Table 7.1 Regulations, the prevalence of HGFs and structural transformation

	Private production	Monopolized production
Private financing	Entrepreneurs – Yes Inventors – Yes Industrialists – Yes Skilled labor – Yes Business angels – Yes Venture capitalists – Yes Actors in secondary markets – Yes Competent customers – Yes All actors present, prevalence of HGFs and fast structural transformation	Entrepreneurs – No Inventors – Limited Industrialists – No Skilled labor – Limited Business angels – No Venture capitalists – No Actors in secondary markets – No Competent customers – Limited Several key competencies missing, imperfectly replaced by government, no HGFs and slow structural transformation
Public financing	Entrepreneurs – Possible Inventors – Possible Industrialists – Possible Skilled labor – Yes Business angels – Possible Venture capitalists – Possible Actors in secondary markets – Possible Competent customers – Limited Potential impediments to presence of all actors, HGFs and to structural transformation, depending on institutional climate	Entrepreneurs – No Inventors – Limited Industrialists – No Skilled labor – Limited Business angels – No Venture capitalists – No Actors in secondary markets – No Competent customers – No Most key competencies missing, imperfectly replaced by government, no HGFs and slow structural transformation

private schools, this will weaken profit incentives for entrepreneurs and reduce business opportunities for venture capitalists. Consequently, there will be no HGFs, and structural transformation will be slow.

A major disadvantage of prohibiting private financing is the signaling from spending decisions by competent customers, since all private customers are excluded. The mixture of private production and public financing is therefore expected to prevent the formation of complete sets of actors with the requisite complementary competencies and, lacking private customers, few HGFs are expected.[19] Table 7.1 provides a summary of the analysis. The benchmark case is private production *and* private financing, when there are no legal restrictions barring the formation of sets of actors possessing all required competencies, rapidly growing firms, and fast structural transformation. The analysis reveals that thriving HGFs require free private provision of goods and services and private financing. Only then can the incentives be (reasonably) harmonized for all required key actors, thereby providing favorable circumstances for HGFs.

THE ORGANIZATION OF LABOR MARKETS, THE PREVALENCE OF HGFs, AND STRUCTURAL TRANSFORMATION

Rapid firm growth and structural transformation presupposes the reallocation of labor from low- to high-productivity firms and industries. Labor studies document massive ongoing restructuring of jobs and workers across firms (Abowd and Kramarz, 1999; Davis and Haltiwanger, 1999; Caballero, 2007). It is reasonable to hypothesize that current and future HGFs are more in need of flexibility and freedom of contracting in order to realize their high growth potential. Institutions hampering the freedom of contracting curtail the possible combinations of factors of production. The large productivity differentials across firms in the same industry indicate that labor productivity controlling for skills/competencies can vary dramatically depending on who is the manager/entrepreneur (Lucas, 1978; Pelikan, 1993; Caballero, 2007).

In this section we shall examine the impact of labor market institutions on the functioning and efficiency of key competencies. We focus on three labor market institutions of particular importance for the economy's ability to generate HGFs and to promote structural transformation: (i) wage-setting institutions; (ii) employment protection legislation; and (iii) the social insurance system.

Wage-setting Institutions

Wage-setting institutions may influence the scope for cooperation between key actors with complementary competencies, and the conditions for (potential) HGFs and structural transformation through several channels. In particular, the wage compression associated with centralized wage bargaining is likely to disadvantage potential HGFs, since an artificially compressed wage structure in both tails of the distribution makes it more difficult for profitable firms with high productivity to use salaries as an incentive to recruit new productive employees, making expansion more difficult to realize. This effect is reinforced if taxes are progressive. Minimum wages set above the market equilibrium level, on the other hand, force low-profit firms with low productivity out of business. Start-ups generally tend to be low-wage firms in the beginning due to their relatively low productivity before they reach the minimum efficient scale of the industry (Audretsch, 2002). Halabisky et al. (2006) demonstrate HGFs to be low-salary companies in the beginning of their life cycle and large firms in slowly growing industries to be high-salary companies. When young potential HGFs realize their growth potential and begin to grow rapidly, salaries start to grow fast. Halabisky et al. conclude (p. 265): 'In other words, for small firms, wage levels were highest in those that grew the fastest'. The finding suggests that a compressed wage structure pegging minimum wages above the market equilibrium level tends to choke potential HGFs in their infancy. They cannot bear high wage costs in the beginning of their life cycle when still developing their product and in the early phase of commercialization before the firm has become more productive and could afford to pay higher salaries.

Empirical studies find HGFs to be younger and smaller than other firms on average and most likely to be in the services sector. Wages are consistently higher at larger firms, even after exhaustive efforts to control for observable worker characteristics and other job attributes (Oi and Idson, 1999). Old firms pay higher wages than new firms on average and industries in the low end of the wage distribution are found in services, not in manufacturing.[20] Hence, the negative effect of wage compression is reinforced by the fact that wage compression disadvantages firms that are most likely infant HGFs.

Also, centralized wage-setting institutions disadvantage potential HGFs by implementing standard rate compensation policies that closely tie wages to easily observable job and worker characteristics such as occupation, education, experience, and seniority.[21] In their study of the size–wage structure in the US manufacturing sector, Davis and Haltiwanger (1996) find that residual wage dispersion declines sharply with establishment size in standard human capital regressions that relate worker earnings to sex, education, experience, and job tenure.

Given the large intrafirm differences in productivity and productivity growth, in particular in young and rapidly expanding industries and young firms (Caballero, 2007), it follows that the functioning of the cooperation of different key actors needed for HGFs is impaired if wages are set in negotiations far from the individual workplace, and therefore not taking these facts into proper account.

Employment Protection Legislation

There are large cross-country differences concerning employment protection legislation (EPL) (Skedinger, 2010). There is a risk that rigid labor market legislation locks in employees in current firms and industries, which is at odds with the needs of rapidly growing firms. For instance, strict application of the principle of 'last in–first out' in the case of redundancies implies that tenure at the current employer becomes relatively more important for labor security than individual skill and productivity. This fact increases an employee's opportunity cost of changing employers or of leaving a secure salaried job. There may be room for making exceptions from the 'last in–first out' rule. Often this requires union consent, and exceptions are therefore granted through negotiations between the employer and the union, not by the employer. Irrespective of skill, an employee can never be sure of the outcome of such negotiations. Hence, there will always be an opportunity cost, also for high-skill workers, to give up a long-tenured position for a new job. This will make it more difficult for rapidly expanding firms to hire skilled workers. The risk of growth-dampening bottlenecks in production increases.

The empirical findings about churning and restructuring give reasons to believe that, in particular, strict employment security provisions and other regulations that restrict contracting flexibility are more harmful for enterprises that would like to grow rapidly. As an employer learns about a worker's abilities over time, or as those abilities evolve with experience on the job, the optimal assignment of the worker to various tasks is likely to change. The scope for task reassignment within the firm can be expected to rise with firm size. In an unfettered labor market, optimal task reassignment often involves mobility between firms, and such mobility is higher when the initial employment relationship involves a small, often young, business. For instance, Schnabel et al. (2008) report that employment stability (measured as time employed in the same firm) is higher and the risk for becoming unemployed lower in incumbent firms than in newly founded firms. Moreover, both the rate at which workers separate from jobs and the rate at which employers destroy job positions decline with the size, age, and capital intensity of the employer (Brown and Medoff, 1989; Davis and Haltiwanger, 1999). Bartelsman et al. (2004, p. 4) claim that there is much more churning among young and small firms compared to old and large ones. In a meta-analysis of employment creation studies, van Praag and Versloot (2007, p. 360) conclude that 'employment dynamics are larger in entrepreneurial firms'.[22] These patterns in worker separation and job destruction rates suggest that any costs imposed by EPL are likely to fall more heavily on younger, smaller, and less capital-intensive (often service) employers. Since HGFs are overrepresented in these categories, this implies that a stringent EPL disproportionately burdens HGFs. Another important argument is provided by the 'varieties of capitalism' literature (Hall and Soskice, 2001), where it is argued that employment protection legislation harms particularly innovative firms and start-ups because these firms are faced with an exceptional degree of uncertainty and have a special need for flexibility.

If regular employment is highly regulated there may be strong incentives to devise arrangements that circumvent these regulations. In several European countries new forms of flexibility have emerged, leading to more job opportunities (Blau and Kahn, 1999; Skedinger, 2010). The most important of these arrangements are increased self-employment, the emergence of an underground economy where the government refrains from enforcing regulations, and increased reliance on temporary employment.[23] It is likely that part of the increase in self-employment in recent years has been driven by such considerations. For the self-employed, compensation and working hours are totally unregulated and no labor security is mandated. Also, very small firms may be able to avoid unionization and the signing of collective agreements, and therefore benefit from greater freedom of contracting. This room to maneuver is likely to be lost once the firm size exceeds a certain threshold. Therefore, these evasive measures do little to help HGFs and welfare-enhancing structural transformation. Instead, they tend to create a system with a large share of economic activity occurring in small firms without the ability or the aspiration to become HGFs.[24]

The differential effect of labor market regulations may go a long way towards explaining why the rate of self-employment is fairly low in the US, while it is very high in Italy. One may hypothesize that in the US the really good entrepreneurial firms are more likely to grow rapidly, while the onerous regulation, possibly in combination with the high tax rates on labor income, makes it difficult and risky to build large firms in Italy. Instead, the firms tend to remain small and resort to a strategy of cooperation with other small firms in clusters (Lazerson and Lorenzoni, 1999).

The Social Insurance System

The design of the social insurance system also affects the conditions for HGFs and structural transformation. One argument in favor of a relatively generous insurance system is that it enhances structural transformation. It is plausible that a rapid structural transformation is correlated with a high turnover of jobs, making people temporarily unemployed. A well-functioning insurance system will then provide income security during periods of unemployment, making people more supportive of fast transformation. A counterargument is that too generous a social insurance system may in practice work as a source of income substituting for paid employment. In this case, the social insurance system increases the reservation wage, which is likely to hamper structural transformation.

The design of the social insurance system may also affect individuals' incentives to establish and expand firms. Sinn (1996) argues that by providing insurance for unfavorable outcomes, an extensive and generous public social insurance system can in principle encourage individuals to pursue entrepreneurial endeavors. This is a valid theoretical argument but it is an open question whether it is important empirically. At first sight it appears more clear-cut that a generous welfare system makes it less costly to bear uncertainty as an entrepreneur or transfer to a risky job in an entrepreneurial firm. In labor markets where job security is closely linked to job tenure, this may no longer hold; what matters is the opportunity cost, that is, how much an employee has to give up in terms of income security if (s)he transfers to self-employment or a risky job in an entrepreneurial firm.

We can illustrate this point by comparing the situations in Sweden and Denmark. In Denmark, generous welfare systems are combined with weak job security mandates, sometimes called 'flexicurity' (Andersen, 2005). In Sweden, the situation is very different. If employment with the current employer has lasted for a long time, and the employer is unlikely to be forced to shut down, the system in reality provides income security for the individual.[25] By contrast, somebody who voluntarily gives up a tenured position for self-employment may often end up having no more security than what is provided by social welfare, and this presupposes that the individual depletes all his/her own assets. Hence, the construction of the public income insurance systems in combination with the EPL tends to penalize individuals who assume entrepreneurial risk. As a result, the opportunity cost of giving up a tenured position in Denmark is substantially lower than in Sweden.

A final point concerns the design of the supplementary pension system and other important benefits that may be tied to employment, notably health insurance. Supplementary pension plans that are not fully actuarial and individualized contain elements of redistribution and risk-sharing across individuals in a group, for example, the white-collar workers in a certain industry. The pension benefit level may be disproportionately tied to the wage level achieved at the end of the professional career. To the extent that this is true, the mobility of (older) workers across firms is greatly discouraged, as is the hiring of elderly unemployed.

THE TAX CODE, THE PREVALENCE OF HGFs, AND STRUCTURAL TRANSFORMATION

The tax system is particularly important for the issue discussed here. Taxes invariably influence transactions in that they create a wedge between the net receipt of sellers and gross costs of buyers of a service or a good. Hence, taxes greatly influence the incentives to acquire and apply productive knowledge as well as the possibility to reallocate factors of production to more productive areas. Taxes can create lock-in effects of labor and capital. In a former section we identified six distinct categories of actors crucial for HGFs. However, the tax code only imperfectly acknowledges these categories; there is no specific tax on income from entrepreneurial effort or inventive activity. Instead, based on provisions in the tax code, individual income will be classified as labor income, capital income, and/or corporate income, and within each of these categories there may be further provisions influencing the effective tax rate. In what follows we shall examine how the incentives for the different categories of key actors are affected by the tax system.

Labor Taxation and Sales Tax/VAT

The level and progressivity of labor taxation (including mandatory social security contributions) affect employees directly, by determining the incentives for work effort, labor supply (on the extensive and intensive margin), occupational choice, career aspirations, and the propensity to upgrade and learn new skills. Most obviously, high and progressive labor taxes lower the rate of return on productive skills, and therefore they are likely to reduce the supply of skilled workers.[26] They also slow down restructuring and the reallocation of people across firms, since it becomes more costly to obtain the net wage differential necessary to induce a person to quit his/her current employment position.

To the extent that inventors are taxed as wage-earners their incentives are also affected by the tax code for labor income. The same is true for industrialists (those who carry out the function of the Schumpeterian imitator and the Schumpeterian entrepreneur in later phases), unless they have a large ownership share in the firm they manage, which is usually not the case for large firms.

The level and progressivity of labor income taxation also indirectly affect the industry structure from the demand side. High rates of personal taxation tend to make it more profitable to shift a large share of service production to the informal economy, in particular into the 'do-it-yourself' sector.[27] Cross-country comparisons of industry-level employment also point to considerable scope for substitution of certain economic activities between the market and non-market sectors (Freeman and Schettkat, 2005; Rogerson, 2006).

As a result, the emergence of a large, efficient service sector competing successfully with unpaid work is less likely in countries with high rates of personal taxation. Consequently, important opportunities for commercial exploitation and entrepreneurial business development become less accessible. When services are provided by professionals, incentives emerge to invest in new knowledge, to develop more effective tools, to develop superior contractual arrangements, to create more flexible organizational structures, and so forth. Put simply, higher rates of personal taxation discourage the market provision of goods and services that substitute closely for home-produced services.[28]

The incidence of commodity taxation generally falls on final domestic consumers, while intermediate goods and exports are exempted. Hence, the effects of these taxes on the different actors are similar to the effects of labor taxation although there is no progressivity. Generally, there is considerable differentiation in sales/VAT taxation across countries and commodity groups.

Taxation of Stock Options

One mechanism to encourage and reward individuals supplying key competencies to a firm is the use of stock options. In ideal circumstances this can provide incentives that closely mimic direct ownership. This is likely to be most important for employed inventors, entrepreneurs and industrialists in certain industries where options are an effective response to agency problems.

The efficiency of stock options is highly dependent on the tax code. If gains on stock options are taxed as wage income when the stock options are tied to employment in the firm, some of the incentive effect is lost. This is particularly true if the gains are subject to (uncapped) social security contributions and if the marginal tax rate is high.

The situation is very different if an employee who accepts stock options can defer the tax liability to the time when the stocks received upon exercise of the options are eventually sold. The effectiveness is further reinforced if there are no tax consequences to the employee upon the granting or the exercise of the option and if the employee is taxed at a low capital gains rate when the stock acquired through the exercise of the option is sold. In the latter case the tax risk of the options is pushed back to the government. This accomplishes two things: it increases the potential profit from the stock options and it allows budget-constrained individuals to sell stocks whenever they choose to do so. It is noteworthy that the US changed the tax code in the early 1980s along the latter lines, which paved the way for a wave of entrepreneurial ventures in Silicon Valley and elsewhere (Misher, 1984; Gompers and Lerner, 2001).

Taxation of Venture Capital and Private Equity Activity

Venture capitalists often fill a crucial role in the development of a small entrepreneurial high-growth venture by converting high-risk opportunities to a more acceptable risk level through portfolio diversification, and adding key competencies that the firm may be lacking. This is achieved by means of developing arrangements that align the incentives of the three actors – investors, venture capitalists, and entrepreneurial start-ups (Zider, 1998; Gompers and Lerner, 2001). The extent to which this is possible is also largely governed by the tax code for stock options, capital gains, and whether pension funds are allowed to invest in high-risk securities issued by small or new companies and venture capital funds.

The tax systems of many countries evolved before complicated ownership structures involving venture capital/private equity (VC/PE) financing even existed.[29] Sophisticated mechanisms were needed to provide high-powered incentives for a number of actors in addition to the final equity holders. In fact, the modern VC industry in the US could not evolve until the tax system was changed in key respects: sharp reductions in the capital gains tax, new legislation in 1979 allowing pension funds to invest in high-risk securities issued by small or new companies and VC funds, and stock option legislation of 1981 that made it possible to defer the tax liability to the time when the stocks were sold rather than when the options were exercised (Fenn et al., 1995).

In the US, investments by VC firms are taxed at low rates. The returns that venture capitalists receive when the companies they help build are sold (so-called 'carried interest') are taxed at the 15 percent capital gains rate. For the founders of the start-up the capital gains tax rate may be half of that level (up to a high cap), since half of the gains is tax exempt if the stock has been held for at least five years.

In Sweden, by contrast, domestically domiciled VC and PE firms are at a disadvantage relative to other firms. Until 2003 dividends were taxed threefold: at a rate of 28 percent in both the firm itself and the VC firm and, when applicable, at 30 percent at the owners' level. Since 2003 there has been no taxation at the level of the VC or PE firm. And, business angels that take an active part in the management of the firms in which they invest are taxed at a higher rate. Likewise, the income of the general partners in VC firms and income from stock options tied to employment are taxed as wage income. Thus, the high rates of taxation of entrepreneurs, general partners of VC firms and the owners of the VC firms or the business angels result in a substantial reduction in the after-tax return on activities typical of VC firms in the US. This may be an important factor explaining the fact that few Swedish firms founded in recent decades have grown to a large size.[30]

Corporate Taxation

Following extensive tax reforms, corporate tax rates throughout the OECD countries have come down from very high levels in the 1980s. Cross-country variations in the statutory corporate tax rates remained large until recently. For instance, in the early 2000s it exceeded 50 percent in Germany (by 2009 the German corporate rate had been lowered to roughly 16 percent) while it was no higher than 24 percent in Ireland and 18 percent in Hungary. In general, there was a discrepancy between statutory and effective corporate income tax rates stemming from mechanisms such as tax-reducing depreciation rules, inventory valuation rules, and other more *ad hoc* tax reductions that may be country or industry specific.[31] Seen from the perspective of the individual firm, opportunities for lowering the effective tax rate induce behavioral responses by firms, and to the extent that these opportunities differ depending on firm and industry characteristics, effects on HGFs and on structural transformation can be expected.

Taxation of Current Capital Income

Current capital income consists of interest income and dividends on equity holdings. Tax systems may differ in important respects here: (i) labor income and capital income can be summed and taxed according to the same tax schedule, and if the income tax is progressive this may result in very high taxes on capital income, in particular if the tax rate applies to nominal as opposed to real returns; (ii) capital income can be taxed separately from labor income, at either a flat or a progressive rate with or without inflation adjustment; (iii) dividends may be taxed at a lower rate, reflecting the fact that dividends as opposed to interest payments are not a tax-deductible business cost for the firm; and (iv) the tax code may put restrictions on the payment of dividends to the owners of closely held firms in order to prevent active owners from converting labor income into capital income taxed at a lower rate.[32] Moreover, tax systems may differ as to whether deduction of interest payments is allowed (in real or nominal terms).

Hence, the tax code pertaining to current capital income has large incentive effects, especially for entrepreneurs and the functioning of secondary markets. In particular, if taxation is nominal and tax rates are high, the real rate of taxation – that is, the combined effect of nominal taxation and inflation on the real rate of return on an investment – can easily exceed 100 percent even at moderate inflation rates. On the other hand, this may be largely offset by tax deductibility of interest payments, and if certain investments are tax favored, opportunities for tax arbitrage arise.[33]

Taxation of Capital Gains

Most of the economic return from the successful building of an HGF comes in the form of a steeply increased market value of its stock rather than as dividends or large interest payments to the owners. As a result, the taxation of capital gains on stock holdings has large effects on the incentives to create wealth through the fostering of HGFs.

There are large differences across countries and over time. In some countries the tax rate is zero or very low on capital gains on long-term holdings of equity, thereby providing strong incentives for entrepreneurs to create value by investing money and effort in their own business, and to give other key actors (industrialists and business angels) ownership stakes in the firm if their competencies are required. In other countries the reverse may be true, that is, the tax system penalizes owners of stock in closely held firms relative to owners of stock in listed firms in order to prevent owners of profitable small businesses from saving on taxes relative to the case where they are regular employees.[34]

Moreover, the capital gains tax may differ across different types of owners, where some types of owners, such as institutional investors and offshore trust funds, are taxed at lower rates than individuals. This is likely to spur an endogenous response in the ownership structure of the business sector towards the tax-favored owner categories. Generally, if individual stock holdings are disfavored relative to institutional holdings this affects the functioning of secondary markets, giving more effective control rights to fund managers and less to final owners. In the case that owner competence is a scarce resource and ownership matters for potential HGFs, such tax rules tend to inhibit the emergence and growth of HGFs (see Pelikan, 1993). Empirical results demonstrate that the success of HGFs often is due to individual owners 'of flesh and blood' playing a decisive role in critical phases of the life cycles of HGFs. These individuals have often generated their wealth through their own entrepreneurial activities when younger, and then become business angels or venture capitalists. Institutional holdings are managed by employees with other backgrounds lacking the experience and competence of these individual owners, which probably can only be acquired through learning by doing as entrepreneurs and private investors. Arguably, this competence is among the most valuable competencies in a market economy. An individual possessing this competence will therefore not work as an employee in general, but in his/her private company to fully reap the return on the competence.

Taxation of Asset Holdings

There are several types of taxes levied on asset holdings where the tax is decoupled from the return. This is true for taxes on wealth, property, and inheritance. In cases where these taxes are non-zero, the rules for how taxable wealth is assessed in the business sector are particularly important in our context. Successful entrepreneurs, venture capitalists, and actors in secondary markets have been shown to be highly sensitive to these kinds of taxes.[35] In some systems corporate wealth may be exempted, which would spur investment in entrepreneurial ventures by key actors. Alternatively, corporate wealth may be taxed heavily, while other assets such as pension savings or art objects are exempted. Hence, taxes on asset holdings influence both the absolute and relative return on asset accumulation. In most cases where such taxes are levied, the calculations are complicated; certain assets may be exempted and the imputed value used as the basis for assessments may be far below the market value. Again, HGFs tend to depend on individual owners during certain critical phases in their life cycle, and taxes on asset holdings that give incentives for private individuals to shun direct ownership of unlisted stock are expected to affect HGFs negatively.

Taxation at the Ownership Level

To get a better understanding of the effect of the tax system on the prevalence of HGFs and the speed of structural transformation the combined effect of different taxes on the incentives to establish firms with high-growth ambitions have to be taken into account, including differences caused because of different sources of finance. For our purposes it is important to highlight whether there are any differences between small individually owned firms (incorporated or unincorporated) and institutionally owned firms, which are either listed or unlisted.

Estimating, in real terms, the size of the marginal tax burden faced by private firms for investment in real capital is a painstaking task requiring that we consider the overall effects of several different taxes, such as corporate taxation with its specific rules for depreciation and valuation, as well as the taxation of interest income, dividends, capital gains, and wealth.

Table 7.2   *Effective marginal tax rates for different combinations of owners and sources of finance in Sweden, 1980 and 1994 (real pre-tax rate of return = 10%)*

	Debt	New share issues	Retained earnings
1980			
Households	58.2	136.6	51.9
Tax-exempt institutions	−83.4	−11.6	11.2
Insurance companies	−54.9	38.4	28.7
1994			
Households	32.0/27.0[†]	28.3/18.3[†]	36.5/26.5[†]
Tax-exempt institutions	−14.9	21.8	21.8
Insurance companies	0.7	32.3	33.8

Note: [†]Excluding wealth tax, the wealth tax on unlisted shares was abolished in 1992. All calculations are based on the actual asset composition in manufacturing. The following inflation rates were used: 1980: 9.4%, 1994: 3%. The calculations conform to the general framework developed by King and Fullerton (1984). The average holding period is assumed to be 10 years. A negative tax rate implies that the rate of return after tax is greater than before tax. For instance, a tax rate of –83.4 percent for a debt-financed investment owned by a tax-exempt institution in 1980 tells us that a real rate of return of 10 percent before tax becomes 18.34 (10 − (−8.34)) percent after tax, while a real rate of return of 10 percent before tax for a debt-financed investment owned by a household becomes 4.18 (10 − 5.82) after tax.

Sources: Södersten (1984), and calculations provided directly by Jan Södersten and reproduced with permission from Jan Södersten.

In addition, we need to consider how these tax schedules differ across different types of investors. A correct estimate of the tax burden must take into consideration which type of real capital the firms invest in, how these investments are financed, and who the firm's owners and creditors are. Estimates have been made for a number of countries using the methodology developed by King and Fullerton (1984).

We will use the Swedish tax system to illustrate how tax schedules affect HGFs. Table 7.2 presents effective marginal tax rates for different combinations of owners and sources of finance for Sweden in 1980 and 1994. Three categories of owners and sources of finance are identified, and the effective marginal tax rate is calculated assuming a real pre-tax rate of return of 10 percent. A negative number means that the real rate of return is greater after tax than before tax.

The table highlights several aspects of the tax system that are potentially important determinants of HGF activity. First, in 1980 debt financing received the most favorable tax treatment and new share issues the least favorable. Second, the taxation of households as owners was much higher than for other categories. In fact, more than 100 percent of the real rate of return was taxed away for a household buying a newly issued share. Third, tax-exempt institutions benefited from a large tax advantage relative to the other two categories of owners. Tax-exempt institutions had a substantial relative tax advantage throughout when investing in newly issued shares.[36] Fourth, insurance companies were in an intermediate position in terms of effective taxation. As shown by Davis and Henrekson (1997), the tax system favored large and old manufacturing firms. By implication, a tax system of this type penalized many of the key attributes characterizing HGFs. Distortions of such magnitude most certainly have a negative effect on the way the actors with different but complementary competencies can cooperate, thereby harming the capability of generating rapidly growing firms; in particular entrepreneurs, venture capitalists, actors in secondary markets, and HGFs in their infancy are likely to be negatively affected.

A series of tax reforms in Sweden from 1985 until 1994 entailed a substantial 'leveling of the playing field' for different types of owners and sources of finance. The tax changes of 1993–94, primarily the abolition of wealth tax on unlisted stocks and on dividends at the investor level, and the lowering of capital gains taxation to 12.5 percent, brought about a dramatic leveling of taxation for different owners and different means of finance compared to the situation in 1980. Taxation on financing by owner equity, regardless of whether it takes the form of a new issue of shares or of earnings plowed back into the firm, became largely the same for households as for other categories of ownership.[37] This should have a positive effect on the generation and growth of HGFs and on structural transformation.

Symmetry in the Tax Treatment of Business Profits and Losses

It has been argued that governments can provide insurance for business owners by taking part of profits in good times and offsetting losses in bad times (Domar and Musgrave, 1944; Sinn, 1996). If individuals are risk averse, such insurance encourages the risk-taking central to all entrepreneurial activity.

A number of arguments have been put forward to counter this proposition. For instance, it is not valid under progressive taxation and, under most tax codes, that losses be offset against future profits only. It could well be that misdirected forms of insurance only serve to encourage new business ventures among those who are not Schumpeterian entrepreneurs (de Meza, 2002).

In this respect there are also large differences across countries. For instance, Cullen and Gordon (2006) show that the asymmetry in the tax treatment of business profits and losses is greater in Sweden than in the US.[38] In the US, the asymmetry actually runs the other way in some cases. Cullen and Gordon (p. 17) write: 'For individuals in the top bracket, risk taking in start-up firms is heavily subsidized in the US, but tax penalized in Sweden'. This is due to the fact that in the US, business losses can in certain cases be offset against tax reductions based on the progressive labor tax schedule.

The usual tax asymmetry discourages risk-taking activities even for risk-neutral owners. Since start-up activities are often risky, this effect is stronger for new firms than for incumbents. This difference is aggravated to the extent that small firms have more volatile profit streams and fewer opportunities to apply losses in some units to reduce taxes on the gains accruing to other units. For closely held firms, the disincentive to pursue risky activities is even stronger insofar as risk-averse owners have much of their wealth tied up in the firm. As regards the previously reported evidence that HGFs tend to be young, it is conceivable that such a policy has negative effects on entrepreneurial activities in general and HGFs in particular.

Taxation of Savings

Given the level of wealth or national savings, the composition of national savings is not neutral in its impact on entrepreneurship and small business development. The manner in which savings are channeled to various investment activities influences the type of business organization that can obtain credit. Pension funds, for example, are both relatively risk averse and have difficulties handling smaller individual investments. Therefore, they are less likely to channel funds to entrepreneurs than business angels or VC firms. Hence, if the government forces individuals to carry out a large part of their savings through a national pension fund system, small business credit availability will suffer relative to an alternative policy and institutional arrangements that allow for greater choice by individuals regarding their savings and investments. But apart from such forced measures, the tax system may provide forceful incentives regarding the level and channeling of savings.

A tax system that encourages reliance on savings schemes that escape capital taxation typically restricts the final owner's control of the assets. In doing so, the tax treatment of financial assets and property encourages the accumulation of illiquid assets controlled by large financial institutions rather than assets under the direct control of the final owner. A typical case is pension assets that cannot be withdrawn until a person reaches the retirement age. Personal financial assets with these characteristics cannot be used by the asset holder as working capital either in an existing owner-operated business or to start a new owner-operated business. In particular, this would affect entrepreneurs and venture capitalists and, hence, the generation and early growth of HGFs.

If entrepreneurial talent and VC competence are unevenly distributed, policies that decrease the likelihood of equity constraints for the entre-preneurially talented and those with talent for being venture capitalists are likely to be beneficial policies. The only efficient means of increasing this likelihood is to pursue economic policies that promote private wealth accumulation across the board, and in ways that do not preclude or severely circumscribe that the wealth may be used as equity in entrepre-neurial ventures.[39]

CONCLUDING DISCUSSION

We argue that analyses of firm growth in general, and the economic con-tribution of HGFs in particular, benefit from being evaluated in a broader context of structural transformation. Rapid growth of some firms on the one hand requires entry of new firms from which to 'recruit' high-growth candidates and, on the other, the contraction and exit of other firms to free up resources for expanding firms. The essence of structural trans-formation is the reallocation of means of production from certain uses to more productive ones. Thus, the economy transforms into new struc-tures; it changes form. Without this dynamic reallocation, the growth of firms would be held back, irrespective of their inherent growth potential. Empirical studies demonstrating HGFs to be of particular importance for driving structural transformation should be paid particular attention.

The successful commercialization of innovations – new productive knowledge – by HGFs depends on actors with complementary compe-tencies that work together. The high degree of complexity in production combined with the specifics of human capital makes successful interaction among actors with different key competencies and roles difficult but also highly rewarding when successful. Most (potential) HGFs fail, but the few that succeed account for a substantial part of growth and development in their industries.

Bringing together the specialized, non-transferable competencies of dif-ferent actors into a well-functioning whole is invariably difficult, even with favorable institutions and public policies, and almost impossible in any other setting. Favorable economic institutions are likely to be of particular importance for the emergence of HGFs, both because of the sensitiveness of competencies to the design of institutions and because of the high social return in terms of growth and job creation.

Our analysis emphasizes the complementary character of institutions.[40] There is no 'quick fix' that will boost the frequency of HGFs. If policy-makers want to improve conditions for HGFs, our analysis suggests that they need to adopt a broad approach and implement a wide array of complementary institutional reforms. Hence, creating appropriate conditions for growth based on effective constellations of key actors with complementary competencies places great demands on government policies. As is pointed out by many research scholars, picking winners in this chaotic world is virtually impossible and the only winning strategy is 'to let 1000 flowers bloom' (Birch, 2006, p. 198). The perpetual search by economic actors for profits that exceed the risk-adjusted rate of return available for passive investors leads to a situation in which entrepreneurship, talent and ownership skills are channeled to the most promising areas and supplied in the best possible quantities. This increases the probability that new business opportunities will be developed and exploited to their full potential. This process creates the organizational and structural capital that is an indispensable component in all successful enterprises. The potential entrepreneur can always refrain from developing and using his/her skills and remain an employee with a fixed salary; the venture capitalist can choose to remain passive instead of supplementing his/her financial investment by supplying management skills, and so on.

Our analysis is confined to highly developed countries with basic institutions, such as secure property rights and the rule of law, in place. We have identified three bundles of institutions which are likely to be particularly important for the prevalence of HGFs and for rapid structural transformation: labor market regulations, the tax system, and the degree of free enterprising (the right of private entrepreneurs to establish and provide goods and services with a profit).

Labor market regulations can be expected to influence incentives for potential HGFs and existing HGFs, by restricting the freedom of contracting and thereby curtailing the possible combinations of factors of production. The need for experimentation in order to find more efficient factor combinations is likely to be larger in new firms and industries in general, and in current and potential HGFs in particular.

The most important channel by which labor market institutions affect HGFs is by hampering the supply of skilled workers to firms undergoing expansion and/or change. Given the large worker flows required in a dynamic economy, it will be harder to recruit workers with the competencies needed: the opportunity cost of leaving a tenured position goes up for the employees; the fixed cost of hiring goes up when a bad recruitment becomes more costly to reverse; there may be threshold effects that make firms hesitant to expand beyond a certain size; and a great deal of entrepreneurial effort may need to be expended on evasive rather than directly productive activities.

A fundamental insight from our analysis is that experimentation and selection takes place not only across firms, but also between workers and other key actors (notably entrepreneurs) whose productivity is only revealed while working. If temporary contracts are used systematically in order to circumvent regulations tied to permanent employment, industries and business ideas that depend on high-skilled labor and on-the-job learning are disadvantaged. Legal and institutional hurdles that prevent firms from laying off workers that underperform discourage potential HGFs from expanding. Depending on how labor markets are regulated and how these regulations interact with the social insurance system, the opportunity cost of becoming self-employed is affected. When social security benefits are closely tied to tenured positions and the employee has tenure at a low-risk employer, the opportunity cost increases sharply. If employees who establish their own business lose part of their social security entitlements, this can be expected to impact negatively on the recruitment of entrepreneurs.

The analysis reveals that tax systems typically contain many asymmetries giving rise to distortions concerning, for instance, ownership and firm age, which is expected to have a negative effect on the way actors with different but complementary competencies can cooperate, and hence on the ability to generate HGFs. Despite recent trends towards tax harmonization within the EU and the OECD, it is clear that there exist innumerable combinations of tax rates and tax provisions giving rise to different blends of ownership structure, financing structure, industry structure, size distribution of firms, and employment dynamics across countries.

Even seemingly neutral taxation may give rise to distortions if, for instance, some actors and firms are more likely to be financially constrained, notably small firms.[41] Such examples are corporate taxation, taxation on savings, and taxation on private wealth where small and young firms to a larger extent rely on retained earnings and private equity. In our view, this is an important determinant of cross-country differences in the prevalence of HGFs. Likewise, the regulatory (tax) burden is likely to fall more heavily on small and young firms (and hence on potential HGFs), since the concomitant administrative costs have a large fixed component that is unrelated to the size of the firm.[42]

Of the three categories of institutions we have discussed, monopolization of production poses the greatest obstacle to the creation and joint functioning of actors with complementary competencies which are instrumental in the generation of HGFs. While high taxes and labor market regulations also impinge on the creation of critical competencies and the actions of key actors embodying these competencies, there is often some scope for (costly) tax evasion and circumvention of labor market regulations. Government monopolization of production considerably constrains the evolution of contestable markets, where critical entrepreneurial and venture capitalist competencies can be developed and acquired through learning. De facto prohibition of profit-driven organizations has the same effect. Consequently, there will be no HGFs.

Moreover, the more complicated and the less stable the regulations, the more they benefit large incumbent firms, that is, firms with a low probability of becoming HGFs. Generally, we find distortions introduced by the three bundles of institutions analyzed to disfavor the kind of firms that have been found to be overrepresented among HGFs, namely young, small, and service sector firms. The policies may also enforce one another.

To summarize the effects of the institutions on HGFs we characterize institutions that provide a favorable environment for 'dynamic capitalism', the experimental process of creative destruction facilitating the joint functioning of agents with different but complementary competencies and HGFs; see Table 7.3.

Even in advanced economies, there is a large untapped economic potential which can be unleashed by institutional changes, such as the opening up of closed markets for entrepreneurial competition. This can be expected to have a positive effect on the emergence of the requisite specialized actors and the prevalence of HGFs. The effect would be more pronounced if tax structures and labor market institutions simultaneously were adjusted in order to stimulate the emergence of more effective cooperation of the different types of actors, and institutions were made more neutral with respect to firm attributes, type of ownership, and source of finance. The two most important conclusions from this analysis are that (i) institutions have far-reaching effects, and (ii) to identify these effects on HGFs, the respective institutions have to be studied in depth. The Devil is in the detail!

It is appropriate to end with a word of caution and point out that the relationship between institutions, entrepreneurship and other productive competencies, and growth is currently only partly understood. Much more research in this respect is called for to gain a fuller understanding both qualitatively – which are the key institutions and how they interact with one another – and quantitatively. To be able to quantify the effect of changes in a specific institution such as a key tax rate or labor security

Table 7.3   Institutions favoring dynamic capitalism, the emergence of HGFs and structural transformation

Institution	
Marginal tax rate	Low
Personal tax on capital income	Low
Personal tax on capital gains	Low
Tax on stock options	Low
Degree of tax neutrality across owner categories	Neutrality
Degree of neutrality across sources of finance	Neutrality
Personal taxation of asset holdings	No, or exemption for equity holdings
Corporate tax rate	Low statutory rate, low effective rate, neutral across types of firms and industries
Symmetric tax treatment of profit and losses	Yes
Labor security mandates	Portability of tenure rights
Design of pension plans	Fully actuarial
Wage-setting arrangements	Decentralized and individualized
Production of welfare services/ merit goods	Sizable private production, contestability
Financing of welfare services/merit goods	Government ensures basic high-quality supply, then private financing
Profit-driven organizations	Fully allowed
Government role in income insurance	Provide flexicurity

mandates, empirical research requires heterogeneity of institutions such as in cross-country comparison or instances of 'clean' changes in a particular institution. Here, a great deal can be learnt from labor economics, where considerable knowledge has been gained from the study of quasi experiments, often using instrumental variable techniques; see Angrist and Krueger (2001). There are many possible instances that could be utilized. Let us just mention two: (i) the different strategies by universities *vis-à-vis* the involvement of their faculty in the commercialization of research (Siegel et al., 2003); and (ii) the lessening of the employee protection legislation in Sweden in 2001 for firms with fewer than 10 employees (Lindbeck et al., 2006).

Furthermore, institutions do not come out of thin air; they emerge and develop in a specific context.[43] In propitious circumstances, informal and formal institutions evolve in ways that encourage economic growth by facilitating the entrepreneurial exploitation of economically valuable knowledge. However, this is by no means guaranteed. History is replete with examples where the evolution of institutions supporting dynamic capitalism has been severely hampered and even totally blocked.

NOTES

1. See, for instance, Bartelsman et al. (2004, 2005), Birch (2006), Brown et al. (2006), Caballero (2007), and Fogel et al. (2008) for empirical evidence that churning and growth are strong correlates. A suggested explanation is that churning accelerates the discovery procedure of new business opportunities and a rapid reallocation of resources from unsuccessful to successful firms (for example, Johansson, 2005).
2. For early evidence, see Birch and Medoff (1994) and Storey (1994). More recent studies include Schreyer (2000) and Acs and Mueller (2008). The literature is summarized in Henrekson and Johansson (2010).
3. Furthermore, a formal institution that is not enforced is likely to lose its practical relevance, and effective formal institutions become codified in society in the form of norms, habits, and other informal institutions. In short, informal institutions are endogenous, that is, the consequence of a certain set of policies and formal institutions – see, for example, Kasper and Streit (1998) and Lindbeck et al. (1999) – *and* effective formal institutions are consistent with existing informal institutions (Williamson, 2009).
4. Schumpeter (1934, p. 63): 'It is just this occurrence of the "revolutionary" change that is our problem, the problem of economic development in a very narrow and formal sense . . . By "development", therefore, we shall understand only such changes in economic life as are not forced upon it from without but arise by its own initiative from within'.
5. Relating to Hayek (1937, 1945, 1978), this can be seen as the generation and use of new productive knowledge.
6. Schumpeter (1934, p. 68): 'The carrying out of new combinations means, therefore, simply the different employment of the economic system's existing supplies of productive means – which might provide a second definition of development in our sense'.
7. See Eliasson and Eliasson (1996) and Johansson (2010) for a further discussion. The idea of the importance of complementary competencies to generate growth is recognized by a number of research scholars. See, for instance, Phelps (2007, p. 553) for a discussion in conformity with our analysis.
8. A profitable venture for the individual entrepreneur may, however, have a zero or negative social rate of return. Productive entrepreneurs perform entrepreneurial activities where the social outcome is positive and based on wealth generation (Baumol, 1990).
9. See Wright (2007) for an overview of the different categories and Prowse (1998) for an analysis of the function of the private equity market. Gompers and Lerner (2001) offer a comprehensive analysis of the importance of venture capital for innovation and firm growth. See also Landström (2007).
10. Two famous examples are the difference between Route 128 in Boston and Silicon Valley (Saxenian, 1996) and the distinct difference between East and West Germany (Fritsch, 2004).
11. See, for example, Hibbs and Locking (2000).
12. In this context, private firms can be seen as 'universities' for educating talented people (see Eliasson and Vikersjö, 1999). In line with this way of reasoning, small firms may function as a cost-efficient mechanism to identify, select, and develop entrepreneurial, industrial, and venture capital competencies. Failures are less costly and learning costs lower in small firms because small values are at stake (Lucas, 1978).
13. Hart et al. (1997, p. 1131) argue that the focus on quality changes from innovative

activities differs from traditional approaches in the literature on regulation and pro-curement, for example, Laffont and Tirole (1993), who study issues such as adverse selection and moral hazard stemming from incomplete information in contracting.

14. This should be separated from the rate of innovation for inputs purchased by the government from private firms, such as pharmaceuticals and medical equipment. Winston (1998) provides empirical examples of how the transfer of ownership from the government to private actors positively affects the creation and adoption of new technologies.

15. OECD (2005, p. 130) defines a market-type mechanism as 'encompassing all arrange-ments where at least one significant characteristic of markets is present'.

16. One reason could be that the government wants to ascertain that service providers offer a minimum level of quality, for instance, concerning health care. Shleifer (1998) sug-gests that in the case where monitoring costs are high and private firms have incentives to shirk on quality, a government-managed organization may even have some advan-tages over private alternatives. These alternative mechanisms can mitigate the problems associated with the removal of market forces, but are unlikely to fully offset the costs, especially since the market can be combined with alternative ways of influencing pro-ducers (Le Grand, 2007).

17. One of the best-known examples is the health-care provider Capio, which was founded in Sweden in 1994. In 2008 Capio had 16,500 employees in eight countries. There are also several large operators in elderly care, which are gradually becoming multinational as well.

18. This was explicitly suggested by a government expert investigation in Sweden in 2002 (SOU, 2002, p. 31).

19. An exception is when the government purchases goods and services for its core activi-ties, such as national defense.

20. Garen (1985) and Kremer (1993) develop theoretical models that explain the systematic sorting of more productive workers to larger employers as an efficiency-enhancing outcome in economies with heterogeneous, imperfectly substitutable labor.

21. Blanchflower and Freeman (1992), Blau and Kahn (1996) and Freeman (1998) provide evidence that unions and other centralized wage-setting institutions compress wages among observationally similar workers by promoting standard rate compensation policies.

22. They define entrepreneurial firms as smaller and younger firms.

23. Arai and Heyman (2004) report that temporary job flows in Sweden in the 1990s were as much as 10 times higher than job flows for permanent contracts. See also Shane (2008).

24. These opposing effects are also consistent with the findings of Robson (2003) and Torrini (2005), who do not find any relationship between the rate of self-employment and the degree of regulation of labor markets in rich countries.

25. This was true until 2006, but beginning in 2007 the Swedish government has imple-mented numerous measures that reduce the generosity and eligibility of the social insur-ance system for the unemployed.

26. The incentives to acquire human capital through formal schooling may be strong thanks to low or zero tuition fees, subsidized student loans and housing financed by taxes, while high marginal taxes abate the incentives to use and further develop that kind of capital.

27. This basic insight constitutes an important point of departure in recent work in the theory of optimal taxation. The theoretical results of Kleven et al. (2000) and Piggott and Whalley (2001) strongly suggest that the optimal tax structure involves a relatively low tax rate on those market-produced services that could alternatively be produced in the household sector. See also Jansson (2006).

28. See Davis and Henrekson (2005), Rogerson (2006) and Dew-Becker and Gordon (2008) for assessments of these effects across OECD countries.

29. VC and PE ownership involves several layers of ownership: private ownership stake by

founders and key personnel, ownership share by VC/PE firm, ownership stake by VC/ PE partners (often indirect), investor stake in the VC/PE fund, and final beneficiaries of institutions investing in VC/PE funds.

30. In 2004, among the 100 largest firms in Sweden, including firms formed by government and firms established by foreigners, there were 34 firms originally founded by Swedish entrepreneurs. The median year of establishment of these firms was 1908 and none was founded after 1970 (Axelsson, 2006).

31. See, for example, King and Fullerton (1984) and the studies contained therein.

32. In this respect it is noteworthy that in the US, dividends in the so-called 'S-corporations' are only taxed at the level of the owner's personal income tax (Cullen and Gordon, 2006).

33. Fukao and Hanazaki (1987) provide systematic evidence of such effects for OECD countries in the 1970s and 1980s.

34. This is the case in Sweden, where the legislator is concerned that owners of closely held firms do not convert labor income to capital income by paying themselves dividends taxed at 30 percent rather than wages taxed at the marginal tax rate for labor income. The scope for dividend payments is therefore restricted to a relatively small percentage of the equity capital paid in by owners. Similar provisions raise the capital gains tax on small businesses (Agell et al., 1998). In recent years it has normally been 43 percent for small closely held firms instead of the regular 30 percent, since half of the capital gain has been taxed as wage income.

35. See Rosen (2005) for an overview. In Sweden the emigration of successful entrepreneurs was extensive due to very high effective taxes on wealth and inheritance, particularly during the 1970s and the 1980s (Lindqvist, 1990).

36. Tax-exempt institutions by definition pay no tax on interest receipts, dividends or capital gains. This category includes charities, scientific and cultural foundations, foundations for employee recreation set up by companies, pension funds for supplementary occupational pension schemes, and the National Pension Fund.

37. These rules were only in place for one year, and the differential across owner categories and sources of finance increased again in 1995 when taxation of dividends at the investor level was reintroduced and the capital gains tax was raised to 30 percent.

38. Asymmetry refers to a situation whereby the effective tax rate on business profits is greater than the fraction of business losses shared by the government through the tax system.

39. Pelikan (1988) provides forceful arguments supporting this view.

40. The same conclusion is made by researchers in different fields of economic research. For instance, Orszag and Snower's (1998) study of the complementarity of different policies in the area of unemployment provides an interesting parallel, showing how the effectiveness of one policy depends on the implementation of others.

41. See, for instance, Beck et al. (2005) and Angelini and Generale (2008).

42. This is recognized in a number of countries identifying the regulatory burden itself as an impediment to economic development, in particular for young and small firms (see, for example, European Commission, 2007).

43. The literature trying to explain institutional change or the lack thereof is currently expanding fairly rapidly. See, for example, Kasper and Streit (1998, ch. 12), Boettke and Coyne (2009) and Zweynert (2009).

REFERENCES

Abowd, John M. and Francis Kramarz (1999), 'The analysis of labor markets using matched employer–employee data', in Orley Ashenfelter and David Card (eds), *Handbook of Labor Economics*, Vol. 3, Amsterdam: Elsevier, pp. 2629–710.

Acemoglu, Daron, Simon Johnson and James A. Robinson (2005), 'Institutions as the fundamental cause of long-run growth', in Philippe Aghion and Steven Durlauf (eds), *Handbook of Economic Growth*, Amsterdam: Elsevier, pp. 385–472.

Acs, Zoltan J. and Pamela Mueller (2008), 'Employment effects of business dynamics: mice, gazelles and elephants', *Small Business Economics*, **30** (1), 85–100.

Adema, Willem (2001), 'Net social expenditure: 2nd edition', OECD Labor Market and Social Policy Occasional Papers, No. 52, Paris: OECD.

Adema, Willem and Maxime Ladaique (2005), 'Net social expenditure, 2005 edition: more comprehensive measures of social support', OECD Social, Employment and Migration Working Papers, No. 29, Paris: OECD.

Agell, Jonas, Peter Englund and Jan Södersten (1998), *Incentives and Redistribution in the Welfare State: The Swedish Tax Reform*, London: Macmillan.

Andersen, Torben M. (2005), 'The Danish labor market – from excess to shortage', in Martin Werding (ed.), *Structural Unemployment in Western Europe: Reasons and Remedies*, Cambridge, MA: MIT Press, pp. 75–102.

Andersen, Torben M. (2008), 'The Scandinavian model – prospects and challenges', *International Tax and Public Finance*, **15** (1), 45–66.

Angelini, Paolo and Andrea Generale (2008), 'On the evolution of firm size distributions', *American Economic Review*, **98** (1), 426–38.

Angrist, Joshua D. and Alan B. Krueger (2001), 'Instrumental variables and the search for identification: from supply and demand to natural experiments', *Journal of Economic Perspectives*, **15** (4), 69–85.

Arai, Mahmood and Fredrik Heyman (2004), 'Temporary contracts and the dynamics of job turnover', *Economics Bulletin*, **10** (4), 1–6.

Audretsch, David B. (1995), *Innovation and Industry Evolution*, Cambridge, MA: MIT Press.

Audretsch, David B. (2002), 'The dynamic role of small firms: evidence from the US', *Small Business Economics*, **18** (1), 13–40.

Audretsch, David B. and Maryann P. Feldman (2003), 'Small-firm strategic research partnerships: the case of biotechnology', *Technology Analysis and Strategic Management*, **15** (2), 273–88.

Audretsch, David B. and Michael Fritsch (2002), 'Growth regimes over time and space', *Regional Studies*, **36** (2), 113–24.

Axelsson, Sten (2006), 'Entreprenörer från sekelskifte till sekelskifte – kan företag växa i Sverige?', in Dan Johansson and Nils Karlson (eds), *Svensk utvecklingskraft*, Stockholm: Ratio, pp. 57–97.

Bartelsman, Eric J., John Haltiwanger and Stefano Scarpetta (2004), 'Microeconomic evidence of creative destruction in industrial and developing countries', Policy Research Working Paper Series No. 3464, World Bank, Washington, DC.

Bartelsman, Eric J., Stefano Scarpetta and Fabiano Schivardi (2005), 'Comparative analysis of firm demographics and survival: evidence from micro-level sources in OECD countries', *Industrial and Corporate Change*, **14** (3), 365–91.

Baumol, William J. (1990), 'Entrepreneurship: productive, unproductive, and destructive', *Journal of Political Economy*, **98** (5), 893–921.

Baumol, William J. (2004), 'Entrepreneurial enterprises, large established firms and other components of the free-market growth machine', *Small Business Economics*, **23** (1), 9–21.

Beck, Thorsten, Asli Demirgüc-Kunt and Vojislav Maksimovic (2005), 'Financial and legal constraints to growth: does firm size matter?', *Journal of Finance*, **60** (1), 137–77.

Bhidé, Amar (2008), *The Venturesome Economy: How Innovation Sustains Prosperity in a More Connected World*, Princeton, NJ: Princeton University Press.

Birch, David L. (1979), *The Job Generation Process*, MIT Program on Neighborhood and Regional Change, Massachusetts Institute of Technology, Cambridge, MA: MIT Press.

Birch, David L. (2006), 'What have we learned?', *Foundations and Trends in Entrepreneurship*, **2** (3), 197–202.

Birch, David L. and James Medoff (1994), 'Gazelles', in Solomon C. Lewis and Alec R.

Firm growth, institutions, and structural transformation 211

Levenson (eds), *Labor Markets, Employment Policy and Job Creation*, Boulder, CO and London: Westview Press, pp. 159–67.

Blanchflower, David G. and Richard B. Freeman (1992), 'Going different ways: unionism in the US and other OECD countries', *Industrial Relations*, **31** (Winter), 156–79.

Blau, Francine D. and Lawrence M. Kahn (1996), 'International differences in male wage inequality: institutions versus market forces', *Journal of Political Economy*, **104** (4), 791–837.

Blau, Francine D. and Lawrence M. Kahn (1999), 'Institutions in the labor market', in Orley Ashenfelter and David Card (eds), *Handbook of Labor Economics*, Vol. 3, Amsterdam: Elsevier, pp. 1399–461.

Boettke, Peter J. and Christopher J. Coyne (2009), 'Context matters: institutions and entrepreneurship', *Foundations and Trends in Entrepreneurship*, **5** (3), 135–209.

Brown, Charles and James Medoff (1989), 'The employer size–wage effect', *Journal of Political Economy*, **97** (5), 1027–59.

Brown, Clair, John Haltiwanger and Julia Lane (2006), *Economic Turbulence: Is a Volatile Economy Good for America?*, Chicago, IL: University of Chicago Press.

Caballero, Ricardo (2007), *Specificity and the Macroeconomics of Restructuring*, Cambridge, MA: MIT Press.

Cullen, Julie B. and Roger H. Gordon (2006), 'How do taxes affect entrepreneurial activity? A comparison of US and Swedish law', mimeo, University of California, San Diego, CA.

Davis, S.J. and J. Haltiwanger (1996), 'Employer size and the wage structure in US manufacturing', *Annales d'Économie et de Statistique*, **41/42**, 323–67.

Davis, Steven J. and John Haltiwanger (1999), 'Gross job flows', in Orley Ashenfelter and David Card (eds), *Handbook of Labor Economics*, Vol. 3, Amsterdam: Elsevier, pp. 2771–805.

Davis, Steven J. and Magnus Henrekson (1997), 'Industrial policy, employer size and economic performance in Sweden', in Richard B. Freeman, Birgitta Swedenborg and Robert Topel (eds), *The Welfare State in Transition: Reforming the Swedish Model*, Chicago, IL: University of Chicago Press, pp. 353–97.

Davis, Steven J. and Magnus Henrekson (2005), 'Tax effects on work activity, industry mix and shadow economy size: evidence from rich-country comparisons', in Ramón Gómez-Salvador, Ana Lamo, Barbara Petrongolo, Melanie Ward and Etienne Wasmer (eds), *Labour Supply and the Incentives to Work in Europe*, Cheltenham, UK and Northampton, MA, USA: Edward Elgar, pp. 44–104.

de Meza, David (2002), 'Overlending?', *Economic Journal*, **112** (477), F17–F31.

Dew-Becker, Ian and Robert J. Gordon (2008), 'The role of labor market changes in the slowdown in European productivity growth', NBER Working Paper, No. 131840, National Bureau of Economic Research, Cambridge, MA.

Domar, Evsey D. and Richard A. Musgrave (1944), 'Proportional income taxation and risk-taking', *Quarterly Journal of Economics*, **58** (3), 388–422.

Eliasson, Gunnar and Åsa Eliasson (1996), 'The biotechnical competence bloc', *Revue d'Economie Industrielle*, **78** (1), 7–26.

Eliasson, Gunnar and Kurt Vikersjö (1999), 'Recruiting in a European company', *Vocational Training*, **12** (1), 14–19.

European Commission (2007), 'Models to reduce the disproportionate regulatory burden on SMEs', Enterprise and Industry Directorate-General, Report of the Expert Group, Brussels: European Commission.

Fenn, George, Nellie Liang and Stephen D. Prowse (1995), 'The economics of the private equity market', Washington, DC: Board of Governors of the Federal Reserve System.

Flamholtz, Eric G. (1986), *Managing the Transition from an Entrepreneurship to a Professionally Managed Firm*, San Francisco, CA: Jossey-Bass.

Fogel, Kathy, Randall K. Morck and Bernard Yeung (2008), 'Big business stability and economic growth: is what's good for General Motors good for America?', *Journal of Financial Economics*, **89** (1), 83–108.

212   *Handbook of research on entrepreneurship and regional development*

Fogel, Robert W. (1999), 'Catching up with the economy', *American Economic Review*, **89** (1), 1–21.
Freeman, Richard B. (1998), 'War of the models: which labour market institutions for the 21st century', *Labour Economics*, **5** (1), 1–24.
Freeman, Richard B. and Ronald Schettkat (2005), 'Marketization of household production and the EU–US gap in work', *Economic Policy*, **20** (41), 6–50.
Fritsch, Michael (2004), 'Entrepreneurship, entry and performance of new business compared in two growth regimes: East and West Germany', *Journal of Evolutionary Economics*, **14** (5), 525–42.
Fritsch, Michael and Pamela Mueller (2004), 'Effects of new business formation on regional development over time', *Regional Studies*, **38** (3), 961–75.
Fritsch, Michael and Pamela Mueller (2006), 'The evolution of regional entrepreneurship and growth regimes', in Michael Fritsch and Jürgen Schmude (eds), *Entrepreneurship in the Region*, New York: Springer, pp. 225–44.
Fritsch, Michael and Florian Noseleit (2009), 'Investigating the anatomy of the employment effects of new business formation', Jena Economic Research Paper 2009–001, Friedrich Schiller University and Max Planck Institute of Economics, Jena.
Fukao, Mitsuhiro and Masaharu Hanazaki (1987), 'Internationalization of financial markets and the allocation of capital', *OECD Economic Studies*, No. 8, 35–92.
Galbraith, John K. (1956), *American Capitalism: The Concept of Countervailing Power*, Boston, MA: Houghton Mifflin.
Galbraith, John K. (1967), *The New Industrial State*, London: Hamish Hamilton.
Garen, John E. (1985), 'Worker heterogeneity, job screening, and firm size', *Journal of Political Economy*, **93** (4), 715–39.
Gerschenkron, Alexander (1962), *Economic Backwardness in Historical Perspective*, Cambridge, MA: Harvard University Press.
Gompers, Paul A. and Josh Lerner (2001), *The Money of Invention: How Venture Capital Creates New Wealth*, Cambridge, MA: Harvard University Press.
Halabisky, David, Erwin Dreessen and Chris Parsley (2006), 'Growth in firms in Canada, 1985–1999', *Journal of Small Business and Entrepreneurship*, **19** (3), 255–68.
Hall, Peter and David Soskice (2001), *Varieties of Capitalism: The Institutional Foundations of Comparative Advantage*, Oxford: Oxford University Press.
Haltiwanger, John and C.J. Krizan (1999), 'Small business and job creation in the United States: the role of new and young businesses', in Zoltan J. Acs (ed.), *Are Small Firms Important? Their Role and Impact*, Boston, MA, Dordrecht and London: Kluwer Academic Publishers, pp. 79–97.
Hart, Oliver, Andrei Schleifer and Robert W. Vishny (1997), 'The proper scope of government: theory and an application to prisons', *Quarterly Journal of Economics*, **112** (4), 1127–61.
Hayek, Friedrich A. (1937), 'Economics and knowledge', *Economica*, **4** (1), 33–54.
Hayek, Friedrich A. (1945), 'The use of knowledge in society', *American Economic Review*, **35** (4), 21–30.
Hayek, Friedrich A. (1978), 'Competition as a discovery procedure', in Chiaki Nishiyami and Kurt Leube (eds), *The Essence of Hayek*, Stanford, CA: Hoover Institution Press, pp. 361–81.
Henrekson, Magnus and Dan Johansson (2010), 'Gazelles as job contributors – a survey and interpretation of the evidence', *Small Business Economics*, **35** (2), 227–44.
Hibbs, Douglas A. and Håkan Locking (2000), 'Wage dispersion and productive efficiency: evidence for Sweden', *Journal of Labor Economics*, **18** (4), 755–82.
Jansson, Jan-Owen (2006), *The Economics of Services. Development and Policy*, Cheltenham, UK and Northampton, MA, USA: Edward Elgar.
Johansson, Dan (2005), 'The turnover of firms and industry growth', *Small Business Economics*, **24** (5), 487–95.
Johansson, Dan (2010), 'The theory of the experimentally organized economy and competence blocs: an introduction', *Journal of Evolutionary Economics*, **20** (2), 185–201.

Jones, Charles I. (2001), 'Was an industrial revolution inevitable? Economic growth over the very long run', *Advances in Macroeconomics*, **1** (2), 1028–48.

Kasper, Wolfgang and Manfred E. Streit (1998), *Institutional Economics*, Cheltenham, UK and Northampton, MA, USA: Edward Elgar.

King, Mervyn A. and Don Fullerton (1984), *The Taxation of Income from Capital: A Comparative Study of the United States, the United Kingdom, Sweden and West Germany*, Chicago, IL: University of Chicago Press.

Kirchhoff, Bruce A. and Patricia G. Greene (1998), 'Understanding the theoretical and empirical content of critiques of U.S. job creation research', *Small Business Economics*, **10** (2), 153–69.

Klepper, Steven and Kenneth L. Simons (2005), 'Industry shakeouts and technological change', *International Journal of Industrial Organization*, **23** (1–2), 23–43.

Kleven, Henrik J., Wolfram F. Richter and Peter B. Sørensen (2000), 'Optimal taxation with household production', *Oxford Economic Papers*, **52** (3), 584–94.

Kremer, Michael (1993), 'The O-ring theory of economic development', *Quarterly Journal of Economics*, **108** (3), 551–76.

Laffont, Jean-Jacques and Jean Tirole (1993), *A Theory of Incentives in Regulation and Procurement*, Cambridge, MA: MIT Press.

Landström, Hans (2007), *Handbook of Research on Venture Capital*, Cheltenham, UK and Northampton, MA, USA: Edward Elgar.

Lazerson, Mark H. and Gianni Lorenzoni (1999), 'The firms that feed industrial districts: a return to the Italian source', *Industrial and Corporate Change*, **8** (2), 235–66.

Le Grand, Julian (2007), *The Other Invisible Hand: Delivering Public Services through Choice and Competition*, Princeton, NJ and Oxford: Princeton University Press.

Lerner, Josh and Robert P. Merges (1998), 'The control of technology alliances: an empirical analysis of the biotechnology industry', *Journal of Industrial Economics*, **46** (2), 125–56.

Lindbeck, Assar, Sten Nyberg and Jörgen W. Weibull (1999), 'Social norms and economic incentives in the welfare state', *Quarterly Journal of Economics*, **114** (1), 1–35.

Lindbeck, Assar, Mårten Palme and Mats Persson (2006), 'Job security and work absence: evidence from a natural experiment', IFN Working Paper No. 660, Research Institute of Industrial Economics, Stockholm.

Lindqvist, Hans (1990), *Kapitalemigration*, doctoral dissertation, Economic Research Institute, Stockholm School of Economics.

Lucas, Robert E. (1978), 'On the size distribution of business firms', *Bell Journal of Economics*, **9** (2), 508–23.

Maddison, Angus (2009), http://www.ggdc.net/Maddison/Historical_Statistics/vertical-file_03-2009.xls (accessed 23 September 2009).

Misher, Norman (1984), 'Tax consequences of exercising an incentive stock option with stock of the granting corporation', *The Tax Executive*, July, 357–63.

Mokyr, Joel (1990), *The Lever of Riches: Technological Creativity and Economic Progress*, Oxford: Oxford University Press.

North, Douglass C. (1990), *Institutions, Institutional Change, and Economic Performance*, Cambridge: Cambridge University Press.

North, Douglass C. and Robert Thomas (1973), *The Rise of the Western World: A New Economic History*, Cambridge: Cambridge University Press.

OECD (2005), *Modernising Government: The Way Forward*, Paris: OECD.

OECD (2006), *Economic Outlook*, vol. 80, December, Paris: OECD.

Oi, Walter and Todd L. Idson (1999), 'Firm size and wages', in Orley Ashenfelter and David Card (eds), *Handbook of Labor Economics*, Vol. 3, Amsterdam: Elsevier, pp. 2165–214.

Orszag, Mike and Dennis J. Snower (1998), 'Anatomy of policy complementarities', *Swedish Economic Policy Review*, **5** (2), 303–43.

Parker, Simon C., David J. Storey and Arjen van Witteloostuijn (2010), 'What happens to gazelles?', *Small Business Economics*, **25** (2), 203–26.

Pelikan, Pavel (1988), 'Can the imperfect innovation systems of capitalism be outperformed', in *Technical Change and Economic Theory*, edited and compiled by the Maastricht Economic Research Institute on Innovation and Technology, New York: Columbia University Press, pp. 370–98.

Pelikan, Pavel (1993), 'Ownership of firms and efficiency: the competence argument', *Constitutional Political Economy*, **4** (3), 349–92.

Phelps, Edmund S. (2007), 'Macroeconomics for a modern economy', *American Economic Review*, **97** (3), 543–61.

Piggott, John and John Whalley (2001), 'VAT base broadening, self supply, and the informal sector', *American Economic Review*, **91** (4), 1084–94.

Prowse, Stephen D. (1998), 'The economics of the private equity market', *Federal Reserve Bank of Dallas, Economic Review*, 3rd Quarter, 21–34.

Robson, Martin T. (2003), 'Does stricter employment protection legislation promote self-employment?', *Small Business Economics*, **21** (3), 309–19.

Rogerson, Richard (2006), 'Understanding differences in hours worked', *Review of Economic Dynamics*, **9** (3), 365–409.

Rosen, Harvey S. (2005), 'Entrepreneurship and taxation: empirical evidence', in Vesa Kanniainen and Christian Keuschnigg (eds), *Venture Capital, Entrepreneurship and Public Policy*, Cambridge, MA: MIT Press, pp. 251–79.

Rosenberg, Nathan and Luther E. Birdzell (1986), *How the West Grew Rich: The Economic Transformation of the Industrial World*, New York: Basic Books.

Saxenian, AnnaLee (1996), *Regional Advantage. Culture and Competition in Silicon Valley and Route 128*, Cambridge, MA: Harvard University Press.

Schnabel, Claus, Susanne Kohaut and Udo Brixy (2008), 'Employment, stability of entrants in newly founded firms: a matching approach using linked employer–employee data from Germany', Discussion Paper No. 9, Institut für Arbeitsmarkt- und Berufsforschung, Nürnberg.

Schreyer, Paul (2000), 'High-growth firms and employment', OECD Science, Technology and Industry Working Papers, 2000/3, Paris.

Schumpeter, Joseph A. (1934), *The Theory of Economic Development*, New Brunswick, NJ and London: Transaction Publishers.

Schumpeter, Joseph A. (1942), *Capitalism, Socialism and Democracy*, New York and London: Harper & Brothers.

Shane, Scott A. (2008), *The Illusions of Entrepreneurship*, New Haven, CT: Yale University Press.

Shleifer, Andrei (1998), 'State versus private ownership', *Journal of Economic Perspectives*, **12** (4), 133–50.

Siegel, Donald S., David Waldman and Albert N. Link (2003), 'Assessing the impact of organizational practices on the relative productivity of university technology transfer offices: an exploratory study', *Research Policy*, **32** (1), 27–48.

Sinn, Hans-Werner (1996), 'Social insurance, incentives and risk-taking', *International Tax and Public Finance*, **3** (3), 259–80.

Skedinger, Per (2010), *Employment Protection Legislation: Evolution, Effects, Winners and Losers*, Cheltenham, UK, and Northampton, MA, USA: Edward Elgar.

Smith, Adam (1776), *The Wealth of Nations*, Chicago, IL: University of Chicago Press.

Södersten, Jan (1984), 'Sweden', in King and Fullerton (eds), pp. 87–148.

SOU (2002), *Vinst för vården* (Profit in the Health Care Sector), 2002:31, Stockholm: Ministry of Social Affairs.

Storey, David J. (1994), *Understanding the Small Business Sector*, London: Routledge.

Torrini, Roberto (2005), 'Cross-country differences in self-employment rates: the role of institutions', *Labour Economics*, **12** (4), 661–83.

van Praag, C. Mirjam and Peter H. Versloot (2007), 'What is the value of entrepreneurship? A review of recent research', *Small Business Economics*, **29** (4), 351–82.

van Praag, C. Mirjam and Peter H. Versloot (2008), 'The economic benefits and costs of entrepreneurship: a review of the research', *Foundations and Trends in Entrepreneurship*, **4** (2), 65–154.

von Hippel, Eric (2007), 'Horizontal innovation networks – by and for users', *Industrial and Corporate Change*, **16** (2), 293–315.

Williamson, Claudia R. (2009), 'Informal institutions rule: institutional arrangements and economic performance', *Public Choice*, **139** (3–4), 371–87.

Winston, Clifford (1998), 'U.S. industry adjustment to economic regulation', *Journal of Economic Perspectives*, **12** (3), 89–110.

Winter, Sidney G. (1984), 'Schumpeterian competition in alternative technological regimes', *Journal of Economic Behavior and Organization*, **5** (3), 287–320.

Wright, Mike (2007), 'Private equity and management buy-outs', in Landström (ed), pp. 281–314.

Zider, Bob (1998), 'How venture capital works', *Harvard Business Review*, November–December, 131–9.

Zweynert, Joachim (2009), 'Interests versus culture in the theory of institutional change', *Journal of Institutional Change*, **5** (3), 339–60.

8   Inadvertent infrastructure and regional entrepreneurship policy
Maryann P. Feldman, Lauren Lanahan and Jennifer M. Miller[1]

INTRODUCTION

Policies to promote entrepreneurship have become increasingly common as an economic growth strategy. Formally defined as government initiatives that influence the formation, viability, and commercial success of new firms, entrepreneurship policy is particularly relevant at the regional or subnational level given that entrepreneurs tend not to relocate when starting their firms. Yet local governments must rely on national governments to manage a wide array of macroeconomic and other broad-scale factors. Actions at the national level can have inadvertent consequences at the regional level. Tension often arises between federal preemption in the regulation of commerce and direction of national science and technology policy and the need for regionally calibrated policies (Feller, 1992; Spence and Murray, 1999). These inadvertent consequences become even more evident over time as economies in the developed world transform from large-scale, standardized, national manufacturing to a more flexible system of global competition, integrated value chains, and knowledge work. Legacy policies more appropriate for an older historical era can both directly and indirectly influence the strategies available for regional entrepreneurship in unexpected and surprising ways.

The objective of this chapter is to consider entrepreneurship policy in a regional context.[2] While evaluations exist for specific programs of initiatives that provide funding or incubator space, there are few attempts to consider the overarching theme of how public policy affects regional entrepreneurship. The US is a particularly fruitful environment to consider regional policy. The 50 states provide rich 'laboratories of democracy' where specialized entrepreneurship policies have been tried and tested (Osborne, 1988). Policymakers in subnational units in other federal systems, such as Canada, Germany, and Australia, commonly referred to as states, provinces, or Länder – have similar latitude in both policy design and discretionary funding to support locally tailored programs that promote regional entrepreneurship. Moreover, smaller jurisdictions are frequently engaging in entrepreneurship policies as places try to encourage new firm formation and growth. The European Union faces similar concerns as individual nations have every incentive to craft policies that offer some advantage to small, entrepreneurial firms.

This chapter begins by describing four case studies of US policies that have inadvertent effects on entrepreneurship. The first case examines the role of enforcing employment covenants not to compete in the development of high-technology clusters. The second case considers the institutional relationship of health insurance to employment and identifies implications for entrepreneurship, especially in the transition to self-employment. The third case evaluates the role of size-based employment regulation in the growth of new firms and creation of quality jobs. The fourth case describes the role of antitrust legislation as a constraint on cooperative research and innovation. For each of the four sections, we consider the theoretical basis through which the policies are thought to influence entrepreneurial activity, examine one or more national policies and their stated intent, highlight related regional policy responses, and review evidence from existing research. Table 8A.1 in Appendix 8A summarizes the empirical literature relevant for each of the four cases. Our intention is to review the evidence from academic studies and to offer concerns, insights, and implications for regional entrepreneurship policy. As should be expected, the policy involvement of multiple, overlapping jurisdictions leads to conflict over entrepreneurship policies, with interesting implications for the realization of encouraging and promoting entrepreneurship. We conclude by offering suggestions for future research.

NON-COMPETE AGREEMENTS, AGGLOMERATION ECONOMIES, AND REGIONAL INNOVATION

Recent studies have found evidence that non-compete agreements affect entrepreneurial endeavors when workers leave one company to start another (Gilson, 1998; Almeida and Kogut, 1999; Valletta, 2002; Fallick et al., 2006; Marx et al., 2007; Garmaise, 2009). The most successful entrepreneurs are often spawned from incumbent firms in an industry (Gompers et al., 2005; Klepper and Sleeper, 2005; Chatterji, 2009). If a worker is prohibited from competing with a former employer, he/she is limited in the ability to start a new company or to join an existing start-up that competes in the same technology or market. Dating as far back as the Industrial Revolution, non-compete agreements have been present in legal codes around the world to provide a degree of protection for incumbent firms (Decker, 2002). The intention of these agreements is to safeguard established firms' human and business capital and intellectual property; however, scholars have recently raised concerns that the enforcement of non-compete agreements potentially reduces labor mobility (Gilson, 1998; Feldman and Audretsch, 1999; Marx et al., 2007; Garmaise, 2009). Given that labor mobility is a defining feature of both innovative regional industry clusters and agglomeration economies, scholars have raised concerns that this policy may hinder economic growth by slowing spillovers and decreasing market efficiency in the match between employees and employers (Samila and Sorenson, 2011).

The state of California is the subject of much of the theoretical and empirical research for non-compete agreements. While the vast majority of states do enforce a non-compete agreement, there is considerable variation by state in four critical features – geographic proximity, duration of the contract, nature of restricted activity, and employee compensation. To briefly elaborate, some states have the jurisdiction to enforce non-competition in regions beyond the market of the current firm (for example, Missouri) while others are more constrained to the immediate market (for example, Virginia). Some states have the legal right to enforce a three-year non-compete contract (for example, Pennsylvania) while others can enforce only up to two years (for example, Florida) (Garmaise, 2009). Tennessee and Florida may only enforce non-compete agreements for employees with specialized training, whereas Georgia 'can ban an employee from trading with any current clients of the firm, even if the employee has no contact with the client' (Vanko, 2002, p. 14). Up until the mid-1980s, only 10 of the 50 US states (Alaska, California, Connecticut, Minnesota, Montana, North Dakota, Nevada, Oklahoma, Washington, and West Virginia) did not enforce any aspect of non-compete agreements (Malsberger et al., 2002). As of 2004, however, only California and North Dakota fell into this category.

The history of California's policy begins in 1872 when California adopted a comprehensive civil code. This provision of the code was not a strategic entrepreneurship policy passed by California lawmakers. As noted by Gilson (1998), 'Rather, the California prohibition [is] a serendipitous result of the historical coincidence between the codification movement in the United States and the problems confronting a new state in developing a coherent legal system out of its conflicting inheritance of Spanish, Mexican, and English law' (p. 5). Section 16600 of the California Business and Professions Code states that 'every contract by which anyone is restrained from engaging in a lawful profession, trade or business of any kind is to that extent void'. State courts have consistently prevented the enforcement of non-compete agreements, thus relaxing the competitive restraints between employers and employees (Valletta, 2002).

Gilson (1998) advanced an intriguing hypothesis regarding this feature of California law. In his comparative case study of the high-tech sectors of Silicon Valley in California and Route 128 in Massachusetts, a state with enforcement of non-competes, he argued that the non-enforcement of non-compete in California was the enabling factor of the creation of knowledge-based agglomeration economies in Silicon Valley. That is to say, California's non-enforcement of non-compete led to increased levels of labor mobility, a factor that has been identified as a mediator of agglomeration economies and their innovation outputs (Almeida and Kogut, 1999; Feldman, 1999). Gilson's hypothesis stands in contrast to Saxenian (1985, 2006) who attributed Silicon Valley's high intraregion labor mobility to culture or Hyde (1998) who emphasized trade secrets law.

To support his argument, Gilson presents a four-stage model of industrial district formation and development. He attributed both districts' formation to initial conditions and resulting agglomeration economies. In a path-dependent development process, the next stage depended on the new initial conditions and their resulting agglomeration economies. He found support for the first three stages in Saxenian's historical account of the development of Silicon Valley, but disagreed that culture was the best explanation. Instead, he attributed Silicon Valley's more extensive development to the resolution of a collective action problem that allowed all firms to benefit from the agglomeration economies of high labor mobility through the non-enforcement of non-competes. Although high labor mobility is of greater overall benefit to the region's firms, any given firm would have an incentive to enforce a non-compete agreement upon its own employees. Section 16600 effectively eliminates the collective action problem by nullifying non-competes for all California employers.

Gilson's comparative case study of the high-tech sectors in California and Massachusetts serves as the cornerstone for understanding the potential economic repercussions of non-compete agreements. Building upon his work, several further elaborations and tests of Gilson's hypothesis have looked at how this law has played out in other states and in other industries. Valletta (2002) provides empirical support for Gilson's hypothesis in the highly innovative computer services sector. By focusing on 15 states with the highest technology employment density, he found evidence that yearly employment growth in computer services was correlated with non-enforcement of non-compete. Results were generally consistent with Gilson's hypothesis, but they were not definitive. Some states with non-compete enforcement also showed more growth in computer services – specifically, Massachusetts, New Hampshire, Arizona, and Washington (although Washington's pattern can be explained by Microsoft's presence).

Fallick et al. (2006) conducted an empirical test using archival data to examine Gilson's proposition that California's failure to enforce non-competes facilitated labor mobility and agglomeration economies. Results from their analysis found that employees moved between computer-industry firms more often in Silicon Valley than they did in information technology (IT) clusters where states enforced non-competes. Computer-industry interfirm mobility was higher in California than in other states and interfirm mobility in Silicon Valley and California was higher in all industries. They noted that other industries in California do not enjoy the same beneficial agglomeration economies as the Silicon Valley's computer industry; and they found that regional benefits of labor mobility in Silicon Valley depended on the benefits from shared tacit knowledge outweighing losses from reduced employer incentives to invest in human capital. Thus, they suggest the phenomenon observed by Gilson can be considered an interaction between legal structure and local industry characteristics.

Marx et al. (2007) tested Gilson's theory in a natural experiment related to non-compete policy changes in Michigan. In 1985, with the passage of the Michigan Antitrust Reform Act (MARA), the state of Michigan repealed MCL 445, which resulted in the enactment of a non-compete clause. By using Michigan for a unique case study, their results from a difference-in-difference approach suggested that labor mobility decreased after the state reversed the non-compete policy. Moreover, prominent innovators, including 'star' researchers and 'specialist' inventors, were especially hard hit by the change in legislation with labor mobility decreasing an additional 14 and 17 percent for these two groups, respectively.

Garmaise (2009) examined non-compete agreements across the 50 US states and the District of Columbia. Drawing from Malsberger et al.'s (2002) research, whose work has served as a critical legal resource pertaining to US non-compete agreements, Garmaise designed an enforceability index for each state to assess variation in this policy design by state and the subsequent consequences for differing economies. The results from his analysis provide support for Gilson's hypothesis that stricter non-compete policies yield lower degrees of labor mobility, especially among executives. In addition, he found evidence that tougher enforcement of the non-compete policy led to a decrease in research and development (R&D) and a decrease in capital employee expenditures.

These studies provide convincing evidence that non-compete policies do adversely affect entrepreneurship. As scholars continue to study the relationship between this policy and the subsequent economic activity, it is important to recognize how the design and implementation of non-compete laws vary by jurisdiction. Given the fluctuating nature of the legal code due to state repeals and legal amendments, there is potential for illuminating longitudinal studies in this area. Only Garmaise (2009) examined the heterogeneity of this law on a national US scale, so there remains considerable work to be done in understanding how variations of this policy and its actual enforcement affect regional economies. Future work could consider how non-compete agreements affect larger firms with markets spanning multiple legal jurisdictions from states to countries.

In addition to the US, a number of countries have versions of non-compete agreements (McElroy and Haleen, 2009; Samila and Sorenson, 2011; Stewart and Greene, 2010). The design of these agreements varies by country and reflects the national legal system. In their recent discussion of non-compete clauses, Stewart and Greene stressed that policymakers continue to balance the appropriate level of autonomy that should be granted to employees and protection provided for employers. In Australia, non-compete agreements have been introduced primarily to protect firms with confidential information and direct personal contacts (ibid.). Although Stewart and Greene did not directly discuss the inadvertent consequences of non-compete policies, Samila and Sorenson argue that innovation and entrepreneurship suffer as a consequence of these practices. In the case of Ontario, Canada, despite the high levels of R&D conducted at local universities and firms, high flows of venture capital, and active support from the local government, the region's high-tech sector has struggled to develop. According to Samila and Sorenson, 'part of the answer may reside in the way common law in Canada effectively bars management-level employees from leaving to competing firms, even in the absence of actual non-compete clauses' (p. 25). Thus, the lack of labor mobility, in part related to non-competitive pressures, seems to inhibit innovation and growth for the high-tech sector. There is considerable potential to expand to include international case studies and comparative examinations of different regional economies and non-compete agreements. Moreover, given the increasing propensity for firms to function on an international scale, it would be interesting to examine how these agreements affect individual firms or markets that operate internationally, spanning multiple legal boundaries.

In terms of economic development policy, these studies raise a critical question for policymakers: do industries benefit more from agglomeration economies or from intellectual property protection (Gilson, 1998)? What is the right balance? Audretsch and Feldman (1996) indicate that knowledge-intensive industries are the most likely to benefit from agglomeration economies made possible by labor mobility. However, further research could clarify which industries are most sensitive to labor mobility and benefit most from agglomeration economies. Blocking the enforcement of non-competes with legislation is one policy approach to consider. If that is infeasible, other policy approaches to facilitate labor mobility or to encourage firms to voluntarily reduce reliance on non-competes could be explored.

HEALTH INSURANCE AND ENTREPRENEURSHIP

Entrepreneurship is fundamentally connected to the acceptance of business risk, but it is also often associated with some level of personal risk. We begin this section with a review of the history of employer-sponsored health insurance in the US, then present theoretical and empirical support for the effect of employer-based health insurance on entrepreneurship. Next, we discuss how state and local policy approaches to health insurance for the self-employed have influenced entrepreneurship regionally in the US. We conclude with a few international perspectives on the relationship between entrepreneurship and the social safety net.

Unlike the highly visible public welfare states common in Europe, the US has an inadvertent and divided social safety net (Gottschalk, 2000; Hacker, 2002). Tax exemption of employer and employee medical benefits expenditures codified in the 1954 US tax code provided a cost advantage to benefits provided through the workplace (Thomasson, 2003). These employer-provided benefits became institutionalized when, as an anti-inflation measure during and immediately after the Second World War, employers were encouraged to provide health insurance rather than increase wages (Howard, 1997, 2006). Unions negotiated benefits for their members and the provision of similar benefits was also a key strategy of nonunion firms for remaining union free. This outgrowth of a rather informally implemented anti-inflation measure set the US on a distinctly different path of benefits provision compared to other countries and has had a broad impact well beyond the temporary suppression of wages. The employer-based institutional structure of providing health insurance led to isomorphism in the provision of elements of the social safety net as a diverse array of programs – including pensions; tax-deferred savings programs; dental and vision care; life, disability, and long-term care insurance; and dependent care tax credit programs.

As reported by the Ewing Marion Kauffman Foundation (2007), employer-based health insurance creates a barrier to entrepreneurship by presenting would-be entrepreneurs with the risk of inaccessible or unaffordable health insurance for themselves and their families. This barrier has three components. First, there is the tax deductibility of premiums.

Only since 2003 have the self-employed been able to deduct 100 percent of their health insurance premiums from US federal income tax, and they are still subject to profitability and filing requirements (Gumus and Regan, 2007). Second, entrepreneurs face higher costs for health insurance compared to the lower premiums negotiated by employers for their group plans. Third, entrepreneurs may face higher costs in or exclusion from individual insurance markets due to their own or family members' pre-existing or emergent health conditions. In combination, these mechanisms have been said to create job lock, preventing those currently employed from pursuing self-employment or other opportunities (Buchmueller and Valletta, 1996; Brunetti et al., 2000). While the original income tax-exemption-based distinction had been almost eliminated, the constellation of enabling institutions around employer-provided benefits remained.

Empirical studies using varied research designs have supported the premise that access to health insurance makes people more likely to transition into self-employment. Wellington's (2001) design is based on the rationale that people with health insurance through a spouse will be more likely to become self-employed. By further considering that men over 40 are likely to place a higher value on health insurance, she confirmed a statistically significant relationship between spousal health insurance and transitions to self-employment. Fairlie et al. (2008) applied two identification strategies to matched data from consecutive years. Their first strategy compared workers' transitions based on their access to alternative health insurance coverage and incidence of family health problems. Individuals with no alternative source of health insurance and those whose family members anticipate high health expenses were found to be less likely to make transitions to self-employment. They also used a regression discontinuity design that examined initial Medicare eligibility and found that business ownership increased in the month people turned 65. While limits on health insurance premium deductibility from federal income tax are consistent throughout the US, states have experimented with deductibility from state income tax, providing natural experiments to test the effect of deductibility on self-employment transitions. By looking at variation in state and national tax treatment over a five-year period, Heim and Lurie (2009) found that individuals were more likely to become self-employed and less likely to leave self-employment when self-employed individuals could deduct health insurance premiums from federal and state income taxes. These findings are consistent with the mechanisms of unfavorable treatment of entrepreneurs in the tax system and individual insurance market.

Studies have found small but fairly consistent effect sizes. Wellington's (2001) analysis indicates that self-employment would increase by 2.3 to

224 Handbook of research on entrepreneurship and regional development

4.4 percentage points for husbands and 1.2 to 4.6 points for wives, if an alternative source of health insurance were available. Fairlie et al. (2008) found that access to health insurance through a spouse was associated with a 1.0 percentage point increase in transitions to self-employment compared with a base transition rate of 3.0 percent and that business ownership jumped 3.6 percentage points at age 65. However, access to insurance through a spouse is only as secure as the spouse's job, and effects from a guaranteed alternative are expected to be larger. Heim and Lurie (2009) found that tax deductions for health benefits were associated with a 0.9 percentage point increase in transitions into self-employment and a 3.3 percentage point decrease in exits from self-employment, resulting in an increase of 1.2 to 1.7 percentage points in the probability of partial or total self-employment. The somewhat smaller magnitude of the effects found by Heim and Lurie are consistent with the fact that tax deductions do not address the higher costs and uncertainty of insurance purchased individually rather than through an employer.

A few studies, however, have found mixed or contradictory evidence. Holtz-Eakin et al. (1996) found that employer-provided health insurance was inversely related to the probability that a worker would transition to self-employment. That relationship, however, was no longer statistically significant after controlling for other employee benefits, such as pensions. While controlling for these benefits eliminated the effect for health insurance, these benefits are all elements of the employer-based welfare state. The findings may be consistent with the idea that the employer-based welfare state as a whole has a negative effect on entrepreneurship. Holtz-Eakin et al. also tested several longitudinal models without finding a statistically significant effect for the availability of health insurance through a spouse. Their research design assumed that '[i]f health insurance affects transitions, then the incremental effect of being covered on a spouse's plan should be to generate a greater probability of making a transition for an individual with an employer-provided plan than for an individual without such a plan' (1996, p. 225). One interpretation of these results suggests that having a spouse with health insurance had the *same* enabling effect on transitions to self-employment for persons with and without health insurance through their own employment.

Zissimopoulos and Karoly (2007) analyzed factors affecting self-employment among older workers, a population more likely to be self-employed. Their results were mixed with no clear evidence that availability of health insurance through a spouse or through retiree health insurance had an enabling effect on entrepreneurship. The authors speculated that perhaps spousal coverage through active employment was not secure. This may be especially plausible for older workers with declining health, plans to retire soon, or employers encouraging early retirement. Another possible explanation is that workers with retiree health insurance have typically spent a long career at a single large employer. Such workers may be less likely, based on personal traits or work experience, to be interested in self-employment.

Within the US, some state and local governments initiated reforms in advance of national reforms. One challenge to state and local health-care reform efforts in the US is the legal doctrine of ERISA (Employee Retirement Income Security Act) preemption, which gives federal law jurisdiction over employee benefit plans (Gregory, 1986). State and local governments have worked around this constraint in a few cases, providing additional opportunities for researchers to understand the effect of health insurance access on entrepreneurship.

One state policy option has been to focus on the individual insurance market, either through tax policy or regulation of insurance companies. Heim and Lurie (2009) observed effects of variation in the exemption of health insurance costs from state income tax. State income tax rates vary considerably and the number of states that allowed 100 percent deduction of premiums for purchases of individual health insurance increased from 9 to 40 over the study period of 1999 to 2004. DeCicca (2010) examined the impact of New Jersey's 1993 Individual Health Coverage Plan and found an increase in self-employment estimated at 1.1 to 1.6 percentage points. He suggested that this shift was associated with this policy's provisions to increase access to individual health insurance plans by establishing pure community rating, renewability, and availability requirements. New Jersey's plan was the most comprehensive of similar reforms by eight states between 1993 and 1996. Trends in self-employment were compared between New Jersey and Pennsylvania, an adjacent state that did not implement such reforms. The increase in self-employment was greater among older, unmarried, and less healthy individuals, the groups one would expect to experience the greatest benefit from access to an additional source of health insurance.

A second regional policy option has been to improve access to health care and insurance while countering the potential for employers to act as free-riders with a pay-or-play provision requiring companies to pay into a public fund if they do not provide health insurance to their workers (Monahan, 2006). Reforms of this type have been enacted in the state of Massachusetts and the city of San Francisco. A study of state-level reforms enacted in 2006 in Massachusetts found a detrimental effect on new firm formation within the portion of the Boston metropolitan area adjacent to the neighboring state of New Hampshire (Jackson, 2010). This reduction in entrepreneurial activity may have been because of an employer mandate that imposed a cost burden on small firms. Jackson observed that either suppression or displacement of entrepreneurial activity could explain his findings. Since the study focused on part of a single metropolitan area that spanned two states, at least some displacement seems highly likely, pointing to a challenge in coordinating health-care reform with economic growth at the regional level.

Although we find no evaluation yet of this program's impact on self-employment or small business, San Francisco provides an example of a policy approach to increase health-care access at the municipal level. Two main elements of the city's Health Care Security Ordinance (HCSO) are a health access program and an employer mandate to provide health insurance for companies. These programs could expand access to health care for the self-employed by providing access to basic local health-care services through the health access program and by increasing the availability of insurance through employed spouses. A survey of health access program participants found that 13 percent of them were self-employed (Kaiser Family Foundation, 2009).

The Patient Protection and Affordable Care Act (PPACA) of 2010 represents a significant modification of the US social safety net. Although many aspects of PPACA are uniform across the US, individuals will be able to purchase insurance from state-level exchanges. An effectively functioning exchange could serve as a source of competitive advantage for states that provide ready access to health insurance for the self-employed and favorable conditions for small businesses seeking or required to provide coverage for their workers. The increased availability of health insurance to the self-employed in the US may increase demand and opportunities for organizations that serve and encourage entrepreneurs, as well as shift the demographic mix of those using their services.

While the US is widely considered exceptional in its approach to health care, we can extend some implications about the social safety net and entrepreneurship to an international context. First, although the US case highlights the importance of access to health insurance as a facilitator to entrepreneurship, entrepreneurship is sometimes considered a weak spot in the otherwise highly innovative Scandinavian countries (Henrekson, 2005). Ilmakunnas and Kanniainen (2001) provide cross-country analysis of the relationship between entrepreneurship and the welfare state using data from 20 countries, primarily in Europe but also including the US, Canada and Japan. They find that a more extensive welfare state has a negative effect on entrepreneurship, but also suggest that treating entrepreneurs differently from employees in terms of social insurance, such as unemployment benefits, discourages entrepreneurship.

Second, while high levels of access to health-care predominate in

Europe, other high-growth economies are still developing modern systems of health-care access. In China, for example, the provision of health insurance for the self-employed was used for regional economic development. Xu et al. (2007) examine changes in health insurance coverage between 1998 and 2003. They began their survey in 1998 when China introduced a new Urban Employee Basic Health Insurance Scheme (BHIS), which was intended to increase coverage and control costs. This program was even more closely tied to employment than the systems it replaced. Xu et al. reported that the number of self-employed people in China's urban areas increased by almost three million between 1996 and 2000, but that this group was largely ineligible for this and other mainstream health insurance plans. Policy responses at the municipal level in Guiyang and the Urumuqi Autonomous Region included allowing the self-employed to buy into the BHIS by paying the full premium, which typically receives a government or employer subsidy.

Overall, considering the US and other findings about the role of health insurance and entrepreneurship, the implication for regional economic development is that there are potential advantages from designing social welfare programs so that entrepreneurs are not at a disadvantage over other workers. European 'flexicurity' initiatives, which attempt to balance flexibility and security of the labor force, may be a fruitful approach to encourage economically optimal movements among various levels and types of labor force participation, including entrepreneurship (Wilthagen and Tros, 2004).

SIZE-BASED REGULATION AND THE GROWTH OF ENTREPRENEURIAL FIRMS

Policymakers realize the importance of supporting entrepreneurial ventures in large part because of their potential to grow and create good jobs. The creation of good, high-quality jobs contributes to the wellbeing of workers, their families, and their communities. Yet legislation to improve the quality of jobs – protection from unlawful discrimination, leave entitlements, minimum wages, and so on – also creates a challenging web of costs and legal risks for small, growing firms. For that reason, broad, size-based exemptions from employment regulations have a long history in the US. Yet Shane (2009) observes that broad-based exemptions based on size rather than targeting high potential firms may support marginal businesses and may not be effective policy for supporting entrepreneurship. This section examines multiple policy approaches to size-based exemptions and their predicted and observed effects on small business.

We begin with a brief historical timeline of US employment legislation and the exemptions provided for small firms. To avoid imposing burdensome costs of compliance on small firms, US legislation establishing employee rights typically exempts businesses below a certain size. In fact, such consideration is required by two federal laws, the Regulatory Flexibility Act of 1980 and the Small Business Regulatory Enforcement Fairness Act of 1996. Table 8.1 provides a timeline summarizing the coverage provisions of key pieces of legislation establishing employee rights. Coverage provisions vary in the size cutoff of the exemption and the role of geographic location, hours worked, and tenure in determining who counts as an employee. Coverage provisions based on tenure provide some relief for young firms, but new employees are included in counts used to determine firm size and eligible for coverage within one year.

Size-based exemptions from legislation are relevant to the study of entrepreneurship and innovation because entrepreneurial firms start small, but hopefully their growth is not hindered by regulation. Most obviously, when a small firm has been exempted from compliance with certain employment and regulatory policies their internal policies and operating procedures are designed accordingly. Once the firm starts to grow, a new policy regime is applied and the firm must adapt its compliance. As firms grow, they proceed through a thicket of regulation, which imposes what is essentially a tax on their growth as resources are deployed to policy compliance. Of particular interest is the potential for microeconomic and resource dependence factors to keep small firms small and to result in predominantly low-quality jobs.

A microeconomic perspective predicts that costs of regulation affect individual firms at the margin. Consider a growing firm with 14 employees. For such a firm, the marginal cost of adding an employee now includes the cost of compliance with the Americans with Disabilities Act (ADA) for all 15 employees. Microeconomics predicts that such a firm will be less likely to grow to 15 or more employees than it would have been without the law. The firm might remain small or be more likely to fail if its inability to attain its optimal size of 15 or more employees is a significant drain on efficiency. A similar argument could be made for a firm with 49 employees at a single site or within 75 miles, subject to the Family and Medical Leave Act (FMLA), which applies to firms with 50 or more employees within 75 miles, or for any other regulation applied based on the number of employees (Baum, 2003). The microeconomic perspective takes into account the negative effects the costs of legislation may have on firm survival, and how those costs would influence firm hiring behavior at the margin.

Table 8.1   Coverage and key provisions of select US federal employment regulations

Year	Regulation	Coverage	Summary of key provisions
2010	Patient Protection and Affordable Care Act and Health Care and Education Reconciliation Act	50 or more full-time equivalent employees	Beginning in 2014, requires employers to offer qualifying health insurance to employees
1993	Family and Medical Leave Act	Employers with 50 or more employees. Employees at worksites with 50 or more employees within 75 miles	Requires provision of up to 12 weeks of leave, which can be unpaid, as parental leave or for serious health conditions
1992	Americans with Disabilities Act	15 or more employees for each working day in each of 20 or more calendar weeks in the current or preceding calendar year	Prohibits discrimination against the disabled and requires reasonable accommodations
1988	Worker Adjustment and Retraining Notification Act	'[E]mployers are covered by WARN if they have 100 or more employees, not counting employees who have worked less than 6 months in the last 12 months and not counting employees who work an average of less than 20 hours a week'	Requires advance notice of layoffs of specified numbers of employees
1986	Consolidated Omnibus Budget Reconciliation Act (COBRA) health benefit provisions, an amendment to the Employee Retirement Income Security Act (ERISA) of 1974	'[A]ll employers maintaining such plan normally employed fewer than 20 employees on a typical business day during the preceding calendar year' 'Group health plans for employers with 20 or more employees on more than 50 percent of its typical business days in the previous calendar year . . . Both full and part-time employees are counted . . . Each part-time employee counts as a fraction of an employee, with the fraction equal to the number of hours that the	Requires employers to allow separated workers to maintain enrollment in employer-sponsored health plans for a limited time, typically 18 months to 3 years

Table 8.1   (continued)

Year	Regulation	Coverage	Summary of key provisions
		part-time employee worked divided by the hours an employee must work to be considered full time'	
1967	Age Discrimination in Employment Act	'[A] person engaged in an industry affecting commerce who has twenty or more employees for each working day in each of twenty or more calendar weeks in the current or preceding calendar year: Provided, That prior to June 30, 1968, employers having fewer than fifty employees shall not be considered employers'	Prohibits discrimination against workers age 40 and above
1967	Executive Order 11246	50 or more employees and $50,000 or more in business with the US federal government as a contractor or subcontractor	Requires qualified affirmative action plans for women and minorities
1964	Title VII of the Civil Rights Act	15 or more employees for each working day in each of 20 or more calendar weeks in the current or preceding calendar year	Prohibits discrimination based on race, sex, religion, and national origin
1938	Fair Labor Standards Act	As amended in 1990: annual gross volume of sales made or business done is less than $500,000. Numerous additional industry-specific exemptions	Establishes minimum wage and requires overtime payments to qualifying employees

Bradford (2004) observes that there is scant economic literature on small-business exemptions from regulation. Studies of the effects of regulation usually examine compliance costs through *ex ante* cost projections, *ex post* surveys or calculations of firm expenditures and *ex post* estimates of the effects of regulation on observable performance levels, such as firm size. These studies rarely address exemptions explicitly. He explains that the first two methods are vulnerable to political manipulation and that the third frequently does a poor job of studying small business, which is often exempt or subject to weaker regulation. Bradford's review of empirical economic studies of all three types leads him to the conclusion that there are lasting economies of scale in costs of regulation, primarily due to fixed costs. However, he also concluded that variable costs have an effect. Examples of each of these types of studies are presented below.

Phillips (2002) provides an *ex ante* microeconomic model of the impact of expanding the FMLA both to include paid leave and to cover smaller firms. Phillips projects that such changes would result in an average increase in annual costs – including reduced sales, overtime, and management resources – of $30,000 to $50,000 per firm and approximately 60,000 lost jobs nationwide. An *ex post* firm cost calculation by Crain and Hopkins (2005) found that the cost of US federal workplace regulation is higher on a per-employee basis in midsize (20–499 employee) firms than in the smallest (fewer than 20 employee) firms. For the smallest firms, workplace regulation has a smaller per-employee cost than economic, environmental, or tax policy. In an outcome-based *ex post* study, Baum (2003) found relatively little impact on employment and wages from the FMLA and state-level maternity leave legislation. This analysis is perhaps due to the Act extending benefits to relatively few workers who did not already have comparable benefits.

Bradford (2004) develops an economic model to understand the efficiency of exemptions for small business. Starting from the assumption that a regulation is economically efficient if applied universally, his model holds that size-based exemptions are efficient if they result in a greater net benefit than if the law were applied to all firms. However, he notes that transaction costs associated with exemptions may change the net costs and benefits. Some of the transaction costs he considers are costs to regulators to develop efficient exemptions, higher enforcement costs associated with regulating coverage as well as behavior, information costs, and waste from strategic behavior by firms in an attempt to avoid regulation, as resource dependence theory suggests.

Resource dependence theory can be applied to consider a fuller range of strategic responses and therefore a variety of potential unintended consequences. Pfeffer and Salancik's (1978) resource dependence theory emphasizes strategic action by organizations to manage power relationships, reduce uncertainty, and maintain access to critical resources. Oliver (1991) elaborated a theoretical framework for applying resource dependence theory to predict whether organizations' strategic responses to external institutional pressures will take the form of acquiescence, compromise, avoidance, defiance, or manipulation. From the perspective of entrepreneurship policy, the firm responses that Baumol (1990) would describe as unproductive – including avoidance, defiance, and manipulation – are not desirable. Existing legislation anticipates some level of strategic avoidance responses when it specifies how temporary, part-time, and seasonal workers should be counted. However, technology has enabled an increasing variety of strategic responses, such as automation, outsourcing, and off-shoring.

Child's (2005) taxonomy of interfirm links provides a framework to consider potential strategic responses. Some possible strategic responses by organizations attempting to avoid regulation by keeping headcount low are sourcing agreements (including those for services), joint ventures (discussed at greater length in the following section), and divestitures. Mergers and acquisitions represent another possible strategy, since they allow costs of regulation to be spread over a larger group. Policy and firm-level factors may influence firm responses to exemptions through the control exercised by enforcement agencies or alignment of policies with organizational goals (Oliver, 1991).

Fewer empirical studies have considered strategic responses beyond a microeconomic perspective. Studies of unfair dismissal, minimum wage and maternity leave policies in the UK reviewed in Edwards et al. (2004) and the results of 18 small-firm case studies presented in the same paper are analyzed in terms of the economic context, institutional theory, legal reasoning, and industrial relations. These scholars theorize that the failure of these studies to find evidence of harm to small businesses may be due to the informality of small businesses facilitating flexible compromise responses, such as individually negotiated payments or scheduling flexibility in place of legal entitlements, or regulatory effects being outweighed by the effect of competitive conditions. An alternative explanation might be that the UK experience differs from the US experience.

Within the US, there is substantial state and local variation in employment regulations. States and municipalities are free to enact laws that create stronger protections than those put in place by federal law, though they do not enjoy the same discretions for increasing flexibility. It is common for states rather than the federal government to apply employment laws to smaller firms. Further, some states and multi-state regions, such as the Southern states, position themselves as business friendly with minimal employment regulations.

The WARN Act, which requires employers of sufficient size to give notice of plant closings and mass layoffs, provides an example of state-level variation (Prucino and Poloche, 2009). Several states have enacted stricter standards by requiring notice from smaller companies, requiring application of the policy for layoffs affecting fewer employees, and sometimes assessing greater penalties for noncompliance. The WARN Act and many of its state-level counterparts contain provisions to help local governments prepare to assist laid-off workers in transition. This notice supports local economic development and allows government agencies, labor unions, and other intermediary organizations to help workers prepare for new opportunities, sometimes including entrepreneurship, self-employment, and jobs in emerging industries (Osterman, 2004; Eberts, 2005). Questions for further research include whether regional economies benefit more from expanding layoff notice requirements to more employers, applying requirements to smaller layoff events, imposing greater penalties for noncompliance, or engaging intermediaries more strategically in the layoff process.

Jackson's (2009) study of the Massachusetts health insurance reform attributed a negative effect on new firm foundation to an employer mandate to provide health insurance if a firm has 11 or more employees. Because he studied a single metropolitan area that spanned two states, his finding of reduced firm formation might have been due to displacement, though it was not directly tested. In some cases, it may be easy for new firms to be displaced from one jurisdiction to another. It would be useful for future research to focus on examining the evidence for displacement and particularly the effect of displacement on firms that create high- and low-quality jobs.

US policy stands in contrast with recent legislation in Australia. With the implementation of Fair Work Australia in 2010, Australia has recently reduced state-level variation with national standards and eliminated size-based exemptions from some of its key employment regulations related to family leave and unfair dismissal (Gollan, 2009). Three of the main objectives of Australia's recent reform show an awareness of the potential for strategic response and concern about job quality. These include: (i) providing workplace relations laws that are fair to employees and flexible to employers, and promote productivity and economic growth; (ii) ensuring a guaranteed minimum safety net of fair, relevant, and enforceable wages and conditions; and (iii) ensuring that the guaranteed minimum safety net cannot be undermined (ibid., p. 261). These reforms provide an opportunity for scholars to study the creation of good-quality jobs in small firms.

Shane's (2009) warning about the inefficiency of broad-based exemptions as an approach to foster entrepreneurship and Bradford's (2004) concerns about the economic efficiency of exemptions suggest that regional public policy practitioners might reconsider size-based exemptions from employment regulation or create policies that are phased incrementally. The worst outcome is the displacement from one state or region to another in response to inconsistencies in regulation and differing costs of compliance. In an increasingly global economy, national legislation might lead to cross-border displacement. Future research should focus on the ways firms respond strategically to regulation and on the relative success of high- versus low-regulation approaches to foster economic growth and the creation of high-quality jobs. These strategic responses may also affect competition on an industry level, and this is another important topic for future research.

ANTITRUST, COLLABORATIVE RESEARCH, AND INNOVATION

Antitrust legislation has historically focused on regulating the activities of large industrial firms dominating a large portion of the market and thus impeding competition. Over the past 30 years, however, in response to an increasing trend of interfirm collaborations, antitrust legislation has shifted its focus toward encouraging research joint ventures (RJVs) for firms and industries involved with innovative activities (Caloghirou et al., 2003). This has most notably pertained to firms in the R&D sectors. The topic of antitrust legislation and RJVs has received considerable attention from scholars and policymakers because technological innovation is widely perceived to be one of the critical factors driving economic activity and growth (Benfratello and Sembenelli, 2002; Branstetter and Sakakibara, 2002). In this section we first consider the theoretical implications of these changes in legislation and research practices, and discuss the factors that affect these collaborations on the international, national, and regional levels. We then use the US as a case study to review the historical timeline of the policy changes related to RJVs over the past century, and conclude by considering implications for policy and future research.

Since the 1980s, scholars have noticed a stark shift in the nature of interfirm collaborations from equity to non-equity agreements (Katz, 1986; Kattan, 1993; Branstetter and Sakakibara, 2002; Caloghirou et al., 2003). Sharing the concern that innovative research is closely related to inherent market failures, firms began forming research consortia to reduce the potential for wasteful duplications and other risks that are associated with innovative research endeavors. This led to the emergence of joint ventures, defined by the Organisation for Economic Co-operation and Development as activities between two or more firms involved in the following activities: (i) buying or selling operations; (ii) natural resource exploration, development and/or production operations; (iii) R&D operations; and (iv) engineering and construction operations (OECD, 1986). Although certain implications of the RJV policies are disputed, many policymakers support this anticompetitive reform since it provides an opportunity for firms to pool the costs of research, internalize knowledge spillovers, attain economies of scale and scope, and arguably increase R&D activity (Katz, 1986; Kattan, 1993; Katsoutacos and Ulph, 1998; Benfratello and Sembenelli, 2002; Branstetter and Sakakibara, 2002; Silipo, 2008). While empirical evidence is not extensive, scholars have also found RJVs to be the preferred form of collaboration given the increased levels of symmetry among firms, cost-sharing, risk-sharing, spillovers, and complementarities associated with this form of research (Silipo, 2008).

Scholars have also identified a number of shortcomings with RJVs (Katz, 1986; Kattan, 1993; Benfratello and Sembenelli, 2002). In his influential welfare analysis of cooperative research practices, Katz argued that the level of *ex post* product market competition decreases for cooperative research practices. Because of the decrease in the price of production resulting from the collaborative effort, firms decrease their output to preserve their profits. According to Katz, this decrease in R&D output ultimately leads to a decrease in social welfare. Kattan also raised concerns over the free-rider problem affiliated with cooperative endeavors. He points out how conducting research in an open environment places firms in a more vulnerable position compared with the traditional competitive market environment. In addition to these concerns, scholars have identified cultural barriers, administrative costs, information asymmetries, moral hazard, and transaction costs that make contracting imperfect as further shortcomings with RJVs (Kattan, 1993; Barkema et al., 1996; Benfratello and Sembenelli, 2002).

There remains a contentious debate among policymakers, scholars, and researchers over the benefits and consequences of RJVs. Should policymakers encourage collaborative research practices at the expense of traditional market competition? Or should research remain within the bounds of the firm, despite the potential for wasteful duplication and a lessening of incentives to innovate? In the literature, strong cases are made for both RJV reform and antitrust reform. We discuss the balance of these two policies further in our case study analysis of US policies related to cooperative R&D research. Before doing so, we first review the implications of RJVs on the international, national, and regional levels.

The Japanese government was the first nation to actively promote RJV activities. Starting in the 1950s, the Japanese government took an active role in R&D by encouraging full public dissemination of research results and by providing subsidies for collaborative R&D expenditures (Branstetter and Sakakibara, 2002). Prompted by Japan's success and increased levels of R&D competitiveness, many countries in North America, Europe, and Asia followed suit. With the global spread of these policy reforms, these collaborative endeavors came to extend into the international realm. Research from the MERIT-CATI database found that the number of new international collaborations increased over 200 percent from the early 1970s to the 1990s (Caloghirou et al., 2003). These research collaborations not only increased the incentives for firms to innovate, but they also provided an advantageous avenue for firms to expand beyond their industrial and even national bounds. In Hennart's (1991) study of international RJVs, specifically between Japan and the US, he found that firms were more likely to engage in international collaborative endeavors for the following reasons: (i) to increase diversification; (ii) to enter a foreign country for the first time; (iii) to gain access to resources that are controlled locally; and (iv) to combine complementary inputs.

In analyses of RJVs on a national level, scholars have also sought to identify the various dynamics and firm characteristics that promote innovations and decrease the anticompetitive consequences of these research collaborations (Kattan, 1993; Branstetter and Sakakibara, 2002). Although many nations had adapted RJV reforms, Japan remained a leader in innovation throughout the 1980s and 1990s. Evidence from Branstetter and Sakakibara's longitudinal analysis of Japanese research consortia attributes Japan's success to specific policy measures. In addition to subsidies for collaborative research and mandates to fully disseminate research results, the Japanese government encouraged collaboration among firms with complementary research assets and assigned patents to the research consortia rather than to the individual firms. Other studies have found that RJVs are most successful in facilitating innovation if the collaboration occurs during the preliminary stages of research. Specifically, Branstetter and Sakakibara, and Benfratello and Sembenelli (2002) argue that RJVs are most effective when the firms focus on basic research rather than applied. Under these measures, firms are encouraged to cooperate during the initial phases of research when the costs and risks are high while still constraining them to compete in the post-innovation product market (Benfratello and Sembenelli, 2002). On a final note, scholars and policymakers have found that RJVs are more successful in promoting innovation in the high-growth sectors (Hennart, 1991; Kattan, 1993). Using the company rather than the venture as the unit of analysis, Vonortas (1997) found telecommunications to be the leading technology field for RJV participants. Participating firms tended to be in machinery and electrical equipment, with 8 percent of participating entities making up 47 percent of all memberships. Vonortas was surprised to find strong service-industry participation, but this may be due to RJVs being used to facilitate links between customers and suppliers or RJVs allowing non-manufacturers to participate in R&D in areas outside their general scope of work.

While no studies were found that examine RJVs on a regional or state level, results suggest that RJV reforms have varying implications for different industries across regional economies. Given that scholars have found RJVs to be more effective in the high-growth industries, there is considerable room for additional research to examine the effects of this reform on different industrial regions. What are the implications of RJVs in regional economies with varying degrees of R&D? Are RJVs more effective in regions with a stronger high-growth focus, or are they more beneficial for emerging economies? These are some of the avenues that scholars could consider exploring to improve our understanding of these policies. We now turn to the US to more closely examine the RJV and antitrust policy reforms and their implications for innovation.

Hart (2001) describes the history of antitrust in the US as a series of stages alternating between concentration and deconcentration of market power. The *laissez-faire* formative period resulted in the introduction of a legal framework that limits the ability of firms to engage in cooperative action, including R&D. This series of antitrust measures – to prevent firms with market power from colluding to reduce output and thus raise prices and profits – was introduced through a number of policy measures: section 1 of the Sherman Act (1890), section 7 of the Clayton Act (1914), section 2 of the Sherman Act, and section 5 of the Federal Trade Commission Act (1914) (Wright, 1986). During this formative period some industries consolidated to avoid penalties for collaboration with competitors, which allowed these firms to support greater investments in R&D (Hart, 2001).

During the New Deal, increased antitrust enforcement led to decon-centration and thus heightened competition from the 1940s to 1970s. Throughout this period there was an emphasis on in-house R&D rather than acquisitions of small, innovative companies because mergers were closely scrutinized under the structure–conduct–performance standard. This was followed by a period known as 'Chicago School concentration-ism', based on economic arguments that considered almost all markets contestable and emphasized the competitive effects of potential market entrants. From this perspective, concentration, encouraging greater collaboration, was considered favorable to R&D based on the Schumpeterian argument that large firms are free to innovate without fear that the gains would be disproportionately misappropriated by competitors.

As American high-technology firms lost market share in the 1980s, however, blame fell in part on excessive regulation of competition. As a result, policymakers passed the National Cooperative Research Act (NCRA) of 1984, which created provisions for collaboration in R&D in the form of RJVs to reduce economic costs associated with research (Caloghirou et al., 2003). The current era, beginning in the 1990s, is char-acterized by a high-technology focus and return to deconcentration. In the face of technological advances and global competition, much debate arose concerning the need to adapt antitrust enforcement.

Bringing this history into the context of the debate over collaborative research, Jorde and Teece (1990) argued that the NCRA fell short of the needed flexibility to protect collaborative research from the damage and deterrence effects of US antitrust law. Because innovation was now under-stood to be a nonlinear, cumulative, and often simultaneous activity, they found that the NCRA's coverage that was limited to research activities provided insufficient protection for developing and commercializing new products. They argued that innovation required R&D to be closely integrated with manufacturing, procurement, and especially marketing functions to allow for rapid feedback and mid-course adjustments. Noting the more supportive legal framework for collaboration in Europe and Japan, they advocated for extension of the NCRA's registration protection to the entire commercialization process and adoption of a certification that would exempt research and innovation collaborations that are expected to increase market competition from antitrust suits. Jorde and Teece's argument for this broad extension of the NCRA rests on the principle that innovation leads to economic growth, the idea that firms need to adopt appropriate organizational forms to succeed as innovators, and the assertion that global industries with rapidly changing technology are unlikely to form cartels.

Brodley (1990), on the other hand, argued against this reform. He noted that antitrust enforcement has not been aggressive and stated that only minimal reforms were needed to address issues of perceived antitrust prosecution risk. He claimed that 'innovation collaboration appears capable of injuring competition when the collaboration includes substantially the whole market and when entry barriers exist' (p. 98). In these cases, collaboration can have anticompetitive effects on research, downstream, and input markets. Scott (1988) added to these concerns by showing that the NCRA may have induced R&D collaboration beyond socially optimal levels. Although Brodley did acknowledge the antitrust risks in the areas of production and marketing joint ventures involving small firms and experimental production collaboration among large firms, he argued for more limited reforms, which included coverage of experimental joint production under the NCRA.

Link (1996) examined RJVs between 1984 and 1994, roughly the same time period of the original NCRA reform. He found that RJVs were most commonly found in the communications and electronics industries, which was consistent with the expectation that spillovers motivate collaboration. Environmental, health, and safety research topics were the leading types of RJVs. Foreign affiliates and universities were the most common external partners in RJVs although the involvement of foreign affiliates declined over time. In another study drawing from RJV data through 2003, Link and Scott (2005) found that RJV registration peaked in the mid-1990s and declined sharply thereafter. Universities' participation in RJVs increased, however, especially as partners in large ventures. Using data from 1990 to 1994 from the same source, Röller et al. (2007) found evidence to support their prediction that variance in firm size within an industry influences the suitability of the RJV structure. Large firms will tend not to form RJVs with small firms because the RJV tends to reduce industry asymmetry and therefore large-firm profitability.

The adequacy of the legal framework for cooperative research has continued to be a subject of debate. Drawing on his cyclical and dynamic model, Hart (2001) claimed that precedents from earlier periods are difficult to apply to current antitrust issues. Some of his suggested approaches to ensure appropriate consideration of antitrust issues include greater transparency about the role of technology in antitrust decisions, more antitrust enforcement personnel with technological expertise, and consideration of the interaction between public R&D funding and antitrust.

Increased attention to new economy issues provided substantial motivation for the creation of the Antitrust Modernization Commission (AMC) in 2004. The Commission received 192 public comments on issues such as merger enforcement, civil remedies, immunities and exemptions, the relationship of intellectual property to antitrust, information-sharing in standards development working groups, and post-grant review of patents (AMC, 2007; see also Hemphill, 2005). Only 12 of the comments were related to new economy issues, however. As a result, the Commission made two recommendations with respect to antitrust and the new economy: (i) there is no need to revise the antitrust laws to apply different rules to industries in which innovation, intellectual property, and technological change are central features; and (ii) for industries in which innovation, intellectual property, and technological change are central features, antitrust enforcers should carefully consider market dynamics in assessing competitive effects, and they should ensure proper attention to economic and other characteristics of particular industries that may have an important bearing on a valid antitrust analysis (AMC, 2007, p. 9). Although the Commission recommended merger reforms and repeal of the Robinson–Patman Act of 1936 (a price-discrimination statute intended to protect small retailers), the report was primarily an affirmation of the existing antitrust laws (AMC, 2007; Carlton, 2007).

In one sense, the Commission's report leads to the conclusion that the antitrust environment for collaborative research is appropriate and likely to remain stable. On the other hand, the Commission may not have been adequately informed about new economy issues due to limited public comment on those topics. Recent events including the extended recession, the renewed focus on national innovation policy – including metrics from the Bureau of Economic Analysis and platforms from the nation's first Chief Technology Officer – and increased federal investment in science and technology may motivate the US to revisit the legal framework for cooperative research in the near term (Lohr, 2009). While support of domestic manufacturing is understandable, the telecommunications and electronics industries doing the most collaborative research rely heavily and increasingly on overseas production. The gains from flexibility in manufacturing may outweigh gains from collaboration, essentially negating much of the 1993 reform. The suitability of the US antitrust environment for collaborative research and innovation remains an important area for empirical investigation.

As this discussion has shown, both the policy of cracking down on industry collaboration through antitrust measures and the contrary policy of encouraging collaboration through RJVs have their benefits and limitations in promoting innovation and economic activity. These policies have considerable implications for both the nature of R&D activity and subsequent levels of innovation, entrepreneurship, and economic growth. As the US case has shown, this remains an ongoing debate for policymakers, especially with shifts in the national and global economies. As policymakers seek to improve antitrust and RJV policies that promote innovation, scholars must strive toward a deeper understanding of the implications both policies have on varying economies. Scholarship and policy decision-making would benefit from careful comparative consideration of RJV and antitrust policies with other aspects of national innovation systems (Silipo, 2008).

CONCLUSION

The four cases examined in this chapter illustrate the potential for entrepreneurship and innovation to be shaped by a wide variety of public policies with both direct and indirect implications for innovation. These four cases serve as examples of the breadth of policies that can have inadvertent effects on this critical aspect of the economy. Non-compete enforcement may influence firm structure and foster the growth of high-tech clusters through the interaction of geographic and industry characteristics. The institution of employer-provided health insurance may shape the individual characteristics of entrepreneurs and the size and geographic location of their growing firms. Employment regulation with exemptions based on headcount may influence firm structure, industry, and geographic location of growing entrepreneurial firms. Antitrust legislation and enforcement may influence the structure of firms and industries and the nature of innovative output from collaborative research.

The inadvertent consequences of policy for entrepreneurship and innovation are certainly not limited by the cases considered here. Other relevant cases are the tax treatment of investments in human and other types of innovative capital; the effects of immigration policy on attraction and retention of top scientific talent; and the introduction of new medical innovations through the price points of reimbursement through public health programs. In addition, policies related to intellectual property, as it applies to innovation, also have many unintended consequences.

As these cases illustrate, when policies are developed to promote entrepreneurship, they are enacted in a context of other policies that already act as constraints or catalysts to their proposed effects. This context should be considered when designing and advocating policies that foster entrepreneurship. Researchers and policymakers studying and advocating for policies that support entrepreneurship and innovation should not limit their focus, but rather should attend to a broad spectrum of policies and consider any potential inadvertent effects these policies may have for firms. The heightened importance of entrepreneurial ventures in the new economy means that it is increasingly important to consider the effects of any proposed or existing policy on innovative and growing ventures.

NOTES

1. Authors are listed alphabetically. We would like to acknowledge funding from the National Science Foundation under SBE-0947814 and CHE-9876674. We thank Michael Fritsch, Paul Tippett, and Richard Blackburn for comments and suggestions.
2. Hart (2003) provides a review of the development of US entrepreneurship policy while Parker (2005) provides a review of policy initiatives that directly affect entrepreneurship. Carlsson (2006) and Wolfe and Gertler (2006) discuss cluster development policies with a specific focus on new business formation.

REFERENCES

Almeida, P. and B. Kogut (1999), 'Localization of knowledge and the mobility of engineers in regional networks', *Management Science*, **45** (7), 905–17.

Antitrust Modernization Commission (AMC) (2007), *Report and Recommendations*, Washington, DC.

Audretsch, D.B. and M.P. Feldman (1996), 'R&D spillovers and the geography of innovation and production', *American Economic Review*, **86** (3), 630–40.

Barkema, H.G., J.H.J. Bell and J.M. Pennings (1996), 'Foreign entry, cultural barriers, and learning', *Strategic Management Journal*, **17** (2), 151–66.

Baum, C.L. (2003), 'The effect of state maternity leave legislation and the 1993 Family and Medical Leave Act on employment and wages', *Labour Economics*, **10** (5), 573–96.

Baumol, W.J. (1990), 'Entrepreneurship: productive, unproductive, and destructive', *Journal of Political Economy*, **98** (5), 893–921.

Benfratello, L. and A. Sembenelli (2002), 'Research joint ventures and firm level performance', *Research Policy*, **31** (4), 493–507.

Bradford, C.S. (2004), 'Does size matter: an economic analysis of small business exemptions from regulation', *Journal of Small and Emerging Business Law*, **8** (1), 1–38.

Branstetter, L.G. and M. Sakakibara (2002), 'When do research consortia work well and why? Evidence from Japanese panel data', *American Economic Review*, **92** (1), 143–59.

Brodley, J.F. (1990), 'Antitrust law and innovation cooperation', *Journal of Economic Perspectives*, **4** (3), 97–112.

Brunetti, M.J., K. Nayeri, C.E. Dobkin and H.E. Brady (2000), 'Health status, health insurance, and worker mobility: a study of job lock in California', paper presented at the California Work & Health Survey Research Conference, December, available at: http://ucdata.berkeley.edu/pub_list.php?recid=2 (accessed March 21, 2001).

Buchmueller, T.C. and R.G. Valletta (1996), 'The effects of employer-provided health insurance on worker mobility', *Industrial and Labor Relations Review*, **49** (3), 439–55.

Caloghirou, Y., S. Ioannides and N.S. Vonortas (2003), 'Research joint ventures', *Journal of Economic Surveys*, **17** (4), 541–70.

Carlsson, B. (2006), 'The role of public policy in emerging clusters', in P. Braunerhjelm and M.P. Feldman (eds), *Cluster Genesis: Technology Based Industrial Development*, New York: Oxford University Press, pp. 264–78.

Carlton, D.W. (2007), 'Does antitrust need to be modernized?', *Journal of Economic Perspectives*, **21** (3), 155–76.

Chatterji, A.K. (2009), 'Spawned with a silver spoon? Entrepreneurial performance and innovation in the medical device industry', *Strategic Management Journal*, **30** (2), 185–206.

Child, J. (2005), *Organization: Contemporary Principles and Practice,* Malden, MA: Wiley-Blackwell.

Crain, W.M. and T.D. Hopkins (2005), 'The impact of regulatory costs on small firms', *Small Business Research Summary*, **264** (1), 1–87.

DeCicca, P. (2010), 'Health insurance availability and entrepreneurship', Upjohn Institute Working Paper No. 10-167, W.E. Upjohn Institute for Employment Research, Kalamazoo, MI.

Decker, K.H. (2002), *Covenants Not to Compete*, New York: John Wiley & Sons.

Eberts, R.W. (2005), 'After the doors close: assisting laid-off workers to find jobs', *Economic Perspectives*, **29** (2), 75–86.

Edwards, P., M. Ram and J. Black (2004), 'Why does employment legislation not damage small firms?', *Journal of Law and Society*, **31** (2), 245–65.

Ewing Marion Kauffman Foundation (2007), *On the Road to an Entrepreneurial Economy: A Research and Policy Guide*, Kansas City, MO.

Fairlie, R.W., K. Kapur and S.M. Gates (2008), 'Is employer-based health insurance a barrier to entrepreneurship?', RAND Working Paper Series, No. WR-637-EMKF.

Fallick, B., C.A. Fleischman and J.B. Rebitzer (2006), 'Job-hopping in Silicon Valley: some evidence concerning the microfoundations of a high-technology cluster', *Review of Economics and Statistics*, **88** (3), 472–81.

Feldman, M.P. (1999), 'The new economics of innovation, spillovers and agglomeration: a review of empirical studies', *Economics of Innovation and New Technology*, **8** (1), 5–25.

Feldman, M.P. and D.B. Audretsch (1999), 'Innovation in cities: science-based diversity, specialization and localized competition', *European Economic Review*, **43** (2), 409–29.

Feller, I. (1992), 'American state governments as models for national science policy', *Journal of Policy Analysis and Management*, **11** (2), 288–309.

Garmaise, M.J. (2009), 'Ties that truly bind: noncompetition agreements, executive compensation, and firm investment', *Journal of Law, Economics, and Organization*, Advance Access, 1–50.

Gilson, R.J. (1998), 'The legal infrastructure of high technology industrial districts: Silicon Valley, Route 128, and covenants not to compete', *New York University Law Review*, **74**, 575–629.

Gollan, P.J. (2009), 'Australian industrial relations reform in perspective: beyond work choices and future prospects under the Fair Work Act 2009', *Asia Pacific Journal of Human Resources*, **47** (3), 260–70.

Gompers, P., J. Lerner and D. Scharfstein (2005), 'Entrepreneurial spawning: public corporations and the genesis of new ventures, 1986 to 1999', *Journal of Finance*, **60** (2), 577–614.

Gottschalk, M. (2000), *The Shadow Welfare State: Labor, Business, and the Politics of Health Care in the United States*, Ithaca, NY and London: ILR Press.

Gregory, D. (1986), 'Scope of ERISA preemption of state law: a study in effective federalism', *University of Pittsburgh Law Review*, **48** (1), 427–90.

Gumus, G. and T. Regan (2007), 'Tax incentives as a solution to the uninsured: evidence from the self-employed', University of Miami Working Paper 0709, Miami, FL.

Hacker, J. (2002), *The Divided Welfare State: The Battle over Public and Private Social Benefits in the United States*, New York: Cambridge University Press.

Hart, D.M. (2001), 'Antitrust and technological innovation in the US: ideas, institutions, decisions, and impacts, 1890–2000', *Research Policy*, **30** (6), 923–36.

Hart, D.M. (2003), *The Emergence of Entrepreneurship Policy: Governance, Start-ups, and Growth in the US Knowledge Economy*, New York: Cambridge University Press.

Heim, B.T. and I.Z. Lurie (2009), 'The effect of health insurance premium subsidies on entry into and exit from self-employment', unpublished working paper, Office of Tax Analysis, US Department of the Treasury.

Hemphill, T.A. (2005), 'Modernizing U.S. antitrust law: the role of technology and innovation', *Business Economics*, **40** (2), 70–74.

Hennart, J.F. (1991), 'The transaction costs theory of joint ventures: an empirical study of Japanese subsidiaries in the United States', *Management Science*, **37** (4), 483–97.

Henrekson, M. (2005), 'Entrepreneurship: a weak link in the welfare state?', *Industrial and Corporate Change*, **14** (3), 437–67.

Holtz-Eakin, D., J.R. Penrod and H.S. Rosen (1996), 'Health insurance and the supply of entrepreneurs', *Journal of Public Economics*, **62** (1–2), 209–35.

Howard, C. (1997), *The Hidden Welfare State: Tax Expenditures and Social Policy in the United States*, Princeton, NJ: Princeton University Press.

Howard, C. (2006), *The Welfare State Nobody Knows: Debunking Myths about U.S. Social Policy*, Princeton, NJ: Princeton University Press.

Hyde, A. (1998), 'Silicon Valley's high-velocity labor market', *Journal of Applied Corporate Finance*, **11** (2), 28–37.

Ilmakunnas, P. and V. Kanniainen (2001), 'Entrepreneurship, economic risks, and risk insurance in the welfare state: results with OECD data 1978–93', *German Economic Review*, **2** (3), 195–218.

Jackson, S. (2010), 'Mulling over Massachusetts: health insurance mandates and entrepreneurs', *Entrepreneurship Theory and Practice*, **34** (5), 909–31.

Jorde, T.M. and D.J. Teece (1990), 'Innovation and cooperation: implications for competition and antitrust', *Journal of Economic Perspectives*, **4** (3), 75–96.

Kaiser Family Foundation (2009), *Survey of Healthy San Francisco Participants*, Menlo Park, CA, available at: http://www.healthysanfrancisco.org/files/PDF/HSF_Satisfaction_Survey_Kaiser.pdf (accessed March 21, 2011).

Katsoutacos, Y. and D. Ulph (1998), 'Endogenous spillovers and the performance of research joint ventures', *Journal of Industrial Economics*, **46** (3), 333–57.

Kattan, J. (1993), 'Antitrust analysis of technology joint ventures: allocative efficiency and the rewards of innovation', *Antitrust Law Journal*, **61**, 937–73.

Katz, M.L. (1986), 'An analysis of cooperative research and development', *RAND Journal of Economics*, **17** (4), 527–43.

Klepper, S. and S. Sleeper (2005), 'Entry by spinoffs', *Management Science*, **51** (8), 1291–306.

Link, A.N. (1996), 'Research joint ventures: patterns from Federal Register filings', *Review of Industrial Organization*, **11** (5), 617–28.

Link, A.N. and J.T. Scott (2005), 'Universities as partners in U.S. research joint ventures', *Research Policy*, **34** (3), 385–93.

Lohr, S. (2009), 'Can governments till the fields of innovation?', *New York Times*, 21 June p. BU3, available at: http://www.nytimes.com/2009/06/21/technology/21unboxed.html?_r=1&hpw (accessed March 21, 2011).

Malsberger, B.M., S.M. Brock and A.H. Pedowitz (2002), *Covenants Not to Compete: A State-by-State Survey*, Washington, DC: BNA Books (Bureau of National Affairs).

Marx, M., D. Strumsky and L. Fleming (2007), 'Noncompetes and inventor mobility: specialists, stars, and the Michigan experiment', Harvard Business School Working Paper 07-042, Cambridge, MA.

McElroy, A.C. and P. Haleen (2009), 'A widening gap? An overview of US and EU antitrust rules for franchisors', *Franchise Law Journal*, **29** (1), 23–31.

Monahan, A.B. (2006), 'Pay or play laws, ERISA preemption, and potential lessons from Massachusetts,' *University of Kansas Law Review*, **55** (5), 1203–32.

Oliver, C. (1991), 'Strategic responses to institutional processes', *Academy of Management Review*, **16** (1), 145–79.

Organisation for Economic Co-operation and Development (1986), *Competition Policy and Joint Ventures*, Paris: OECD.

Osborne, D. (1988), *Laboratories of Democracy*, Boston, MA: Harvard Business School Press.

Osterman, P. (2004), 'Labor market intermediaries in the modern labor market', in R.P. Giloth (ed.), *Workforce Intermediaries for the Twenty-first Century*, Philadelphia, PA: Temple University Press, pp.155–69.

Parker, S.C. (2005), 'The economics of entrepreneurship: what we know and what we don't', *Foundations and Trends in Entrepreneurship*, **1** (1) 1–54.

Pfeffer, J. and G. Salancik (1978), *The External Control of Organizations: A Resource Dependence Perspective*, New York: Harper Row.

Phillips, B.D. (2002), 'The economic costs of expanding the Family and Medical Leave Act to small business', *Business Economics*, **37** (2), 44–55.

Prucino, D.L. and S. Poloche (2009), 'State plant closing and mass layoff laws can pose pitfalls to unwary employers', *Employment Relations Today*, **36** (3), 81–101.

Röller, L.H., R. Siebert and M.M. Tombak (2007), 'Why firms form (or do not form) RJVS', *Economic Journal*, **117** (522), 1122–44.

Samila, S. and O. Sorenson (2011), 'Non-compete covenants: incentives to innovate or impediments to growth', Working Paper 10-02, Danish Research Unit for Industrial Dynamics.

Saxenian, A. (1985), 'The genesis of Silicon Valley', in P. Hall and A. Markusen (eds), *Silicon Landscapes*, New York: HarperCollins, pp. 20–34.

Saxenian, A. (2006), *The New Argonauts: Regional Advantage in a Global Economy*, Cambridge, MA: Harvard University Press.

Scott, J.T. (1988), 'Diversification versus co-operation in R&D investment', *Managerial and Decision Economics*, **9** (3), 173–86.

Shane, S. (2009), 'Why encouraging more people to become entrepreneurs is bad public policy', *Small Business Economics*, **33** (2), 141–9.

Silipo, D.B. (2008), 'Incentives and forms of cooperation in research and development', *Research in Economics*, **62** (2), 101–19.

Spence, D.B. and P. Murray (1999), 'Law, economics, and politics of federal preemption jurisprudence: a quantitative analysis', *California Law Review*, **87**, 1125–207.

Stewart, A. and J. Greene (2010), 'Choice of law and covenants not to compete: Australia: choice of law and the enforcement of post-employment restraints in Australia', *Comparative Labor Law and Policy Journal*, **31** (1), 305–30.

Thomasson, M.A. (2003), 'The importance of group coverage: how tax policy shaped U.S. health insurance', *American Economic Review*, **93** (4), 1373–84.

Valletta, R. (2002), 'On the move: California employment law and high-tech development', *FRBSF Economic Letter*, August 16, 3.

Vanko, K.J. (2002), 'You're fired – and don't forget your non-compete: the enforceability of restrictive covenants in involuntary discharge cases', *DePaul Business and Commercial Law Journal*, **1** (1), 1–48.

Vonortas, N.S. (1997), 'Research joint ventures in the US', *Research Policy*, **26** (4–5), 577–95.

Wellington, A.J. (2001), 'Health insurance coverage and entrepreneurship', *Contemporary Economic Policy*, **19** (4), 465–78.

Wilthagen, T. and F. Tros (2004), 'The concept of "flexicurity": a new approach to regulating employment and labour markets', *Transfer: European Review of Labour and Research*, **10** (2), 166–86.

Wolfe, D.A. and M.S. Gertler (2006), 'Local antecedents and trigger events: policy implications of path dependence for cluster formation', in P. Braunerhjelm and M.P. Feldman (eds), *Cluster Genesis: Technology Based Industrial Development*, New York: Oxford University Press, pp. 243–64.

Wright, C.O.B. (1986), 'National Cooperative Research Act of 1984: a new antitrust regime for joint research and development ventures', *High Technology Law Journal*, **1** (1), 133–94.

Xu, L., Y. Wang, C. Collins and S. Tang (2007), 'Urban health insurance reform and coverage in China using data from National Health Services Surveys in 1998 and 2003', *BMC Health Services Research*, **7** (1), 37.

Zissimopoulos, J.M. and L.A. Karoly (2007), 'Transitions to self-employment at older ages: the role of wealth, health, health insurance and other factors', *Labor Economics*, **14**, 269–95.

APPENDIX 8A

Table 8A.1   Institutional factors shaping entrepreneurship: review of selected empirical studies

Study	Data and methodology	Results
Non-compete agreements and agglomeration economies		
Almeida & Kogut (1999)	Logistic regression of patent and patent citation data from the semiconductor industry, 1980–1995	Local labor mobility mediates agglomeration economies
Audretsch & Feldman (1996)	OLS and 3SLS state-level analysis of Small Business Administration's innovation database of new products introduced in 1982	Geographic concentration of production depends on how important new knowledge is to a given industry
Fallick, Fleischman & Rebitzer (2006)	2SLS model using Current Population Survey, 1994–2001	Employees moved between computer-industry firms more often in Silicon Valley than they did in IT clusters where states enforced covenants not to compete; computer-industry interfirm mobility was higher in California compared to other states; and interfirm mobility in Silicon Valley and California was higher in all industries
Feldman & Audretsch (1999)	Poisson regression analysis of data from Business Week, Small Business Administration's innovation database, County Business Patterns, and Yale Survey of R&D managers, 1975–1982	A concentration of firms engaged in complementary activities but sharing a common science base is more conducive to innovation than is local specialization
Garmaise (2009)	Time-series and cross-sectional analyses using Standard and Poor's Execu-comp and Compustat data. Designed an enforceability index of state-level non-compete legislation to consider two theoretical models	Stricter non-compete policies yield lower degrees of labor mobility. Tougher enforcement of the non-compete policy led to a decrease in R&D and a decrease in capital employee expenditures

Table 8A.1   (continued)

Study	Data and methodology	Results
Non-compete agreements and agglomeration economies		
Gilson (1998)	Narrative case studies of Silicon Valley and Route 128	California's legal system, which does not enforce covenants not to compete, has enabled knowledge-based agglomeration economies in Silicon Valley, allowing the region to surpass Route 128
Marx, Strumsky & Fleming (2007)	Difference-in-differences and Cox event-history analyses of patent data, 1960–2006	When Michigan began enforcing covenants not to compete in the mid-1980s, intrastate mobility of inventors decreased. The effect was larger for 'star' and 'specialist' inventors
Samila & Sorenson (2011)	Panel data of US metropolitan areas from 1993 to 2002. Narrative of Canadian implications resulting from non-compete practices	For states enforcing non-compete agreements, evidence from analysis suggests that an increase in venture capital has a positive effect for the number of patents, start-ups and employment
Stewart & Greene (2010)	Legal analysis of Australia's subnational non-compete covenants	Call for Australian legal consideration of international and state/territorial complications that arise from variations in non-compete covenants
Valletta (2002)	Regression analysis of state-level employment and salary growth data from the American Electronics Association, 1995–2000	Some evidence that employment growth in computer services benefitted from the lack of non-compete enforcement in California and Colorado
Health insurance and new ventures		
Brunetti et al. (2000)	Logistic regression model using California Work and Health Survey, 1998–1999, and Current Population Survey, 1997–1998	Even after implementation of COBRA continuation of coverage, and shortly after implementation of HIPAA continuity of coverage, this study finds evidence of reduced worker mobility based on objective measures of health status

Table 8A.1   (continued)

Study	Data and methodology	Results
Health insurance and new ventures		
Buchmueller & Valletta (1996)	Probit model using Survey of Income and Program Participation, 1984	Finds evidence of reduced worker mobility based on health status, with a stronger effect for women than for men
Fairlie, Kapur & Gates (2008)	Difference-in-differences and regression discontinuity probit models using Current Population Survey, 1996–2006	Access to health insurance through a spouse associated with a 1 percentage point increase in transitions to entrepreneurship compared with a base transition rate of 3 percent
Gumus & Regan (2007)	Difference-in-differences analysis of Current Population Survey data, 1996–2006	Incremental reforms in the tax code to allow the self-employed to deduct 25–100% of the cost of health insurance resulted in an increased probability of purchasing coverage. However, many of the self-employed still did not purchase health insurance
Heim & Lurie (2009)	Fixed effects regression using instrumental variables using panel data from tax returns, 1999–2004	Tax deductibility of health insurance was associated with a 0.9 percentage point increase in transitions to self-employment and a 3.3 percentage point decrease in the probability of exiting self-employment
Holtz-Eakin, Penrod & Rosen (1996)	Cross-sectional analysis of 1984 Panel Survey of Income Dynamics and longitudinal analysis of Survey of Income and Program Participation, 1984–1987	Found no evidence that an alternate source of health insurance through a spouse was associated with an increased probability of becoming self-employed
Jackson (2010)	Binomial probability, time series, and random effects regression models using census data, patent records, and firm records from the Info U.S.A® business directories, 2006–2007	Found no evidence that Massachusetts health insurance reform resulted in an increase in entrepreneurship, possibly due to the employer mandate feature of the legislation

Table 8A.1 (continued)

Study	Data and methodology	Results
Health insurance and new ventures		
Thomasson (2003)	Probit and tobit estimations based on Nationwide Family Surveys conducted by the National Opinion Research Center, 1953 and 1958	The tax subsidy increased group health coverage and formalized the institution of employment-based health insurance
Wellington (2001)	Difference-in-differences analysis of Current Population Survey, 1993	Self-employment would increase from 2.3 to 4.4 percentage points for husbands and 1.2 to 4.6 points for wives if a guaranteed alternative source of health insurance were available
Zissimopolous & Karoly (2007)	Longitudinal analysis of panel data from Health and Retirement Survey, 1992–2000	No clear evidence that availability of health insurance through a spouse or through retiree health insurance has an enabling effect on entrepreneurship
Employment regulation and the growth of new ventures		
Baum (2003)	Difference-in-differences model using data from the National Longitudinal Survey of Youth, 1986–1994	Maternity leave legislation has only negligible effects on employment and wages
Crain & Hopkins (2005)	*Ex post* calculation of firm costs using data from published studies and reports	Costs of workplace regulation are highest for mid-size firms and workplace policies have a smaller impact than economic, environmental, or tax policies in small firms
Edwards, Ram & Black (2004)	Eighteen case studies of small firms in the UK	Employment regulation has little effect on small firms
Phillips (2002)	National Federation of Independent Business Regulatory Impact Model	Expansion of FMLA to cover smaller firms would result in an average increase in annual costs of $30,000–50,000 per firm and approximately 60,000 lost jobs

Table 8A.1   (continued)

Study	Data and methodology	Results
Antitrust regulation in an entrepreneurial economy		
Benfratello & Sembenelli (2002)	Empirical analysis of European RJVs under two programs: EUREKA and Framework Programs for Science and Technology (FPST). Supplemental data from AMADEUS	Firms affiliated with EUREKA have experienced improvement in their performance post-policy. Performance was based on labor productivity, total factor productivity, and price cost margin
Branstetter & Sakakibara (2002)	Large sample econometric study of Japanese government-supported research consortia	Results suggest that participation in research consortia was correlated with higher levels of firm R&D spending and that participation raised research productivity. Found support that research consortia had positive spillover effects
Branstetter & Sakakibara (2002)	With the research consortia as the unit of analysis, they created a mapping of Japanese research consortia practices using data from Japanese and US Patent Office	Consortia outcomes are positively associated with R&D spillovers, and the outcomes are negatively associated with the product market competition
Hennart (1991)	Survey of Japanese subsidiaries in US in 1985. Data from Toyo Keizai's 1987 questionnaire to Japanese corporations	Evidence that Japanese investor ownership is driven by same transaction costs that influence US investor ownership
Kattan (1993)	Legal analysis of technology joint ventures in US	Discussion of the benefits (shared risk, ease of entry to market, and decrease in duplication of research) and shortcomings (free-rider problem and potential for suboptimal investments) resulting from RJV policies
Link (1996)	Quantitative descriptive analysis of CORE database with venture-level information from the Federal Register, 1984–1994	Communication services industry is the sector with the most RJVs, followed by electronic/electrical. Environmental, health and safety research topics are the leading types of RJVs identified

Table 8A.1   (continued)

Study	Data and methodology	Results
Antitrust regulation in an entrepreneurial economy		
Link & Scott (2005)	Probit regression analysis of CORE database, 1984–2003	Larger RJVs are more likely to include universities because conditions are more favorable to appropriate research outcomes
Röller, Siebert & Tombak (2007)	Endogenous switching model and rare events logit model using data from CORE database, 1990–1994	Firms in less concentrated industries increased their R&D intensities. Firms in more concentrated industries are less likely to form RJVs. The presence of large RJVs makes it less likely that other RJVs will form. The results support cost-sharing as a motivation to form an RJV
Vonortas (1997)	Quantitative descriptive analysis of National Cooperative Research Act Research Joint Venture firm-level database information from the Federal Register, 1985–1995	RJVs most prevalent in telecommunications technology. Machinery and electrical equipment firms strongly represented. Some evidence of RJVs engaged in generic research. General upward trend in number of RJVs registered annually

9 Universities, entrepreneurship, and local economic development

Thomas Åstebro and Navid Bazzazian[1]

INTRODUCTION

The last 30 years have seen an increasing rate of spin-offs from university research: the Association of University Technology Managers (AUTM) which collects quantitative data on licensing activities at US universities and research institutions reports 3,376 spin-offs between 1980 and 2000, and another 2,885 between 2001 and 2007. This acceleration is not confined to the US. There is a concomitant increase in other countries across the world. An increasing fraction of academics are engaging in entrepreneurial activities (Thursby and Thursby, 2007) and more companies are started based on research at universities than these numbers reveal since not all spin-offs are disclosed to universities and faculty may also start up businesses that are not based on university intellectual property rights (IP).[2] While university spin-offs have been increasing in absolute terms, licenses of university patents to established firms strongly dominate over spin-offs as a form of technology commercialization. In 2007 there were eight times as many executed licenses to each university spin-off. However, spin-offs are becoming relatively more important as the relationship was even larger a decade ago; 12 licenses per start-up in 1996 (AUTM data).

This literature review spans several areas of research with a focus on the impact of universities on local entrepreneurship and economic development. There is also some original research; several secondary datasets are re-analyzed and we add some primary interview and case data from a few universities.[3] We do not examine the broader economic impacts of universities on local economies such as the effects of students' consumption. For a recent review of the latter literature, see Goldstein (2009). Local is defined from the city level and sometimes up to the state/province. We mostly treat the university as the unit of analysis and ask first, 'What role do universities play in stimulating local economic development through entrepreneurship?' and second, 'What can a university do to encourage entrepreneurship to increase local economic development?'. However, it is also important to recognize that many university decisions are driven by state allocation of funding for higher education and research and so we shall also consider at times the state as the implicit decision maker.

In many countries the role of the university has recently expanded to include the creation of local economic development. This goal expansion has not been without its critics. More importantly, the role of creating local economic development has become an important point on many political agendas. In this perspective, this literature review is both timely but also frustrated in the lack of documented causal effects.

This is a critical literature review which will question some current dogma. It will not cite or review all previous articles in the field. Instead, for recent comprehensive reviews, see Rothaermel et al. (2007) and Djokovic and Souitaris (2008). We start with an exposé of the history of university-based entrepreneurship. We then continue to review research on the distribution of return to innovation, the entrepreneurial university, technology transfer/technology licensing, the importance of students/alumni as founders of start-ups, science parks and incubators, entrepreneurship education, local and regional conditions, and finally local and regional impacts. There is then a concluding section.

This review will start out by analyzing whether social welfare is maximized through private ownership of university research and the impact of the increased private protection of these rights on welfare. We shall ask whether it makes sense for society to have universities increase their direct involvement in commercialization of their research. There exist a fair number of studies showing that the size, age, and expenditure of technology licensing offices (TLOs) are positively correlated with university licensing revenues and spin-off rates, possibly suggesting that activities should be expanded to promote commercialization (Siegel et al., 2007a). But the causation is unclear and we shall examine the role of TLOs critically. We shall also discuss the matter of unintended consequences of recent regulatory and normative changes with respect to commercialization of university research.

Further, we shall discuss whether maximizing local entrepreneurship necessarily maximizes total welfare. For example, maximizing licensing revenues may produce greater welfare than maximizing spin-off rates, or vice versa. Universities can differ regarding these goals (Belenzon and Schankerman, 2009). It may be difficult for one university to generate local spin-offs, for example due to adverse local economic conditions such as lack of local complementary resources (for example, local industry, venture capital, and relevant labor force) or due to strong public service norms among its scientists. However, licensing of research, theoretically, is not constrained by the availability of local resources, and so may be preferred in such instances. Several additional goal conflicts appear to exist. For example, the royalty rate allocated to the researchers has been shown to raise university licensing income (Lach and Schankerman, 2008) but reduce spin-off rates (Di Gregorio and Shane, 2003). Further, consulting and university–industry collaborative research may not be maximized if a university focuses on maximizing spin-off rates. Finally, the university conditions that maximize the commercialization of research may not maximize research quality or output.

It is important, therefore, to compare the various outcomes from university research on social welfare: free knowledge dissemination, licensing, start-ups, and consulting. Only a few articles have attempted such comparative analysis of opportunity costs currently hampering policy conclusions. The existing literature which discusses the role of universities for local economic development, and more ambitiously that which addresses cluster formation, has yet to show conclusively how universities create local economic development through entrepreneurship formation. We shall present as much evidence as can be assembled at this time on the impact of universities on local economic development. We shall discuss, for example, the role of TLO policies, faculty quality, science parks and incubators, the role of teaching entrepreneurship, and finally the role of students versus faculty, as a source of local economic growth.

We shall also bring forward arguments and review evidence on university policies and regulation regarding ownership of university-created intellectual property. Starting with the US and the Bayh–Dole Act, there have been wide-ranging recent changes in such policies across Europe. Some early evidence has been appearing and it is time to take stock as to whether these policy changes are likely to be effective.

Finally, we shall ask whether much of past research and practice on commercializing research from universities may have missed the target. Most past research and practice has focused on the productivity of technology transfer licensing offices, investigating TLO practices and university policies as antecedents of spin-off rates. For recent reviews of this literature, see Shane (2004) and Siegel et al. (2007a). However, our hypothesis is that the majority of local entrepreneurial economic development affected by universities is in the form of start-ups created by former students. If this hypothesis is confirmed then the recent transformation of university goals and practices toward increasing spin-off rates and new firm creation by university faculty and researchers may be misguided.

THE HISTORY OF UNIVERSITY-BASED ENTREPRENEURSHIP

Universities have not traditionally been concerned with commercialization of research.[4] Their two long-established goals have been to provide education and to conduct research. In the late nineteenth century, teaching and research at European universities, in particular the British and French systems, was primarily theoretical in nature. In contrast, the key motive for the creation of the natural science- and engineering-based universities in Germany, and later the creation of the 'land-grant' universities in the US, was to produce students for agriculture and industry (Noble, 1977). These schools catered to local demands for skilled employees and their structure and goals thus varied widely. For example, the University of Akron supplied skilled personnel for the local rubber industry, and became well-known for rubber and later polymer chemistry research (Mowery et al., 2004, p. 12). Contrasting this local dependency of US higher education institutions, federal funding of academic research was not strong and amounted only to 25 percent of total university research funding in the mid-1930s (ibid., p. 23). The local focus created strong incentives for collaboration between academics and industry in the US, Germany and the European countries which copied the German system, such as Sweden and Denmark.[5] The university–industry links were, on the other hand, rather weak in countries such as Britain and France. University research rose in importance at unequal paces across Europe and the US but was a well-established activity at well over 100 US universities by the start of the First World War (Murmann, 2003).

A third motive for universities has been to provide service to society, where the latter only quite recently has been interpreted to include the commercialization of research. In fact, universities until recently have been barred from conducting profit-making activities, have been prohibited from owning equity, and have thus had little stake in the direct commercialization of research. For example, in 1934 the President and Fellows of Harvard University responded to the commercialization efforts by faculty in its medical school by decreeing that 'no patents primarily concerned with therapeutics or public health may be taken out by any member of the university, except with the consent of the President and Fellows; nor will such patent be taken out by the university itself except for dedication to the public' (Palmer, 1948, p. 75). The two reasons for this sharp restriction on university actions are well known: the economics of science (Nelson, 1959; Arrow, 1962) and the sociology of science (Merton, 1973).

The economic argument states that since research primarily produces information, and the cost of transmitting information is typically quite low, the optimal allocation would be for close to unlimited distribution of the information. In this interpretation, research is deemed a public good that should be free for all and its generation paid through taxes (Samuelson, 1954). Three difficulties appear if the producing monopolist tries to commercialize the research. First, the specific feature of research as information makes it difficult to trade: the prospective buyer upon inspection of the good has acquired it for free, implying a market failure where information will be undertraded (Arrow, 1962). Second, the economic value of research is difficult to forecast, leading to downward pressure on its price (Nelson, 1959). Third, information is very hard to keep private and a large fraction of the private information typically 'spills over' to competitors. A large portion of the value of information may thus not be priced but appropriated by other parties for free. All three things considered, the private market for information is assumed to be very problematic, leading to the traditionally assumed underinvestment under a private ownership/market-based model. To counter this underinvestment, governments assign property rights to ideas – patents. Nevertheless, patents are not a panacea to the difficulties of trading information as they may not protect the owner sufficiently (for example, Gans and Stern, 2000). These market failures reinforce the suggestion of an optimal system where the production of information is subsidized by the government and the producer provides the information for free. This has indeed been the main argument for government funding of university-based science for the past 50 years (for example, Dasgupta and David, 1994; Noll, 1998) and the reason why university scientists were either discouraged or outright prohibited from patenting their discoveries for much of this century, in particular in the field of medicine (Mowery et al., 2004).

In any setting it is important to create appropriate incentives for the researcher to exert maximum effort. When public research is not for sale, other incentives than monetary must prevail. Merton (1973) as well as Dasgupta and David (1994) argue that the norms of science to a large extent replace the need for monetary incentives.[6] A key reinforcement of these norms for the researcher in a university is the value of priority of discovery. Being the first to discover in science carries strong positive reputational value and in addition may be directly tied to material rewards such as salary and access to research facilities. Inherent in this system is the need to disclose findings publicly as soon as possible, thus achieving the societal goal of free information dissemination.

In a historical perspective, university patenting and licensing of inventions have thus not been important as a vehicle for technical change. Rather, other forms of transfer of knowledge from university researchers have dominated, such as publications and reports, informal contacts, meetings and conferences, consulting, contract research, the movement of students, and cooperative research (Cohen et al., 2002). Patenting was indeed a rare activity among faculty for most of this millennium. Mowery et al. (2004, p. 47) report a total of less than 50 patents granted to universities in the US in 1925, rising slowly to approximately 100 in 1969.

Reflecting this paucity, relatively few universities were directly involved in managing patenting activities until the 1970s. Two of the earliest patent management organizations in the US, the Research Corporation, established 1912, and the Wisconsin Alumni Research Foundation (WARF), established in 1924, were both originated by university researchers but incorporated as independent entities. This organizational form reflected both the lack of interest by university administrators in patenting research, as well as the obvious tension it created with the scientific ethos of universities. Land-grant universities were the most active in patenting and several of those created copies of the WARF structure during the 1930s. Notably, most US universities lacked patent policies before the Second World War. Several that had patent policies either discouraged patenting or outright prohibited it by faculty. Patent policies developed and spread in the 1950s and 1960s but most universities did little to promote patenting or still took a dim view of it. In some universities such as the Massachusetts Institute of Technology (MIT), Columbia (except in medicine) and Stanford, the inventors retained the rights to their inventions and could do with these as they pleased.[7]

University research rose to prominence only after the Second World War, and in the first decades after the war it was primarily in leading institutions such as MIT, where many important war efforts were converted into sustained research efforts. A driving force was the massive expansion of federal research funding. Academic research budgets rose almost sixfold in constant dollars between 1935 and 1960 and more than doubled again by 1965. During this period the federal government became the largest supplier of research funds, providing more than 60 percent by 1960 (Mowery et al., 2004, p. 23).

During the 1970s the rate of patenting at universities rose dramatically and became more dispersed. Close to 350 patents were issued to universities in 1975, compared to approximately 100 in 1969. University patents per research dollar also started to increase in the 1970s (Henderson et al., 1998), reflecting a shift in faculty behavior and incentives during that decade. Further, industry funding of research and development (R&D) increased from approximately US $200 million per year throughout the 1960s to approximately $500 million per year in 1980 (constant 2000 dollars: NSF, 2007). All these numbers continued to grow in the 1980s and 1990s. In parallel, and surely a function of this growth, the number of

TLOs and the number of spin-offs started to rise. Reflecting this broadening of licensing and spin-off activities Mowery and Sampat (2001) report that there were only six TLOs in 1960, rising to 25 in 1980.

A particularly important phenomenon explaining the rising rate of patenting and industry funding of university research was the germination of biomedical research in the 1970s. This was in turn driven by a large increase in federal funding of molecular biology. Thus, while biomedical patents grew in number by 295 percent from 1970 to 1980, other university patents grew 'only' by 90 percent during the same period (Mowery et al., 2004, p. 56).

The change in the commercial focus of university research in biomedical research forever altered the way that industry and university researchers work together. Patent applications covering techniques for modifying living organisms had been accumulating at the US Patent Office during the 1970s – US Patent and Trademark Office (USPTO) officials refused to examine them until a decision could be reached on the patentability of such matters. Finally in the case *Diamond vs. Chakrabarty* on June 16, 1980 the US Supreme Court decided in favor of patenting living organisms created by mankind.

Prior to 1980, industry and university worked closely together with different goals in mind. For example, one industry representative at Monsanto, a large US-based biotech firm, stated: 'Our scientists are awarded for an economic return . . . Academic scientists are rewarded and promoted based on publications' (Charles, 2001, p. 22).[8] After the Supreme Court decision, universities had to change. One lucid example is the case of Mary-Dell Chilton who arrived at Washington University in St. Louis in 1980 to lead a lab working on using a microbe, *Agrobacterium*, as a vehicle for transforming plant cells. Monsanto offered funds to help Chilton's transition to Washington University and continued to pay her as a consultant. There were no formal conditions placed on this funding. Monsanto's headquarters was located just five miles away and their researchers had full access to her lab's work, participated in meetings, obtained lab samples, and freely discussed ideas. 'We weren't even required to write a report' one university researcher stated, and another said, 'We talked to those guys two or three times a week' (ibid., pp. 17–18). Very little information about what was going on at Monsanto flowed back though. At Monsanto they were busy writing patents on experiments based on the ideas and materials obtained from Washington University. It all came to a head at the Miami Winter Symposium on Molecular Genetics of Plants and Animals on 18 January 1983, where Chilton and a competing university lab in Ghent together announced findings on how to genetically alter plants. However, a representative of Monsanto who was unannounced also climbed onto the stage and joined in the announcement. Monsanto that day distributed a press release stating they had filed a patent on the process one day earlier. Monsanto stole the thunder, and within days the news was on *Wall Street Journal*'s front page crediting Monsanto as the inventor. However, Chilton had secretly heard that Monsanto were going to release something 'big' and had sent in a patent application a few days earlier.[9] The colleague at Ghent had learned the same and while their filing reached the USPTO on the day of the conference, one day after Monsanto's, their European application reached the European Patent Office (EPO) before Monsanto's and they were subsequently awarded priority in Europe. Several other crucially important patent applications that were submitted during the 1970s, such as Cohen and Boyer's application on recombinant DNA were awarded shortly after the *Diamond vs. Chakrabarty* ruling and further cemented the new norm that patenting of university biomedical research was from now on big business.

In parallel, US federal policy towards patenting of university research had become a topic of debate in the 1970s after the release of several federal reports.[10] Since there was no federal policy but university patenting was increasing, especially in the biomedical field, federal agencies started to define their own policies, which varied. By the 1970s, US universities were able to patent the results of federally funded research, sometimes under restrictions. The lack of uniformity (Senators Birch Bayh and Bob Dole testified that federal 'policy' in fact consisted of more than 20 different agreements with various federal agencies) created a pressure for standardization. Attention also was rising on patenting restrictions imposed on research funded by agencies such as the Department of Health, Education and Welfare (HEW). In September 1978, Senator Dole criticized HEW for 'stonewalling' university patenting. Testimony at hearings also focused on lagging US productivity growth and innovativeness, suggesting that improvement could be accomplished by further regulation, a rather unusual position taken in the US. Other witnesses suggested that giving ownership to universities would create greater incentives for inventors and universities to commercialize their research. The result was the Bayh–Dole Act, signed into law in December 1980. It replaced the 22 institutional agreements with a uniform policy giving universities rights to any patent resulting from grants funded by federal agencies, and expressed support for negotiation of exclusive licenses between universities and industry based on such grants. Further amendments and subsequent regulations removed some restrictions and added that universities should share licensing royalties with inventors.

After 1980 the distribution of patenting and commercialization activities have both deepened but also widened considerably across universities.

While 96 patents were granted to 28 US universities in 1965, US university patenting grew to 386 patents granted to 79 US universities in 1980, continuing to grow to 3,258 patents granted to 155 universities in 2007. Patenting intensity changed from about 3.5 patents per patenting university in 1965, to 4.9 per patenting university in 1980, to about 21 per patenting university in 2007. Following this growth, 21 universities established TLOs before 1980, with the majority being added in the next two decades: 55 TLOs were added in the 1980s, 66 in the 1990s and only 12 new ones between 2000 and 2007, to a total of 154 in 2007. The growth of TLOs obviously has abated and we shall see only a smattering of universities add TLOs in the next decade.

The number of university spin-offs has risen concomitantly. The yearly number of recorded spin-offs has risen from approximately 59 start-ups in 1991 reported by 98 universities, to 366 spin-offs from 141 universities in 2000, and to 502 spin-offs from 155 universities by 2007. These numbers reflect an increase both in the number of institutions reporting data and for each reporting entity.

Little systematic data about spin-offs exists before the AUTM started collecting such in 1991. For example, MIT faculty reported two spin-offs to their TLO in 1980. Of course, reporting to the TLO was voluntary at this time and there could be unreported entities. Indeed, using an alternative data source we find vastly larger spin-off counts. A survey by Roberts and Eesley (2009) of MIT alumni indicates that 42 responding faculty at MIT who prior to that were MIT students self-reported starting three firms that year. Using this base and correcting for survey non-response rates, the total number of faculty start-ups by MIT alumni in 1980 was 28.[11] Adding an equivalent start-up rate by non-MIT alumni among the MIT faculty results in a count of 54 start-ups by all MIT faculty in 1980.[12] This exercise tells us two things: (a) the AUTM/TLO reported data may only cover a tenth of the actual spin-offs by faculty at spin-off active institutions, and (b) already by 1980 there was substantial spin-off activity by faculty at leading institutions.

We now continue by examining the 'productivity' of universities, assuming that patent disclosures as inputs and patent applications, licenses, and spin-offs are outputs. Using AUTM data for the six-year period from 1996 to 2001 for which 25 engineering schools consistently report data, the number of invention disclosures increased by approximately 6.5 percent per year, the number of patent applications increased by 16 percent per year, while executed licenses and the number of start-ups increased by 19.5 and 8 percent per year, respectively.[13] These schools spun off an average of three firms per year. Looking at the same institutions from 2001 to 2007, the number of invention disclosures[14] increased by approximately 6.5

percent per year, the number of patent applications increased by 11 percent per year, while executed licenses and the number of start-ups increased by approximately 4 and 1 percent per year, respectively. These schools now spin off an average of four firms per year. Data from US medical schools and hospitals which continuously report data show similar trends.[15] These schools spun off an average of 2.2 firms per year from 1996 to 2001 and now spin off an average of three firms per year.

These data show some consistent patterns across the engineering and medical schools:

- The percentage of patents issued per disclosure has been going up, from approximately 33 percent to 55 percent (65 percent for engineering) over 12 years from 1996 to 2007, indicating increased TLO efficiency, or increased disclosure quality, or both.
- The number of licenses executed per patent has been going down from 78 percent (88 percent for engineering) to 43 percent in 2007 for both types of schools, indicating a decrease in TLO efficiency, market saturation, or a decrease in commercialization quality of patents, or all three.
- The number of licenses executed per disclosure has been flat over the years at approximately 30 percent because the above two trends cancel each other out.
- The number of start-ups per patent has been going down from 6 percent (7.5 percent for engineering) to 5 percent in 2007 for both types of schools, indicating a decrease in TLO efficiency, market saturation, or a decrease in patent quality, or all three.

A more rigorous analysis on the sources of growth in university licensing was performed by Thursby and Thursby (2002) (they exclude, however, an analysis of spin-off rates). They model technology commercialization as a three-stage production process: (i) disclosure, (ii) patenting, and (iii) licensing, involving multiple inputs in each stage. Using AUTM data for the 1994–98 period (note the shorter period than the one we use) they find that much of the growth in university commercial activity stems from input growth. A negative growth rate in licensing is interpreted as that as the number of disclosures and patents goes up per university, the marginal commercial quality of inventions goes down, rather than a change in research focus by faculty. Much of the average growth in disclosures and patenting over the period is due to marginal and average performing universities catching up in activity to the most prolific universities by increasing their inputs.[16]

While university spin-offs have been increasing in absolute terms, it should be noted that licenses of university patents to established firms strongly dominate over spin-offs as a form of research commercialization. In 2007 there were eight times as many executed licenses to each university spin-off at the above fixed set of universities. However, spin-offs are becoming relatively more important as the relationship was even larger a decade ago: 12 licenses per start-up in 1996 (AUTM data).

Changing pro-research-commercialization attitudes have meant regulatory changes also in Europe and elsewhere in the last decade. For example, university charters have changed to include a stronger role of universities to participate in societal activities both in Belgium (in 1996) and Sweden (first in 1975 in rather vague terms and then in 1996 in more explicit terms).[17] These changes have led directly to more open reporting by universities of their activities, but also indirectly, changing interpretations by university administrators of the role of universities. It has been argued that the 1996 change in Sweden has been interpreted as mainly being about the commercialization of research (Goldfarb and Henrekson, 2003; Jacob et al., 2003).

Europe did not start from the same position as the US. European faculty inventors typically owned their IP through what is commonly referred to as the 'Professor's Privilege'. The incentive problem referred to in the US was thus not present; inventors knew they had the right to their ideas and were free to commercialize them without fearing holdups by funding agencies. Nevertheless, a government task force appointed by the Swedish government (SOU, 1998) still recommended a Bayh–Dole Act copy in 1998.[18] In fact, the recommendations were supporting even stronger university control than what the US regulators found acceptable: the task force recommended that universities in their right as employer could withhold publication of research results of their employees until a patent application had been submitted.[19] Neither the suggested change of the Professor's Privilege, nor the publication limitation on research stood up to critique. Indeed, the Swedish government subsequently rejected the fundamental idea that collaboration with industry is all about access to resources (IP). It stated: 'It is important from an overall aspect of quality that universities develop good collaboration with external interests . . . without jeopardizing their integrity' (Regeringens Proposition, 1998/99:94, p. 3). A similar discussion was waged in Canada, where the authorities decided that no change was motivated in the current regulation allowing universities to decide whom takes control rights of IP. However, in many other countries, Bayh–Dole-type acts invoking *de jure* ownership by the employer (university) were enacted in Belgium in 1999, in Denmark in 2000, in Germany and Austria in 2002 and in Norway in 2003. Italian legislators, however, bucked the trend and *introduced* the Professor's Privilege in 2001 on the reverse intuition that individual scientists may have a greater incentive to patent than the university which employs them.

Several authors have been critical of the rapid and uncritical adoption of Bayh–Dole-type legislation in parts of Europe (Mowery and Sampat, 2005; David, 2007; Kenney and Patton, 2009). Some have argued that it is unrealistic to assume that burdening the university with the task of producing commercial-relevant output will have anything but marginal effects on technological change (David, 2007). Others have shown that the Bayh–Dole Act was not responsible for the growth in patenting in the US and is on this ground not a reason to be emulated (Mowery et al., 2004; Mowery and Sampat, 2005). Yet others have pointed to data showing that even under the Professor's Privilege, European scholars do transfer their knowledge to industry. For example, Lissoni et al. (2008) find that the dearth of patents assigned to universities due to the Professor's Privilege in France, Sweden, and Italy can be explained by the high rate by which businesses are assigned patents by academics: approximately 60 percent.[20] However, that does not mean that European university researchers are lagging behind their US counterparts. Rather, European academic inventors are *more* active at patenting their research than their US counterparts.[21] Computing the share of professors that patent, Lissoni et al. find approximately 4 percent in Sweden, Italy and France, while the comparable figure for the US for the same period is 2.3 percent.

In Europe, university researchers have typically collaborated freely and frequently with industry, often assigning ownership of their IP to the industrial collaborator. For example, as much as 50 percent of Swedish university researchers report ongoing research collaborations with private firms (Lööf, 2005). In the biotech drug discovery sector, industry–university collaborations seem particularly prevalent. Valentin and Jensen (2007) report that among biotech firms specializing in drug discovery, Swedish firms have university co-inventors on patent applications on average 43 percent of the time, while their Danish counterpart firms have university co-inventors on patent applications on average 22 percent of the time.[22] These outcomes appear to be based on interactions where the industrial partner typically makes available access to the firm's research capabilities, may support a PhD student, provides consulting income or laboratory funding, and takes ownership rights of IP but relinquishes publication rights (Goldfarb and Henrekson, 2003).

Commercialization of university research through spin-offs may be less frequent in Europe than in the US, but even that assumption can be questioned. For example, approximately 13 percent of Swedish university scientists have had some experience commercializing their own research, through licensing, spin-offs or other forms. Approximately 35–40 percent of those, or 5 percent, commercialized their research through starting a new business (Lööf, 2005). These data appear to be of approximate equal magnitudes to the US where close to 90 percent of university ideas were commercialized by methods other than the establishment of new firms (Goldfarb and Henrekson, 2003).

It is even possible that there has been a negative effect on the rate of technological change through the implementation of Bayh–Dole-type acts in various European countries. We have three examples. In January 2000 the Danes enacted a Bayh–Dole-inspired legislation, the Law on University Patenting (LUP).[23] Valentin and Jensen (2007) evaluate the impact of this policy change on the contributions of university scientists to patent applications by dedicated biotech firms specializing in drug discovery, comparing Denmark to Sweden where the industry shares a number of historical and structural features. Difference-in-difference regressions show an increasing fraction of participation by university scientists in industry research in Denmark up to 2000, a temporary spike in the last quarter of 2000, followed by a 13 percent reduction in the share of Danish domestic academic inventors to patent applications made by Danish biotech firms, relative to Sweden over the four years 2001–04. The argument for this LUP-induced relative decline is that the previous bilateral agreements between university scientists and firms are complicated by the introduction of a third party at the table, as well as the obviously reduced ownership incentive to the firms of engaging in these agreements (ibid.). Further, Cambridge University experienced a decrease in the number of biotech spin-offs after Bayh–Dole enforcement (Breznitz, 2009). Finally, professors' joint patenting with firms decreased from 441 to 155 (65 percent) at Tohoku University two years after the university started to enforce the recent Bayh–Dole-type act while university-assigned patents increased dramatically from 27 to 324, leaving the total number of patents unchanged before and after (Takahashi and Carraz, 2009). In this case it appears that there has been a substitution of assignments from firms to universities with no net increase.

Nevertheless, government financial support to TLOs to effectuate 'technology transfer' has been increasing. France started supporting 31 incubators in 2000 and Germany created 22 new TLOs in 2002. In Germany these regionally operating TLOs each serve a group of universities and were fully funded for a start-up period and given training and other support. Public programs to finance university spin-offs have also been rising in numbers and fund volume. France implemented a program in 1999; Germany started the EXIST program in 2000; Italy incorporated the Quantica Fund in 2005, and Belgium created a spin-off program for post-docs in 2002, largely modeled on the German experience. We highlight two examples: EXIST and Flügge. EXIST is a federally funded part of the German government's 'Hightech Strategy for Germany' and is co-financed by the European Social Fund (ESF), while Flügge[24] is a Bavarian initiative. EXIST provides several forms of support:

- Gründerstipendium is a one-year salary stipend of €2,500 per month for PhDs (€2,000 for Master's degree students up to five years after degree completion, €800 for current students) for up to three founders plus an additional €22,000 for other start-up costs.
- Forschungstransfer supports outstanding research projects at universities where expensive and risky development activities are targeted; Phase I: to demonstrate the technological feasibility (< €350,000 over 18 months), Phase II: further development work to reach market and commence operations (< €150,000 with matching funds of €50,000 required).
- EXIST III promotes projects at universities and research institutions for creating a culture of entrepreneurship. EXIST III provides start-up grants to universities and other research institutes to strengthen their spin-off activities and processes.

Flügge was created in 1997 and is aimed towards innovative university spin-offs in the seed or start-up phase. It offers young graduates and university employees a salary as part-time workers at their university for a period of two years while they work on creating their start-up. According to a brochure released by Flügge, the program has supported 99 projects at universities and 15 at technical institutes totaling 324 people over 10 years; 76 percent have reached the market, 4 percent have been sold, 7 percent liquidated, and 13 percent are still working towards commercialization.[25]

Switching back from Europe to North America, an interesting comparison to the US is Canada since many Canadian universities operate in similar ways and conditions to US schools. In contrast to the US, spin-off activities are very concentrated in Canada – four universities account for 57 of the 141 spin-off companies in a study by NSERC (2005). Compared to most countries, Canada has a long tradition of state involvement to promote the use of scientific research, with a large number of programs at federal and provincial levels.[26] Using a very broad definition, one survey identified 178 initiatives that represented an expenditure of Canadian dollars (CAD) 3.2 billion a year (Gault and McDaniel, 2004). Among the more important for university spin-offs is the National Research Council (NRC) funded Industrial Research Assistance Program (IRAP) which has been in operation for over 60 years (Kolodny et al., 2001).[27] Its singular most important feature is its 240 industrial technology advisors (ITAs) who are located in 100 communities across Canada. Not surprisingly then, about half the Canadian university spin-offs have received IRAP funds (Rasmussen, 2008). Similarly to several initiatives in Europe, a more directed program was launched by NSERC in the 1990s to support universities' TLO activities. The rather small program (for Canadian measures) contributes to a small share of a TLO's budget, but is considered particularly important for some of the smaller TLOs. A total of CAD 19 million was awarded for the years 2005–08. Group awards provide funding for groups of institutions to undertake cooperative activities and broaden existing capabilities.

All the major Canadian research universities now have a TLO. Their tasks, organization, and size differ and the number of technology transfer staff varies from one person up to 30 on some campuses; the national average is 3.8 (AUCC, 2003). In 2003, Canadian universities spent CAD 36.4 million on IP management, with an average distribution of institutional base funding (29 percent), institutional one-time allocations (10 percent), IP commercialization revenues (for example, licensing, cashed-in equity) (36 percent), and external sources (25 percent) (Read, 2005). That is, although there exists a rather large state involvement to promote commercialization of research, the licensing revenues and cashed-in equity from spin-offs cover only one-third of IP management costs. Canada thus seems much less effective than the US system, which appears to approximately break even.

While the Canadian universities underperform when compared with their US counterparts in terms of TLO productivity, they create considerably more spin-off companies than their US counterparts, when counting the number of companies created per dollar of research (Clayman, 2004). On the other hand the licensing income per dollar of research is lower in Canada than in the US. Clayman interprets the data as a Canadian deficiency. He states that Canada is well known for not having enough established companies that can commercialize technology from universities. This explains the lower licensing revenues, and the higher rate of start-up formation per dollar of research in Canada.

Possibly the most important point of comparison with the US is that Canadian universities have a diversity of approaches to IP ownership. Among its 20 largest universities, the creator is awarded control rights in eight cases, in another eight cases the university takes control rights, and the remaining four have joint ownership or case-by-case negotiations.[28] A comparison of the two groups of eight universities shows essentially no difference at all on the number of licenses, patents, license income, and spin-offs with the allocation of control rights (ibid.).

The increased commercialization of university research may have other negative unintended consequences. From a positive perspective, increased private protection of research results increases the incentives to commercialize the research by the owner of the property right. It may also increase the efficiency of the market for ideas, encourage further investment in the idea by the owner, and mitigate disincentives to disclose and exchange knowledge (Merges and Nelson, 1990; Gans and Stern, 2000). However, Merges and Nelson (1990) and Scotchmer (1991) highlight the possibility that the assertion of property rights on only one or two key upstream, foundational discoveries may significantly restrict follow-on research. In a general model of comparative statics, it is possible to show that under plausible parameter values society will lose out while the owner benefits when obtaining private rights to research (Mukherjee and Stern, 2009). Further, Heller and Eisenberg (1998) and Shapiro (2000) suggest that in the specific case of patents granted on research tools which are needed to conduct research (such as the 'OncoMouse'),[29] this has created barriers to the acquisition of licenses and other rights that may make it too burdensome to permit research that would otherwise have been scientifically and socially valuable.

As one example, Louis et al. (2001) examined the effect of scientific norms and commercialization incentives on secrecy. They surveyed 847 clinical and non-clinical life sciences faculty across 49 US top-funded universities who had published at least one article and had received research funding from industry.[30] Forty-three percent of the basic researchers replied that they had been denied access to materials or software from other researchers in the past three years, while only 27 percent of the applied researchers replied that this was the case. Basic researchers were also significantly more likely than applied researchers to deny others' requests for access of their own results or material. Evidently, and maybe unexpectedly fast,[31] the prior Mertonian ethos of free access to information had by the late 1980s largely disappeared and been replaced by a culture of secrecy even stronger among basic researchers than among those who work directly with established companies testing their new drugs.

In multivariate analysis, the higher probability of *being denied* research material for basic researchers held up after controlling for research budget, tenure, gender, and entrepreneurial involvement, the last being insignificant. However, being a basic researcher was not a significant predictor for *denying* others' requests, while the coefficient for entrepreneurship was positive and significant in denying others' requests, all else equal. As well, the more successful the researchers in terms of obtaining funding, the more secretive they were. Our interpretation of these regressions is that those who engage in commercializing their own research become more secretive about their research results, and that this effect trumps whatever culture of openness exists in that community. That is, individual-level business incentives are far stronger than scientific norms. The more researchers become engaged in commercializing their own research, the less sharing of research materials and results we can expect. The net effect on social welfare is unclear: society may gain by providing increased private benefits and thus greater incentives to commercialize, but may also lose due to increased secrecy and thus less information diffusion.

Confirming the increased secrecy observed by Louis et al. (ibid.), Walsh et al. (2007) survey 507 academic researchers in genomics and proteomics and find that researchers that have a history of commercial activity are likely to deny 1 percent more requests to their research material (cell lines, reagents, and so on) to other researchers than those who are not commercially active. Their research also shows that if a TLO is involved in fielding a request, there is a 2 percent lower probability of receiving a requested material. While denials are still relatively infrequent they may affect research considerably when appearing if the technology is sufficiently important. Walsh et al. focus on three very important proteins and find that approximately 15 percent of projects exhibit adverse effects due to patents on the material and 3 percent abandoned projects due to inability to access the material. While these results may appear small to the outsider, insiders are voicing considerable concern about the delays caused on research from the added bureaucracy to scientific material transfers imposed by the Bayh–Dole Act.[32] Further, the effect of granting patents to scientific projects appears to lead to between a 10 to 20 percent reduction in the number of citations to the research publication related to the patent (Murray and Stern, 2007), illustrating broader negative effects of (potential) commercialization of research than simply access to research material. Nevertheless, it is unclear whether the observed negative effects on sharing of research materials and diffusion of knowledge extend far beyond the areas of the life sciences.[33]

To sum up this section, there are several explanations for the increasing trend toward more university spin-offs: the rising importance of the biotech sector, the passage of the Bayh–Dole Act,[34] judicial decisions that have expanded what is patentable and provided stronger protection for patents, increased financing of research by industry, changing university guidelines and behavior, changes in the scientific ethos of faculty and researchers, policymakers' growing pro-spin-off attitudes, and the general public's increasing acceptance of a university that engages in/produces commerce. The increasing trend is not limited to the US. It is widespread across industrialized countries, which in several cases have implemented replica versions of the Bayh–Dole Act as well as created many other programs to stimulate academic entrepreneurship.

However, it is far from clear that this is an optimal situation. The well-known arguments for why the market fails to appropriately price university inventions remain. We have noted that in areas where intellectual property is easier to protect through patents, such as in biomedical applications, the rate of patenting is much greater than in other fields. Since patenting laws over time in various ways have strengthened the rights of patent holders, this suggests that the failures of the market-based mechanism have decreased. However, this does not imply that private ownership is the socially most efficient mechanism for commercializing university research, even in the biotech field. The increased tendency by researchers to claim private ownership rights to research appears to reduce overall rates of technological change by limiting or delaying future researchers' rights to follow-on invention or access to materials that were previously exempt from limits to use. The increased involvement by universities to control IP appears to stifle such access even further. Such recently implemented *de jure* university control also appears to have reduced university–industry collaborative research in several countries. The increased role of commerce has also changed incentives to researchers to become more secretive.[35] The institutional scientific norms that worked in favor of free dissemination of research results have permanently changed, at least in the biotechnology field. We are left with researching and debating what the appropriate university actions and agency structures should be at universities given this new regime.

THE RETURN TO ENTREPRENEURSHIP AND (UNIVERSITY) INNOVATION

The typical start-up originating from a university is a very rare breed. Every year there are about two million start-ups in the US (Shane, 2008). Approximately 7 percent of them are high-tech, and only about 3 percent of the founders consider their businesses to be 'technologically sophisticated' (ibid., p. 30). In comparison, the registered number of spin-offs from US universities, hospitals, and research institutions in 2000 was 554 (AUTM, 2006). The median number of start-ups (from those reporting to AUTM, which are the top research-oriented schools) was two, while the top producer (MIT) generated 23 spin-offs in 2006.

These start-ups are not likely to be profitable, on average. Available evidence consistently shows that the distribution of return to innovation is highly skewed, with most patents/inventions producing no value

(Schankerman and Pakes, 1986; Schankerman, 1998; Harhoff et al., 1999; Scherer and Harhoff, 2000; Åstebro, 2003; Hall et al., 2005; Giuri et al., 2007; Thursby and Thursby, 2007). For example, Åstebro finds that for independent inventors only the top 3 percent break even but the top 0.5 percent earn rates of return above 1,400 percent. Similarly, Scherer and Harhoff (2000) compute that the top 10 percent of all Harvard patents provided 84 percent of the gross economic value.

Consistent with the studies cited above, Thursby and Thursby (2007) use data from the AUTM and report annual median licensing net income (including cash-in of spin-off equity stakes) per university to be around $30,000 if one excludes sponsored research. This return is hardly worth the effort if one considers the median legal fees ($462,000) and salary costs ($638,000) for operating a TLO. That is, most universities are not likely to make any money on their TLO activities. Indeed, further evidence from AUTM provides sobering figures: relative to the AUTM universities' total 2006 US patent applications of 10,748 there were 500 start-ups produced, or a ratio of 4.6 percent. We hasten to say that not all patent applications are made to produce spin-offs, but the licensing revenues of the research are equally low and far apart. Thursby and Thursby report that only 0.48 percent of all active licenses generated licensing income of $1 million or more. Thus, one should reasonably expect few spin-offs from each university, the average spin-off to be unprofitable, and only a very small fraction of those that are profitable to have large returns.

Another example of the stunningly skewed distribution of returns from university inventions is found in the case description on the Research Corporation (RC) in Mowery et al. (2004, ch. 4). The Research Corporation was founded in 1912 by Frederick Cottrell as a third-party technology transfer agent to help academics patent and license their inventions. The RC began accepting donations of patents from academics in the 1920s. Among the most important was a process for synthesizing vitamin B1 developed in 1932 by Robert R. Williams at the University of California. In 1937 it signed an invention administration agreement with MIT which laid grounds for RC becoming the largest US intermediary for licensing of university patents for the next 40 years. By its 1947 Annual Report it had handled 40 MIT inventions and a handful of others, but these had yet to produce any significant returns. The Annual Report noted:

> [T]he handling of inventions for educational institutions can be successful only if . . . a large number of potentially valuable inventions can be administered . . . unless a sizeable number of such inventions is available for administration the numerical odds of unsuccessful developments to successful ones would render the management under such circumstance too great a risk. (RC, 1947, p. 3)

The RC subsequently expanded and managed several hundred other US universities' patents obtaining approximately 300 disclosures in 1955, and peaking at approximately 500 disclosures in 1975. But this increased flow of disclosures did not produce any large increase in patents or, more importantly, in gross royalties (Mowery et al., 2004, Figures 4.3 and 4.4). In fact, between 1945 and 1985, while accepting at least 9,000 disclosures and patenting approximately 980 inventions, the RC's top five inventions stood for between 72 and 98 percent of yearly royalty income (ibid., Table 4.1). Typically these top inventions were biomedical. Facing the expiration of its last lucrative patent in 1975 the RC noted: 'while it is possible that other substantial income producing inventions will become available in the future, it will be a rare occurrence' (1947, p. 3).

The evidence consistently shows that universities are confronted with a 'jackpot' economy. They may earn spectacular returns as that demonstrated by Stanford University and the University of California combined licensing revenues from the Cohen–Boyer patent on recombinant DNA of US$255 million up until 2001 (Bera, 2009) or in the case of Google, in which Stanford's 2 percent ownership share returned $33.4 million on the day of Google's initial public offering (IPO) in 2004.[36] But the likelihood that this happens is extremely low. In fact, universities need to produce a very large number of patentable inventions every year in order to break even on their TLO activities (Scherer and Harhoff, 2000). The data from the RC suggest that a steady flow of over 300 disclosures a year, many in the most commercially interesting biomedical technology field, does not guarantee break-even. Note that only MIT, recently, with 507 disclosures per year and Stanford with 459 disclosures per year (last three-year averages) clearly surpass this flow (see Table 9.1). Indeed, the RC's net royalty income drew negative for the first time in 1976 and remained negative for six consecutive years. Consequently, the RC closed the division managing patents in 1987 and transferred the activities to an independent for-profit organization.

Despite the sometimes hilarious popular press articles stating the 'university return to R&D' quoting the latest statistics from AUTM, universities apparently cannot expect to more than break even on their TLO operations. For universities with small research funds and faculty it thus seems both extremely risky and wasteful to spend money on promoting licensing and spin-off creation. The typical university in fact cannot manage its TLO towards refunding its operations with licensing income, nor use the meager revenues, which may vary widely from year to year, to offset the much larger external funding from state and federal funding agencies. This conclusion then begs the question what other form of administrative support a university might provide to stimulate, or at least assist, their researchers who would like to commercialize their inventions. Some suggest that letting market mechanisms rule will produce more appropriate mechanisms (Litan et al., 2007; Kenney and Patton, 2009). An alternative currently practiced in Germany is to enlist mandated intermediaries which pool their invention commercialization services across a number of universities.[37] This decreases inefficiencies associated with the skewed distribution of returns, provides a steadier return for the university, enhances bargaining power, and pools knowledge and enhances learning in interfacing with firms. But it may also lead to commercialization efforts that are too far removed from the inventors to be efficient (a recurrent problem even for TLOs, see Jensen and Thursby, 2001). Such an intermediary was tested and found wanting with the case of the RC in the US. Another alternative is to leave commercialization in the hands of the inventor. We shall say more about alternative options to TLOs in a later section.

Despite the gloomy statistics, there seems to be a qualitative difference between university-based start-ups and start-ups in general. The propensity of university-based start-ups to become listed as a public company is estimated by Goldfarb and Henrekson (2003) to be at least 8 percent, 114 times the rate for all US start-ups during the same period. This propensity is much higher for MIT: 257 times (Shane, 2004, p. 30). In Canada, approximately 10 percent of all spin-offs have gone public, which is a larger fraction than among spin-offs in the US. Over half of Canadian spin-offs that have gone public are biotech firms (Niosi, 2006).

University-based start-ups also seem to create many more jobs than the typical start-up. AUTM data show 83 employees per spin-off during the 1980–99 period, while the number of employees for the typical start-up with employees is 3.8 (Shane, 2008, p. 65). Other countries also show high rates of employment from spin-offs. One study found an average of 44 jobs in the UK (Charles and Conway, 2001), spin-offs from the University of Linköping in Sweden appear to have generated on average 12.3 employees, the University of Twente in the Netherlands 4.8, the University of Liège in Belgium 10, and Queens University in Northern Ireland 10.6 (Blair and Hitchens, 1998).[38] Moreover, Blair and Hitchens estimated that the spin-offs in Northern Ireland and the UK employed three times the number of university graduates than regular firms.

Further, AUTM (2002) report that out of 3,376 spin-offs from member universities between 1980 and 2000, 68 percent remained operational in 2001. Although these numbers do not allow us to compute yearly survival rates, it would seem that the survival of university start-ups is higher than for the general start-up. The survival rate of spin-offs from leading universities looks much higher. Shane (2004, p. 31) estimates that 80 percent of MIT spin-offs started between 1980 and 1996 survived 1997, and Lowe (2002) reports that only 6 percent of the University of California system ever ended up in bankruptcy.

But comparing apples and oranges is not the right way to make a case for supporting university spin-offs. Ensley and Hmieleski (2005) showed that university spin-offs were significantly lower in performance than a comparison sample of new technology-based firms in terms of cash flow and revenue growth, and that their top-management teams were less dynamic and more homogeneous. Unfortunately the tests were simple *t*-tests and not in a multivariate setting. However, in a multivariate regression of venture-backed firms, Zhang (2009) finds that university spin-offs that were venture backed (8.6 percent of all venture-backed start-ups, the vast majority in biomedical and software) have a higher survival rate but are not significantly different from other venture-backed start-ups in terms of the amount of venture capital raised, the probability of completing an IPO, the probability of taking a profit, or the size of employment. It is notable that the university spin-off sample showed significant lower probability of taking a profit, and lower employment size in univariate *t*-tests, but that these differences disappeared in multivariate analysis when industry dummies were introduced.

To conclude this section, data show that universities are not likely to earn any money on promoting the commercialization of their research. In fact, it appears that only the top two producers of disclosures in the US – Stanford and MIT – are likely to avoid prolonged periods of losses on the universities' costs for managing their IP. From a strict revenue perspective, universities should thus be advised not to spend effort on commercialization promotion. Spin-offs from universities appear no different from other high-tech start-ups. While a few universities historically have had large impacts, particularly through some spectacularly successful licenses, most have not, simply because there are very few faculty spin-offs, and most spin-offs do not employ very many or grow very much. The median rate of spin-offs is two a year for the top 100 research universities in the US.

THE ENTREPRENEURIAL UNIVERSITY

This section will review research that examines variation in rates of spin-offs as a function of varying university characteristics that are not related to invention disclosure rules, contractual design rules, or the organization of the TLO. These last three issues represent an area of research that is presented in the next section. In this section we shall consider such issues as the role of university culture, faculty quality, invention inputs, and the role of non-TLO university policies such as leave of absence and use of university resources.

The rate of spin-offs varies quite considerably across universities. Much of this is due to the large variation in inventive inputs – not all universities produce any significant number of inventions, while some produce a lot. All input metrics one could reasonably think of except number of patents (amount of federal R&D spending, amount of industry R&D spending, number of invention disclosures, and faculty quality) have been found to positively affect licensing revenues (see Table 9.2). For spin-offs the results are not so clear-cut. Patenting was found not to affect spin-offs in two studies, while faculty quality, federal R&D spending, and invention disclosures typically had positive effects. The impact of industry R&D spending was unclear (see Table 9.3). Most of these results have been obtained through cross-sectional analysis where typically only selected input metrics were introduced due to strong multicollinearity between them. However, faculty quality seems to have enough independent variation for its effect to survive inclusion of all input quantity metrics. Once one uses panel-data models the results are less obviously positive because there has been a declining effectiveness trend for the licensing-income-to-patent-counts and number-of-spin-offs-to-patent-counts. Due to data and analysis limitations one should not draw too strong conclusions regarding the role of any particular input quantity metric.

If one roughly controls for the degree to which a university is science based by computing the rate by which disclosures 'produce' spin-offs, Table 9.1 reports the three-year average proportion of spin-offs per disclosure. The universities were chosen to match Table 4.1 in Shane (2004). The table indicates that there is some considerable variation in the rate of spin-offs across universities even after controlling for invention production. Excluding the University of Miami, the variation is on the order of 5:1. However, the data lack the very large variation that Shane drew up from the same universities because he used data from only one year, and there is enormous year-to-year variation in spin-off rates. For example, New York University was noted as having a spin-off ratio of 0.41 in 2000, but over the three years 2005–07 it ended up a bit above average with 0.04.

There are likely many variables that affect cross-university variation in start-up rates that are outside the control of the university, such as regional economic differences, differences in state regulation, and historical reasons. We have explored historical reasons in the previous section and will discuss regional economic differences later on. We continue by discussing general university policies and university culture, which are arguably under some control of the institution.

Table 9.1   *Spin-off rates as a fraction of disclosures by various US universities reporting to AUTM (2005–2007 year averages)*

University	Disclosures	Spin-offs	Ratio
Boston University	106.0	3.67	0.03
Columbia University	322.0	12.00	0.04
Georgia Institute of Technology	337.7	8.67	0.03
Iowa State University	125.3	3.33	0.03
Johns Hopkins University	346.0	5.00	0.01
Massachusetts Institute of Technology	507.3	22.33	0.04
New York University	104.7	4.67	0.04
Northwestern University	158.3	7.33	0.05
Ohio State University	158.7	3.33	0.02
Pennsylvania State University	138.3	3.33	0.02
Purdue Research Foundation	247.3	9.33	0.04
Rutgers, the State University of NJ	116.0	1.33	0.01
Stanford University	459.5	6.50	0.01
SUNY Research Foundation	278.0	10.50	0.04
University of Florida	286.7	10.67	0.04
University of Georgia	104.7	2.00	0.02
University of Maryland, College Park	113.7	5.33	0.05
University of Miami	45.7	0.00	0.00
University of Michigan	301.3	7.67	0.03
University of North Carolina, Chapel Hill	107.7	2.33	0.02
University of Pennsylvania	304.7	5.00	0.02
University of Pittsburgh	184.0	7.00	0.04
University of Rochester	142.0	4.67	0.03
University of Southern California	144.3	4.67	0.03
University of Texas, Austin	121.3	4.67	0.04
University of Virginia Patent Foundation	181.7	5.33	0.03
WARF/University of Wisconsin Madison	430.0	5.67	0.01

The assumption is that general university policies can have large effects on entrepreneurs' behavior (for example, Shane, 2004). Most of this wisdom has been based on case evidence documented by, for example, Kenney and Goe (2004) comparing UC Berkeley and Stanford, Roberts (1991) and Shane (2004) studying MIT entrepreneurs, Clarke (1998) and Wright et al. (2007) examining several European universities, Hsu and Bernstein (1997) comparing MIT and Harvard, Feldman and Desrochers (2003, 2004) examining Johns Hopkins University, and Mowery and Ziedonis (2001) examining founders of spin-offs from Lawrence Livermore labs. These case studies highlight the different effects of policies and unwritten norms such as taking equity in start-ups, restrictions on part-time work/

leave of absence, use of university resources, and providing seed capital. While illuminating examples are provided, the case analysis researcher decides which potential causes to highlight, and it is difficult to evaluate the marginal role of any potential policy or norm.

With respect to culture, we saw in a previous section that over time the scientific ethos has given way to a more commercial culture driven by money, particularly in the biomedical sciences.[39] Some US universities have been slower to accept this greater commercial orientation, for example Johns Hopkins. While a leading research university, it is considered a late entrant into post-Bayh–Dole technology transfer style, displaying an open 'abhorrence to engage in activities that might involve proprietary restrictions on knowledge dissemination' (Feldman and Desrochers, 2003, p. 6). Maybe surprisingly, even leading creators of spin-offs such as MIT and Stanford have been very cautious and have resisted completely caving in to a 'commercialization ethos'. For example, the long-time director of the MIT TLO at a conference on the topic 'Secrecy in Science' in 1999 stated:

> The situation at M.I.T., with its transition from industrial support being a relatively minor fraction of the research budget to being almost a quarter of the budget, is instructive. If you go back about seven or eight years ago, the administrators at M.I.T. were being berated for their inflexibility in insisting on such 'absolutes' as freedom of publication and payment of full costs. We insisted that we would not delay publication beyond about 30 days (in rare cases 60, and sometimes less than 30 days in the more rapidly moving fields). Even that delay in publication was only for the purpose of identifying inventions on which patents should be filed and filing them. No restraint on the content of the publication of our results was (or is) allowed. We also insisted that we would not get into that other race to the bottom caused by bargaining on indirect cost rates ('Well, you've got the lab anyway so don't charge industry overhead'). And we reiterated our belief in the primacy of investigator-initiated projects and those that would allow meaningful participation by students . . . M.I.T. recently had a consortium with a number of other universities involving what we considered egregious intellectual property terms. After trying literally for years to resolve the issues on fair terms, in the face of major amounts of money promised which made it very, very difficult for our more needy brethren to say 'No', M.I.T. was finally forced to walk away – unilaterally because the other university administrators were under too much pressure to accept the terms. The end of the story though, was happy: a second leading university then threatened to join us in walking away, and the industrial funders realized that they could not continue an advanced program without the scientific leaders. We all came back to the table and negotiated an acceptable agreement. (Nelsen, 1999)

Further, European universities are still early in their conversion to a more commercial culture. For example, Keck (1993) reported that the intellectual orientation of German professors at that time made them averse to exploiting new ideas for commercial purposes even as they might have been encouraged to do so by their administrators. In our interviews in Germany we found a strong open science ethos still to be present among faculty.[40]

The 'commercial culture' of a university may reasonably be related to its spin-off activities. A 'commercial' orientation of a university or department may be more prone to support spin-off generation than a university, faculty or department that is more oriented towards fundamental science. Unfortunately there is very little evidence of the role of culture/norms in an all-else-equal comparison.

In a rare exception, Louis et al. (1989) obtained 778 survey responses from biomedical faculty across 40 US top-funded universities and merged these responses with university administrators' responses from the same schools. The survey time (1985) represents a point where there were considerable changes at leading US universities in policies and procedures *vis-à-vis* commercialization of research. We focus on their work explaining the probability of faculty becoming an entrepreneur. There was significant variation in entrepreneurship: the mean chance of being an entrepreneur was 7 percent, while the top quartile universities had fractions of faculty entrepreneurship between 26 percent (Harvard) and 44 percent (MIT).

Perhaps the most controversial result was that the multivariate analysis showed no effect for university-wide administrative support on the rate of entrepreneurship after controlling for group norms and individual-level effects. Variables such as whether the institution is a state or private school, whether seed money was available or not, the number of professional employees in the patent office, how strong the university's relationships with industry have been in the past, and a summary scale indicating the number of mechanisms the university has for commercializing research (for example, holding equity in firms employing faculty, investing venture capital in faculty firms) were not predictive, all else equal. However, personal activities including obtaining consulting income, obtaining industry funding for research and patenting together explained about 10 percent of the variation in entrepreneurship, while local norms, measured as the university proportion of entrepreneurs, explained another 5 percent of the variance.

We highlight the work by Louis et al. (ibid.) as their results are based on a large set of micro-level data and multivariate analysis, but also because the results go against received wisdom. At first sight there is a perplexing difference in the results between Louis et al.'s examination and those that study the effects of university policies on entrepreneurship rates using cross-university data, where the latter group generally find some type of effect (see Siegel et al., 2007a). The differences in results can be explained in two ways. First, the latter set of studies relies only on aggregate cross-university data (typically from AUTM) and so these can only compare aggregate university-level causes. Differences across universities in individual behavior or group-level norms are not measured and so these studies suffer from omitted variables bias if such behavior and norms are correlated with policies and procedures. Second, Louis et al. measure group-level norms as the university average of the dependent variable – the proportion of faculty being entrepreneurial. This is an endogenous variable; it does not measure norms *per se* but the outcome of norms. Therefore, it should be instrumented, which the authors fail to do. Further, this measure may be a function of university-level policies, and by construction of the analysis, the university policies may fail to become significant when introduced together with the endogenous variable on the right-hand side. While the reported study may suffer from specification error, many of the null effects from similar university-level mechanisms have been confirmed in the later studies by Di Gregorio and Shane (2003), Friedman and Silberman (2003), and Markman et al. (2009). Using individual-level commercialization data is important to figure out the relative role of university, group, and individual effects, but the study by Louis et al. (1989) likely overstates the effect of group norms and understates the effects of university-level policies. It would have been interesting if the authors had replaced the measured norms with fixed university effects to find what the boundary of all potential non-individual university effects would be, and how these university-specific effects varied across universities.

Two recent articles in clever ways corroborate the importance of scientific, peer, and department leadership norms in affecting entrepreneurial behavior, albeit measured by proxy (Stuart and Ding, 2006; Bercovitz and Feldman, 2008). Stuart and Ding study the role of peer influence on the probability of a university-employed life scientist becoming a founder or member of the scientific advisory board of a US biotechnology company between 1961 and 2002. They were more likely to do so when their department colleagues were also more likely to become entrepreneurs. This measure suffers from the same endogeneity problem as in Louis et al.'s study, but Stuart and Ding examine causality in more detail by detailing probable correlates of influence mechanisms. The effect was larger when their peers were prestigious scientists, and they were more likely when their coauthors had become entrepreneurs, particularly when the coauthors were well connected in industry and when the link was established prior to the time when the coauthor had become an entrepreneur. The manifested social influence could be twofold; by influencing attitudes towards the acceptability of commercial activities or by providing channels for information exchange and contacts. Notably, the propensity to commercialize and the social influence were the largest in the emergence of the industry and among the star scientists and elite institutions; the probability became more widespread with time and the social influence became less strong.

Bercovitz and Feldman (2008) find that the decision to disclose inventions across 15 matched departments within the medical schools of Duke and Johns Hopkins universities is strongly influenced by three effects: disclosing norms where the faculty was initially trained, the observed behavior of department chairs, and the observed behavior of department peers of the same rank.[41] These effects are strong and present under a host of control variables measuring the scientific quality of the individual researcher, and including fixed department effects. There were no significant university-level differences. The authors show concern that their peer measure is endogenous.[42] They therefore ran an additional model that includes an 'other' cohort variable; the average disclosure rate over those individuals in the same department but of a different rank, as well as the own cohort variable. In this specification the latter variable remains positive and significant while the former is positive while not significant. This test indicates that there is less cause for concern that the cohort variable is a function of unobserved department-level effects. The authors were also able to perform some tests that seemed to reject an alternative explanation that individuals predisposed to disclosure were differentially hired to departments supportive of commercialization of research, although they did not consider these tests conclusive. In addition to the above-mentioned articles, several others more indirectly show that university culture, group norms and human capital considerations are most important in affecting the rate of university start-ups according to Siegel et al. (2007b).

In summary, universities vary tremendously in their apparent degree of commercialization of research, maybe by a factor of five, even after controlling for the amount of IP that is produced (disclosed). While many different university factors have been highlighted, most of these seem to wash out after controlling for the university's commercial culture. There are still questions as to the validity of this finding and more research is needed at the project/individual level to confirm/reject the latter claim. The strongest predictors of commercialization rates are at the individual level, but scientific norms at the department, peer, and university levels as well as scientific quality also matter. There is some evidence that local norms towards commercialization are declining in importance over time as positive held views towards private commercialization of research are becoming more widespread.

TECHNOLOGY TRANSFER/TECHNOLOGY LICENSING

This section reviews models and empirical evidence on the role of university policies with respect to economic development objectives, the organization of technology licensing and transfer activities, and researcher incentives. The amount of research on this topic is probably the largest among all research topics reviewed in this chapter. Thankfully, others have recently reviewed this material and so we shall refer to their summaries whenever possible (Rothaermel et al., 2007; Siegel et al., 2007a; Djokovic and Soutaris, 2008). In this section we highlight new research results. We focus our discussion on the possibilities for adverse unintended effects of university policies and designs. Given the potential for goal conflict between maximizing total licensing revenue and local start-up generation, it is important to first understand how licensing revenues are affected by university policies and designs. We then move on to discuss the role of university policies and designs for spin-off rates.

Most empirical research on the role of university policies and design for licensing and spin-offs has been focusing on the productivity of TLOs. Most research has also been based on aggregate data by each university, comparing inputs and outputs across universities in production-function models of licensing revenues. Many have used the same data, the annual survey by AUTM. A few brave ones have hand-collected similar data (for example, from the UK) and fewer yet have studied individual-level or project-level data (see Tables 1 and 2 in Siegel et al., 2007a). Studies collecting individual-level data are the most interesting as they can investigate the role of university policies while controlling for individual and sometimes peer effects (for example, Louis et al., 1989; Zucker et al., 1998b, 2000; Zucker and Darby, 2001; Audretsch et al., 2005a; Lowe and Gonzalez-Brambila, 2007; Bercovitz and Feldman, 2008). Articles focused on start-ups will be given most space here. In reviewing the literature explaining licensing income, Siegel et al. (2007a, p. 649) conclude that the key impediments to effective patenting and licensing tend to be organizational in nature:

> These include problems with differences in organizational cultures between universities and (small) firms, incentive structures including both pecuniary and non-pecuniary rewards, such as credit towards tenure and promotion, and staffing and compensation practices of the TTO [TLO] itself.

Details on the estimated role of university policies, procedures, organization, and norms for licensing revenues are summarized in Table 9.2. However, simply listing associations often hides complex relationships,

Table 9.2   *Effects on university licensing revenue of various conditions**

Variable	Positive and significant	Zero effect	Negative and significant
Incentive structure			
Royalty shares to faculty	Friedman and Silberman (2003), Link and Siegel (2005), Lach and Schankerman (2008)		
Royalties to department	Markman et al. (2009)		
TLO staff salary		Markman et al. (2009)	
TLO staff bonuses	Belenzon and Schankerman (2009)		
Input metrics			
Faculty quality	Foltz et al. (2000), Rogers et al. (2000), Thursby and Kemp (2002), Markman et al. (2009)	Lach and Schankerman (2008)	
Federal R&D spending	Foltz et al. (2000)[a]		
Industry R&D spending		Siegel et al. (2003a)	
Invention disclosures	Siegel et al. (2003a), Belenzon and Schankerman (2009)		
Patents			
TLO design			
Age of TLO	Rogers et al. (2000), Friedman and Silberman (2003), Siegel et al. (2003a), Powers and McDougall (2005)	Chapple et al. (2005), Markman et al. (2009)	
Number of TLO staff	Rogers et al. (2000), Foltz et al. (2000), Thursby and Kemp (2002), Siegel et al. (2003a), Chapple et al. (2005), Lach and Schankerman (2008),[b] Markman et al. (2009)	Siegel et al. (2003a)	
External legal expenditures	Siegel et al. (2003a), Chapple et al. (2005)		

Table 9.2   (continued)

Variable	Positive and significant	Zero effect	Negative and significant
University type			
University with medical school	Belenzon and Schankerman (2009)	Friedman and Silberman (2003), Siegel et al. (2003a), Lach and Schankerman (2008)	Thursby and Kemp (2002),[b] Chapple et al. (2005), Anderson et al. (2007)[b]
Land grant university	Friedman and Silberman (2003),[b] Link and Siegel (2005)	Siegel et al. (2003a)	
Private university	Thursby and Kemp (2002)[b]	Friedman and Silberman (2003), Anderson et al. (2007), Belenzon and Schankerman (2009)	
Local economic conditions			
High-tech density	Friedman and Silberman (2003), Chapple et al. (2005), Lach and Schankerman (2008) for private universities, Belenzon and Schankerman (2009)		Lach and Schankerman (2008) for public universities

Notes:
*   The table only covers studies conducting multivariate analysis with university licensing revenues as the dependent variable.
a. Federal R&D support becomes insignificant when environmental/institutional variables are excluded from the model.
b. Significant only at 10 percent.

and ignores the potential for reverse causation. For example, Siegel et al. (2003a) find that increasing TLO staff increases the number of licenses executed but has no effect on total licensing revenues. Apparently TLO staffs make themselves busy. Further, the same authors find that external legal expenditures increase total licensing revenues but decrease the number of licenses executed. In this case outside lawyers may be negotiating harder, focusing on bigger deals and getting more out of less for the university than university-employed lawyers. Other potential explanations for the latter finding are reverse causality – that universities hire outside advice on larger deals, or that it represents litigation expenses.

Therefore, rather than detailing the empirical studies listed in Table 9.2 we move on to discuss the particular agency situation when there is a university and a researcher with a research project that potentially can be commercialized in various ways. We then introduce the TLO as an intermediary between the inventor and the market and discuss optimal organizational design. This will serve to highlight the potential agency problems and will give a useful background to the empirical literature.

We use the model developed by Lowe (2006) as a framework for analyzing the various parties' incentives. Lowe's base case is where the inventor starts out owning the invention fully.[43] The model has three stages and to our knowledge is the most complete characterization of the agency problem, as it involves both the option that an invention is licensed to a third party (modeled by, for example, Jensen and Thursby, 2001)[44] or is commercialized by the inventor.[45] In stage one, the inventor discloses an invention[46] and offers a licensing contract to an outside firm. In the second stage, if the firm accepts the offer, the inventor chooses an effort level to transfer know-how. The effort level is not contractible. The firm chooses output and pays the inventor in the third period. If the firm rejects the offer, the inventor decides whether to do nothing, or to start a firm on his/her own. In the third stage the firm earns profits and pays royalties. A key feature of the model is that the inventor will improve the probability of successful development with increased effort and that the marginal value of the effort is scaled by the degree to which the effort is tacit.

There are five main findings:

1. When considerable effort is required it is always better for the inventor to found the firm him/herself rather than obtaining royalty from a licensee.
2. Inventions not requiring effort from the inventor for technology transfer are optimally licensed for a fixed fee.
3. There exists a separating equilibrium where some inventors with low opportunity cost of their time start firms, and others with high opportunity costs license their invention for a royalty rate. Given a distribution of inventor opportunity costs, this equilibrium is more efficient than all inventors licensing or all inventors starting firms.
4. When an inventor starts a firm based on a university license any positive royalty rate that remains in the contract between university and the inventor reduces the level of the final goods output (value of the inventor's firm) below the output under a simple contract between the inventor and the outside firm without the university as an intermediary. The university gains, but for society this gain is more than

offset by a reduction in total output. The inventor is also worse off because of the decrease in output and sharing royalties with the university. However, a 'pure fixed fee contract' (which could be in terms of equity) does not distort output and provides a Pareto-efficient solution.

5. If the university TLO is able to bid up the selling price of firms (through for example engaging in an auction) then inventors may be better off and the university no worse off.

The model predicts that introducing a TLO as an intermediary will have negative consequences on total economic efficiency, except if the TLO is able to find multiple buyers of the inventor's business to sufficiently bid up the selling prize. Even the latter case does not guarantee overall system improvements, or improvements for all inventors, as competing bids must bring up the selling prize enough to compensate for efficiency losses introduced by the TLO tax reducing total output, and because some positive net present value projects will not be actively marketed by the TLO. Other theoretical models similarly propose that the TLO has an advantage over the inventor as an information aggregator (Hoppe and Ozdenoren, 2005; Macho-Stadler et al., 2007). The rationale is that the TLO sees more projects than the individual inventor and thus may have lower search costs for potential partners, a benefit which will be passed on to the inventor.

While some TLOs are noted to be very helpful, it is questionable whether *all* TLOs provide useful services. For example, Audretsch et al. (2005a) quote a scientist saying:

> I refuse to work with the TTO [TLO]. They have destroyed any of my commercial work. I have given up on any sort of commercial enterprises with my TTO. I don't think any of my colleagues have attempted to commercialize anything here the past six years. (p. 25)

and another as stating:

> My commercial spirit stops at the TTO [TLO] door. (p. 25)

Indeed, various researchers have found TLOs to have a high rate of staff turnover, and staff to have insufficient business and marketing experience (for example, Siegel et al., 2003a). Surveying firms, Hertzfeld et al. (2006) found that firms expressed great difficulties dealing with TLOs, citing the same problems as Siegel (2003a) discovered. As a result, in some cases firms decided to bypass the TLO and deal directly with the inventor.

In a study bound to be controversial, Audretsch et al. (2005a) found in multivariate analysis that scientists who self-identified their TLO as being helpful had a higher probability of licensing their invention but a lower probability of starting up a firm based on their invention. Further, those who transferred ownership rights to their TLO had a higher probability of licensing their invention but a lower probability of starting up a firm based on their invention, compared to those who did not transfer rights to their TLO. Finally, they uncovered that TLOs that were more efficient in terms of converting patent applications to patents positively impacted on the probability of licensing inventions, but did not affect start-up rates. The authors interpret these results as indicating a bifurcation in TLO skills – TLOs appear to know how to sell licenses but not how to help inventors who want to commercialize their research on their own. We interpret these results as indicating differences in incentives. TLO employees typically have greater and more immediate personal benefit from selling a license than from helping an inventor to start a business.[47]

While there might be potentially superior benefits to using a TLO in some cases, Kenney and Patton (2009) argue that such a service in no way motivates a *de jure* allocation of ownership to the TLO. Their arguments are as follows. Suppose that the inventor knows best how to commercialize his/her invention. Then there is no need for the inventor to pay for the TLO service and since *de jure* TLO ownership implies extracting royalty from the start-up, taxing the project this way leads to lower social welfare (Lowe, 2006). Suppose instead that the TLO has superior knowledge. The inventor will realize this after contacting the TLO and will contract for the services at fair market value, or sell the rights to the TLO. Gains from trade will emerge. Suppose instead that the TLO is initially allocated the rights but the inventor is the most effective commercialization agent, a not unlikely case when key technical information is highly tacit and inalienable (Thursby and Thursby, 2007).[48] The TLO will have to either negotiate an effort agreement with the inventor or allocate royalties as incentive. However, an effort agreement is unenforceable when tasks are tacit. And in the latter case the incentive is always less than if the inventor owned the firm and the inventor will thus underperform, partly due to the tax extracted by the TLO, but also due to the loss in output (Lowe, 2006). The only remaining solution which turns out Pareto superior is if the TLO charges a fixed fee for its service which in itself does not require *de jure* TLO ownership.

An additional complication from introducing a TLO with *de jure* ownership is that industry negotiates with the TLO but the TLO does not credibly represent the inventor as the TLO cannot enforce compliance by the inventor for successful technology transfer. Industry would thus prefer to negotiate directly with the inventor in order to provide stronger assurances of adequate technology transfer, be it in a licensing or other form of contract, and the rationale for the existence of a TLO is on this account thus also questioned.[49]

From Canada we can ascertain whether assigning control rights to the university implies increased efficiency. Canadian universities are free to choose how to allocate control rights over IP. For example, in the city of Vancouver the University of British Columbia takes control rights, while at Simon Fraser University its inventors are allocated control rights. Among the 20 largest universities, the creator takes control rights in eight cases, in another eight cases the IP is university owned, and the remaining four have joint ownership or case-by-case negotiations. Analysis of the Canadian AUTM data comparing the 16 top universities with clear differences in allocation of control rights suggests that universities that claim ownership of IP do not have a record of more successful exploitation of IP on any outcome measure (Clayman, 2004).

In sum, if the inventor is the default owner, superior allocation of rights will always occur. Conversely, *de jure* TLO ownership is only economically efficient when (a) the TLO performs valuable services, and (b) the TLO charges the inventor a fixed fee for its services. But if a TLO is providing valuable services, these can be contracted at will and *de jure* allocation is inefficient (Kenney and Patton, 2009). Either way, allocation of rights should rest most efficiently with the inventor.

It has been argued that an open market for commercialization services will guarantee the provision of superior skills (Litan et al., 2007; Kenney and Patton, 2009). Indeed, there are many privately operated invention evaluation and marketing services available, some with considerable experience and reputation, and the number of intermediaries and their menu of different services is growing.[50] It is important to understand that a market for commercialization services does not suffer nearly the same difficulties as the market for inventions. It is comparatively much simpler to price an invention marketing service than it is to price an invention (as the TLO-centric model implicitly does). This is an additional argument for why control rights should initially rest with the inventor – offers of marketing and patenting services should be fairly easy to evaluate by the inventor and services are likely to be provided at close to marginal costs, while default decisions on equity-sharing by the TLO are unlikely to lead to efficient allocations and appropriate incentives.

Introducing a TLO as a mandated technology transfer agent may have additional negative effects on technological change. The starting point of interaction between an inventor and the TLO at most universities is the disclosure by a researcher of an invention to the university. Post-Bayh–Dole, all US universities now require such disclosures, although in countries such as Sweden which maintain the Professor's Privilege there is no such requirement.[51] A researcher loses some and gains some by disclosing the invention. As discussed above, the researcher may potentially gain help in commercializing the invention. Since disclosure is mandated he/she also avoids potential censure or prosecution, and loses the guarantee of keeping all returns for him/herself, reducing his/her incentive to commercialize. In most US universities the researcher retains about 30 percent ownership rights, which means that he/she loses 70 percent directly on disclosure. If the benefits of using the TLO are small and the potential penalties small, the inventor has a large incentive not to disclose.[52] A fair number of spin-offs indeed go unregistered by universities. According to Markman et al. (2008) 42 percent of professors who patented bypassed the TLO, while Audretsch et al. (2005a) put this number at 30 percent for their sample of university researchers obtaining NIH Cancer Institute grants. Further, in direct contravention with the Bayh–Dole Act, 26 percent of all faculty patents in the US under the Bayh–Dole Act were directly assigned to firms (Thursby et al., 2009). However, not all of these non-employer assignments are sinister. Many could be due to research consulting engagements, where assignment to the client is legal and the faculty inventor's contribution is properly acknowledged on the patent. It is not clear what useful recourse a university has if it uncovers that a faculty member has commercialized IP without its disclosure and the university also has some legal rights to the IP. Forcefully extracting rents from the spin-off or imposing penalties on the non-reporting employee may have negative repercussions on university reputation, contributions to endowments, and future entrepreneurship. Kenney and Patton (2009) illustrate this with the cases of Marc Andreessen[53] and Jim Clark.[54]

As a case in point, in our interviews at a European university which recently came under Bayh–Dole-type regulation, the TLO administrators found the following effects upon implementing *de jure* ownership with mandatory disclosure:

- faculty disclose but are uncooperative in further interactions with the TLO;
- faculty with established industry collaborations started to withhold information about their activities, or simply stopped claiming IP;
- faculty state invention as having zero commercial opportunity, thus leading to immediate release of university ownership claims.

Examining this negative incentive to disclose, Siegel et al. (2007a, p. 643) recommend that 'the university needs to have proper incentive schemes in place, specifying an adequate share for the inventors in royalties or equity'. Indeed, Thursby et al. (2009) find that the greater the inventor royalties the greater the probability that the IP is assigned to the university employer.[55] However, any share less than 100 percent reduces the incentive to disclose. One might ask why universities have attached *de jure* ownership to the requirement by faculty to disclose. If universities want to maximize disclosures it would seem more reasonable *not* to claim ownership by default upon disclosure. Further, it appears from Bercovitz and Feldman (2008) that disclosure is a function of department norms, university norms, as well as scientific norms. That is, there are other ways of raising disclosure rates.

After disclosure follows patenting. The TLO's decision on what to patent may diverge from what is in the inventor's best interest. For example, where TLOs have a reputation of presenting high quality inventions to industry, the TLO may have an incentive to not pursue some projects with positive expected net present value because losing the reputation by not delivering a certain quality level may be very costly for the TLO (Macho-Stadler et al., 2007). Further, even in the absence of reputational effects, since the returns functions of the TLO are different from the inventors' the TLO may not pursue some projects with positive expected net present value.[56]

Finally, as already alluded to, the TLO may be biased towards executing a license with an established company because: (a) licenses generate royalty income sooner than start-ups and many TLO officers are incentivized to maximize royalty income; (b) TLOs have a budget to manage and so may be more likely to take cash now than a risky option; (c) start-ups often require exclusive licenses which makes it a more risky proposition for the TLO;[57] and (d) a licensing contract is likely easier to execute for TLO personnel than an equity deal (Debackere and Veugelers, 2005; Thursby and Thursby, 2007; Belenzon and Schankerman, 2009). These incentives may not always be in the interest of the inventor.

In fact, there is good evidence that TLO officers have incentives that are not aligned with inventors' incentives. Approximately 70 percent of university central administrators report that 'royalties/license fees' is extremely important as a measure of success for their TLO, while only 36 percent of them mention 'number of inventions commercialized' as extremely important (Jensen and Thursby, 2001). The survey also asked TLO officers what they think faculty considers most important. Incongruously, the TLO officers know that their goals are different from those of faculty. Approximately 75 percent of TLO officers state that 'obtaining sponsored research funds' is extremely important for faculty, while 36 percent report that they believe 'number of inventions commercialized' is extremely important for faculty.

Nevertheless, if a TLO adopts incentive pay for its staff (in particular merit pay and bonus) it increases university licensing income per license by between 30 and 40 percent, a substantial amount given that the mean licensing income per active license was $38,900 and yearly number of executed licenses per university was 29 in the data (Belenzon and Schankerman, 2009). This benefits universities but also inventors. Private universities are significantly more likely to adopt these incentives than public universities. However, incentive pay does not affect the fraction of spin-offs to licenses that are created. That is, the university seems only able to incentivize staff for generating licensing income, not for generating start-ups.

Moving on to discuss inventors' incentives, it is likely that allocating greater royalty shares to inventors increases their efforts. Indeed, universities that allocate greater ownership shares to inventors have larger licensing income (Friedman and Silberman, 2003; Link and Siegel, 2005; Lach and Schankerman, 2008). The impact is much larger at private universities than at publicly operated universities (ibid.). This differential effect is probably due to the TLOs at the private universities being more effective at finding firms willing to purchase/license the IP, in part because private universities impose fewer constraints and rules on their TLOs. In such places, a percentage point increase in royalty share means proportionally more in the inventor's pocket. In most private universities allocating a dollar more licensing income to the inventor raises total royalty income by more than a dollar. However, if universities expect competing universities to match changes in their royalty share, this net gain is only present in a small set of universities. Importantly, the incentive effect is twofold: it raises faculty effort at the margin, and it sorts scientists across universities. The second effect implies that more commercially oriented researchers would tend to join universities that allocate greater royalty shares to inventors.

Faculty effort affects both the number of inventions and their quality, and both should be increasing functions of effort incentives. Lach and Schankerman find that the primary incentive effect of raising the royalty rate is to raise the quality rather than the quantity of inventions. Importantly, raising the royalty rate at private universities by *one percentage point* will generate *4.3 percent more* licensing income, given the same number of licenses. The effect of a percentage increase in the royalty rate on the number of executed licenses is about half of that. Interestingly, the authors reject the idea that the inventors are *only* motivated by cash considerations – when they decompose the incentive into private cash and laboratory funding, the effect for laboratory funding is about *twice* the size of private cash, and both effects are statistically significantly different from zero. In public universities it appears that incentive effects are much weaker; many of the reported incentive effects turn out to be insignificant. These results illustrate that university central administrators and TLO officers alike currently may not fully understand how to most efficiently increase licensing income using university policies as a lever. If they knew, they would allocate as much effort as possible to maximize lab funding to their researchers since this produces the greatest licensing income per dollar unit cost. But instead, according to Jensen and Thursby (2001), increasing lab funding is only a secondary goal for university central administrators and a distant fourth-ranked goal for TLO officers, but a top-ranked goal for researchers. The last is, of course, consistent with the estimates of Lach and Schankerman (2008).[58]

While licensing revenues increase with inventors' royalty rates, two publications (Di Gregorio and Shane, 2003; Markman et al., 2009) show that the number of start-ups is reduced by an increase in the royalty rate granted to inventors. However, the negative effect of inventor royalties on start-up rates is not consistent – Lockett and Wright (2005) find a positive effect and two additional studies find null effects (see Table 9.3). Di Gregorio and Shane interpret their result as indicating an increase in the opportunity cost of starting a business for an academic. Their argument is as follows: when the royalty rate increases, the income increases for the inventor who licenses the invention to a third-party firm and so licensing of the invention is encouraged. But if the inventor owns the firm, an increase in the royalty rate does not increase his/her earnings through profits because the inventor is indifferent between income through royalty payments from his/her own firm and payment in the form of residual income (profits). We do not find this a convincing argument due to a two-stage argument. First, as the inventor's royalty share increases, the university's share decreases proportionally and the tax on the firm decreases, leading to greater pre-tax returns for the inventor-owner. Second, while the inventor's royalty income is recorded as personal taxable income which is directly taxable, the inventor's residual income from the firm is net of expenditures before being taxed. The firm can deduct expenses before profits; as well, business taxes are typically lower than personal taxes so the effective tax rate on residual income is typically lower than on royalties. It thus seems reasonable to assume that because pre-business income increases and because the effective taxation on invention rewards is lower when owning a firm than when declaring the reward as personal income, greater royalty rates should increase the incentive to commercialize inventions through a start-up over licensing. Nevertheless, it could be that the incentive to start a business is reduced by *any* royalty rate as it functions as a tax on the start-up (Lowe, 2006). It remains to be determined whether and why increased inventor royalty rates may decrease spin-off rates. One probably needs project-level data to understand this problem better.

This section has reviewed models and evidence concerning the formation

Table 9.3   Effects on number/probability of spin-offs of various conditions

Variable	Positive and significant	Zero effect	Negative and significant
Incentive structure			
Royalty shares to faculty	Lockett and Wright (2005)	Louis et al. (1989), Friedman and Silberman (2003)	Di Gregorio and Shane (2003), Markman et al. (2009)
Royalties to department		Friedman and Silberman (2003), Markman et al. (2009)	
Taking equity in start-up by university	Di Gregorio and Shane (2003)	Louis et al. (1989)	
University venture capital fund		Louis et al. (1989), Di Gregorio and Shane (2003)	
Licensing for cash		Markman et al. (2009)	
Sponsored research agreements		Markman et al. (2009)	
Equity agreements		Markman et al. (2009)	
Local development objective		Belenzon and Schankerman (2009)	
Input metrics			
Faculty quality	Zucker et al. (1998b), Di Gregorio and Shane (2003), O'Shea et al. (2005), Powers and McDougall (2005), Markman et al. (2009)		
Federal R&D spending	O'Shea et al. (2005)		
Industry R&D spending	O'Shea et al. (2005), Powers and McDougall (2005)	Louis et al. (1989), Di Gregorio and Shane (2003)	
Invention disclosures	Di Gregorio and Shane (2003), O'Shea et al. (2005), Belenzon and Schankerman (2009)	Friedman and Silberman (2003)	

Table 9.3   (continued)

Variable	Positive and significant	Zero effect	Negative and significant
Input metrics			
Patents		Louis et al. (1989), Di Gregorio and Shane (2003)	
TLO design			
Age of TLO	Powers and McDougall (2005)	Friedman and Silberman (2003), Lockett and Wright (2005)	Markman et al. (2009)
Number of TLO staff	O'Shea et al. (2005), Markman et al. (2009)	Louis et al. (1989), Di Gregorio and Shane (2003), Lockett and Wright (2005)	
Expenditure on IP protection	Lockett and Wright (2005)		
TLO staff salary	Markman et al. (2009)		
TLO staff bonuses		Belenzon and Schankerman (2009)	
University type			
Incubator	Markman et al. (2009)	Colombo and Delmastro (2002), Di Gregorio and Shane (2003), Lee and Osteryoung (2004), O'Shea et al. (2005), Rothaermel and Thursby (2005), Squicciarini (2009)	
Science park		Louis et al. (1989)	
University with medical school		Louis et al. (1989), Friedman and Silberman (2003), Lockett and Wright (2005), O'Shea et al. (2005), Belenzon and Schankerman (2009), Markman et al. (2009)	
Land grant university		Louis et al. (1989), Friedman and Silberman (2003), O'Shea et al. (2005), Markman et al. (2009)	

Table 9.3   (continued)

Variable	Positive and significant	Zero effect	Negative and significant
University type			
Private university		Louis et al. (1989), Friedman and Silberman (2003), O'Shea et al. (2005), Markman et al. (2009)	Belenzon and Schankerman (2009)
Local economic conditions			
Venture capital availability	Powers and McDougall (2005)	Di Gregorio and Shane (2003), Markman et al. (2009)	Zucker et al. (1998b)
High-tech density	Belenzon and Schankerman (2009)	O'Shea et al. (2005)	

of firms based on intellectual property developed through research at universities. TLOs are in most empirical work considered as having a positive effect. However, whether this is due to causation, reverse causation, or common determination has not been shown. In addition, the theoretical work is much more skeptical as to the potential benefits of introducing or enlarging TLOs. Further, there are dissenting empirical data as to the value of TLOs, and in particular to the value of assigning control rights over IP to the TLO by default. Further, the research clearly shows that incentives matter, both for TLO officers and for researchers. A consensus seems to be forming that TLO officers are strongly incentivized to license IP, but much less interested in helping inventors to start businesses. Researchers, on the other hand, bring in more licensing income to the university than the university loses by awarding the inventor greater royalty shares, but the greatest 'bang for the buck' may be when productive researchers are simply awarded more laboratory funding. More research using project-level data and good experimental design with analysis of treatment effects is sorely needed to explore incentive effects, contractual design, market design, and TLO process management impacts. Research using the AUTM data will continue to be plagued by interpretation problems with respect to causality.

The empirical evidence exclusively covers patents and start-ups by faculty and staff. Existing empirical work (in particular all the work based on AUTM data) does not cover firms started by students because these are typically not using IP based on university funding.[59] So, if a group of students get together (before or after graduating) to start a business, this is not typically counted as a university spin-off.[60] In the next section we shall review what little evidence there is of student spin-off activity. It turns out that this activity is probably of an order of magnitude larger than faculty spin-offs, at least in terms of number of firms.

STUDENT/ALUMNI START-UPS

Most past research and practice has focused on the productivity of technology transfer from university research, investigating TLO practices, university policies, and sometimes faculty cultures as antecedents of spin-off rates. We contend that the majority of local entrepreneurial economic development imparted by universities is in the form of start-ups created by former students, and that start-ups by university faculty and researchers constitute a minority of the local economic impact simply because these are very few. Our claim is based on two points. The first point is that there are many more students than faculty. A rule of thumb would be a ratio of 30 graduated students per year per faculty. If, as indicated in an MBA alumni survey that we conducted at the University of Toronto, there are on the order of 10 percent of students who create start-ups in the first three years after graduating, we obtain one student start-up per faculty per year (0.10*30/3). Since a faculty member teaches over approximately 25 years it stands to reason that students' start-ups greatly outnumber start-ups by the average faculty. If each faculty member starts one business in his/her lifetime, the ratio is 25:1 in favor of students; if more plausibly one in four faculty members starts one business in his/her lifetime, the ratio is 100:1 start-ups in favor of students.

There are no general data on the rate by which students start up new businesses upon graduation, but there are several university-specific alumni surveys that give indications of the magnitude. Recent alumni surveys have been conducted on Harvard MBAs (Lerner and Malmendier, 2007), Stanford MBAs (Lazear, 2005), and students from Tsinghua University[61] in China (Eesley et al., 2009), Halmstad University in Sweden (Eriksson, 1996), and MIT (Hsu et al., 2007; Roberts and Eesley, 2009). The percentages of students from these programs starting businesses are approximately 5 percent at Harvard Business School (HBS) (1997–2004 students), 24 percent each from MIT, 24 percent from Stanford Business School and Tsinghua, and finally 36 percent from an engineering program at Halmstad University.

In computing a student-to-faculty proportion of spin-offs, we shall feature most prominently the survey of all living alumni from MIT as it contains a wealth of information. In Roberts and Eesley's (2009) report,

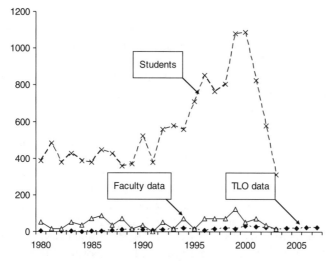

Notes: TLO data (black diamonds) as reported by the MIT TLO to AUTM. Student and faculty data are from Roberts and Eesley (2009). Faculty data computed as follows: The number of current MIT faculty responding to the Roberts and Eesley survey who are MIT student alumni reported starting 66 companies during 1980–2003. Each start-up is multiplied by the product of the inverses of the two survey non-response rates = 2.425*3.906. To approximate the number of spin-offs by *all* MIT faculty we compute the fraction of MIT faculty in the mechanical and electrical engineering departments in 2000 who were MIT alumni (53 percent). This gives an additional scale-up factor of (1 + 0.47/0.53).

Sources: AUTM (1996–2007); Charles Eesley from Stanford University.

Figure 9.1   *Number of faculty spin-offs and student start-ups from MIT between 1980 and 2007*

23.5 percent of the alumni indicated that they had founded at least one company.[62] A special extract of these data made by Charles Eesley revealed 388 firms started by former students in 1980 growing to 710 in 1995 and to 1,089 started in 2000, subsequently to decline to 313 started in 2003.[63] These numbers indicate an enormous response to the dot-com boom, both up and down. In comparison, the number of TLO-registered spin-offs by MIT faculty and staff were two in 1980, growing to 14 in 1995 and 23 in 2006. (Note again that the number of registered spin-offs from MIT is leading among all US universities.)

The cumulative student spin-offs from MIT thus outnumbered officially registered faculty spin-offs by a ratio of 48:1 between 1980 and 2003 (Figure 9.1). Should one accept that the number of unregistered faculty spin-offs is somewhere between 30 and 45 percent (Audretsch et al., 2005a;

Markman et al., 2008) the ratio is still on the order of 20–25:1. However, using instead as one source of information the MIT alumni survey and counting the data on MIT students who stayed and became MIT faculty (survey extract by Charles Eesley, and making several additional assumptions: see notes to Figure 9.1) we obtain a ratio of 12:1. Consequently, under any reasonable assumption the number of student start-ups is at least one order of magnitude larger than faculty start-ups.

Almost all MIT alumni founders (89 percent) started their companies where they were living at the time. The largest percentage (65 percent) indicated that they were living there because this was where they had been employed, and 15 percent indicated that that's where they attended university (often MIT). When asked what factors influenced the location of their companies, the most common responses (in order) were: (i) where the founders lived, (ii) network of contacts, (iii) quality of life, (iv) proximity to major markets, and (v) access to skilled professional workers. Taxes and the regulatory environment were rated as less-important factors (Roberts and Eesley, 2009). In BankBoston's survey of MIT spin-offs (BankBoston, 1997), Massachusetts survey firms ranked access to MIT and to other universities ahead of low business cost; in every other region of the country, business cost was more important than contact with universities.

It is therefore not surprising that the state benefiting most from jobs from MIT alumni is Massachusetts with 6,900 active MIT alumni firms and one million jobs. The 6,900 alumni firms generate worldwide sales of about $164 billion — 26 percent of the sales of all Massachusetts companies – a truly astounding proportion. However, there has been a shift towards locating in California with about 22 percent of MIT graduates starting their companies there in the 1990s, growing from 10 percent in the 1950s, while still leaving about 26 percent locating in Massachusetts. California has thus benefited greatly from MIT alumni with 4,100 alumni firms and 526,000 jobs (Roberts and Eesley, 2009).[64]

Each successive MIT graduating class was found to generate proportionally more entrepreneurs. Furthermore, alumni of more recent cohorts are also starting their first companies sooner and at earlier ages (BankBoston, 1997; Roberts and Eesley, 2009). The median age of first-time entrepreneurs has gradually declined from about age 40 (1950s) to about age 30 (1990s). Correspondingly, the average time lag between graduation and first firm founding has dropped from approximately 18 years (1950s) to as low as four years (1990s), although data truncation artificially deflates the latter figure (ibid.).

A critical influence on these start-ups is the effect of 'positive feedback' arising from early role models and successes. In particular, the alumni survey by Roberts and Eesley shows that while 17 percent of those who eventually formed companies chose MIT to study for its entrepreneurial environment in the 1950s, 42 percent of those 1990s graduates who formed companies claim they were attracted to MIT by its reputed entrepreneurial environment. Student-run activities (mostly many different clubs) are pointed to as the major reason for the vast number of student spin-offs. Importantly, student-run activities were initiated already in the 1950s and have grown organically and slowly. Faculty are assessed to be more important in terms of stimulating students' start-ups through their research and openness to entrepreneurship rather than as founders of start-ups. Furthermore, the MIT TLO office took a very non-interventionist role (see, for example, Pfeiffer, 1997; Nelsen, 2007) and MIT did not provide many courses on entrepreneurship (Pfeiffer, 1997). In fact, from 1961, only one course in entrepreneurship was taught at MIT until 1990. There has been a late growth in a variety of support activities and courses in entrepreneurship at MIT since the mid-1990s, but these cannot be said to have had any impact on the trend that began in the 1950s.

Students from MIT may have been exceptionally well endowed with favorable local conditions explaining the high spin-off creation rates by MIT students and alumni. There has been a large amount of applied engineering research done at MIT, an early development of the venture capital industry in Boston, and a large supply of potential co-founders and employees (BankBoston, 1997; Roberts and Eesley, 2009). Nevertheless, we have been able to find an antithesis where none of these conditions exists/existed and where a large proportion of engineering students still manage to start up new businesses, albeit maybe of smaller average size.

The antithesis to MIT is Högskolan i Halmstad in Sweden and a short background is required to appreciate the data. Halmstad has close to 90,000 inhabitants. The local economy is a mixture of different small-scale operations with no venture capital, research labs, or research-driven businesses. Instead, trade and services are important due to seasonal tourism. The largest private company employs 600, while 75 percent of inhabitants are employed in companies with 10 or fewer employees.

A small teachers' college was created in Halmstad in 1973 from which the university was formed in 1983 through a general university reform; it is one of the youngest universities in Sweden.[65] In the mid-1980s it was focused on teachers' education and shorter degree programs. Not until 1997 was the university granted the right to employ full professors; prior to that the teaching staff had lower-status positions. The first PhD was conferred as late as 1999. In 2008, Högskolan i Halmstad had some 50 degree programs, 5,000 full-time (11,500 total) students, approximately 40 professors and a research budget of 88 MSEK (US$ 8 million). The number of Halmstad students graduating is 55 percent of those graduating from Chalmers University of Technology in Göteborg, but Halmstad has an R&D budget of only 6 percent of that of Chalmers.

One of the first new programs created in 1979 was 'Innovation Engineering'. It received the nickname the 'Inventor program' and it quickly attracted students from across the country, many with prior work experience. The program aimed at combining broad engineering knowledge with business skills. A Mechatronics program was started next, followed by Computer Engineering.

The percentage of alumni starting new businesses from the Innovation Engineering and Computer Engineering programs was estimated through a survey in 1992 to be 36 and 21 percent, respectively (Eriksson, 1996). Since many start-ups were team based, the fraction of unique spin-offs was somewhat lower – 28 and 16 percent, respectively. To explain the large rate of start-ups from the 'Inventor program', Eriksson points out that in that program students' thesis projects are geared towards developing a technical idea into a product, usually in cooperation with established local companies. Further, Eriksson argues that Halmstad University experienced exceptionally large institutional changes which ended up creating a supportive environment for entrepreneurship. The program's closeness to industry and the students' independence and greater maturity are further explanations.

Even the research laboratories produce considerably more student spin-offs than faculty spin-offs at Halmstad University. In a study of 15 spin-offs from the Center for Research on Embedded Systems, Berggren and Lindholm-Dahlstrand (2008) found that 12 (80 percent) were formed by former students and only three by research staff. Twelve of these firms (80 percent) maintain a head office in Halmstad. The first wave of student-entrepreneurs (1988–96) 'were inspired by the unique Innovation Engineering programme and the spirit of new settlement that surrounded the university at the time' (ibid., p. 50). A second generation of entrepreneurs started after 2000 as more resources were given to the university's incubator and venture capital became available from Högskolan i Halmstad. Also, some of the first generation of student entrepreneurs returned to the university, became discussion partners, network providers, and in some cases provided financing for ventures in the second wave (ibid., pp. 50–51).

This illuminating case provides great hope for universities which lack the ecosystem that MIT has developed for itself over many decades. The case shows that even in situations with considerable local resource constraints there appear to be actions that a university can take to create local economic development, primarily through graduating engineering students. The role of university policies and TLO activities may have had some impact, but most important at Halmstad and similar to MIT was the engineering programs' industry orientation and spirit of entrepreneurialism. The case also reinforces the lesson from MIT of the importance of peers (entrepreneurs returning to the university) influencing students' decisions to start up businesses. Importantly, many of the spin-offs remained close to their alma mater, just as in the case of MIT, even though local economic conditions may not have been ideal.

There is a more formal econometric study that indicates the role of students' peers in improving the quality of spin-offs. Lerner and Malmendier (2007) use allocation of students to sections in the Harvard MBA program as an instrument for peer effects, claiming that assignment to sections is random.[66] They find that a one standard deviation increase in the share of peers with pre-HBS entrepreneurial background in a section decreases the share of the section going into an entrepreneurial role after graduation from 5 to 4 percent. This effect is driven by the diminishing rate of unsuccessful entrepreneurs after graduation: students in sections with more pre-HBS entrepreneurs are less likely to start unsuccessful businesses. Finally, sections with few prior entrepreneurs have a considerably higher variance in their rates of unsuccessful entrepreneurs. They argue that these results are consistent with intra-section learning, where the close ties between students in a section lead to an enhanced understanding of the merits of proposed business ideas. Because the authors analyze not individual- but section-level data, an alternative interpretation is that entrepreneurs start again after obtaining their MBA, but with better ideas.[67] Better ideas could be obtained through coursework, for example, rather than from peer interaction.

Returning us from peer effects and local norms to the role of university policies, Franklin et al. (2001) interview policy-setters and administrators at universities in the UK and distinguish between academic and 'surrogate' (external) entrepreneurs. Universities creating the most start-ups are claimed to be those that have the most favorable policies towards enlisting surrogate entrepreneurs. Our inclination is to extend the authors' definition to encompass students as surrogate entrepreneurs. Students may be more flexible in adopting business attire than the university inventors, certainly have lower opportunity costs in doing so, and are in reasonably good supply so that it is possible to develop a talent market. The drawbacks of using students as surrogate entrepreneurs are that students may not have the technical expertise and may still be too 'green' to be able to carry a business forward effectively. Such drawbacks may be solved if an effective talent market is developed and the inventor remains with the business to complement students' lack of technical expertise. We shall illustrate this point with another case.

Chalmers Tekniska Högskola (University of Technology), a Polytechnique/Institute of Technology located in Göteborg (population 500,000), was founded in 1829 through a donation from a business person. It has always had close interaction with local industry. Large local employers such as Volvo, SKF, and Ericsson typically hire a considerable number of engineers from Chalmers every year. A large minority (10 percent) of new high-tech firms in Göteborg are direct spin-offs from universities by faculty and researchers, and an additional 21 percent are 'indirect' spin-offs by former faculty and researchers who have spent some time working in industry before starting their business (Lindholm-Dahlstrand, 1999). This means that the region has almost twice as many university spin-offs among high-tech firms as the country as a whole and experiences a disproportionate impact of Chalmers compared to other regions with universities. Chalmers has had a steady stream of spin-offs, with the first recorded in 1946, 13 ventures recorded in 1980, growing to 22 in 1985 and declining to 10 in 1994 (Wallmark, 1997; data include active students' spin-offs, when available).

Chalmers went through radical changes in their innovation ecosystem during 1994–2007, precipitated by several events. First, in 1994 Chalmers became private, only the second of two Swedish universities at that time.[68] Chalmers appointed a new Chair in Innovation at its fledgling incubator in 1993. His first task was to create a modest seed financing fund at Chalmers by appropriating 20 million SEK (approx. US$2 million) from a 1994 government privatization loan. Two additional early-stage venture capital funds were subsequently created, reaching 300 million SEK and 115 million SEK, respectively, before closing. These were the first venture capital pools with university investment in Sweden. A new building for the incubator was bought and opened in 1999. However, the most radical impact on spin-offs from Chalmers was the Entrepreneurship School (E-School) founded in 1997, the first of its kind in Sweden.

The idea was to pair high-quality Chalmers undergraduate students with inventions from Chalmers' laboratories to create spin-offs. The E-School was designed to combine formal lectures with giving the students the task of creating real companies. This is now a two-year International Master Program. The first intake contained 12 students and with a steady rate E-School now admits 20 students each year from approximately 100 applicants. Applicants are screened through a three-stage process, where those that are not open to new ideas, with low self-efficacy, low stamina, and low creativity are screened out. Most applicants have an undergraduate engineering degree from Chalmers.

A key feature of the program is that students do *not* bring their own venture idea. Instead, the projects are based on promising inventions developed by faculty and staff at Chalmers, and to a small but increasing degree inventions developed by researchers outside Chalmers. A double-sided competitive selection process clears the market. A contract is signed where the inventor is left with a third ownership rights, the students in the project obtain a third conditional on continuing the project after graduation, and Chalmers obtains the remaining third. Each project's expenses (approximately 20,000–30,000 SEK for patent work, legal, and other) are paid by Chalmers. The inventor agrees in writing to provide reasonable efforts (typically two days a month). After finishing E-School, approximately half the students continue in the newly incorporated businesses in a leading position, and many take the next step to the incubator. Approximately 80 percent of the businesses remain in the region. The students often return to Chalmers as guest speakers, providing contract research (surprisingly more in absolute terms than from the region's larger firms) and their start-ups provide many opportunities for undergraduate theses work. The E-School produced two start-ups in its first year of operations, increasing to six in 2007.

Having discussed the dominance of student start-ups over faculty start-ups, and giving three examples of different mechanisms that universities can use to stimulate the creation of student start-ups, we now move to discussing their relative local impact. Using Swedish matched employer–employee records, Baltzopoulos and Broström (2009) are able to statistically estimate the effect of studying at a particular university on the probability that a student locates his/her start-up in the region of the university as opposed to another region. Seventy-one percent of the entrepreneurs graduating from university start their business in the region where they were born. If the university were in the same region as they were born, this probability increases to 87 percent. However, if the university where they studied were located in another region than where they were born, the probability of locating in the region where they were born decreases to 26 percent. Further, among those who moved to study at a university in another region, 51 percent start up the business in the same region as the university, 22 percent move to another region altogether, and as previously reported 26 percent move back home to start their business. The university thus serves as a strong magnet to start-ups by alumni and breaks the otherwise very strong 'home bias' that entrepreneurs have.

One might ask why students are more likely to locate their start-up close to their alma mater. There are probably many reasons. Studying spin-offs started by PhD students, post-docs and former research assistants, Heblich and Slavtchev (2009) find that the likelihood of these being located in the region of the parent university increases with the number of professors at the parent university in the specific academic discipline, but not with the number of professors at other universities in the region in the specific academic discipline. The degree to which the advisor of the students had R&D collaboration with local industry also affected the probability of locating locally. Because the data are cross-sectional, the authors cannot eliminate common unmeasured causes. However, in the analysis comparing the effect of the number of professors from the parent university with the number of professors from other universities in the region, regional conditions are held constant. In another more descriptive study (BankBoston, 1997), it was found that just under half of MIT alumni spin-offs in Massachusetts report regular contact with MIT; the major purpose of these contacts was consulting with faculty members, continuing professional education, and company recruiting. About one in five firms outside Massachusetts remains in touch with MIT. The results suggest strong effects of ties between professors and students as an explanation for why students' start-ups remain close to their alma mater.

In closing, we have seen both anecdotal and systematic data showing that up to 80 percent of students' spin-offs remain extremely close to their alma mater, even if the local environment lacks important resources, as in the case of Halmstad. The importance of universities for creating local economic development through start-ups may therefore be considerably underestimated by looking exclusively at faculty spin-offs where absolute numbers are much smaller. Another conclusion is that it is within universities' clear realm to produce local economic development simply by graduating more students. Indeed, Andersson et al. (2004, 2009) show that the establishment/expansion of new universities such as Halmstad enhances regional productivity and innovativeness. However, they also find that the elasticity of regional productivity growth is higher with respect to the number of faculty employed than the number of students graduated. Nevertheless, the gross effects of students' start-ups likely outnumber the gross effects of faculty spin-offs. In terms of the relative number of start-ups data are sparse, but the MIT case indicates a student-to-faculty spin-off ratio of up to 48:1. A low estimate is 12:1. Universities serve as magnets of skilled engineers and scientists and many students who create a start-up stay put. Peer effects, local norms, and ties to professors seem to be important for locating closely. More research is needed using alumni surveys, preferably in panel data form to eliminate omitted variable bias related to the co-variation of university location and economic activity. These surveys will be able to identify new and exciting evidence regarding start-ups' location patterns, their magnitudes, and their causes.

SCIENCE PARKS AND INCUBATORS

Science parks located close to universities were first built in the 1950s in the US (for example, Stanford Research Park and the Research Triangle Park in North Carolina) and then in the late 1960s in Europe.[69] The best-known European park may be Sophia Antipolis outside Nice, which was constructed in 1969. The number of science parks grew rapidly in the 1980s and 1990s, and by 1999 there were 46 such parks in the UK and 364 in Italy (Colombo and Delmastro, 2002; Siegel et al., 2003b).

Science parks were built based on several arguments. First, large firms wanted closer access to university research in more informal ways than are accomplished by reading scientific journals and attending conferences. Indeed, academic articles show the importance of proximity to the transfer/spillover of knowledge from universities to established firms' labs (for example, Jaffe, 1989; Acs et al., 1992, 1994; Mansfield and Lee, 1996; Adams, 2002; Furman and MacGarvie, 2007). For example, Mansfield and Lee found that firms prefer to work with local universities (within 100 miles of the corporate lab) and that firms support local applied research of less distinguished faculties nearly as much as faculty in top schools, though basic research supported by firms takes place mostly at top schools. Second, a science park or business incubator may facilitate the process of research commercialization by university researchers by providing easy access to business resources while allowing the researcher to still continue at his/her lab/university position. A third argument is that agglomerating firms in a park/building may lead to positive spillover between them. The two last arguments have not been the target of much research and currently we do not know whether there are any such positive effects, gross or net of their costs.

Most research on science parks shows that science parks have no positive impact on firm performance compared to firms not located in science parks (for example, Westhead and Storey, 1995; Westhead, 1997; Lindelöf and Löfsten, 2003, 2004; Siegel et al., 2003b). However, other differences have sometimes been found, such as in employee composition, R&D intensity and innovation orientation. For a recent review of this literature, see Siegel et al. (2003b). Most studies typically select a set of science parks, survey their members and then choose a matched comparison group based on a set of criteria, typically firm age, ownership status, industry, and region, and survey these over the same time period, or allow the comparison group to be randomly sampled from some common pool. Most studies have only performed univariate statistics, which confounds impact on performance with self-selection into science parks.

A small set of studies have tried to control for observable tenant differences through multivariate regressions when estimating a science park effect. Of course, the science park dummy is biased if it is endogenous, and no-one really believes that it is not. Firms choose to belong to parks for the very reasons stated above. For example, Lindelöf and Löfsten (2003) found that tenants reported nearness to universities to be the most important location criterion, while off-park firms reported proximity to customers to be of higher importance in their location choice. Choosing to locate in a science park may depend on many firm characteristics such as degree of business contacts, access to financing, workforce skills, and origin of idea.

Such choice-based variation should be controlled for to accurately estimate the effect of science park membership on performance. However, so far there have been no studies using instrumental variable techniques or propensity score matching to handle self-selection based on observable differences, so there remains much room for improvement in this literature. Self-selection is important to analyze as it can cause quite unexpected results, as illustrated by Westhead and Batstone's (1998) work. They found that tenants in non-managed parks (which provided fewer resources to tenants) had lower failure rates than tenants in managed parks. It may be that poorer businesses select science parks that provide more resources, but that such provisions do not matter (or matter only marginally compared to the differences in 'pre-treatment' performances) for business performance. One possible step forward would be to instrument science park choice with the geographical distance to the university from which the founder received his/her degree.[70] Sampling would then have to be conditioned on founders with university degrees. The key identifying assumption, which is testable, is that the distance from the graduating institution to the firms' location affects the choice of setting up business in a science park, but does not directly affect business performance.

As an example of the state of the art we refer to Colombo and Delmastro (2002), who examined a sample of Italian start-ups either located in science parks or incubated with a sample of high-technology start-ups matched on industry, age, and region. The science park/incubated firms had significantly more PhDs and employees with graduate degrees, and a larger number of founders had previously been employed at universities. Surprisingly, the science park firms were not more innovative or research intensive, although they had easier access to local financing, were more involved in EU R&D projects, and there was more networking. In a one-equation multivariate regression there was a significant difference in firm size between science park and off-park firms controlling for ownership status, start-up size, firm age, number of founders, and founder skills. The estimates implied a 55 percent annual growth rate for science park firms and a 30 percent growth rate for off-park firms during the first years. But the authors did not include access to finance, EU project status and cooperation agreement status in the regression – maybe because they considered those variables endogenous and they did not endogenize the business park status dummy.

In a more recent article, Squicciarini (2009) tries to control for unobservable firm effects by estimating a time-to-next-patent model for firms that at some time moved to a science park in Finland. Unobservable firm characteristics are assumed fixed before and after the move and not related to the move and thus deemed irrelevant. The author finds that moving to a science park increases the likelihood of patenting which could indicate a productivity-increasing effect. However, the author also finds that firms moving to parks with a university lab present have the chance of patenting decreased by 90 percent. It does not make sense to interpret this as a productivity depressor through spillovers. Spillovers are never that strong – the average number of tenants is 87 so the characteristics of a single tenant on others cannot make that much difference. Rather, it is more likely that firms that join science parks with university labs are less likely to patent for some reason. While worthy, this approach apparently does not solve the problem of correcting for self-selection.[71]

It may be that science parks vary widely in what they offer tenants and that these different offerings should be distinguished to better measure the effect of science parks (Siegel et al., 2003b). However, even if there are significant effects of only some types of parks with some specialized offerings while others provide no benefits (and there are no self-selection issues) the prior average null result is still informative. Further, if the reasons to join parks with different characteristics vary it is even more important to distinguish pre-choice differences in a selection equation to accurately assess the impact of belonging to a science park or incubator on business performance.

Most incubators have been established relatively recently, but are quite common in or around universities.[72] Among the top 100 US spin-off producing universities, about 35 percent had an incubator in 1998 (Di Gregorio and Shane, 2003). The small but consistent set of findings on incubators shows that incubators have zero effect on spin-off and patenting rates (Colombo and Delmastro, 2002; Di Gregorio and Shane, 2003; Lee and Osteryoung, 2004; O'Shea et al., 2005; Rothaermel and Thursby, 2005; Squicciarini, 2009). Many incubators, both located off- and on-university, have been closed since the year 2000 because they have been losing money.

In summary, the literature that evaluates the role of science parks and incubators is in its infancy. It appears reasonable that firms self-select to join science parks and incubators and so models must account for this. One study finds that firms that do poorly join more actively managed science parks and that this effect dominates over potential productivity-enhancing effects. It would be bittersweet if this result holds up under further scrutiny because it implies that the best university strategy would be not to operate a science park.

ENTREPRENEURSHIP EDUCATION

Teaching entrepreneurship in academic institutions started in 1947 when Myles Mace taught the first entrepreneurship course in the United States at Harvard Business School (Katz, 2003). Entrepreneurship education started to become more prevalent after the University of Southern California launched the first MBA concentration in entrepreneurship in 1971, and the first undergraduate concentration in 1972 (Kuratko, 2005). In the early 1980s, 300 universities had courses in entrepreneurship education in their curriculum. By the early 1990s, over 1,050 universities in the US were reporting courses in entrepreneurship education (Solomon et al., 1994). Today, entrepreneurship education has expanded to more than 2,200 courses at over 1,600 US schools (Kuratko, 2005).

The logic of entrepreneurship education is more aligned with the aims of economic development than with those of advanced education (McMullan and Long, 1987). However, the link between entrepreneurship education and entrepreneurial activity is not straightforward. Entrepreneurs do not necessarily set up their companies directly upon graduation. Even though the average time lag between graduation and starting a business has dropped from 18 years in the 1950s to four years in the 1990s (MIT data; Roberts and Eesley, 2009), the multiplicity of reasons for engaging in entrepreneurship makes it difficult to measure the effect of entrepreneurship education on entrepreneurial activity. Some researchers contend that manifestation of students' intentions as new venture creation is an ultimate success factor of an entrepreneurship program (Clark et al., 1984; McMullan and Long, 1987).

Researchers have begun to investigate the effects of entrepreneurship education. However, this work is still very preliminary. Most attempts only evaluate the impact of entrepreneurship programs on students' stated intentions to start a business. None of the studies we found clearly evaluated the impact on actual start-ups. Some researchers propose that entrepreneurship education affects students' opinion about entrepreneurship and their perception of starting a new business (Rasmussen and Sorheim, 2006). Bird (1988) postulated that starting a new business is driven by entrepreneurial intentions. This led to the use of 'intention models' in entrepreneurship research.

Research on entrepreneurial intentions draws on psychology (Ajzen, 1987, 1991; Bagozzi et al., 1989). Intentions are argued to be the best predictor of planned behavior, particularly when the behavior is considered rare and hard to observe, or involves unpredictable time lags (Azjen, 1991; Madden et al., 1992). Since starting a new business is a rare and hard to observe behavior it is exactly the type of planned behavior for which intention models are well suited (Bird, 1988; Katz and Gartner, 1988).

A variety of intention models have been developed. Maybe the most notable one is Ajzen's (1991) theory of planned behavior, which identifies three attitudinal antecedents that drive intentions. The first is the 'attitude towards the behavior' and refers to an individual's favorable/unfavorable perception of the behavior in question. The second predictor is 'subjective norms', a social factor that refers to an individual's perceived social pressure to engage or not engage in the behavior. The third antecedent is 'perceived behavioral control' which refers to perceived ease or difficulty of performing the behavior and mirrors an individual's past experience, perceived impediments, and obstacles toward the behavior. The theory of planned behavior predicts that the greater the positive attitude and subjective norm toward behavior, and the greater the perceived behavioral control, the greater should be an individual's intention to perform the behavior. An intention model specific to the field of entrepreneurship is conceptualized by Shapero (1975, 1985).

Some empirical studies argue that there is a positive impact of entrepreneurship courses/programs at universities on students' start-up decisions (for example, Clark et al., 1984; van Clouse, 1990) as well as the perceived attractiveness and feasibility of starting a new business (for example, Tkachev and Kolvereid, 1999; Fayolle and Lassas-Clerc, 2006).[73] But these studies rarely involve control groups, pre-test–post-test settings, or control for existing predisposition towards entrepreneurship. Three exceptions are Peterman and Kennedy (2003), Souitaris et al. (2007), and Oosterbeek et al. (2008) who use pre-test–post-test control group designs.

Peterman and Kennedy (2003) and Souitaris et al. (2007) investigate the effect of a five-month enterprise education program, and an elective entrepreneurship course for science and engineering students, respectively, on perceptions towards entrepreneurship. Both adopted a pre-test–post-test control group design to measure changes in students' perceived desirability and perceived feasibility of starting a new business. Both found a significant increase in both perceived desirability and feasibility of starting a business for the group exposed to the entrepreneurship course, whereas the control group's perceived desirability and feasibility remained unchanged. Souitaris et al. (2007) also find that the change in desirability, feasibility, and control affected intentions. However, the results of these studies should be interpreted with caution. First, treatment was not randomized, meaning that students self-select into the courses. Even though prior attitudes are measured, unmeasured attitudes may be correlated with the treatment effect. Second, only the effects on intentions are tested, not the impact on observed behavior.

In a carefully executed study, Oosterbeek et al. (2008) analyze the impact of a compulsory entrepreneurship program on entrepreneurial competencies and intentions using an instrumental variable approach in a difference-in-difference framework. They exploit the fact that the program was offered to students at one location of a school but not to students at another location of the same school by comparing differences in pre-post measures at both locations. Self-selection of students into different locations is controlled by using relative distance from the campus to the location of the students' place of living prior to enrolling in post-secondary education as an instrument. They find two surprising results which stand in sharp contrast to previous studies. First, the effect of the entrepreneurship program on students' self-assessed entrepreneurial skills is not significant. Second, there is a significant negative effect on students' entrepreneurial intentions. The authors argue that the results might be related to the content of the entrepreneurship program which enabled students to obtain a more realistic perspective of themselves as well as an entrepreneurship career in general. In a recent study by von Graevenitz et al. (2010), results are similar to those found by Oosterbeek et al. (2008). They report a decline in students' entrepreneurial propensity after taking a compulsory entrepreneurship course. To explain the results, they use a Bayesian learning model in which the entrepreneurship program generates signals that help students to evaluate their own aptitude for an entrepreneurial career. Importantly, the model distinguishes between two types of students, entrepreneurs and employees, whose beliefs about their actual type and consequently about their entrepreneurial abilities are updated during the entrepreneurship program. The results from Oosterbeek et al. and von Graevenitz et al. make it clear that it is important to control for self-selection. Prior results reporting positive impacts may be entirely consistent with the last two studies reporting negative impacts since it might be that those with unmeasured positive prior attitudes self-select into entrepreneurship programs and self-report large gains in attitudes, while those with prior neutral or skeptical views select not to take the course, or, if it is compulsory, self-report no change (or decreases) in subsequent attitudes. Thus, one conclusion might be that entrepreneurship programs often preach to the choir.

The relation between entrepreneurship education and actual start-ups is still not clear. Perhaps this is due to the significant time lag between the intention and the actual start-up activity which dilutes the causal relationship between them. Souitaris et al. (2007) tried to compensate for this by measuring several actions (such as raising capital) as proxies for starting up. They found no link between these actions and change in intentions. As previously reported, Lerner and Malmendier (2007) find that among HBS MBAs, a one standard deviation increase in the share of section peers with pre-HBS entrepreneurial background decreases the share of the section going into an entrepreneurial role after graduation from 5 to 4 percent, but increases the rate of successful start-ups. They argue that these results are consistent with intra-section learning, where the close ties between students in a section lead to better business ideas. An alternative interpretation is that entrepreneurs start again after obtaining their MBA, but with better ideas. Better ideas could be obtained through coursework, for example. Whether or not entrepreneurship education induces more, or better, business start-ups is an avenue for future research.

LOCAL AND REGIONAL CONDITIONS

Universities are located across varying conditions, some are in locations with considerable infrastructure and economic activity, others are located in more rural areas. An immediate question is whether university supply effects are just spurious – spin-off rates may be determined fully by local demand conditions. If there are independent university effects one might ask whether regional conditions affect the ability of a university to produce spin-offs. We remind the reader that most universities have very little spin-off activity. Licensing deals are on the order of 10 times the magnitude and may be more important in gross terms. There is little systematic research on the effect of local economic conditions in the context of university spin-offs. The few studies we know of are reviewed next.

First, geographical proximity to universities is positively correlated with regional start-up rates in high-tech industries (for example, Zucker et al., 1998a; Stuart and Sorenson, 2003; Audretsch and Lehmann, 2005; Audretsch et al., 2005b; Rothaermel and Ku, 2008). Among these studies only Rothaermel and Ku employ unit (MSA) fixed effects to exclude cross-sectional common causes.[74] Some of these associations are thus indeed likely to be from cross-sectional common causation, as illustrated by, for example, Heblich and Slavtchev (2009), who find that several local demand conditions affect the probability that PhD students, post-docs, and research assistants locate their spin-off close to their parent university.

However, when analyzing the role of these variables in 'structurally weak regions'[75] only GDP/capita remains an important local demand determinant, while the coefficient for the number of professors at the parent university doubles in size. Thus, when local demand conditions are weak, any increase in university supply conditions has double the effect on local spin-off rates. An even stronger indication that the parent university really does matter for local spin-offs is that when the authors introduce a measure of the number of professors in the academic field of the entrepreneurs in the region, this has a significant positive effect only for professors at the parent university. The number of professors at other universities in the region has null effect. Since the two measures are comparing counts of professors within the same region, cross-regional variation cannot explain this difference. That is, the size of the parent university does play an important role for whether a spin-off is placed locally or not.

Access to venture capital may be one important local economic characteristic that conditions university spin-off rates and their location. However, various measures of local venture capital activity did not affect the rate of university spin-offs in the studies by Di Gregorio and Shane (2003) and Markman et al. (2009), or had a negative marginal effect (Zucker et al., 1998a).[76] Only Powers and McDougall (2005) obtained statistically significant positive effects. These varying results stand in contrast to the result that geographical proximity to venture capital is positively correlated with regional start-up rates in high-tech industries (for example, Stuart and Sorenson, 2003). Zucker et al. (1998a) argue that the typically observed positive effect of local venture capital is due to omitted variable bias – venture capital is attracted to universities with star researchers and once that variation has been appropriately controlled for the remaining effect is negative. Access to local venture capital may not matter for university spin-offs for reasons that have not yet been fully explored. Clearly, more research is warranted on this topic.

Several researchers have examined the effect of the local density of high-tech firms (Friedman and Silberman, 2003; Chapple et al., 2005; O'Shea et al., 2005; Lach and Schankerman, 2008; Belenzon and Schankerman, 2009).[77] If demand is localized, universities in areas with more high-tech activity should license more inventions from a given pool of inventions, and obtain more revenue. High-tech density turns out to have a large average positive effect on the generation of licensing revenue (Friedman and Silberman, 2003; Chapple et al., 2005; Belenzon and Schankerman, 2009). The effect on number of spin-offs was positive in Belenzon and Schankerman (2009), but not in the study by O'Shea et al. (2005).[78]

Lach and Schankerman (2008) find that the effects on licensing income of local high-tech density are quite different between private and public universities. Private universities in the top quartile high-tech areas have about 6 percent higher licensing revenues than those in the three lower quartiles. However, public universities have about 8 percent higher licensing revenues in the *bottom* quartile high-tech areas compared to those in the three top quartiles. This difference, if robust, remains to be explained. Maybe an answer is to be found in location differences between public and private universities. There is a high likelihood that a private university is located in one of the top metropolitan areas, and among those metropols, higher local demand may indeed positively incentivize university scientists. But for land-grant and other public universities located in more rural areas, local demand may not be strong to begin with. These universities may historically have been forced to orient themselves to more global tech markets. Such an orientation would explain why Belenzon and Schankerman (2009) find licensing income to increase dramatically with high-tech density for public universities in the bottom quartile of the high-tech index. An interaction between the high-tech index and university status will reveal if this hypothesis holds.

In summary, this section reveals that there has been relatively little work on local and regional effects on university spin-off rates. First, it appears clear that universities have effects independent of local economic conditions. Second, it is also clear that there are also common determinants. Among the local conditions, local high-tech density does matter while access to local venture capital may not matter, maybe because venture capital eagerly supplies funds to good opportunities created at universities no matter where they are located.

LOCAL AND REGIONAL IMPACT OF UNIVERSITY SPIN-OFFS

University spin-offs seem to create primarily local economic development, although the evidence here is not systematic.[79] In 1999, AUTM reported that 82 percent of firms formed from university licenses operated in the state where the university was located. By 2007 this number had dropped to 72 percent. At a more aggregate level, Mustar (1997) estimates that 40 percent of all high-tech companies founded in France between 1987 and 1997 were university spin-offs, which is an incredibly large concentration. And Clayman and Holbrook (2003) find that 80 percent of surviving Canadian spin-offs operate in the same region as the university from which they originated. Using a much smaller geographical footprint as a point of evaluation, Roberts (1991) finds that spin-offs from MIT (in Cambridge,

MA) tend to be located in Cambridge, whereas spin-offs from MIT's Lincoln Labs (in Lexington, MA) tend to be located in Lexington.

We performed some complementary analysis on the local concentration of university spin-offs using data from Ludwig Maximilians Universität (LMU), Germany, and from MIT. LMU spun off 96 companies between 1977 and 2009. Approximately 80 percent of these spin-off companies are located within only 20 kilometers of LMU. A similar investigation of 76 spin-offs from MIT between 1980 and 1996 (listed in Shane, 2004, Table 2.2) reveals that approximately 50 percent are located within 20 kilometers of MIT and a little over 70 percent are located less than 100 kilometers from MIT. More generally, Egeln et al. (2004) find that 66 percent of academic spin-offs in Germany locate within 50 kilometers from their university. These data reinforce the suggestion of very local effects.

Turning this around one might ask what proportion of high-tech firms in a region comes from universities? It was found that 17 percent of new tech companies founded in the Cambridge area were university spin-offs (Wickstead, 1985). For the greater Göteborg region, a minority (10 percent) of new high-tech firms are spin-offs from universities by faculty and researchers, while an additional 21 percent are spin-offs by former faculty and post-docs with some post-university work experience (Lindholm-Dahlstrand, 1999). Finally, Goldman (1984) found that as much as 72 percent of high-tech companies in the Boston area in the early 1980s were based on technologies originally developed at MIT laboratories. The variation in the local impact thus seems enormous. If we remove Boston as an extreme outlier we still probably have two cities (Cambridge, UK and Göteborg) which are both much higher on the scale of university local impact than for the typical region. Also, one has to immediately be concerned with causality. The reported cases have long traditions of industrial development in the regions and relatively ample supply of labor, capital, and other infrastructural benefits. Whether the universities are the causes of the spin-offs' location or whether it is simply that these universities are located in fertile ground for start-ups cannot be determined by cross-sectional analysis.

However, one would expect primarily local effects of university spin-offs for several reasons. If the inventor is to be engaged in the spin-off less than full-time then the inventor would want to start up close to his/her main employment location (Zucker et al., 1998b). Also, the inventor may want to use the labs of the university after spin-off to engage in additional research to support the spin-off (Hsu and Bernstein, 1997). Further, the inventor may want to exploit local social networks developed over time by the inventor to support the spin-off. Finally, all else equal, the inventor may prefer not to move households even if leaving his/her job at the university, as moving is costly both socially and economically. However, moving may be useful if current local conditions are not ideal for the spin-off.

To examine more precisely the issue of causality one can look towards Sweden which undertook a conscious spatial decentralization of its higher education system beginning in 1987. Eleven new universities were created and 14 colleges were upgraded in status to create a total of 36 universities. This comes close to a natural experiment and Andersson et al. (2004, 2009) use this exogenous shock to estimate the effect of increased university employment and student matriculation on local productivity growth and patenting. The authors find large increases in local productivity around the new universities and a greater impact on productivity growth than the old established universities. The elasticity is higher with respect to the number of researchers employed than the number of students graduating. The effects are very local: about 75 percent of the effect occurs within 100 kilometers of the municipality containing the new institution. In their 2009 paper, the authors employ IV (instrumental variables) estimation and test their exogeneity assumption, finding good instruments and that the assumption holds. They also establish positive effects of the number of researchers employed on local patenting activity, finding strong effects. When they compare the economic effects of increased university investment in pre-existing universities (in older, denser, urban regions) with equivalent investments in the new institutions (in less dense, rural regions) the results suggest that the decentralization policy has led to an increase in aggregate output and aggregate creativity in Sweden.

Rather than comparing new versus old universities, Belenzon and Schankerman (2009) compare the local economic effects of private versus public universities. They found that private universities are much less likely to pursue local development objectives than public universities. Universities with strong local development objectives generate about 30 percent less income per license, but at the same time, such universities generate about 28 percent more licenses. Such universities also have a proportionally greater number of non-exclusive licenses which might promote the number of licenses executed. Further, these universities are more likely to generate proportionally more in-state start-up companies while the total number of spin-offs is not affected. Belenzon and Schankerman conclude their paper by highlighting the importance of comparing the benefits of local development objectives to alternative policies, such as maximizing licensing income from university inventions. They find that it would be socially more efficient to maximize licensing income, using the additional income to finance local economic development in other ways, rather than to directly pursue local development objectives by directing university policy.[80]

In a follow-up paper the same authors (Belenzon and Schankerman, 2010) ask whether a local development objective might be motivated if one also considers the indirect value of scientific research. They do so by examining knowledge flows using data on citations to university patents and scientific publications. As has previously been found, knowledge spillovers fall sharply with distance up to about 150 miles. A new result is that state borders strongly constrain such diffusion, controlling for distance. Such effects may be due to varying state policies. Also interesting is that part of this state border effect is related to the local and regional development objectives of university TLOs, such that the more local the development objective of the TLO, the more important is the state border effect. Thus, potentially both state and university policy matters for the degree to which there are indirect effects on local economic development. Thus, the conclusions from Belenzon and Schankerman (2009) must be tempered since there are offsetting benefits of a local development objective in terms of more localized knowledge spillovers. The offset is currently not monetized so it is by no means clear how large the value of such knowledge spillovers is in comparison with the monetary benefits of following a strategy-maximizing licensing income.

A related literature on local economic effects is that on 'clusters'. A regional technology cluster is defined by Porter (1998, p. 78) as a 'geographically proximate group of interconnected companies and associated institutions in a particular field, linked by commonalities and complementarities'. Most of the existing theories of clusters of innovative activity focus on agglomeration economics and externalities (for example, Krugman, 1991; Jaffe et al., 1993; Audretsch and Feldman, 1996; Saxenian, 1996). Within this literature one asks whether universities can support the formation of clusters. Popular examples such as MIT and Stanford come to mind, but the academic literature is particularly weak in testing for causation (for a critique of this literature, see Bresnahan et al., 2001).

To summarize this section, we discover that most spin-offs are located extremely close to their parent, within 50 kilometers. This is close enough to allow person-to-person contact even in densely populated cities. Inferring causality for correlation is not recommended. However, the papers by Andersson et al. (2004, 2009) indicate clear causal effects of increased investments at universities in personnel and matriculation on local labor productivity growth and patenting activity. Interestingly, such growth is much faster in 'structurally weak' regions where the new universities were created, and slower per input in the older established institutions located in 'structurally strong' regions.

CONCLUSIONS

There has been an increased trend in the number of spin-offs generated by universities at the aggregate. This has been driven by, or associated with, an increase in university research activities, increased funding from industry, an increase in privately protected ownership of research at universities, and an increase in licensing of the research for profit. The trend accelerated through the 1970s in association with the biomedical revolution, with implementation of legislation and court decisions conferring stronger private property rights on intellectual work, and with legislation in the US allowing universities to take *de jure* ownership of intellectual work by their researchers. This trend has not been limited to the US but is a widespread phenomenon across the industrialized world. Several European countries have lately copied the US legislation, shifting control rights of intellectual property from the creator to the university employer.

It is not clear that these trends have been good for society. There can be several negative effects and system efficiency may be higher when research is made public rather than private. However, it is difficult to prove the counterfactual and pundits certainly have applauded the apparent rise in innovative output by US universities over the past 40 years. There has also been a rising acceptance by the public that universities engage in commerce, and the public debate over whether privatization of research is good for society has abated.

Against this backdrop, universities are being pressured by local politicians to aid in increasing local economic development. University chancellors and presidents are being asked 'What role does your university play in stimulating local economic development through entrepreneurship?', and they ask themselves 'What can we as a university do to encourage entrepreneurship to increase local economic development?'. Given these questions, universities are increasingly being 'managed' to increase three performance metrics: number of patents, number of licenses, and number of spin-offs. Early evidence of successful TLOs such as those at Stanford and MIT are used as examples to follow. To abide by legislative changes and to increase commercialization of research, universities create TLOs and appoint ever-increasing numbers of administrators and lawyers to manage the commercialization of intellectual property. But it is not altogether clear that such strategies will increase the efficiency of research commercialization. Research so far has not been able to identify causation in this direction. And the creation of TLOs may be as much a response to legislative changes and changes in scientific norms as a cause of increased commercialization.

Unfortunately, the scientific evidence reviewed in this chapter indicates that policy changes at universities typically have very little impact on commercialization of research, and the benefits to the universities of whatever changes are accomplished are marginal. For example, current evidence indicates that creating incubators and science parks on university grounds has no discernible effect on start-up rates. Further, from a theoretical perspective we have reviewed articles showing that introducing TLOs, the most popular method to stimulate commercialization, may likely introduce economic inefficiencies, hold-ups and decision biases that deviate from what is optimal. There is clear evidence that the top 100 US research universities will, on average, just break even on their TLO efforts, and TLOs at Canadian universities return only 36 cents on the dollar of TLO expenditures. The median university among the top US research-based institutions creates less than two academic spin-offs per year and so the relative effects on local economic conditions through these efforts and policies are bound to be marginal.

Nevertheless the evidence also shows that there are a few variables that university chancellors/deans may impact and which do have important positive effects on start-up rates. The first two are the scientific stature of the faculty and the commercialization culture at the university. Positive cultures may be created locally within departments or study programs and apparently may produce a large number of start-ups by students even in the absence of favorable local economic start-up conditions. The third variable is the sheer number of science and engineering students graduating. Increasing expenditures on university staff and students causes increases in local productivity growth and innovation and the marginal effects are much bigger in structurally weak regions. The marginal effects are also larger from faculty counts than from student matriculation, possibly because of greater spillover effects from faculty. However, student start-ups far outnumber faculty spin-offs, and a majority of those start-ups are located close to the university. In terms of gross economic impact, student start-ups thus appear much more important. We know very little about the factors that cause student start-up rates to grow. Two case studies indicate that much is due to student-run activities and the development of positive local norms among students and faculty over time. The evidence is less clear that dedicated entrepreneurship courses and programs do anything to affect start-up rates – what we do know is that they affect students' intentions to start a business. However, sometimes such courses reduce students' intentions to start a business, which may indicate that students get better informed on the vagaries of starting up businesses.

Whatever is accomplished in terms of increased number of spin-offs disproportionally favors local development. Maybe as much as 80 percent of all university spin-offs are and remain locally situated. However, universities that maximize local effects will not maximize their societal impact. Instead, it appears more efficient if universities simply try to maximize licensing revenues and not worry about the number of spin-offs and their locations. This is an implication that should make managing university TLOs simpler. The tendency to restrict the choices of agents is well known in economics to produce inefficiencies and it holds in this case as well.

Early evidence indicates that emulating the Bayh–Dole Act in Europe, which transfers control rights over IP to universities, appears to be a bad idea. Europe is not starting from the agency problem that the US had pre-Bayh–Dole. European professors patent as much or more than US professors and interact as much or more with industry than US professors. Introducing Bayh–Dole-type acts has already had negative consequences on university–industry collaboration in Denmark, and at several universities in other countries. One hopes that the trend of US emulators stops with the countries that have already shifted regimes and that researchers and policymakers are allowed a period to review the impacts before other countries follow in the footsteps of Denmark.

Current research has closed a few doors and opened many others. One of the open and more puzzling questions is the role of inventor incentives. This is clearly a variable at the chancellor's disposal – he/she may change the royalty rate or other transaction conditions. Empirical studies agree with economic theory that increasing the inventor's share of royalties increases total licensing income. The empirical studies, however, show that there is curiously little variation in the rates schedules across universities. The impact on the rate of spin-offs is less clear; two studies even found negative effects. Further, we know very little about why spin-offs tend to locate close to universities. We do not understand the degree to which universities are able to cause local economic development, as opposed to respond to economic development. We would like to know more about culture. We would like to know a lot more about student start-ups. And we would like to know more about the effects of recent implementations of Bayh–Dole-type acts in various European countries.

In closing, asking the university to shoulder local economic development objectives is to ask the university to do something it is not very good at. Is it learning to do so? – slowly but surely. But it is unclear whether this will be more efficient than stimulating other actors that are typically better able to create economic development.

NOTES

1. We would like to thank those who have provided comments and reading suggestions for this chapter: Michael Fritsch, Taylor Aldridge, David Audretsch, Guido Buenstorf, Wes Cohen, Massimo Colombo, Chuck Eesley, Maryann Feldman, Jeff Furman, Aldo Geuna, Brent Goldfarb, David Hsu, Staffan Jacobsson, Martin Kenney, Åsa Lindholm-Dahlstrand, Francesco Lissoni, Ed Roberts, Frank Rothaermel, Mark Schankerman, Scott Shane, Don Siegel, Viktor Slavtchev, Paula Stephan, Toby Stuart, Jerry Thursby, Mirjam van Praag, and Finn Valentin. We would also like to thank those who have generously provided their time to help us collect data: Jean-Marc Bournazel, Gary Dushnitsky, Chuck Eesley, Dietmar Harhoff, Stefan Heumann, Mats Ljungqvist, Michel Safars, Sören Sjölander, and Thomas Pompe. Finally, we would like to thank the people we interviewed.
2. AUTM counts firms based on university IP disclosed to universities' technology licensing office (TLO). Subscribing members of AUTM report these data to the AUTM. Markman et al. (2008) estimate that 58 percent of faculty report their patent to their TLO. If this also goes for start-ups, faculty spin-offs may be twice that reported. Allen and Norling (1991) found that 16.2 percent of faculty in science, engineering, business, and medicine were involved in starting companies but only 4.4 percent, or roughly one-fourth, did so based on their academic research. Fini et al. (2010) show that about two-thirds of businesses started by academics are not based on patented inventions. That is, the use of AUTM data to identify university spin-offs does not count a dominant fraction of faculty spin-offs. The number of faculty spin-offs may thus be four times as high. Our analysis of data from MIT shows that it may even be up to 10 times higher, although that is probably the upper bound since MIT is such a unique institution.
3. Detailed case studies have been assembled on Chalmers Tekniska Högskola and Högskolan i Halmstad (both in Sweden), Ludwig-Maximilian University (Germany), Penn State, Massachusetts Institute of Technology, University of Waterloo (Canada), and Université de Nice Côte d'Azur (France). For further European case studies, see Wright et al. (2007).
4. For a fascinating analysis of the history of US universities, their contribution to technical progress, and their patenting policies and activities, see Mowery et al. (2004). This section reviews their main points, adds some new data, and in particular expands on recent changes to national and university policies in countries other than the US. This section also offers some new interpretations of existing US data.
5. For examples of early twentieth-century university–industry collaboration and interactions see Hounshell and Smith (1988) and Murmann (2003).
6. In Merton's words, these were: universalism, communism, disinterestedness, and organized skepticism. These were reinforced through socialization in graduate school as well as direct sanctioning as exemplified by the patent policy at Harvard University.
7. Faculty at Columbia's medical school were prevented from patenting the results of their research.
8. The following sentences reflect Chapter 1 of Charles (2001).
9. Charles (2001, p. 22) describes how Chilton was not able to get Washington University's patent lawyer interested in filing her claims. On the advice of her corporate lawyer father, she went to the university chancellor and with the help of her department head and a few chosen words obtained a meeting with the patent agent the next day.
10. This paragraph borrows heavily from Mowery et al. (2004, ch. 5).
11. According to special data extracted from the survey by Charles Eesley. We used a scale-up factor of 2,425*3,906 = 9.47. Many thanks to Dr Eesley for his help.
12. Forty-seven percent of mechanical and electrical engineering faculty in 2000 were non-MIT alumni. We took this fraction as a rough indicator of non-MIT alumni among the MIT faculty for all years and across all departments and also assumed that non-MIT alumni were equivalent to MIT alumni in their spin-off propensity.
13. We chose not to use the AUTM data from 1991 to 1995 since these were described by

AUTM as lacking somewhat in quality and having variable definitions different from the subsequent period.

14. Invention disclosure refers to reporting a discovery by a faculty member to the university.
15. The number of invention disclosures increased by approximately 7 percent per year, patent applications increased by 16.5 percent per year, while executed licenses increased by approximately 8 percent per year, and the number of start-ups increased by 13.5 percent per year for 1996 to 2001. For the 2001–07 period, the number of invention disclosures increased by approximately 6 percent per year, the number of patent applications increased by 7 percent per year, while the number of executed licenses and the number of start-ups increased by 3 and 6 percent per year, respectively.
16. Differences in commercial quality and novelty of disclosures and patent applications across universities may also explain the catching up. Thursby and Thursby (2002) include faculty quality in the input function for licensing agreements in an attempt to adjust for such possible differences.
17. There was an extension in 1975 in the university charter to include 'service to the society' and in 1996, two government appointed task forces stated the need for a clear mandate for universities to interact with industry and the rest of society (SOU, 1996:70 and SOU, 1996:89). The university charter's third task was subsequently changed from 'I forskning och utvecklingsarbete ingår att sprida kännedom om verksamheten samt om hur sådana kunskaper och erfarenheter som har vunnits i verksamheten skall kunna tillämpas' to 'Högskolorna skall också samverka med det omgivande samhället och informera om sin verksamhet' (SFS, 1996:1392). [From 'Research and development work includes diffusing knowledge about activities and about how such knowledge can be applied' to 'Universities should cooperate with society and inform about their activities'.]
18. Such an act had already been tabled in 1992 by Högskoleutredningen (SOU, 1992: 7).
19. SOU (1998: 128) recommends that 'Universities should make sure that intellectual property stemming from [university] research is made use of and that research results are made of practical use' (p. 142) and 'The committee considers it important that the role of universities are strengthened when it comes to economic exploitation of research results . . . The committee recommends an agreement where universities rights to patents and other IP are transferred to universities and that rules for economic compensation to the Professor are stated. Associated with this should be an agreement regarding the possibility that publication of research results is held back until a patent application has been submitted' (p. 143).
20. In France, and to a lesser extent in Italy, a sizable share of academic patents is also owned by large governmental research organizations, reflecting the importance of these actors in these countries.
21. Overall, Italian academics represent 3 percent of EPO patents awarded to Italians (Balconi et al., 2004). In Finland, academics represent 8 percent of all patent assignees (Meyer, 2003) and in Norway they represent almost 10 percent of all assignees (Iversen et al., 2007).
22. Valentin and Jensen (2007) report that the degree of university–industry interaction is the major difference between the two countries; they are otherwise very similar with respect to their size, history, number of inventions, and in the number of inventors per invention in this industry.
23. LUP transfers to universities ownership of IP made by Danish university scientists, where prior to that (since 1955) ownership resided with the inventor.
24. The 'Bavarian support program to facilitate the transition to a founder existence'.
25. For evaluations of these programs (most written in German) contact Marianne Kulicke at the Fraunhofer-Institut für System- und Innovationsforschung ISI, Germany.
26. Federal investments in R&D were significantly reduced in the early to mid-1990s as the Canadian government struggled with a growing deficit and public debt. The 1997–98

fiscal year, however, marked the beginning of federal reinvestment in R&D. The federal government's role in financing R&D was clarified and given momentum in 2002 with the launch of Canada's Innovation Strategy. A part of this strategy was to double the university research funding and triple the commercialization performance by 2010. While these targets have not been achieved, this initiative has led to a significant increase in the public funding of university research and a strong commitment of funds to improve the commercialization of research.

27. IRAP's mission is to stimulate innovation in Canadian small- and medium-sized enterprises (SMEs). In the year 2004/05, 2,615 projects were funded and the budget for 2005/06 is CAD 167 million.

28. According to Clayman (2004), universities that take control rights are McMaster, Memorial, McGill, Université de Montréal, and the universities of British Columbia, Guelph, Ottawa, and Saskatchewan. Universities which allocate control to the inventor are Queen's, Simon Fraser University, and the universities of Alberta, Calgary, Manitoba, Toronto, Waterloo and Western Ontario. However, the authors are pretty sure that Toronto takes control rights.

29. The OncoMouse or Harvard mouse is a type of laboratory mouse that has been genetically modified using modifications designed by Philip Leder and Timothy A. Stewart of Harvard University to carry a specific gene called an 'activated oncogene'. The activated oncogene significantly increases the mouse's susceptibility to cancer, and thus makes the mouse suitable for cancer research. The rights to the invention are owned by DuPont. 'OncoMouse' is a registered trademark (http://en.wikipedia.org/wiki/Oncomouse).

30. For ease of understanding the results we label the clinicians conducting 'applied' research and the non-clinicians conducting 'basic' research, although this can be somewhat of a misnomer. An important difference between these groups is that the potential personal monetary payoff to the individual is much higher for the basic researcher, while the applied researcher functions more as a consultant/contract researcher.

31. Recall the case of Mary-Dell Chilton previously mentioned.

32. At http://sciencecommons.org/projects/licensing/empirical-data-about-materials- transfer/ we learn that the Science Commons Materials Transfer Project tries to reduce delays caused by legal transaction costs by introducing standardized agreements and procedures for transferring scientific materials. This site reports several other studies on the increased delays in obtaining research materials which show greater delays and rates of denials than those reported by Walsh et al. (2007).

33. Research on the impact of patent thickets on the rate of technological change in a nonuniversity setting has so far not shown any convincing negative impacts of increased private property protection (for example, Hall and Ziedonis, 2001; Galasso and Schankerman, 2010).

34. However, the Bayh–Dole Act was as much a result of ongoing changes in university funding, the rise of patenting at universities in the 1970s, unrelated declines in US productivity growth, and the impact that opportunities in the biotech sector provided as it was a cause of growth of university patenting in the 1980s and beyond (Mowery et al., 2004).

35. Warning bells have been rung that the increased commercialization of research may have shifted the focus of productive researchers away from research and towards business, or at least driven them to more applied research. In a world where university researchers typically have the greatest comparative advantage to conduct research while commerce has the greater comparative advantage to commercialize it (David, 2007), this sounds like bad news. But a number of articles show that the most productive researchers are also those that patent the most (controlling for fixed individual effects), and that patenting appears to increase scientific productivity, although in the latter case researchers have not yet adequately removed potential common causes (Breschi et al., 2005, 2007; Azoulay et al., 2006, 2007; Calderini et al., 2007; Stephan et al., 2007; Goldfarb et al., 2008; Buenstorf, 2009; Crespi et al., 2010).

36. The all-time top earning inventions for Stanford (between 1975 and 2001) appear to be recombinant DNA, chimeric receptors ($124.7 million), fluorescent conjugates for analysis of molecules ($46.4 million), functional antigen-binding proteins ($30.2 million), fiber optic amplifier ($32.6 million), and FM sound synthesis ($22.9 million). See Page (2007). Created in 1970, Stanford's TLO is considered the 'gold standard' for TLO effectiveness (ibid.; Bera, 2009). Nevertheless, from 441 disclosures and 458 patent applications in 2008, the TLO 'generated' only 87 licenses and only three licenses with income more than $1 million apiece. For a short popular description of Stanford's approach to licensing research, see Bera (2009). For detailed econometric research on research project-level commercialization data at Stanford, see Goldfarb and Colyvas (2005, 2006); Goldfarb et al. (2008).

37. In March 2001, the German Bundesministerium für Wirtschaft und Technologie (Federal Ministry of Economics and Technology) announced a program, 'AktionsProgramm Wissenschaft Märkte', with several actions and some proposals to improve commercialization of university IP. First, they announced seed funding for the creation of a broad infrastructure of patenting offices, created outside of universities and ruled under private law in order to avoid the complications of the restrictive law governing universities. As a result, around 22 patenting offices were created in 2002, each one serving several universities in a region with services that are performance based. For example, the State of Bavaria in 2000 first settled on an arrangement with the Fraunhofer Institute's patent department. But this arrangement was not sustainable as the Fraunhofer Institute was not legally entitled to receive returns on investments. The Bayerische Patentallianz (BayPat) was therefore established in 2007. As a representative of the state, this entity takes 40 percent of university IP, the university takes 30 percent, and the inventor retains 30 percent of equity. Under a standard contract, BayPat funds the filing and marketing of patents while the universities and inventors bear no cost. The university remains the owner of the rights. BayPat acts on a commission basis.

38. It would be interesting to know the medians as it is likely that these employment distributions are skewed.

39. See also Stuart and Ding (2006).

40. This may be a particular result of the German tradition of locating applied research in research institutes and teaching and basic research at universities. Also, faculty in Germany are civil servants with strong public service norms. A similar situation was found in France. See also Lissoni et al. (2008).

41. The impact of scientific/commercialization norms is cleverly measured as the total number of patents applied for by an individual's graduate institution in the five years preceding the date of the faculty member's graduate degree. This was also tried by Stuart and Ding (2006) but it had no effect in their study. The department chair effect was measured as a dummy for whether the chair had disclosed an invention in the prior five-year period. Finally, the peer effect is measured as the percentage of faculty at the same rank within the department who disclosed an invention in the prior five-year period.

42. This study does not suffer from endogeneity to university-level policies since the main variation in Bercovitz and Feldman's data is across departments, not across universities.

43. The allocation of ownership does not matter in a world with no transaction costs (Coase, 1960) and so in this world it does not matter if the university or the inventor is initially assigned ownership of IP. But given the existence of transaction costs, the initial allocation of property rights matters. A normative conclusion drawn from the Coase theorem is that property rights should be assigned to the actors gaining the most utility from them. This is hard/impossible to distinguish *ex ante* and also means that the allocation may vary across projects. As will become clear, however, allocative efficiency is likely the highest, with the inventor initially assigned control rights.

44. Jensen and Thursby (2001) demonstrate that university licensing contracts should include a royalty or outcome-based component as a means to encourage the inventor

to work with the licensee to transfer knowledge. If no further effort is required by the inventor, a fixed fee agreement is efficient.

45. For a recent contribution, see Jensen and Showalter (2010).

46. In this model, disclosure to the university does not entail any change of ownership and so is costless for the inventor.

47. These results can be interpreted in several ways. It is possible that there is self-selection such that scientists with inventions with high commercial prospects are not disclosed to the university TLO, rather than the TLO handling negatively affecting the commercialization probability. The negative effect of the 'TLO helpful' variable on commercialization probability is more difficult to explain by a self-selection argument. Other TLO descriptors, including TLO age, size, and licensing focus, were not significant.

48. The authors found that 82 percent (74 percent when asking industry) of all licensed inventions are in proof of concept or lab-scale prototype stage when licensed, and Jensen and Thursby (2001) document that faculty involvement in commercialization increases the likelihood of commercialization of a licensed invention.

49. Ironically, one of the motivations for the introduction of *de jure* TLO ownership of IP was that industry complained that IP ownership rights were difficult to ascertain and contracts thus difficult to negotiate directly with academic inventors. It appears the Bayh–Dole legislation thus replaced one agency problem with another.

50. See, for example, Åstebro and Gerchak (2001) for a description of one such service that has operated since 1976 and performed over 14,000 invention evaluations. Further, see Myhrvold (2010) for a description of a very large for-profit invention intermediary (Intellectual Ventures) which claims to have raised $5 billion, purchased more than 30,000 patents and so far paid out about $315 million to individual inventors, universities, and other invention producers with the intent of reselling the inventions in repackaged form, licensing them, or directly partaking in their commercialization.

51. It is clear that disclosures have increased in the US post-Bayh–Dole. Thursby and Thursby (2007) report that the percent of disclosures at six selected universities has risen from 2.7 percent of faculty in 1983 to around 10–11 percent in the mid-1990s, where it appears to have leveled off.

52. Needless to say, inventions go undisclosed for many other reasons: they have zero value, the researcher cannot be bothered, or the process of disclosing is perceived to be cumbersome or unfamiliar, or all of those combined.

53. When Marc Andreessen joined James Clark to form Netscape in 1994, they attempted to negotiate a license with the University of Illinois but found the process so frustrating that they ultimately rewrote the browser code entirely. By 1999, the University of Illinois had successfully collected $7 million from the Mosaic copyrights, but the ill feelings of the Netscape founders almost certainly cost the university a far greater amount in lost donations (Reid, 1997, p. 37; Kenney and Patton, 2009, p. 1413).

54. Conversely, the positive experience of James Clark – a professor at Stanford University until he left in 1982 to form Silicon Graphics to exploit the fruits of his university research – was explicitly mentioned in his 1999 decision to donate $150 million to Stanford (Kenney and Patton, 2009, p. 1413).

55. It is not clear what the mechanism is that produces this effect. It might be that increased royalties increase the chance that the IP is disclosed to the university because the inventor loses less. And/or it might be that the economic incentive to assign the IP to an external firm is reduced because the external firm pays more for the IP to the inventor, all else equal. And/or it might be that the inventor prefers to do less consulting with higher inventor royalties, as suggested by Thursby et al. (2009).

56. For details on this argument, see the prior discussion on Lowe (2006).

57. Thursby and Thursby (2007) report that approximately 90 percent of all university start-ups are based on exclusive licenses, while licenses to established firms are approximately 60 percent non-exclusive.

58. The authors are concerned that their cross-university estimates are driven by unobservables, such as the 'commercial orientation' of the university, and try to control

for pre-existing university conditions by its cumulative number of patents issued (and their citations). For the validity of this approach, see Blundell et al. (1999). Lach and Schankerman also perform a large number of robustness checks.

59. Students may on occasion be involved in start-ups through research projects and these may thus be registered.
60. Sometimes the line is blurred, for example Google was started by two Stanford PhD students where the basic idea was laid out in Larry Page's dissertation. Stanford could not easily claim ownership of this IP as it was in the open domain. But since the students relied heavily on Stanford computers in an early phase, and as a token of appreciation by Page and Brin, the university was awarded 2 percent shares of the company in return and most researchers therefore consider Google a 'university spin-off'.
61. Tsinghua University, Beijing, is one of the most selective universities in China, with a focus on engineering.
62. There were two different alumni surveys. The figure is computed based on the first survey where, however, there are no data on the time of founding. New firms are those that employed 10 or more individuals. A second figure of 18 percent reported by Hsu et al. (2007) is based on a follow-up survey reporting businesses started with known founding dates. As well, duplicates started by several students are removed from this number.
63. With students in leading positions. We thank Charles Eesley and Ed Roberts for generously providing the data and their time. These data exclude all MIT faculty spin-offs. Eesley further removed duplicates in cases where a company was founded by more than one alumni and we count all firms founded. The raw response numbers were scaled up by a factor of 9.476 to account for survey non-responses as in Roberts and Eesley (2009).
64. For an earlier evaluation of the impact of MIT on the local economy, see BankBoston (1997).
65. As late as 1977 only six universities operated in Sweden. In addition there were five large technical institutes in Stockholm, Lund, Luleå, Linköping, and Chalmers 'University' of Technology in Göteborg. In addition, there were 14 small colleges. In 1977 there was a university system reform, with the 14 colleges upgraded in status and 11 new universities started in smaller towns of between 25,000 and 100,000 inhabitants. During the first 10 years these new institutions developed rather slowly. Beginning in 1987 there was a substantial expansion. Since 1987 the number of students at these institutions has doubled and by 1998 more than a third of all students in higher education attended one of these colleges (Andersson et al., 2004). Over time these colleges have also obtained greater resources for research.
66. Among Harvard MBAs, approximately 4 percent self-reported to be entrepreneurs (or intending to become) in the MBA program exit survey, varying over the sample years 1997–2004 from a low of approximately 2.5 percent in 2002 to a peak of approximately 10 percent in 2000. The share of successful entrepreneurs was approximately between 0.5 and 1 percent over the years and 5 percent of each section, on average, had worked previously as an entrepreneur. They define a successful business as one that (a) went public, (b) was acquired for greater than $5 million, or (c) in October 2007 or at the time of the sale of the company had at least 50 employees or $5 million in annual revenues.
67. This point was raised by David Robinson.
68. This came about as a challenge/offer from the newly ruling conservative party to privatize one of Sweden's institutes of technology. Chalmers' bid won and it received a loan of approximately US$166 million to jump-start structural changes, to be repaid by 2009. This loan turned out to be instrumental for spin-off activities, as we shall see. The change in legal status allowed Chalmers to accumulate capital from its entrepreneurial activities, which became an important incentive (Jacob et al., 2003). Privatizing also allowed Chalmers, among other things, to set market wages, although that opportunity has been less often used, and to locally determine program offers, which have been a big boon.

69. Science parks are geographically restricted properties housing more than one business tenant that have park and management functions which provide business support of varying kinds to tenant firms.
70. Similar types of identification strategies have been used in other settings with good results (for example, Oosterbeek et al., 2008).
71. In another paper, Squicciarini (2008) estimates a similar hazard model, but matches the sample with non-science park firms. She finds a negative, but only marginally significant effect of belonging to a science park on the chance of patenting. Clearly then, sample construction strategies together with self-selection problems cause estimates that are difficult to interpret.
72. Incubators offer office space and/or business services in return for a combination of fees, typically including taking equity in the start-up.
73. Clark et al. (1984) found that 76 percent of individuals who started their business subsequent to completing a traditional entrepreneurship course rated the course as having a 'large' or 'very large' effect on their decision to start, while only 4.3 percent felt that the course had little or no effect on the decision. Hornaday and Vesper (1982) found that students who elected to take a single course in entrepreneurship were much more likely to subsequently start their own business (21.3 percent were full-time self-employed) than a control group who had not taken the course (14.2 percent were full-time self-employed). Vesper and McMullan (1997) show that entrepreneurship courses help alumni to make better decisions in the start-up process.
74. Stuart and Sorenson (2003) controlled for state fixed effect when the unit of observation was the zip-code area. Not controlling for unit-level fixed effects means that we do not know whether there is common unmeasured causation at the unit level. Zucker et al. (1998a) establish positive effects of the number of top-quality research universities on number of local high-tech start-ups while controlling for the presence of star scientists and some measurable regional conditions without controlling for fixed regional effects.
75. A 'structurally weak region' was defined as a region where the industry of the spin-off had below the national average proportion of employment.
76. Di Gregorio and Shane (2003) check for robustness by measuring local venture capital activity in a number of different ways and consistently discover null effects.
77. In particular, the 'Milken index' of high-tech activity.
78. Schankerman and colleagues and O'Shea et al. (2005) use Blundell et al.'s (1999) suggested method of incorporating pre-sample information to approximate fixed effects. Under some assumptions that are hard to test, this works.
79. In this debate it is sometimes forgotten that universities create much larger local impact through graduating students. However, the universities also generate huge externalities since many students leave the region to take up jobs elsewhere. On this see, for example, Stephan et al. (2004).
80. Since private US universities are more likely than public universities to be located in urban areas, and the authors use a random effects model, there is some concern that the difference in licensing income may also be due to unobserved local demand conditions.

REFERENCES

Acs, Z.J., D.B. Audretsch and M.P. Feldman (1992), 'Real effects of academic research – comment', *American Economic Review*, **82** (1), 363–7.

Acs, Z.J., D.B. Audretsch and M.P. Feldman (1994), 'Research and development spillovers and recipient firm size', *Review of Economics and Statistics*, **76** (2), 336–40.

Adams, J.D. (2002), 'Comparative localization of academic and industrial spillovers', *Journal of Economic Geography*, **2** (3), 253–78.

Ajzen, I. (1987), 'Attitudes, traits, and actions – dispositional predictions of behavior in personality and social psychology', in Leonard Berkowitz (ed.), *Advances in Experimental Social Psychology*, Vol. 20, New York: Academic Press, pp. 1–63.

Ajzen, I. (1991), 'The theory of planned behavior', *Organizational Behavior and Human Decision Processes*, **50** (2), 179–211.

Allen, David N. and Frederick Norling (1991), 'Exploring perceived threats in faculty commercialization of research', in Alistair M. Brett, David V. Gibson and Raymond W. Smilor (eds), *University Spin-off Companies: Economic Development, Faculty Entrepreneurs, and Technology Transfer*, Savage, MD: Rowman & Littlefield, pp. 85–102.

Anderson, T.R., T.U. Daim and F.F. Lavoie (2007), 'Measuring the efficiency of university technology transfer', *Technovation*, **27** (5), 306–18.

Andersson, R., J.M. Quigley and M. Wilhelmsson (2004), 'University decentralization as regional policy: the Swedish experiment', *Journal of Economic Geography*, **4** (4), 371–88.

Andersson, R., J.M. Quigley and M. Wilhelmsson (2009), 'Urbanization, productivity, and innovation: evidence from investment in higher education', *Journal of Urban Economics*, **66** (1), 2–15.

Arrow, K. (1962), 'Economic welfare and the allocation of resources for invention', in Richard R. Nelson (ed.), *The Rate and Direction of Inventive Activity*, Princeton, NJ: Princeton University Press, pp. 609–26.

Åstebro, T. (2003), 'The return to independent invention: evidence of unrealistic optimism, risk seeking or skewness loving?', *Economic Journal*, **113** (484), 226–39.

Åstebro, T. and Y. Gerchak (2001), 'Profitable advice: the value of information provided by Canada's inventor's assistance program', *Economics of Innovation and New Technology*, **10** (1), 45–72.

AUCC (2003), *Action File: Commercialization*, Ottawa, Canada: AUCC Publications.

Audretsch, D., T. Aldridge and A. Oettl (2005a), 'The knowledge filter and economic growth: the role of scientists entrepreneurs', Discussion Papers on Entrepreneurship, Growth and Public Policy, Max Planck Institute of Economics, Jena.

Audretsch, D. and M. Feldman (1996), 'R&D spillovers and the geography of innovation and production', *American Economic Review*, **86** (3), 630–40.

Audretsch, D.B. and E.E. Lehmann (2005), 'Does the knowledge spillover theory of entrepreneurship hold for regions?', *Research Policy*, **34** (8), 1191–202.

Audretsch, D.B., E.E. Lehmann and S. Warning (2005b), 'University spillovers and new firm location', *Research Policy*, **34** (7), 1113–22.

AUTM (1996) to AUTM (2007), *The AUTM Licensing Survey: Fiscal Year 1996–2007*, Norwalk, CT.

Azoulay, P., W. Ding and T. Stuart (2006), 'The impact of academic patenting on the rate, quality, and direction of (public) research output', NBER Working Paper Series, w11917, National Bureau of Economic Research, Cambridge, MA.

Azoulay, P., W. Ding and T. Stuart (2007), 'The determinants of faculty patenting behavior: demographics or opportunities?', *Journal of Economic Behavior and Organization*, **63** (4), 599–623.

Bagozzi, R.P., J. Baumgartner and Y. Yi (1989), 'An investigation into the role of intentions as mediators of the attitude behavior relationship', *Journal of Economic Psychology*, **10** (1), 35–62.

Balconi, M., S. Breschi and F. Lissoni (2004), 'Networks of inventors and the role of academia: an exploration of Italian patent data', *Research Policy*, **33** (1), 127–45.

Baltzopoulos, A. and A. Broström (2009), 'Attractors of talent – universities and regional entrepreneurship', Working paper, Royal Institute of Technology, Stockholm.

BankBoston (1997), *MIT: The Impact of Innovation*, Boston, MA: BankBoston.

Belenzon, S. and M. Schankerman (2009), 'University knowledge transfer: private ownership, incentives, and local development objectives', *Journal of Law and Economics*, **52** (1), 111–44.

Belenzon, S. and M. Schankerman (2010), 'Localized university knowledge spillovers: the effects of state borders and private ownership', working paper, Fuqua School of Business, Duke University, Durham, NC.

Bera, R. (2009), 'The story of the Cohen–Boyer patents', *Current Science*, **96** (6), 760–63.
Bercovitz, J. and M. Feldman (2008), 'Academic entrepreneurs: organizational change at the individual level', *Organization Science*, **19** (1), 69–89.
Berggren, E. and Å. Lindholm-Dahlstrand (2008), 'Creating an entrepreneurial region: two waves of academic spin-offs from Halmstad University', in Bengt Johannisson and Åsa Lindholm-Dahlstrand (eds), *Bridging the Functional and Territorial Views on Regional Entrepreneurship and Development*, Örebro, Sweden: FSF Publication, pp. 35–54.
Bird, B. (1988), 'Implementing entrepreneurial ideas – the case for intention', *Academy of Management Review*, **13** (3), 442–53.
Blair, D.M. and D.M.W.N. Hitchens (1998), *Campus Companies – UK and Ireland*, Aldershot, UK: Ashgate.
Blundell, R., R. Griffith and J. van Reenen (1999), 'Market share, market value and innovation in a panel of British manufacturing firms', *Review of Economic Studies*, **66** (3), 529–54.
Breschi, S., F. Lissoni and F. Montobbio (2005), 'From publishing to patenting: do productive scientists turn into academic inventors?', *Revue d'Économie Industrielle*, **110** (2), 75–102.
Breschi, S., F. Lissoni and F. Montobbio (2007), 'The scientific productivity of academic inventors: new evidence from Italian data', *Economics of Innovation and New Technology*, **16** (2), 108–18.
Bresnahan, T., A. Gambardella and A. Saxenian (2001), 'Old economy inputs for new economy outcomes: cluster formation in the new Silicon Valleys', *Industrial and Corporate Change*, **10** (4), 835–60.
Breznitz, S. (2009), 'More active, less effective? University policy and the biotechnology industry in Cambridge, UK', Working paper, University of Cambridge, Cambridge.
Buenstorf, G. (2009), 'Is commercialization good or bad for science? Individual-level evidence from the Max Planck Society', *Research Policy*, **38** (2), 281–92.
Calderini, M., C. Franzoni and A. Vezzulli (2007), 'If star scientists do not patent: the effect of productivity, basicness and impact on the decision to patent in the academic world', *Research Policy*, **36** (3), 303–19.
Chapple, W., A. Lockett, D. Siegel and M. Wright (2005), 'Assessing the relative performance of UK university technology transfer offices: parametric and non-parametric evidence', *Research Policy*, **34** (3), 369–84.
Charles, D. (2001), *Lords of the Harvest*, Cambridge, MA: Perseus.
Charles, D. and C. Conway (2001), *Higher Education–Business Interaction Survey*, Newcastle upon Tyne: University of Newcastle upon Tyne.
Clark, B.W., C.H. Davis and V.C. Harnish (1984), 'Do courses in entrepreneurship aid in new venture creation?', *Journal of Small Business Management*, **28** (2), 26–31.
Clarke, B.R. (1998), *Creating Entrepreneurial Universities: Organizational Pathways of Transformation*, New York: IAU Press.
Clayman, B.P. (2004), *Technology Transfer at Canadian Universities: Fiscal Year 2002 Update*, Coquitlam: Canada Foundation for Innovation.
Clayman, B.P. and A.J. Holbrook (2003), 'The survival of university spin-offs and their relevance to regional development', CPROST Report to the Canada Foundation for Innovation, Simon Fraser University, Vancouver.
Coase, R.H. (1960), 'The problem of social cost', *Journal of Law and Economics*, **3**, 1–44.
Cohen, W.M., R.R. Nelson and J.P. Walsh (2002), 'Links and impacts: the influence of public research on industrial R&D', *Management Science*, **48** (1), 1–23.
Colombo, M.G. and M. Delmastro (2002), 'How effective are technology incubators? Evidence from Italy', *Research Policy*, **31** (7), 1103–22.
Crespi, G., P. D'Este, R. Fontana and A. Geuna (2010), 'The impact of academic patenting on university research and its transfer', *Research Policy*, **40** (1), 55–68.
Dasgupta, P. and P.A. David (1994), 'Toward a new economics of science', *Research Policy*, **23** (5), 487–521.
David, P.A. (2007), 'Innovation and Europe's academic institutions – second thoughts

about embracing the Bayh–Dole regime', in Stefano Brusoni and Franco Malerba (eds), *Perspectives on Innovation*, Cambridge: Cambridge University Press, pp. 251–78.

Debackere, K. and R. Veugelers (2005), 'The role of academic technology transfer organizations in improving industry science links', *Research Policy*, **34** (3), 321–42.

Di Gregorio, D. and S. Shane (2003), 'Why do some universities generate more start-ups than others?', *Research Policy*, **32** (2), 209–27.

Djokovic, D. and V. Souitaris (2008), 'Spinouts from academic institutions: a literature review with suggestions for further research', *Journal of Technology Transfer*, **33** (3), 225–47.

Eesley, C.E., E.B. Roberts and D. Yang (2009), 'Entrepreneurial ventures from technology-based universities: a cross-national comparison', working paper, Stanford University, Stanford, CA.

Egeln, J., S. Gottschalk and C. Rammer (2004), 'Location decision of spin-offs from public research institutions', *Industry and Innovation*, **11**, 207–23.

Ensley, M.D. and K.A. Hmieleski (2005), 'A comparative study of new venture top management team composition, dynamics and performance between university-based and independent start-ups', *Research Policy*, **34** (7), 1091–105.

Eriksson, E.L. (1996), 'Akademiskt Företagande – från student till företagare', dissertation, Lund University, Lund, Sweden.

Fayolle, A.G.B. and N. Lassas-Clerc (2006), 'Assessing the impact of entrepreneurship education programmes: a new methodology', *Journal of European Industrial Training*, **30**, 701–20.

Feldman, M.P. and P. Desrochers (2003), 'Research universities and local economic development: lessons from the history of Johns Hopkins University', *Industry and Innovation*, **10**, 5–24.

Feldman, M.P. and P. Desrochers (2004), 'Truth for its own sake: academic culture and technology transfer at Johns Hopkins University', *Minerva*, **42** (2), 105–26.

Fini, R., N. Lacetera and S. Shane (2010), 'Inside or outside the IP-system? Business creation in academia', *Research Policy*, **39** (8), 1060–69.

Foltz, J., B. Barham and K. Kwansoo (2000), 'Universities and agricultural biotechnology patent production', *Agribusiness*, **16** (1), 82–95.

Franklin, S., M. Wright and A. Lockett (2001), 'Academic and surrogate entrepreneurs in university spin-out companies', *Journal of Technology Transfer*, **26** (1–2), 127–41.

Friedman, J. and J. Silberman (2003), 'University technology transfer: do incentives management, and location matter?', *Journal of Technology Transfer*, **28** (1), 17–30.

Furman, J. and M. MacGarvie (2007), 'Academic science and the birth of industrial research laboratories in the US pharmaceutical industry', *Journal of Economic Behavior and Organization*, **63**, 756–76.

Galasso, A. and M.A. Schankerman (2010), 'Patent thickets, courts and the market for innovation', *The RAND Journal of Economics*, **41** (3), 472–503.

Gans, J.S. and S. Stern (2000), 'Incumbency and R&D incentives: licensing the gale of creative destruction', *Journal of Economics and Management Strategy*, **9** (4), 485–511.

Gault, F. and S. McDaniel (2004), 'Summary: joint statistics Canada–University of Windsor workshop on intellectual property commercialization indicators', Science, Innovation and Electronic Information Division Working Papers, Windsor, **6**, 38.

Giuri, P., M. Mariani, S. Brusoni, G. Crespi, D. Francoz, A. Gambardella, W. Garcia-Fontes, A. Geuna, R. Gonzales, D. Harhoff, K. Hoisl, C. Lebas, A. Luzzi, L. Magazzini, L. Nesta, O. Nomaler, N. Palomeras, P. Patel, M. Romanelli and B. Verspagen (2007), 'Inventors and invention processes in Europe: results from the PatVal–EU survey', *Research Policy*, **36** (8), 1107–27.

Goldfarb, B. and J. Colyvas (2005), 'Intellectual property rights and entrepreneurship: evidence from university technology transfer', working paper, University of Maryland, College Park, MD.

Goldfarb, B. and J. Colyvas (2006), 'Tacit knowledge, uncertainty and startups', Working paper, University of Maryland, College Park, MD.

Goldfarb, B. and M. Henrekson (2003), 'Bottom-up versus top-down policies towards the commercialization of university intellectual property', *Research Policy*, **32** (4), 639–58.

Goldfarb, B., G. Marschke and A. Smith (2008), 'Scholarship and inventive activity in the university: complements or substitutes?', working paper, University of Maryland, College Park, MD.

Goldman, M.I. (1984), 'Building a Mecca for high technology', *Technology Review*, **87**, 6–8.

Goldstein, A. (2009), 'What we know and what we don't know about the regional economic impacts of universities', in Attila Varga (ed.), *Universities, Knowledge Transfer and Regional Development: Geography, Entrepreneurship and Policy*, Cheltenham, UK and Northampton, MA, USA: Edward Elgar, pp. 11–25.

Hall, B.H., A. Jaffe and M. Trajtenberg (2005), 'Market value and patent citations', *The RAND Journal of Economics*, **36** (1), 16–38.

Hall, B.H. and R.H. Ziedonis (2001), 'The patent paradox revisited: an empirical study of patenting in the US semiconductor industry, 1979–95', *The RAND Journal of Economics*, **32** (1), 101–28.

Harhoff, D., F. Narin, F.M. Scherer and K. Vopel (1999), 'Citation frequency and the value of patented inventions', *Review of Economics and Statistics*, **81** (3), 511–15.

Heblich, S. and V. Slavtchev (2009), 'The location of university spin-offs', working paper, Max Planck Institute of Economics, Jena.

Heller, M.A. and R.S. Eisenberg (1998), 'Can patents deter innovation? The anticommons in biomedical research', *Science*, **280** (5364), 698–701.

Henderson, R.M., A.B. Jaffe and M. Trajtenberg (1998), 'Universities as a source of commercial technology: a detailed analysis of university patenting, 1965–1988', *Review of Economics and Statistics*, **80** (1), 119–27.

Hertzfeld, H.R., A.N. Link and N.S. Vonoartas (2006), 'Intellectual property protection mechanisms in research partnerships', *Research Policy*, **35** (6), 825–38.

Hoppe, H.C. and E. Ozdenoren (2005), 'Intermediation in innovation', *International Journal of Industrial Organization*, **23** (5–6), 483–503.

Hornaday, J.A. and K.H. Vesper (1982), 'Entrepreneurial education and job satisfaction', in Karl H. Vesper (ed.), *Frontiers of Entrepreneurship Research*, Wellesley, MA: Babson College, pp. 526–39.

Hounshell, D.A. and J.K. Smith (1988), *Science and Corporate Strategy: Du Pont R&D, 1902–1980*, New York: Cambridge University Press.

Hsu, D.H. and T. Bernstein (1997), 'Managing the university technology licensing process: findings from case studies', *Journal of the Association of University Technology Managers*, **9**, 1–33.

Hsu, D.H., E.B. Roberts and C.E. Eesley (2007), 'Entrepreneurs from technology-based universities: evidence from MIT', *Research Policy*, **36** (5), 768–88.

Iversen, E.J., M. Gulbrandsen and A. Klitkou (2007), 'A baseline for the impact of academic patenting legislation in Norway', *Scientometrics*, **70** (2), 393–414.

Jacob, M., M. Lundqvist and H. Hellsmark (2003), 'Entrepreneurial transformations in the Swedish university system: the case of Chalmers University of Technology', *Research Policy*, **32** (9), 1555–68.

Jaffe, A.B. (1989), 'Real effects of academic research', *American Economic Review*, **79** (5), 957–70.

Jaffe, A., M. Trajtenberg and R. Henderson (1993), 'Geographic localisation of knowledge spillovers as evidenced by patent citations', *Quarterly Journal of Economics*, **108** (3), 577–98.

Jensen, R. and D. Showalter (2010), 'University inventions licensed through startups', Working paper, University of Notre Dame, Notre Dame, IN.

Jensen, R. and M. Thursby (2001), 'Proofs and prototypes for sale: the licensing of university inventions', *American Economic Review*, **91** (1), 240–59.

Katz, J.A. (2003), 'The chronology and intellectual trajectory of American entrepreneurship education 1876–1999', *Journal of Business Venturing*, **18** (2), 283–300.

Katz, J. and W.B. Gartner (1988), 'Properties of emerging organizations', *Academy of Management Review*, **13** (3), 429–41.
Keck, O. (1993), 'The national system for technical innovation in Germany', in Richard R. Nelson (ed.), *National Innovation Systems: A Comparative Analysis*, Oxford: Oxford University Press, pp. 115–57.
Kenney, M. and W.R. Goe (2004), 'The role of social embeddedness in professorial entrepreneurship: a comparison of electrical engineering and computer science at UC Berkeley and Stanford', *Research Policy*, **33** (5), 691–707.
Kenney, M. and D. Patton (2009), 'Reconsidering the Bayh–Dole Act and the current university invention ownership model', *Research Policy*, **38** (9), 1407–22.
Kolodny, H., B. Stymne, R. Shani, J.R. Figuera and P. Lillrank (2001), 'Design and policy choices for technology extension organizations', *Research Policy*, **30** (2), 201–25.
Krugman, P. (1991), *Geography and Trade*, Cambridge, MA: MIT Press.
Kuratko, D.F. (2005), 'The emergence of entrepreneurship education: development, trends, and challenges', *Entrepreneurship: Theory and Practice*, **29** (5), 577–97.
Lach, S. and M. Schankerman (2008), 'Incentives and invention in universities', *The RAND Journal of Economics*, **39** (2), 403–33.
Lazear, E.P. (2005), 'Entrepreneurship', *Journal of Labor Economics*, **23** (4), 649–80.
Lee, S.S. and J.S. Osteryoung (2004), 'A comparison of critical success factors for effective operations of university business incubators in the United States and Korea', *Journal of Small Business Management*, **42** (4), 418–26.
Lerner, J. and U. Malmendier (2007), 'With a little help from my (random) friends: success and failure in post-business school entrepreneurship', Working paper, Harvard University, Cambridge, MA.
Lindelöf, P. and H. Löfsten (2003), 'Science park location and new technology-based firms in Sweden – implications for strategy and performance', *Small Business Economics*, **20** (3), 245–58.
Lindelöf, P. and H. Löfsten (2004), 'Proximity as a resource base for competitive advantage – university–industry links for technology transfer', *Journal of Technology Transfer*, **29** (3/4), 311–26.
Lindholm-Dahlstrand, Å. (1999), 'Technology-based SMEs in the Goteborg region: their origin and interaction with universities and large firms', *Regional Studies*, **33** (4), 379–89.
Link, A.N. and D.S. Siegel (2005), 'University-based technology initiatives: quantitative and qualitative evidence', *Research Policy*, **34** (3), 253–7.
Lissoni, F., P. Llerena, M. McKelvey and B. Sanditov (2008), 'Academic patenting in Europe: new evidence from the KEINS database', *Research Evaluation*, **17** (2), 87–102.
Litan, R.E., L. Mitchell and E.J. Reedy (2007), 'Commercializing university innovations: alternative approaches', *Innovation Policy and the Economy*, **8**, 31–57.
Lockett, A. and M. Wright (2005), 'Resources, capabilities, risk capital and the creation of university spin-out companies', *Research Policy*, **34** (7), 1043–57.
Lööf, H. (2005), 'Vad ger samarbetet mellan universitet och näringliv', *Tillväxtpolitisk utblick*, ITPS, Nr. 1, January.
Louis, K.S., D. Blumenthal, M.E. Gluck and M.A. Soto (1989), 'Entrepreneurs in academe: an exploration of behaviors among life scientists', *Administrative Science Quarterly*, **34** (1), 110–31.
Louis, K.S., L.M. Jones, M.S. Anderson, D. Blumenthal and E.G. Campbell (2001), 'Entrepreneurs, secrecy, and productivity', *Journal of Technology Transfer*, **26**, 233–45.
Lowe, R.A. (2002), 'Entrepreneurship, invention, and innovation: the commercialization of university research by inventor-founded firms', PhD thesis, Haas School of Business, University of California, Berkeley, CA.
Lowe, R. (2006), 'Who develops a university invention? The roles of inventor knowledge and licensing policies', *Journal of Technology Transfer*, **31** (4), 415–29.
Lowe, R. and C. Gonzalez-Brambila (2007), 'Faculty entrepreneurs and research productivity', *Journal of Technology Transfer*, **32** (3), 173–94.
Macho-Stadler, I., D. Perez-Castrillo and R. Veugelers (2007), 'Licensing of university

inventions: the role of a technology transfer office', *International Journal of Industrial Organization*, **25** (3), 483–510.

Madden, T.J., P.S. Ellen and I. Ajzen (1992), 'A comparison of the theory of planned behavior and the theory of reasoned action', *Personality and Social Psychology Bulletin*, **18** (1), 3–9.

Mansfield, E. and J.Y. Lee (1996), 'The modern university: contributor to industrial innovation and recipient of industrial R&D support', *Research Policy*, **25** (7), 1047–58.

Markman, G.D., P.T. Gianiodis and P.H. Phan (2008), 'Full-time faculty or part-time entrepreneurs', *IEEE Transactions on Engineering Management*, **55** (1), 29–36.

Markman, G.D., P.T. Gianiodis and P.H. Phan (2009), 'Supply-side innovation and technology commercialization', *Journal of Management Studies*, **46** (4), 625–49.

McMullan, W.E. and W.A. Long (1987), 'Entrepreneurship education in the nineties', *Journal of Business Venturing*, **2** (3), 261–75.

Merges, R.P. and R.R. Nelson (1990), 'On the complex economics of patent scope', *Columbia Law Review*, **90** (4), 839–916.

Merton, R. (1973), *The Sociology of Science: Theoretical and Empirical Investigations*, Chicago, IL: University of Chicago Press.

Meyer, M. (2003), 'Academic patents as an indicator of useful research? A new approach to measure academic inventiveness', *Research Evaluation*, **12** (1), 17–27.

Mowery, D.C., R.R. Nelson, B.N. Sampat and A.A. Ziedonis (2004), *Ivory Tower and Industrial Innovation*, Stanford, CA: Stanford University Press.

Mowery, D.C. and B.N. Sampat (2001), 'Patenting and licensing university inventions: lessons from the history of the research corporation', *Industrial and Corporate Change*, **10**, 317–55.

Mowery, D.C. and B.N. Sampat (2005), 'The Bayh–Dole Act of 1980 and university–industry technology transfer: a model for other OECD governments', *Journal of Technology Transfer*, **30**, 115–27.

Mowery, D.C. and A. Ziedonis (2001), 'The geographic reach of market and nonmarket channels of technology transfer', NBER Working Paper 8568, National Bureau of Economic Research, Cambridge, MA.

Mukherjee, A. and S. Stern (2009), 'Disclosure or secrecy? The dynamics of open science', *International Journal of Industrial Organization*, **27** (3), 449–62.

Murmann, J.P. (2003), *Knowledge and Competitive Advantage: The Coevolution of Firms, Technology, and National Institutions*, Cambridge: Cambridge University Press.

Murray, F. and S. Stern (2007), 'Do formal intellectual property rights hinder the free flow of scientific knowledge? An empirical test of the anti-commons hypothesis', *Journal of Economic Behavior and Organization*, **63** (4), 648–87.

Mustar, P. (1997), 'How French academics create high tech companies: conditions of success and failure of this form of relation between science and market', *Science and Public Policy*, **24** (1), 37–43.

Myhrvold, N. (2010), 'Funding Eureka!', *Harvard Business Review*, **88** (3), 40–50.

Nelsen, L. (1999), 'Remarks by Lita Nelsen, M.I.T. Technology Licensing Office', available at: http://www.aaas.org/spp/secrecy/Presents/nelsen.htm (accessed 22 March 2011).

Nelsen, L. (2007), 'The activities and roles of M.I.T. in forming clusters and strengthening entrepreneurship', in Anatole Krattiger, Richard T. Mahoney, Lita Nelsen, Jennifer Thomson, Alan Bennet, Kanikaram Satyanarayana, Gregory Graff, Carlos Fernandez and Stanley Kowalski (eds), *Intellectual Property Management in Health and Agricultural Innovation: A Handbook of Best Practices*, Oxford: MIHR and Davis, CA: PIPRA, available online at www.ipHandbook.org (accessed 12 February 2010).

Nelson, R.R. (1959), 'The simple economics of basic scientific research', *Journal of Political Economy*, **67**, 297–306.

Niosi, J. (2006), 'Success factors in Canadian academic spin-offs', *Journal of Technology Transfer*, **31** (4), 451–7.

Noble, D.F. (1977), *America by Design: Science, Technology, and the Rise of Corporate Capitalism*, New York: Knopf.

Noll, R.G. (1998), *Challenges to Research Universities*, Washington, DC: Brookings Institution Press.

NSERC (2005), *Research Means Business*, Ottawa: National Sciences and Engineering Research Council.

NSF (2007), *Science and Engineering Indicators 2006*, Washington, DC: National Science Foundation.

Oosterbeek, H., C.M. Van Praag and A. IJsselstein (2008), 'The impact of entrepreneurship education on entrepreneurship competencies and intentions: an evaluation of the junior achievement student mini-company program', available at SSRN: http://ssm.com/abstract=1118251 (accessed 22 March 2011).

O'Shea, R.P., T.J. Allen, A. Chevalier and F. Roche (2005), 'Entrepreneurial orientation, technology transfer and spinoff performance of US universities', *Research Policy*, **34** (7), 994–1009.

Page, N. (2007), 'The making of a licensing legend: Stanford University's office of technology licensing', in Anatole Krattiger, Richard T. Mahoney, Lita Nelsen, Jennifer Thomson, Alan Bennet, Kanikaram Satyanarayana, Gregory Graff, Carlos Fernandez and Stanley Kowalski (eds), *Intellectual Property Management in Health and Agricultural Innovation: A Handbook of Best Practices*, Oxford: MIHR and Davis, CA: PIPRA, available at www.ipHandbook.org (accessed 12 February 2010).

Palmer, A.M. (1948), *Survey of University Patent Policies: Preliminary Report*, Washington, DC: National Research Council.

Peterman, N.E. and J. Kennedy (2003), 'Enterprise education: influencing students' perceptions of entrepreneurship', *Entrepreneurship: Theory and Practice*, **28** (2), 129–44.

Pfeiffer, E.W. (1997), *What MIT Learned from Stanford*, available at: http://www.forbes.com/asap/1997/0825/059.html (accessed 7 December 2009).

Porter, M. (1998), 'Clusters and the new economics of competition', *Harvard Business Review*, **76** (6), 77–90.

Powers, J.B. and P. McDougall (2005), 'Policy orientation effects on performance with licensing to start-ups and small companies', *Research Policy*, **34** (7), 1028–42.

Rasmussen, E.A. (2008), 'Government instruments to support the commercialization of university research: lessons from Canada', *Technovation*, **28** (8), 506–17.

Rasmussen, E.A. and R. Sorheim (2006), 'Action-based entrepreneurship education', *Technovation*, **26** (2), 185–94.

Read, C. (2005), 'Survey of intellectual property commercialization in the higher education sector, 2003', Innovation and Electronic Information Division Working Papers, **18** (32).

Reid, R.H. (1997), *Architects of the Web*, New York: John Wiley & Sons.

Regeringens Proposition (1998/1999:94), *Vissa forskningsfrågor*, Riksdagstryck, Stockholm.

Research Corporation (1947), *Annual Report*, New York: Research Corporation.

Roberts, E.B. (1991), 'The technological base of the new enterprise', *Research Policy*, **20** (4), 283–98.

Roberts, E.B. and C.E. Eesley (2009), 'Entrepreneurial impact: the role of MIT', Ewing Marion Kauffman Foundation, Kansas City, MO.

Rogers, E.M., Y. Yin and J. Hoffmann (2000), 'Assessing the effectiveness of technology transfer offices at US research universities', *Journal of the Association of University Technology Managers*, **12**, 47–80.

Rothaermel, F.T., S.D. Agung and L. Jiang (2007), 'University entrepreneurship: a taxonomy of the literature', *Industrial and Corporate Change*, **16** (4), 691–791.

Rothaermel, F.T. and D.N. Ku (2008), 'Intercluster innovation differentials: the role of research universities', *IEEE Transactions on Engineering Management*, **55** (1), 9–22.

Rothaermel, F.T. and M. Thursby (2005), 'University–incubator firm knowledge flows: assessing their impact on incubator firm performance', *Research Policy*, **34** (3), 305–20.

Samuelson, P.A. (1954), 'The pure theory of public expenditure', *Review of Economics and Statistics*, **36**, 387–9.

Saxenian, AnnaLee (1996), *Regional Advantage: Culture and Competition in Silicon Valley and Route 128*, Cambridge, MA: Harvard University Press.

Schankerman, M. (1998), 'How valuable is patent protection? Estimates by technology field', *The RAND Journal of Economics*, **29** (1), 77–107.
Schankerman, M. and A. Pakes (1986), 'Estimates of the value of patent rights in European countries during the post-1950 period', *Economic Journal*, **96** (384), 1052–76.
Scherer, F.M. and D. Harhoff (2000), 'Technology policy for a world of skew-distributed outcomes', *Research Policy*, **29** (4–5), 559–66.
Scotchmer, S. (1991), 'Standing on the shoulders of giants – cumulative research and the patent law', *Journal of Economic Perspectives*, **5** (1), 29–41.
SFS 1996:1392, 'Ändring i Högskolelagen', *Svensk för Fatningsamling*, Stockholm: Swedish Parliament.
Shane, S. (2004), *Academic Entrepreneurship: University Spinoffs and Wealth Creation*, Cheltenham, UK and Northampton, MA, USA: Edward Elgar.
Shane, S.A. (2008), *Illusions of Entrepreneurship: The Costly Myths that Entrepreneurs, Investors, and Policy Makers Live By*, New Haven, CT: Yale University Press.
Shapero, A. (1975), 'Displaced, uncomfortable entrepreneur', *Psychology Today*, **9** (6), 83–8.
Shapero, A. (1985), 'The entrepreneurial event', *Enterprise*, February 5–9.
Shapiro, C. (2000), 'Navigating the patent thicket: cross licenses, patent pools, and standard setting', in Adam B. Jaffe, Josh Lerner and Scott Stern (eds), *Innovation Policy and the Economy*, Vol. 1, Boston, MA: National Bureau of Economic Research and MIT Press, pp. 119–50.
Siegel, D.S., R. Veugelers and M. Wright (2007a), 'Technology transfer offices and commercialization of university intellectual property: performance and policy implications', *Oxford Review of Economic Policy*, **23** (4), 640–60.
Siegel, D.S., D. Waldman and A. Link (2003a), 'Assessing the impact of organizational practices on the relative productivity of university technology transfer offices: an exploratory study', *Research Policy*, **32** (1), 27–48.
Siegel, D.S., P. Westhead and M. Wright (2003b), 'Assessing the impact of university science parks on research productivity: exploratory firm-level evidence from the United Kingdom', *International Journal of Industrial Organization*, **21** (9), 1357–69.
Siegel, D.S., M. Wright and A. Lockett (2007b), 'The rise of entrepreneurial activity at universities: organizational and societal implications', *Industrial and Corporate Change*, **16**, 489–504.
Solomon, G.T., K.M. Weaver and L.W. Fernald (1994), 'A historical examination of small business-management and entrepreneurship pedagogy', *Simulation and Gaming*, **25** (3), 338–52.
SOU 1992:7, *Kompetensutveckling – en nationell strategi*, Stockholm: Utbildningsdepartementet.
SOU 1996:70, *Samverkan mellan högskolan och näringslivet*, Huvudbetänkande av NYFOR, Stockholm: Fritzes.
SOU 1996:89, *Samverkan mellan högskolan och de små och medelstora företagen*. Slutbetänkande av NYFOR, Stockholm: Fritzes.
SOU 1998:128, *Forskningspolitik: Slutbetänkande av Kommittén för översyn av den svenska forskningspolitiken*, Staten offentliga utredningar, Stockholm: Sveriges Riksdag.
Souitaris, V., S. Zerbinati and A. Andreas (2007), 'Do entrepreneurship programmes raise entrepreneurial intention of science and engineering students? The effect of learning, inspiration and resources', *Journal of Business Venturing*, **22** (4), 566–91.
Squicciarini, M. (2008), 'Science parks' tenants versus out-of-park firms: who innovates more? A duration model', *Journal of Technology Transfer*, **33** (1), 45–71.
Squicciarini, M. (2009), 'Science parks: seedbeds of innovation? A duration analysis of firms' patenting activity', *Small Business Economics*, **32** (2), 169–90.
Stephan, P.E., S. Gurmu, A. Sumell and G. Black (2007), 'Who's patenting in the university? Evidence from the survey of doctorate recipients', *Economics of Innovation and New Technology*, **16**, 71–99.
Stephan, P.E., A.J. Sumell, G.C. Black and J.D. Adams (2004), 'Doctoral education and economic development: the flow of Ph.D.s to industry', *Economic Development Quarterly*, **18** (2), 151–67.

Stuart, T. and W. Ding (2006), 'When do scientists become entrepreneurs? The social structural antecedents of commercial activity in the academic life sciences', *American Journal of Sociology*, **112** (1), 97–144.

Stuart, T. and O. Sorenson (2003), 'The geography of opportunity: spatial heterogeneity in founding rates and the performance of biotechnology firms', *Research Policy*, **32** (32), 229–53.

Takahashi, M. and R. Carraz (2009), *Academic Patenting in Japan: Illustration from a Leading Japanese University*, Strasbourg: University of Strasbourg.

Thursby, J., A.W. Fuller and M. Thursby (2009), 'US faculty patenting: inside and outside the university', *Research Policy*, **38** (1), 14–25.

Thursby, J.G. and S. Kemp (2002), 'Growth and productive efficiency of university intellectual property licensing', *Research Policy*, **31** (1), 109–24.

Thursby, J.G. and M.C. Thursby (2002), 'Who is selling the Ivory Tower? Sources of growth in university licensing', *Management Science*, **48** (1), 90–104.

Thursby, J.G. and M.C. Thursby (2007), 'University licensing', *Oxford Review of Economic Policy*, **23** (4), 620–39.

Tkachev, A. and L. Kolvereid (1999), 'Self-employment intentions among Russian students', *Entrepreneurship and Regional Development*, **11** (3), 269–80.

Valentin, F. and R.L. Jensen (2007), 'Effects on academia–industry collaboration of extending university property rights', *Journal of Technology Transfer*, **32** (3), 251–76.

van Clouse, G.H. (1990), 'A controlled experiment relating entrepreneurial education to students' start-up decisions', *Journal of Small Business Management*, **28** (2), 45–53.

Vesper, K.H. and W.E. McMullan (1997), 'New venture scholarship versus practice: when entrepreneurship academics try the real things as applied research', *Technovation*, **17** (7), 349–58.

von Graevenitz, G., D. Harhoff and R. Weber (2009), 'The effects of entrepreneurship education', *Journal of Economic Behaviour and Organization*, **76** (1), 90–112.

Wallmark, J.T. (1997), 'Inventions and patents at universities: the case of Chalmers University of Technology', *Technovation*, **17** (3), 127–39.

Walsh, J.P., W.M. Cohen and C. Cho (2007), 'Where excludability matters: material versus intellectual property in academic biomedical research', *Research Policy*, **36** (8), 1184–203.

Westhead, P. (1997), 'R&D "inputs" and "outputs" of technology-based firms located on and off science parks', *R & D Management*, **27** (1), 45–62.

Westhead, P. and S. Batstone (1998), 'Independent technology-based firms: the perceived benefits of a science park location', *Urban Studies*, **35** (12), 2197–219.

Westhead, P. and D.J. Storey (1995), 'Links between higher-education institutions and high-technology firms', *Omega – International Journal of Management Science*, **23** (4), 345–60.

Wickstead, Segal Q. (1985), *The Cambridge Phenomenon*, Thetford, UK: Thetford Press.

Wright, M., B. Clarysse, P. Mustar and A. Lockett (2007), *Academic Entrepreneurship in Europe*, Cheltenham, UK and Northampton, MA, USA: Edward Elgar.

Zhang, J. (2009), 'The performance of university spin-offs: an exploratory analysis using venture capital data', *Journal of Technology Transfer*, **34** (3), 255–86.

Zucker, L.G. and M.R. Darby (2001), 'Capturing technological opportunity via Japan's star scientists: evidence from Japanese firms' biotech patents and products', *Journal of Technology Transfer*, **26** (1–2), 37–58.

Zucker, L.G., M.R. Darby and J. Armstrong (1998a), 'Geographically localized knowledge: spillovers or markets?', *Economic Inquiry*, **36** (1), 65–86.

Zucker, L.G., M.R. Darby and M.B. Brewer (1998b), 'Intellectual human capital and the birth of US biotechnology enterprises', *American Economic Review*, **88** (1), 290–306.

Name index

Subject index